To   Peteneddie,   *Kushy*

and every member

of the Thix·····t

family,   whenever

they may come

to join us,

from Nan.

P Γ IA

B R K

O F E

N T

ROGER
TORY
PETERSON

JAYS, THRUSHES, AND TANAGERS

1. CANADA (ROCKY MOUNTAIN) JAY
2. CLARK'S NUTCRACKER
3. PIÑON JAY
4. STELLER'S JAY
5. BLUE JAY
6. CALIFORNIA JAY
7. TOWNSEND'S SOLITAIRE
8. GREEN JAY
9. ARIZONA JAY
10. VARIED THRUSH, MALE
11. MOUNTAIN BLUEBIRD, *a*. MALE; *b*. FEMALE
12. WESTERN BLUEBIRD, *a*. MALE; *b*. FEMALE
13. HERMIT THRUSH
14. RUSSET-BACKED THRUSH
15. WILLOW THRUSH
16. WESTERN TANAGER, *a*. MALE; *b*. FEMALE
17. COOPER'S TANAGER, *a*. MALE; *b*. FEMALE
18. HEPATIC TANAGER, *a*. MALE; *b*. FEMALE

A FIELD GUIDE TO WESTERN BIRDS

BY

ROGER TORY PETERSON

of the National Audubon Society

BOSTON

HOUGHTON MIFFLIN COMPANY

The Riverside Press Cambridge

TO
MY WIFE

𝕿𝖍𝖊 𝕽𝖎𝖛𝖊𝖗𝖘𝖎𝖉𝖊 𝕻𝖗𝖊𝖘𝖘
CAMBRIDGE · MASSACHUSETTS
PRINTED IN THE U.S.A.

PREFACE

IT WAS that pioneer, Ernest Thompson Seton, who first tried the idea of pattern diagrams as a method of teaching bird identification. Years ago he published some diagrammatic plates in *The Auk*, showing how Hawks and Owls look in flight overhead.

Those of us who have read Seton's *Two Little Savages* remember how the young hero, Yan, discovered some mounted Ducks in a dusty showcase. This lad had a book which showed him how to tell Ducks when they were in the hand, but since he only saw the live Ducks at a distance, he was frequently at a loss for their names. He noticed that all the Ducks in the showcase were different — all had blotches or streaks that were their labels or identification tags. He decided that if he could put their labels or 'uniforms' down on paper, he would know these same Ducks as soon as he saw them at a distance on the water.

It was on this idea that my *Field Guide to the Birds*, the Eastern counterpart of this volume, was based. It is a handbook designed to complement the standard ornithological works — a guide to the *field-marks* of Eastern birds, wherein live birds may be run down by impressions, patterns, and distinctive marks rather than by the differences of measurements and anatomy that the collector finds useful. The success of this publication prompted Mr. Clinton G. Abbott, Director of the Natural History Museum at San Diego, to ask why I didn't do a similar guide for the West. I dismissed the idea, at first, thinking that although the plan worked out well for eastern North America, it would be almost impossible to do the same thing for the West, where the situation was, it seemed to me, much more confusing. However, after constant prompting and encouragement by Guy Emerson, President of the National Audubon Society, who has had wide field experience in all parts of the country, I decided to give it a try. After tussling with a few of the problems, I came to the conclusion that field identification was no more difficult in the West than in the East, and that most publications made things look more difficult than they were. There was already one excellent handbook in use — Hoffmann's *Birds of the Pacific States* — but this only covered the States of Washington, Oregon, and California, whereas there was hardly a thing that was adequate for most other parts of the West. This guide does not intend to replace Hoffmann's handbook; rather, it could be most effectively used as a companion piece to it. The approach of the two books is quite different. Hoffmann's is especially thorough on the voices and habitats of birds, much more complete than is possible in a book of this size.

The entire manuscript of this book was read and criticized by Guy Emerson and also by Frank Watson and Laidlaw Williams, two of California's most enthusiastic field students. Mr. Ludlow Griscom of Cambridge, Massachusetts, who has as wide a field knowledge of all the birds of North America as any ornithologist, and who has brought the science of field identification to its greatest perfection, also examined the complete manuscript and has given me the benefit of his valuable experience. Mr. Francis H. Allen of West Roxbury, Massachusetts, veteran editor of many widely known ornithological works, has given the text a complete perusal and editorial polishing. Portions of the manuscript were also sent to the following experts for their critical opinions: Irby Davis (Texas and Mexican species), Charles W. Lockerbie (Rocky Mountain birds), Dr. Alden Miller (Owls, Flycatchers, Thrashers, Juncos, etc.), James Moffitt (Ducks and Geese), Dr. Robert Cushman Murphy (oceanic birds), Robert J. Niedrach (Rocky Mountain and Great Plains species), Dr. Robert T. Orr (shore-birds), and Dr. George Miksch Sutton (Mexican and Southwestern birds).

During my trips West which carried me into all the States covered by this book, I have received constant co-operation from numerous well-known bird students who unselfishly put their time and knowledge at my disposal, often spending days driving me around to see the things I wished most to see. I am especially indebted to Edward Chalif of Short Hills, New Jersey; Garrett Eddy and H. W. Higman of Seattle, Washington; Walter Hagenstein of Medina, Washington; H. M. Dubois, Harold S. Gilbert, and other members of the Oregon Audubon Society; Mr. and Mrs. Charles Lockerbie and Dr. A. M. Woodbury of Salt Lake City, Utah; Mrs. Junea Kelly of Alameda, California; Mrs. Amelia Allen, Mrs. Dorothy Dean Sheldon, and Frank Watson of Berkeley, California; Commander Henry E. Parmenter of San Francisco; Laidlaw Williams of Carmel, California; Miss Helen S. Pratt of Eagle Rock, California; James Murdock of Glendale, California; Frank Gander, Lawrence M. Huey, and Lewis Wayne Walker of San Diego, California; Mr. C. A. Harwell, California representative of the National Audubon Society, and his former associates at Yosemite National Park, Vincent Mowbray and Charles Michael; Randolph Jenks and Dr. Charles T. Vorhies of Tucson, Arizona; Mr. and Mrs. Irby Davis of Harlingen, Texas; James Stevenson of Austwell, Texas; and Thomas Waddell of Eagle Lake, Texas.

Dr. Arthur A. Allen and Charles Brand of Cornell University spent an entire week-end with me in their sound laboratory playing off all the sound recordings of birds which were made on their recent trips West. In this way I was able to make a final check on some of the more puzzling bird voices and compare them with my field descriptions. This was especially helpful in analyzing the voice differences in closely related species that could not always be compared conveniently in the field. In interpreting a few of the more difficult bird songs I have resorted to a system of symbols similar to that developed so successfully by Aretas A. Saunders, to whom I offer my apologies.

As for the drawings, Dr. William Sargent helped me immeasurably on the flight patterns of Hawks by his detailed criticism and the loan of his sketches and notes.

In addition to the foregoing, I am also indebted to the following for notes, suggestions, and other aid: Robert P. Allen, Harold H. Axtell, John H. Baker, H. C. Blanchard, Paul Brooks, Margaret Brooks, Brighton Cain, Dr. Clarence Cottam, David Lloyd Garrison, Dr. William T. Helmuth, Joseph J. Hickey, Richard Johnson, John O. Larson, Sigred Lee, Daniel Lehrmann, J. Norman McDonald, L. Nelson Nichols, Dr. H. C. Oberholser, Charles O'Brien, Richard H. Pough, Charles Shell, Alexander Sprunt, Jr., Mrs. Albert H. Stephens, Wendell Taber, Lovell Thompson, Mrs. Whiting Washington, Dr. Alexander Wetmore, Dr. J. T. Zimmer, and especially my wife, Mildred, who has assisted with much of the research and detail work.

For the use of its extensive collections, I wish to thank the American Museum of Natural History in New York City.

References were made to the following works: *Fourth A.O.U. Check-List of North American Birds*, Alexander's *Birds of the Ocean*, Bailey's *Handbook of Birds of the Western United States*, Bailey's *Birds of New Mexico*, Bent's *Life Histories of North American Birds*, Bond's *Birds of the West Indies*, Chapman's *Handbook of Birds of Eastern North America*, Chapman's *The Warblers of North America*, Dawson's *Birds of California*, Dawson and Bowles's *The Birds of Washington*, Eliot's *Birds of the Pacific Coast*, Forbush's *Birds of Massachusetts and other New England States*, Gabrielson and Jewett's *Birds of Oregon*, Grinnell and Storer's *Animal Life in the Yosemite*, Grinnell, Bryant, and Storer's *The Game Birds of California*, Hoffmann's *Guide to the Birds*, Hoffmann's *Birds of the Pacific States*, Howell's *Florida Bird Life*, Kitchin's *Distributional Check-List of the Birds of the State of Washington*, Linsdale's *Birds of Nevada*, May's *The Hawks of North America*, McCreary's *Wyoming Bird Life*, Murphy's *Oceanic Birds of South America*, Myers's *Western Birds*, Niedrach and Rockwell's *The Birds of Denver and Mountain Parks*, Peterson's *A Field Guide to the Birds*, Phillips's *Natural History of the Ducks*, Roberts's *Birds of Minnesota*, Saunders's *A Distributional List of the Birds of Montana*, Saunders's *A Guide to Bird Songs*, Sclater's *A History of the Birds of Colorado*, Simmons's *Birds of the Austin Region*, Sturgis's *Field Book of Birds of the Panama Canal Zone*,

Swarth's *A Distributional List of the Birds of Arizona*, Taverner's *Birds of Canada*, Van Tyne and Sutton's *Birds of Brewster County, Texas*, Witherby's *The Handbook of British Birds*, Wyman and Burnell's *Field Book of Birds of the Southwestern United States*. In addition to the above, numerous local lists and mimeographed publications were consulted, also the files of *The Auk*, *Bird-Lore*, *The Condor*, and *The Wilson Bulletin*.

More than to any others, I owe the completion of this guide to Guy Emerson, who constantly urged me on, and to my wife, who spent altogether too many lonely nights at home during the last three years while I burned the midnight oil in my study.

CONTENTS

CONTENTS

ILLUSTRATIONS

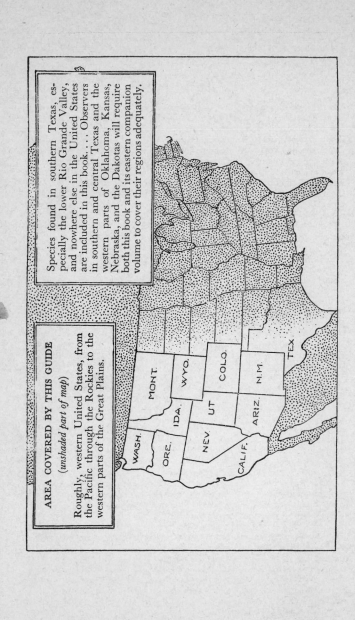

AREA COVERED BY THIS GUIDE

(unshaded part of map)

Roughly, western United States, from the Pacific through the Rockies to the western parts of the Great Plains.

Species found in southern Texas, especially the lower Rio Grande Valley, and nowhere else in the United States are included in this book. . . . Observers in southern and central Texas and the western parts of Oklahoma, Kansas, Nebraska, and the Dakotas will require both this book and its eastern companion volume to cover their regions adequately.

WASH. MONT.

ORE. IDA.

NEV. UT WYO.

CALIF. ARIZ. COLO.

N.M.

TEX.

HOW TO USE THIS BOOK

VETERANS who have watched birds for years will need no suggestions as to ways of using this book. Beginners, however, will do well to bear in mind a few comments that will point to short cuts. A few moments should be spent in familiarizing one's self, in a general way, with the illustrations; the briefest examination of the plates will be sufficient to give the beginner an idea of the shapes of our birds and the groups to which they belong. Ducks, it will be seen, do not resemble Loons; and the Gulls will be readily separable from the Terns. The needle-like bills of the Warblers will immediately distinguish them from the seed-cracking bills of the Sparrows. Birds of a kind — that is, birds that could be confused — are grouped together where easy comparison is possible. Thus, when a bird has been seen in the field, the observer can immediately turn to the picture most resembling it and feel confident that he has reduced the possibilities to the few species in its own group.

In many instances the pictures tell the story without help from the letter-press. This is true of such plates as those illustrating the Swallows, Vireos, Wrens, the diving birds, etc. In every case, however, it is well to check identifications from the drawings by referring to the text. The plates give visual field-marks that may be used in comparing and sorting out species seen in life. The text gives field-marks, size (in inches), manner of flight, voice, range, etc., that could not be pictured, and, in addition, mentions the birds that might, in any instance, be confused with a given species.

In cases where the plates, without the text, do not give definitive identifications, the observer should select the picture that most resembles the bird he saw, and then consult the text. We may, for example, be puzzled by a bird that is certainly a female Merganser. A consultation of the brief descriptions of those birds eliminates the Hooded Merganser because the bird sought had a reddish head — not a dark one. It was seen on the coast, which, so the text tells us, increases the *probability* that it was a Red-breast. And finally, we learn that in the Red-breasted Merganser 'the rufous of the head *blends* into the white of the throat and neck instead of being sharply defined' as in the American Merganser. This characteristic, which accurately describes the bird we have seen, makes the identification certain. This soft merging of color is clearly shown in the plate, but because we had not known what to look for, we failed to notice it.

Far from helping only the beginner who can scarcely tell a Gull from a Duck, it is hoped that the advanced student will find this guide comprehensive enough to be of service in recognizing those accidentals or rarities that sometimes appear in the territory he knows so thoroughly.

Some of the assertions herein contained, of the ease with which certain birds may be distinguished, will possibly be questioned on the ground that older works have stated that they are 'very difficult' or 'impossible' to identify except in the hand.

Doubting Thomases need but take a few trips afield with some of our present-day experts in field identifications to realize the possibility of quickly identifying almost any bird, with amazing certainty, at the snap of a finger. It is but a matter of seeing a bird often enough and knowing exactly what to look for, to be able to distinguish, with a very few exceptions, even the most confusing forms.

Most of the 'rare finds' are made by people who are alive to the possibilities and know what to look for, should they detect anything unusual. It is the discovery of rarities that puts real zest into the sport of birding, a zest that many of us would like to interpret as 'scientific zeal' rather than the quickening of our sporting blood.

Field birding, as many of us engage in it, is a game — a most absorbing game. As we become more proficient, we attempt to list as many birds as we can in a day. The May 'big day' or 'Christmas Census' is the apogee of this sort of thing. Some ornithologists minimize the scientific value of this type of bird work. Truly, it has but little. Recognition is not the end and aim of ornithology, but is certainly a most fascinating diversion, and a tool which the person who desires to contribute to our knowledge of ornithology might profitably learn to master.

The illustrations. The plates and cuts scattered throughout the text are intended as diagrams, arranged so that quick, easy comparison can be made of the species that most resemble one another. As they are not intended to be pictures or portraits, all modeling of form and feathering is eliminated where it can be managed, so that simple contour and pattern remain. Even color is often an unnecessary, if not, indeed, a confusing, factor. In many of the waterfowl, which we seldom see at close range, this is especially true; so most of the diagrams are carried out in black and white. With many of the small birds, however, since color is quite essential to identification, a departure from the monochrome in the illustrations is necessarily made.

Area. The area covered by this book is roughly the United States west of the one hundred and third meridian. This includes the entire States of Washington, Oregon, California, Nevada, Idaho, Utah, Montana, Wyoming, Colorado, Arizona, and New Mexico, and the western part of Texas. In addition, those species which are found in southern Texas, especially in the lower Rio Grande Valley, but nowhere else in the United States, are included in this book. Typical Eastern species or races thereof which occur in the same part of southern Texas will be found in the Eastern counterpart of this volume, *A Field Guide to the Birds.*

Along the western edge of the Great Plains in eastern New Mexico, Colorado, Wyoming, and Montana, a number of strictly Eastern birds have been recorded as stragglers anywhere from one to a dozen times or more. As it is theoretically possible to see almost any Eastern species sooner or later along the western edge of the Great Plains, these are not described here. For eventualities of this sort, bird watchers living east of the mountains should use both books. Following is a list of Eastern strays compiled from published sources:

Broad-winged Hawk (Colo.)
Piping Plover (Colo., Wyo.)
Woodcock (Colo., Wyo.)
Buff-breasted Sandpiper (Colo., Mont.)
Hudsonian Godwit (Wyo., Mont.)
Barred Owl (Colo., Wyo., Mont.)
Red-bellied Woodpecker (Colo.)
Crested Flycatcher (Wyo.)
Carolina Wren (Mont.)
Short-billed Marsh Wren (Colo. and Wyo.; bred in Ut.)
Wood Thrush (Colo.)
Gray-cheeked Thrush (Mont.)

Prothonotary Warbler (Colo. and Wyo.)
Parula Warbler (Colo. and Wyo.)
Magnolia Warbler (w. Tex., Colo., Wyo.)
Black-throated Blue Warbler (N.M., Colo., Wyo.)
Black-throated Green Warbler (Colo. and Mont.)
Cerulean Warbler (N.M. and Colo.)
Blackburnian Warbler (N.M. and Wyo.)
Chestnut-sided Warbler (Colo. and Wyo.)
Bay-breasted Warbler (Mont.)
Palm Warbler (Colo., Wyo., and Mont.)
Connecticut Warbler (Colo.)
Hooded Warbler (Colo.)
Canada Warbler (Colo.)
Scarlet Tanager (Colo. and Wyo.)
Rose-breasted Grosbeak (N.M., Colo., Wyo., and Mont.)
Indigo Bunting (Colo.)
Leconte's Sparrow (Colo.)
Field Sparrow (Colo.; bred in se. Mont.)
Swamp Sparrow (Mont.)

Others will undoubtedly be added to this list. Some of them have even reached the Pacific Coast, where their occurrence is far more accidental. Eastern species, such as the Black-poll Warbler, Tennessee Warbler, and others that migrate *regularly* through eastern Colorado, eastern Wyoming, and eastern Montana, or breed there, are described in the pages of this book.

Although the *A.O.U. Check-List* includes all of Lower California, western Canada, and Alaska, the author found that by sticking strictly to the western United States, he was able to eliminate between two hundred and two hundred and fifty species and subspecies, thereby whittling the book down to practical field-guide proportions. A few of the accidentals, especially seabirds, that have been recorded but once or so and might never be recorded again, are excluded. Others, especially Canadian and Mexican accidentals which have been recorded only two or three times, but might reasonably be looked for in the future, are included.

Range. A thorough acquaintance with any existing State or local list should properly be made by the beginner. The importance of these lists can hardly be stressed too much. The writer has only given an abbreviated account of the ranges of each species; an account of the exact range and seasonal distribution would have more than doubled the size of this handbook. Only the range in the western United States is given. Many species have a much wider distribution. The Mallard, as an example, is found over a large part of the globe.

Subspecies. It is a challenge to the field student to be able to identify some of the more well-marked subspecies, but in this book subspecies are merely listed by name under each species, unless field distinctions are fairly obvious. I have used the words 'no apparent field differences' when identification is very difficult or impossible. Advanced students, referring to skins in their local museums, might work out ways of telling some of these, but a too thorough treatment in these pages might only make the beginner overconfident, and would lead to many errors. A more complete discussion of the subspecies problem will be found in the back of this book. Be sure to read it.

Voice. We make our first identification of a species, as a rule, by sight. Then we become familiar with its song or notes. A 'sizzling trill' or a 'bubbling warble' conveys but a wretched idea of the real effect produced by the voice of any particular bird; they are descriptions and help chiefly to fix in our minds a note or song we have already identified. Voice syllabifications in most standard bird works vary greatly, each author giving his own interpretation. There are a few species whose voices we often hear long before we become acquainted with the bird in life — such birds as the Poor-will and the Owls. Then there are those few, such as the small Flycatchers, that are far more easily recognized by voice than by appearance.

Many birds have a variety of call-notes, and often more than one distinct song. Many Warblers, for example, have two songs. These pages will not attempt to treat the voices of birds more than briefly. In a few difficult cases, in analyzing songs, I have resorted to a system of symbols similar to that used by Aretas Saunders in his Eastern classic *A Guide to Bird Songs*. The serious student should secure a copy of *Birds of the Pacific States* by Ralph Hoffmann. This book, which makes an excellent companion volume to this guide, goes into more detail about voice and notes than I have been able to do in this limited space. Hoffmann's interpretations are much clearer than those of most other writers.

Identification by elimination. Identification by elimination plays an important part in field work. For example, there are six similar species of Junco in the Western States. Only one, the Oregon Junco, occurs normally in the Pacific States, so the student in that area, knowing this, does not usually bother about the other five, once having ascertained the bird in question to be a Junco. If he is on the lookout for rarities (the Gray-headed Junco or the Slate-colored Junco, both of which occur occasionally or rarely in the Pacific States), he looks for Juncos with *gray* sides. Any Junco with *buffy* or *rusty* sides is at once eliminated as being the ordinary species.

Then, of course, there is *elimination by habitat.* One would not expect to find a Rosy Finch in the desert or a House Finch above timber line. Habitats and 'life zones' are very distinct in the West. A visitor coming from the East, where life zones are more uniform, is constantly astonished when told he should look for the Blue Grosbeak only in the willow bottoms, the Plain Titmouse in the oaks or pinyons in the foothills, and not to expect the Steller's Jay below the pines. These altitudinal life zones are very well marked, and each has its own bird life. The beginner should learn what to expect in each one of his local zones. Although this book indicates habitat preferences, it makes little formal mention of zones (other than high mountains, foothills, deserts, valleys, etc.), as the distribution of many species varies somewhat in different parts of the West and at different seasons.

Caution in sight records. One should always use a certain amount of caution in making identifications, especially where rarities are concerned. The ornithologist of the old school seldom accepted a sight record unless it was made along the barrel of a shotgun. Today it is difficult for the average person to secure collecting privileges; moreover, a large proportion of the real rarities show up in parks, preserves, sanctuaries, or on municipal property where collecting is out of the question. There is no reason why we should not trust our eyes — at least after we have acquired a good basic knowledge of the commoner species. Caution should be the keynote. A quick field observer who does not temper his snap judgment with a bit of caution is like a fast car without brakes.

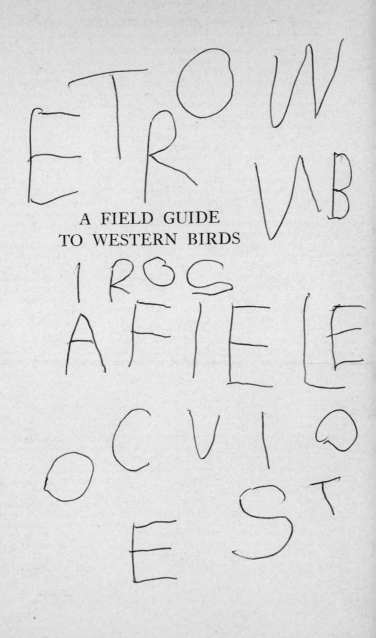

A FIELD GUIDE
TO WESTERN BIRDS

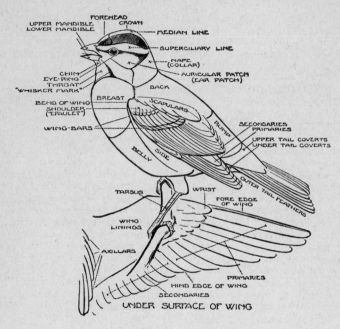

UPPER MANDIBLE
LOWER MANDIBLE
FOREHEAD
CROWN
MEDIAN LINE
SUPERCILIARY LINE
NAPE (COLLAR)
AURICULAR PATCH (EAR PATCH)
CHIN
EYE-RING
THROAT
"WHISKER MARK"
BACK
BREAST
SCAPULARS
BEND OF WING
SHOULDER ("EPAULET")
RUMP
WING-BARS
SECONDARIES
PRIMARIES
UPPER TAIL COVERTS
UNDER TAIL COVERTS
BELLY
SIDE
OUTER TAIL FEATHERS
TARSUS
WRIST
FORE EDGE OF WING
WING LININGS
AXILLARS
PRIMARIES
HIND EDGE OF WING
SECONDARIES

UNDER SURFACE OF WING

TOPOGRAPHY OF A BIRD
Showing terms used in this volume

LOONS: GAVIIDÆ

LARGE swimming birds, larger than most Ducks and with shorter necks than Geese. The sharp-pointed bill is a characteristic feature. Like the Grebes, they are expert divers. In flight the outline is gangly, with a slight downward sweep to the neck and the big feet projecting beyond the tail.

COMMON LOON. *Gavia immer*. Subsp. (Illus., pp. 2, 12.)
Descr. 28–36. Size of small Goose. *Breeding plumage:*— Head and neck glossy black with white collar; back checkered with black and white; under parts white. Adult in this plumage unmistakable. (Pacific Loon has back of head pale gray.) *Winter plumage:* — Mostly grayish; top of head, back of neck, and back dark gray; cheek, throat, and under parts white. In this plumage the bird resembles closely both the Pacific and the Red-throated Loons, but may be recognized by its large size and stouter bill. Its profile is also less snaky. In spite of its name it is no commoner coastwise than the other two species. (See Pacific and Red-throated Loons.) In flight Loons appear like big Mergansers with legs trailing out behind, but with much slower wing-beats than any Duck. On the water, they appear to be long-bodied, low-lying birds. Sometimes they swim with only the head and neck above water. Cormorants resemble Loons but are much blacker, especially in winter, and in flight the longer neck and tail and faster wing-beats are quite evident. Cormorants swim with the bill pointed slightly upward at an angle.
Voice: — On breeding grounds, loud laughing and yodeling calls; at night or before a storm, a rapid ringing *a-oo-oo*.
Range: — Breeds on fresh-water lakes from Can. s. to Wyo., e. Ore., and ne. Calif. (formerly); migrates throughout w. U.S.; winters along Pacific Coast.
Subsp. (No apparent field differences): (1) Common Loon, *G. i. immer*; (2) Lesser Loon, *G. i. elasson*.

PACIFIC LOON. *Gavia arctica pacifica*. (Illus. pp. 2, 12.)
Descr. 23–24. Similar in size to Red-throated Loon. *Breeding plumage:* — The *gray* hind-neck and black throat make good field-marks. *Winter plumage:* — Very similar to the other Loons at this season. About the size of the Red-throated Loon, but with more contrast between dark crown and light cheek and lacking the *speckled* back of that species. Instead, the markings of the back often have a scaly effect. The bill is quite as slender as that of the Red-throat, but is straight, not slightly upturned.

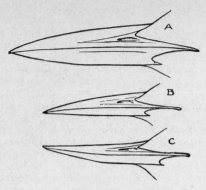

BILLS OF LOONS
A. Common   B. Pacific   C. Red-throated

The Common Loon, which it resembles at a distance in pattern, is a larger bird with a much thicker bill.
Range: — Pacific Coast in migration and winter, occasional at other seasons; accidental inland.

RED-THROATED LOON. *Gavia stellata.* (Illus. pp. 2, 12.)
Descr. 24–27. Smaller than Common Loon; nearer size of Merganser. *Breeding plumage:* — Gray head and *rufous-red* throat-patch unmistakable. *Winter plumage:* — Mainly *grayish* and white in color, like the Pacific Loon, but back speckled with white, giving a paler appearance at long range. In many individuals, the gray on the head and hind-neck is pale, merging into the white and offering none of the black-and-white contrast of the Pacific and Common Loons. The bill of this bird is one of the best field-marks. It seems to be slightly *upturned*, a character that is apparent at a considerable distance. The bills of the Pacific and Common Loons are quite straight.
Range: — Migrant and winter visitant along coast; occasional inland.

GREBES: COLYMBIDÆ

THE Grebes are Duck-like swimming water-birds; poor fliers but expert divers. They may be distinguished from the Ducks by the pointed bill, narrow head and neck, and tailless appearance. The Grebes normally hold their necks quite erect; Loons and Ducks do so mostly when alarmed.

HOLBOELL'S GREBE. *Colymbus grisegena holboelli.* (Illus. p. 12.)
Descr. 18–20. Much larger than any other Grebe, except the Western Grebe; large as a fair-sized Duck. *Breeding plumage:* — Body of bird gray, shading to white below; neck rufous-red; cheeks white; crown black; bill yellowish. *Winter plumage:* — The most familiar plumage. Generally grayish in color; top of head darker; often with a *conspicuous white crescent-shaped mark* on side of head (absent in first-year birds). In flight the bird shows two white patches on each wing. There are several species of birds found in the same waters as this species during the colder months with which it might be confused. The Holboell's Grebe may be distinguished from the Horned and Eared Grebes by its larger size, much heavier head and neck, large dull *yellow* bill, and more uniform gray coloration. (The two smaller Grebes have contrasting white cheeks, white necks, and dark bills.) It can be distinguished from the Loons at long range by its grayer face and neck and dull yellow bill. Loons, on the water, at a distance, appear as long-bodied birds with proportionately shorter necks, whereas the Grebe is a shorter-bodied bird that seems to be all head and neck. In flight, at a distance, this Grebe resembles the female Red-breasted Merganser, but it beats its wings more slowly, has two white patches on each wing instead of one, and holds its neck bent slightly downward — this last a very good field character. The Merganser flies with its neck and body held perfectly horizontal.
Range: — Breeds from n. Wash. and Mont. n.; winters along coast; a rare migrant inland.

HORNED GREBE. *Colymbus auritus.* (Illus. p. 12.)
Descr. 13–15. A small Grebe, typical of lakes, bays, and large bodies of water. *Breeding plumage:* — Head black, with conspicuous buff-colored ear-tufts; neck and flanks rufous-red; back gray; under parts white. *Winter plumage:* — Contrastingly patterned with dark gray and white. Top of head, line down back of neck, and back dark gray; under parts, neck, and cheeks clear white and sharply defined. (See Eared Grebe.)
Range: — Breeds from n. Mont. n.; winters along coast; a few migrate on inland lakes.

EARED GREBE. *Colymbus nigricollis californicus.* (Illus. p. 12.)
Descr. 12–14. *Breeding plumage:* — Smaller than Horned Grebe. Also has buffy facial tufts, but neck *black* instead of chestnut as in that species, and black feathers of crown crest-like instead of flat. *Winter plumage:* — Very similar to that of Horned Grebe. Dark gray and white but dark of head and neck *broader and less clearly defined*, giving a 'dirtier' look. There is

almost invariably a suffused whitish patch in the gray on each side of the head just back of the ear (see diagram). Neck is more slender; bill is slimmer and appears slightly upturned. On the water, the rear parts of the Eared Grebe seem to ride higher.
Range: — Breeds locally, chiefly e. of Cascades and Sierras, from Can. to e. Calif., n. Ariz., and N.M.; winters along entire coast and inland from s. Calif. and N.M. s.

MEXICAN GREBE (LEAST GREBE). *Colymbus dominicus brachypterus.* (Illus. p. 12.)
Descr. 10. A very small dark Grebe, much smaller than the similarly shaped Pied-billed Grebe, with a slender *black* pointed bill instead of a thick pale or pied bill.
Range: — Fresh ponds, marshes, and resacas of s. Tex.

WESTERN GREBE. *Æchmophorus occidentalis.* (Illus. p. 12.)
Descr. 22–29. A large Grebe, with an extremely long, slender neck. In any plumage it is an all *black-and-white* bird. Top of head, line on back of neck, and back, black; cheeks, neck, and under parts white. Bill light yellow. The contrasting black-and-white coloration and single white wing-patch distinguish it from the winter Holboell's Grebe, which has two white patches on each wing. The winter Holboell's Grebe is a gray-looking, instead of a black-and-white, bird.
Range: — Breeds e. of Cascades and Sierras from Can. to n. Calif., Ut., and Colo.; winters along coast; some migrate inland, chiefly w. of Rockies.

PIED-BILLED GREBE. *Podilymbus podiceps podiceps.* (Illus. p. 12.)
Descr. 12–15. A common Grebe of the ponds, creeks, and marshes. *Breeding plumage:* — Gray-brown, darkest on top of head and back; throat-patch and spot across bill black. *Winter plumage:* — Browner, without throat-patch and bill-mark. The thick, *rounded* bill of the Pied-bill will distinguish it in profile at a distance, in any plumage, from the Horned or Eared Grebes with their slender, pointed bills. The Pied-bill has no well-marked white *patches* in the wing as have all the other Grebes.
Voice: — A Cuckoo-like *cow-cow-cow-cow-cow-cow-cowk-cowk-cowk* or *kum-kum-kum*, etc.
Range: — Breeds on fresh-water ponds and marshes throughout w. U.S.; winters in Pacific States and from Ariz. s.

ALBATROSSES: DIOMEDEIDÆ

BLACK-FOOTED ALBATROSS. *Diomedea nigripes.* (Illus. p. 16.)
Descr. 29–36. Wing-spread 7 ft. Albatrosses are birds of the

open ocean, much larger than any Gulls and with wings which are proportionately far longer. These tremendously long saber-like wings and the rigid Shearwater-like gliding and banking identify this species, the only Albatross now found regularly along the Pacific Coast. It is seldom seen from shore. The plumage is dusky above and below, but at close range a whitish face and pale areas toward the tips of the wings can be seen. Some birds, presumably adults, show white patches at the base of the tail; these are usually not seen as often as dark-rumped birds.

Range: — Pacific Ocean, usually offshore.

SHORT-TAILED ALBATROSS. *Diomedea albatrus.*
Descr. 33–37. Wing-spread 7 ft. A white Albatross, with blackish primaries and tip of tail. Formerly regular along Pacific Coast, but thought to have ceased coming during the last generation. However, as individuals are still recorded in Alaskan waters, it should be looked for off the coast of the Pacific States. Its white body will readily distinguish it from the all-dark Black-footed Albatross. The Laysan Albatross, *D. immutabilis*, another white-bodied species, is a remote possibility but has a *black* instead of a white back. The immature Short-tailed Albatross is dark brown and resembles the Black-footed Albatross, but the bill and feet are *pink or flesh-colored*.

SHEARWATERS AND FULMARS: PROCELLARIIDÆ

SHEARWATERS are Gull-like sea-birds, usually found well offshore; uniform dusky, or dark above and white below. Their flight, several flaps and a sail, banking on stiff wings in the wave-troughs, is distinctive. A Shearwater's wings are proportionately narrower than a Gull's and the tail is not so fanlike. Six species occur off the Pacific Coast. Three are of the black-breasted type, three are white-breasted. For convenience, the following table is given to show their proportionate probability of occurrence.

Black-breasted Shearwaters
    1. Sooty Shearwater — abundant
    2. Slender-billed Shearwater — common
    3. Pale-footed Shearwater — very rare
White-breasted Shearwaters
    1. Pink-footed Shearwater — common
    2. Black-vented Shearwater — common
    3. New Zealand Shearwater — rare
Fulmars are Gull-like birds similar to, but more robust than, Shearwaters.

SLENDER-BILLED SHEARWATER. *Puffinus tenuirostris.*
Descr. 14. A dark-bellied Shearwater; looks all black at a distance; can best be told from the Sooty Shearwater by its smaller size and somewhat darker wing-linings. (Sooty has pale grayish-white linings.) The best time to look for this species offshore is in the late fall and early winter after the Sooty Shearwater has decreased in numbers.
Range: — Pacific Coast, chiefly offshore.

SOOTY SHEARWATER. *Puffinus griseus.* (Illus. p. 13.)
Descr. 16–18. Smaller than the California Gull. Uniform dusky brown; under surface of the wings pale or whitish. A Gull-like sea-bird that looks all black at a distance (dark Jaegers always show white at the base of the primaries). This is the commonest Shearwater, great numbers often being seen offshore, especially in late spring, in summer, and in fall. It is the only one frequently seen in abundance from the land.
Range: — Pacific Ocean, along coast and offshore.

BLACK-VENTED SHEARWATER. *Puffinus opisthomelas.*
Descr. 12½–15. A white-breasted Shearwater similar in appearance to the Pink-footed Shearwater but much smaller and with a more rapid wing-motion. It can further be distinguished from the Pink-footed species by white wing-linings and blackish bill (Pink-foot usually has grayer wing-linings and a pale flesh-colored bill). This species is commonest in fall and early winter.
Range: — Chiefly coast of Calif.; occasional in Wash.

PALE-FOOTED SHEARWATER. *Puffinus carneipes.*
Descr. 19½. Very rare. Over a dozen have been taken off Point Pinos, Calif. A dark-bellied Shearwater, a trifle *larger* than the abundant Sooty Shearwater, from which it can be distinguished by its pale *whitish bill, flesh-colored feet,* and lack of pale wing-linings.

PINK-FOOTED SHEARWATER. *Puffinus creatopus.* (Illus. p. 13.)
Descr. 19. Four Shearwaters occur *commonly* off the Pacific Coast. Two appear all black at a distance, and two are two-toned — dark above and white below. The two white-bellied species, the Pink-footed and Black-vented, are frequently associated with the abundant Sooty Shearwaters and can easily be distinguished by size. The Pink-foot is a bit *larger* than the Sooty Shearwater, the Black-vent is much smaller. The present species is an easier and more graceful flier than the Sooty, making fewer wing-strokes. It occurs chiefly in summer and fall. The Pink-foot occurs along most of the coast, the Black-vent chiefly off Calif. (See Black-vented Shearwater.)
Range: — Pacific Coast, offshore.

NEW ZEALAND SHEARWATER. *Thyellodroma bulleri.*
Descr. 16½. This rare Shearwater might be looked for in fall or winter off the coast of Calif. It is a white-bellied Shearwater, and might be told from the two other white-bellied species by the *gray back*, which contrasts conspicuously with the blackish color of the head and tail and wings. The black areas on the primaries and lesser wing-coverts are said to form a wide inverted W when the bird is on the wing. This should be a good mark. At close range the feet are *yellowish* instead of flesh-colored as in the two similar species. It is said to have a different and more airy style of flight.
Range: — Occasional fall or winter visitor to coast of Calif. (most records off Point Pinos). Also recorded in Ore. and Wash.

PACIFIC FULMAR. *Fulmarus glacialis rodgersi.* (Illus. p. 16.)
Descr. 17–19. Slightly smaller than the California Gull. *Light phase:* — Head and under parts white; back and wings gray; wings darker toward tip, but with *no black markings* as in most Gulls; bill yellow. Resembles a California Gull in this phase, but appearance in the air is different. The wings are held quite stiff and the bird glides and scales in the manner of a Shearwater, or even more like an Albatross. *Dark phase:* — Uniform smoky gray; wing-tips darker, bill yellow. In this plumage the bird remotely resembles the Sooty Shearwater but is much paler. The Fulmar's bill is stubbier than a Gull's or Shearwater's, giving a Dove-like appearance to the head. Some Fulmars are mottled with white on the wings. These formerly went under the obsolete name of Rodgers's Fulmar.
Range: — Pacific Coast, offshore, in migration and winter.

STORM PETRELS: HYDROBATIDÆ

THESE Petrels are the little dark birds that flit over the surface of the sea, usually well offshore, in the wake of fishing boats and ocean-going vessels. Three of the five Pacific species are all black in general appearance, and are difficult to tell apart in the field.

FORK-TAILED PETREL. *Oceanodroma furcata.* (Illus. p. 13.)
Descr. 8. A *pearly-gray* Petrel, absolutely unlike all the other Petrels, which are blackish.
Range: — Breeds on ids. off n. Calif. and Ore.; migrates and winters along entire coast, offshore.

BEAL'S PETREL. *Oceanodroma leucorhoa.* Subsp. (Illus. p. 13.)

Descr. 8. A black Petrel with a *conspicuous white rump*. The three other black Petrels have *dark* rumps. The Leach's Petrel of the Atlantic is a race of this species.
Range: — Breeds on ocean ids. from Alaska to Farallon Ids., Calif.; winters offshore from Wash. to s. Calif.
Subsp. (No apparent field differences): (1) Beal's Petrel, *O. l. beali*; (2) Kaeding's Petrel, *O. l. kaedingi*.

BLACK PETREL. *Oceanodroma melania*. (Illus. p. 13.)
Descr. 9. Of the three all-black Petrels found off the coast of southern California in summer, this is the largest and probably the most common. It nests on the Coronados Ids. off San Diego, in company with the less common Socorro Petrel. (See Socorro and Ashy Petrels.) It can be told from those two birds by its larger size, longer wings, and more languid flight (suggestive of Black Tern).
Range: — Calif.; breeds on Coronados Ids. off San Diego; wanders n. to Marin Co.

ASHY PETREL. *Oceanodroma homochroa*. (Illus. p. 13.)
Descr. 7½. The smallest of the three all-black Petrels. At times it can be seen together with the Black Petrel off the coast of central Calif. When such comparison is possible it can be told without much trouble by its decidedly smaller size, shorter wings, and more fluttery flight. At very close range it shows a certain amount of white on the under side of the wings, and it has shorter legs.
Range: — Coast of Calif.; breeds on Farallon Ids. and Santa Cruz Id.

SOCORRO PETREL. *Oceanodroma socorroënsis*.
Descr. 7¾. One of the three all-black Petrels. Breeds in company with the Black Petrel on the Coronados Ids. and is difficult to distinguish from that species. When it can be compared, it will be seen to be smaller and to have a grayer rump. A small percentage of Socorros have a touch of white on the sides of the rump but seldom forming a conspicuous unbroken patch as in the Beal's Petrel. Some authorities consider it but a race of the Beal's Petrel. Its flight is almost exactly like that of that species and consequently quite different from the other two all-black Petrels. Like the Beal's Petrel it leaps about like a Nighthawk; the Black Petrel has a much lazier movement, and the Ashy Petrel a more fluttery flight (R. C. Murphy).
Range: — Coast of s. Calif.; breeds on Coronados Ids. off San Diego.

TROPIC–BIRDS: PHAËTHONTIDÆ

RED-BILLED TROPIC-BIRD. *Phaëthon æthereus.* (Illus. p. 16.)
Descr. 24–40; tail 7½–26. A slender white sea-bird, nearly size of a California Gull, with a *heavy red bill*, black patch through each side of face, and two extremely long *central tail-feathers* — so long and streaming that they could be more easily compared (in length) to those of the Scissor-tailed Flycatcher than to the needle-pointed outer tail-feathers of the Terns. The rapid Pigeon-like flight (steady wing-beats) and the long tail are distinctive. When the bird sits on the water, it rides with its tail cocked like a Wren's.
Range: — Occasional off s. Calif., well offshore.

PELICANS: PELECANIDÆ

EXTREMELY large water-birds with long flat bills and tremendous throat-pouches. Pelicans fly in orderly lines, alternating several flaps with a short sail, each bird in the flock playing follow-my-leader, flapping and sailing in rhythm, apparently taking the cue from the bird in front. In flight they draw their heads back on their shoulders.

WHITE PELICAN. *Pelecanus erythrorhynchos.* (Illus. p. 16.)
Descr. 55–70. Wing-spread 9 ft. A huge white bird with black primaries in the wing and a great yellow throat-pouch. Flies with head hunched back on shoulders, and long flat bill resting on curved neck. Often flies at a great height. Swans have no black wing-tips; the Wood Ibis has black primaries, but flies with neck extended and long legs trailing. The Snow Goose has a similar pattern but is much smaller, flies with neck extended, and has a small bill.
Range: — Breeds locally on inland lakes from Can. s. to s. Calif., w. Nev., n. Ut., and Wyo. (Yellowstone); migrates through interior to Mex.; winters from Calif. s.

CALIFORNIA BROWN PELICAN. *Pelecanus occidentalis californicus.* (Illus. p. 16.)
Descr. 50–54. Wing-spread 6½ ft. A ponderous, dark waterbird with more or less white about the head and neck (in adults). Immatures have dark heads. Flies with its head hunched back on its shoulders and its long flat bill resting comfortably on its curved neck. Its size and flight, a few flaps and a sail, proclaim it a Pelican; its dusky color at once eliminates its white relative.

Range: — Coastal; breeds along coast of s. Calif.; wanders n. after breeding season to Ore. and Wash.; casual in Ariz.

CORMORANTS: PHALACROCORACIDÆ

LARGE dark water-birds, as large as, or larger than, any of the Ducks. To be confused chiefly with the Loons, or Geese, but the tail is longer and wing-action more rapid. In flight, the neck is held slightly above the horizontal (Loon's neck droops slightly). Of course, in winter, when Loons are paler, Cormorants can be told by their very blackness, especially the adults, which are black beneath as well as above. Loons are always clear white below. Flocks of Cormorants usually fly in line or wedge formation very much like Geese and are sometimes called 'Nigger Geese.' A large dark bird perched in an *upright position* on some rock or buoy over the water can hardly be anything else. Swimming, they lie low like Loons, but with necks more erect and snake-like, and bills pointed upward *at an angle*.

DOUBLE-CRESTED CORMORANT. *Phalacrocorax auritus.* Subsp. (Illus. pp. 11, 16.)
Descr. 30–36. Any Cormorant found inland on large bodies of water in w. U.S. can quite safely be called this species. Along the coast it may be told from the other two Cormorants by its bright *orange-yellow* throat-pouch. (See Brandt's Cormorant.)
Range: — Pacific Coast and locally on large bodies of water inland in Calif., Ore., Ut., Ariz., and w. Nev., and along Great Plains.
Subsp. (No apparent field differences): (1) Double-crested Cormorant, *P. a. auritus*; (2) Farallon Cormorant, *P. a. albociliatus*; (3) White-crested Cormorant, *P. a. cincinatus*.

BRANDT'S CORMORANT. *Phalacrocorax penicillatus.* (Illus. pp. 11, 16.)
Descr. 33. About the size of the Double-crested (Farallon) Cormorant but does not have the yellow throat-pouch. Instead it has a *buffy-brown band across the throat* and in the breeding season a *blue* throat-pouch. Young birds are brownish, with paler under parts. Young Double-crested Cormorants are similar in size but usually *whiter* on the under parts, and show the yellow pouch. (If a young Cormorant has a decidedly whitish breast it is a Double-crest; if the breast is buffy or pale brown, it might be a Double-crest but more likely a Brandt's. If the under parts are deep rich brown, the bird is a Brandt's.)
Range: — Pacific Coast.

THIN BILL
DULL RED
THROAT POUCH

YELLOW
THROAT POUCH

BLUE
THROAT POUCH
BUFFY
PATCH

HEADS OF CORMORANTS

A. Baird's   B. Double-crested   C. Brandt's

BAIRD'S CORMORANT. *Phalacrocorax pelagicus resplendens.*
(Illus. pp. 11, 16.)
Descr. 25½. Noticeably smaller than the other two Cormorants,
a good mark when comparison is possible. Much more iridescent and glossy at close range in good light. It can also be
told by its more slender neck, small head, and much *thinner
bill*. In the breeding season (February to June) it has a *white
patch* on each flank near the tail. This is especially conspicuous
in flight. The throat-pouch is dull red, but this can be seen only
at very close range.
Range: — Pacific Coast.

DARTERS: ANHINGIDÆ

WATER-TURKEY. *Anhinga anhinga.*
Descr. 34. Similar to a Cormorant but much slimmer; mainly
blackish with *large silvery patches* on the fore part of the wings,
and with a long white-tipped tail and a *long serpentine neck*;
it perches like a Cormorant, in upright posture, on some tree
or snag, but the neck is much snakier. In flight it progresses
with alternate flapping and sailing, the slender neck extended in
front, the long tail spread fanwise. Females have pale buffy
breasts, males blackish. Immature birds are largely brownish
instead of blackish.
Range: — Occurs on lower Colo. R. near Yuma; casual in N.M.
and Colo.

MAN–O'–WAR BIRDS: FREGATIDÆ

MAN-O'-WAR BIRD. *Fregata magnificens.* (Illus. p. 16.)
Descr. 40. Wing-spread 7½ ft. Voyagers in warmer seas often
see long-winged black birds, with forked Barn-Swallow-like
tails, soaring with great ease. These are the Man-o'-Wars, or
Frigate-birds. Their wings are longer in proportion to the body-
bulk than those of any other sea-bird. *Male:* — Black, with
orange throat-patch. *Female:* — White breast. *Immature:* —
Whole head and under parts white.
Range: — Occasional along coast of s. Calif.

HERONS AND BITTERNS: ARDEIDÆ

Long-legged, long-necked wading birds with long sharp-
pointed bills. In sustained flight their heads are drawn back to
their shoulders. Cranes and Ibises, which are otherwise quite
Heron-like, fly with necks outstretched.

HERONS AND CRANES IN FLIGHT

A. Sandhill Crane   B. Great Blue Heron

MEXICAN GREBE   PIED-BILLED GREBE

SUMMER

WESTERN GREBE   HOLBOELL'S GREBE

SUMMER   WINTER

RED-THROATED LOON

SUMMER   WINTER

PACIFIC LOON

SUMMER   WINTER

COMMON LOON

SUMMER   WINTER

WHITE BREAST
DARK BREAST

SOOTY   SHEAR-
           WATER

PINK-
FOOTED
SHEAR-   WATER

WHITE
PATCHES

SKUA

SQUARE-CUT
TAIL

FORK-
TAILED   PETREL

BLACK
PETREL

PEARLY GRAY

WHITE
RUMP   LIGHT PHASE

ALL DARK

ASHY
PETREL

BEAL'S
PETREL   POINTED
                            CENTRAL
                            TAIL-FEATHERS

PARASITIC
JAEGER

DARK
PHASE

BLUNT
CENTRAL
TAIL-FEATHER

LONG-
TAILED
JAEGER

LONG CENTRAL
TAIL-FEATHERS

POMARINE
JAEGER

SHEARWATERS
PETRELS
AND
JAEGERS

GREAT BLUE HERON. *Ardea herodias.* Subsp. (Illus. pp. 12, 17.)
Descr. 42–52. This great bird, often called 'crane' by country people, stands about four feet tall, and is, next to the Sandhill Crane, the largest wading bird common in the Western States. Its long legs, long neck, and sharp-pointed bill, and, in flight, its drawn-in neck, mark the bird as a Heron. The great size and blue-gray coloration, whiter about the head and neck, identify it as this species.
Voice: — A series of three or four low, hoarse croaks.
Range: — Shores, marshes, lakes, and streams from Can. to Mex.; tends to migrate from colder sections in winter.
Subsp. (No apparent field differences): (1) Great Blue Heron, *A. h. herodias*; (2) Treganza's Heron, *A. h. treganzai*; (3) Northwestern Coast Heron, *A. h. fannini*; (4) California Heron, *A. h. hyperonca.*

AMERICAN EGRET. *Casmerodius albus egretta.* (Illus. p. 17.)
Descr. 37–42. A large Heron of snowy-white plumage, with black legs and feet and a *yellow bill.* The Brewster's Snowy Egret is also white, but is much smaller and has a black or blackish bill instead of yellow.
Range: — Breeds in Ore. and Calif.; wandering birds may be seen along Rio Grande and perhaps elsewhere in w. U.S.

BREWSTER'S SNOWY EGRET. *Egretta thula brewsteri.* (Illus. p. 17.)
Descr. 20–27. The western race of the Snowy Egret. A medium-sized White Heron with a *black bill,* black legs, and *yellow feet.* The American Egret is much larger and has a yellow bill and black feet, almost the reverse in color of those parts in the Snowy.
Range: — Breeds in Calif., Colo., and Ut.; migrates or summers in Wyo., Nev., Ariz., N.M., and w. Tex.

REDDISH EGRET. *Dichromanassa rufescens.* (Illus. p. 17.)
Descr. 29. A medium-sized, shaggy-necked, loose-feathered Heron, larger than a Snowy Egret, smaller than an American Egret. *Dark phase:* — Blue-gray with a pale maroon or buffy brown head and neck, and a *flesh-colored, black-tipped bill. White phase:* — Scarcer; appears like American Egret, but shorter and stouter, legs *bluish.* When it is feeding, the quickest way to pick it out is by its clowning actions. The only *necessary* recognition mark to be remembered for either plumage is the flesh-colored, black-tipped bill.
Range: — Gulf Coast of Tex.; occasional in s. Calif. (San Diego).

LOUISIANA HERON. *Hydranassa tricolor ruficollis.*

Descr. 26. Occasional in southern Calif. A slender, medium-sized Heron, dark in color, with a clear white belly. The contrasting white belly is the key-mark in any plumage.

LITTLE BLUE HERON. *Florida cærulea cærulea.*
Descr. 20–29. *Adult:* — A medium-sized, slender Heron, slaty blue, with a maroon head and neck; legs dark. The adult, like the Green Heron, appears quite blackish at a distance, but the latter bird is smaller with much shorter, more yellow legs. *Immature:* — Snowy white, often with a tinge of blue in the primaries; legs dull *greenish*; bill *bluish* tipped with black. Some Snowy Egrets, especially young birds, are frequently suspected of being Little Blues because of greenish leg coloration. Many Snowys show a stripe of yellow or greenish up the posterior side of the legs as the bird walks away from the observer. The thicker bill, with its bluish base, and the lack of the shuffling foot-motions which are so characteristic of the Snowy, will identify this Eastern species.
Range: — E. U.S.; occasional or accidental in Calif.

ANTHONY'S GREEN HERON. *Butorides virescens anthonyi.*
Descr. 16–18½. A small dark Heron with comparatively short greenish-yellow legs. Elevates a shaggy crest when alarmed. Looks quite black and Crow-like at a distance, but flies with slower, more arched, wing-beats. At close range neck and face are rich chestnut.
Voice: — A series of *kucks* or a loud *skyow.*
Range: — Breeds from Portland, Ore., and s. Ariz. s.; winters from s. Calif. s.

BLACK-CROWNED NIGHT HERON. *Nycticorax nycticorax hoactli.* (Illus. p. 17.)
Descr. 23–28. A chunky, rather short-legged Heron. *Adult:* — The only Heron that is black-backed and pale gray or white below; wings gray. *Immature:* — Brown, spotted and streaked with white. Resembles American Bittern, but gray-brown, rather than rich, warm brown. It beats its wings more slowly and lacks the broad black wing-tips of the Bittern.
Voice: — Call, a flat *quok*, is unmistakable.
Range: — Breeds from e. Wash. and s. Wyo. s. to Mex.; winters n. to Ore. and Ut. (a few).

AMERICAN BITTERN. *Botaurus lentiginosus.* (Illus. p. 17.)
Descr. 23–34. In crossing a marsh we frequently flush this large, stocky brown bird. It is rarely seen perching like the other Herons. The dark wing-tips, contrasting with the warm brown of the rest of the bird, distinguish it from the brown young Night Heron. When silhouetted in flight, the faster wing-beats

and the less curved wings are the Bittern's marks. Contrary
to many a person's preconceived idea, the Least Bittern resembles it but little. The latter bird is much less than half the
size and is contrastingly patterned with buff and black.

Voice: — The pumping, the 'song' of the Bittern, which we hear
in the swamps in the spring might be rendered thus: *oong-ka-
choonk — oong-ka-choonk — oong-ka-choonk*, etc. Distorted by
distance, the *ka* is often the only audible syllable and sounds
like the driving of a stake into the mud. Flushing note, a rapid
throaty *kok-kok-kok*.

Range: — Breeds from Can. s. to s. Calif., cent. Ariz., and n.
N.M. (probably). Winters chiefly from Calif. s. and occasionally as far n. as Ore. and Wash.

LEAST BITTERN. *Ixobrychus exilis*. Subsp. (Illus. p. 17.)
Descr. 12–14. By far the smallest of the Heron family, nearer
size of a Rail. When discovered, it usually flushes close at hand
from its hiding-place in the marsh, flies weakly for a short distance, and drops in again. The *large buff wing-patches* and
black back distinguish it from any of the Rails, which are quite
uniform in coloration. Beginners sometimes call Green Herons
Least Bitterns.

Voice: — The call, a soft *coo-coo-coo* coming from the marsh, is
often the best indication of the bird's presence.

Range: — Breeds in Calif. and e. Ore.; occurs occasionally in
Rocky Mt. States and on Great Plains in e. Wyo. and e. Colo.
Subsp. (No apparent field differences): (1) Western Least
Bittern, *I. e. hesperis*; (2) Eastern Least Bittern, *I. e. exilis*.

WOOD IBISES: CICONIIDÆ

WOOD IBIS. *Mycteria americana*. (Illus. p. 17.)
Descr. 35–47. A very large white Heron-like bird with a dark,
naked head and large black wing-tips; bill long, stout, and *decurved*. Distinguished in flight, at a distance, from the White
Herons by the outstretched neck and the black in the wings and
by the alternate flapping and sailing; from the White Pelican
by its totally different proportions. Young birds are dark gray
with a downy covering on the head and neck.

Range: — Summer visitor to lower Colo. R. in Ariz. and Calif.;
occasional elsewhere in s. Calif. and in other W. States.

IBISES AND SPOONBILLS: THRESKIORNITHIDÆ

WHITE-FACED GLOSSY IBIS. *Plegadis guarauna.* (Illus. p. 17.)
Descr. 22–25. A medium-sized Heron-like bird with a long, *de-curved* bill; largely bronzy-chestnut, but at a distance appears quite black, like a large black Curlew. At close range it shows a white border about the base of the bill. It flies with neck out-stretched, with quicker wing-beats than a Heron, alternating flapping and sailing.
Range: — Breeds or summers from e. Ore., n. Ut., and Wyo. s. to Mex.; winters n. to s. Calif.

ROSEATE SPOONBILL. *Ajaia ajaja.*
Descr. 32. Occasional or accidental in southern California. A *bright-pink* Heron-like bird with a flat spoon-shaped bill. When feeding in the mud the flat bill is swung from side to side. In flight it extends its neck as does an Ibis, but the bird does not sail between wing-strokes so habitually. Immature birds are paler and whiter than adults.

SWANS: CYGNINÆ

VERY large white water-birds, larger and with much longer necks than Geese. Like some of the Geese, they migrate in stringy lines or V-shaped flocks. Their extremely long, slender necks which are fully extended in flight, and the lack of black wing-tips distinguish them from all other large white swimming birds (Snow Goose, White Pelican, etc.). Young birds are tinged with brown.

WHISTLING SWAN. *Cygnus columbianus.* (Illus. p. 24.)
Descr. 48–55. The only wild Swan in most of the West. Usu-ally heard long before the wavering wedge-shaped flock can be detected high in the blue. The much more stream-lined necks, larger size, and lack of black wing-tips eliminate the Snow Goose. Young birds are dingy-looking, not white.
Voice: — High-pitched cooing notes, less harsh than 'honking' of Canada Goose. 'A musical, loud *woo-ho, woo-woo, woo-ho*' (J. Moffitt).
Range: — Winters in Calif., Ore., Ut., and Wyo. (Yellowstone); a migrant in Wash., Mont., and occasionally elsewhere.

TRUMPETER SWAN. *Cygnus buccinator.* (Illus. p. 24.)
Descr. 65. Very rare and local. Larger than Whistling Swan.

BROWN PELICAN
ADULT

WHITE PELICAN

MAN·O'·WAR·BIRD
MALE

IMMATURE

ADULT

DOUBLE·CRESTED CORMORANT

RED·BILLED TROPIC·BIRD

BAIRD'S CORMORANT
ADULT IN BREEDING PLUMAGE
(ABOVE)

LIGHT

BLACK·FOOTED ALBATROSS

DARK

FULMAR

BRANDT'S CORMORANT
ADULT

WHITE-FACED GLOSSY IBIS

LEAST BITTERN

WOOD IBIS

AMERICAN BITTERN

GREEN HERON

ADULT

SANDHILL CRANE

IMMATURE

BLACK-CROWNED NIGHT HERON

SNOWY EGRET

ADULT

BLACK-CROWNED NIGHT HERON

AMERICAN EGRET

GREAT BLUE HERON

DARK PHASE

REDDISH EGRET

LONG-LEGGED WADERS

Adults can usually be distinguished from the Whistling Swan at close range by the *all-black bill* without the yellow basal spot, but this is not infallible, as some Whistlers lack this spot. Perhaps it is best distinguished from transient Whistlers by its deeper voice in the localities where it is resident.

Voice: — Much louder, lower-pitched, and more bugle-like than that of Whistling Swan.

Range: — Breeds in Yellowstone Park, Wyo., Red Rock Lake, Mont., and neighboring lakes; also a migrant and winter resident in this area. Formerly more widely distributed.

GEESE: ANSERINÆ

LARGE waterfowl; larger, heavier-bodied, and with longer necks than Ducks. In flight some species assemble in V-formation. As is not the case with most Ducks, sexes are alike at all seasons. They are more terrestrial than Ducks and feed mainly on land (except Brant); are to be looked for in grass or grain or stubble fields.

CANADA GOOSE. *Branta canadensis.* Subsp. (Illus. p. 24.)
Descr. The most widespread Goose in the West and the only one that breeds there; a brownish bird with black head and neck that contrast strikingly with the light-colored breast. The most characteristic mark is the white patch that runs from under the chin on to the side of the head. Few people are unfamiliar with the long strings of Geese passing high overhead in V-formation. Their musical honking or barking often heralds the approach of a flock long before it can be seen.

Voice: — A deep double-syllabled 'honking' note, *ka-ronk* or *ha-lunk, ha-lunk*.

Subsp. COMMON CANADA GOOSE. *B. c. canadensis.*
> 35–42. Much larger than the White-fronted or the Snow Goose. The best-known race and the only one that breeds in w. U.S. Breeds from ne. Calif., n. Nev., n. Ut., and Wyo. n. into Can.; winters from Wash. and Yellowstone Park s. into Mex.
> WHITE-CHEEKED GOOSE. *B. c. occidentalis.*
> 35. Slightly smaller than Canada Goose, with dark, chocolate-colored under parts. Winters along the coast from Puget Sound to n. Calif. (Del Norte and Humboldt Cos.). 'Voice higher-pitched than Common Canada, intermediate in tone between this form and Lesser Canada Goose' (J. Moffitt). The coastal habitat, dark under parts, and higher voice will identify this race.
> LESSER CANADA GOOSE. *B. c. leucopareia.*

25–34. A medium-sized Goose, much smaller than the Canada Goose or about the size of the Snow and White-fronted Geese, with which it often associates. Some birds are dark, some quite light. Under parts usually lighter than Cackling Goose. Winters from Wash. to Mex., very abundant in interior valleys of Calif. Voice considerably higher pitched than Common Canada but lower than Cackling Goose: *lo-ank*, *lo-ank*, *a-lank*, *a-lank* (J. Moffitt).

CACKLING GOOSE. *B. c. minima.*
23–25. Hardly larger than a Mallard, slightly smaller, stubbier-necked, and with darker under parts than the Lesser Canada Goose, with which it often associates. In some Cackling Geese there is another partial white collar near the base of the black neck, but this is not a good subspecific character, as individuals of other races sometimes show this. The flight notes are an extremely high-pitched yelping *yelk*, *yelk*, *a-lick*, *a-lick*, or *lick*, *lick*, *lick* (J. Moffitt). Winters mainly in Sacramento and San Joaquin Valleys of California.

AMERICAN BRANT. *Branta bernicla hrota.*
Descr. Accidental in w. U.S. Similar to Black Brant but under parts *light*. In the common species the dark of the under parts extends clear to the vent. Both species have light flanks. On the water the two would be almost indistinguishable.

BLACK BRANT. *Branta nigricans.* (Illus. p. 24.)
Descr. 23–29. A small Goose, much smaller than the Common Canada; size of the Cackling Goose. It is strictly coastal, bunching in large, irregular flocks rather than in the strings or V-formation of most other Geese. The Brant resembles the Canada Goose somewhat, but has a black head, neck, and under parts instead of a black head and neck contrasting with a light breast. In other words, the fore parts of a Brant are black to the waterline; a Goose's breast flashes white above the water. The Brant has a small white patch on the neck instead of a large white patch on the face. Then, too, as with all smaller birds, its wing-beats are less slow and labored.
Voice: — A throaty *krrr-onk*, *krrr-onk* (J. Moffitt).
Range: — Winters in the larger bays and lagoons along the Pacific Coast; casual inland.

EMPEROR GOOSE. *Philacte canagica.* (Illus. p. 24.)
Descr. 26. Size of a White-fronted Goose. A rare visitor to the Pacific States. *Adult:* — A small blue-gray Goose handsomely scaled with black and white; identified by its *white head and hind-neck*; distinguished from the even rarer Blue Goose, which

also has a white head and neck, by its *black throat*, and, at
very close range, by the yellow or orange legs (the Blue Goose
has pink legs). Immature birds are not so distinctly marked
and have the head and neck dusky, speckled with white. In
flight this species is very characteristic with its short neck,
short wings, and quick, stiff wing-beats.
Range: — A regular straggler in winter s. to Ore., and occasionally Calif.

WHITE-FRONTED GOOSE. *Anser albifrons.* Subsp. (Illus.
p. 24.)
Descr. 27–30. Smaller than Common Canada Goose; similar in
size to Lesser Snow and Lesser Canada. The commonest Goose
in the Pacific States. *Adult:* — At a distance gray-brown, showing no contrast of black neck and light breast as in the Canada.
When flying overhead the more uniform color below is at once
apparent. At closer range it shows a pink bill, a clear white
patch *on the front of the face*, black marks on the belly, and yellow or orange feet. *Immature:* — Dusky, with *yellow* feet, but
otherwise without the distinctive marks of the adult. No other
common Goose has yellow feet.
Voice: — Flight note, *kah-lah-a-luck*, high-pitched 'tootling,'
usually uttered from one to three times; various other notes
(J. Moffitt).
Subsp. WHITE-FRONTED GOOSE. *A. a. albifrons.*
Migrates chiefly through Pacific States, rare in
Rocky Mt. region, winters in Calif.
TULE GOOSE. *A. a. gambeli.*
A large dark race that winters in the Sacramento
Valley, Calif. Can be told in flight by large size, longer
neck, and slower wing-beats. Voice harsher and deeper
than above race.

LESSER SNOW GOOSE. *Chen hyperborea hyperborea.* (Illus.
p. 24.)
Descr. 23–30. A *white* Goose, smaller than the Canada, with
black wing-tips. Young birds are duskier, but still pale enough
to be recognizable as Snow Geese.
Voice: — Notes similar to White-front but single-noted, not
'tootling.' 'Flight notes: loud, nasal, resonant *whouk-
whouk, houck*, uttered singly, twice, or rarely three times'
(J. Moffitt).
Range: — Occurs in migration in most of W. States. Winters
in Pacific States, chiefly Calif.

BLUE GOOSE. *Chen cærulescens.*
Descr. Would be most apt to occur in company with Snow or
White-fronted Geese. *Adult:* — A dusky Goose with a white

head and neck (see Emperor Goose). *Immature:* — Dusky in color, much darker than young Snow Goose; very similar to immature White-front, but has *pink* legs instead of yellow, and paler bluish wings.
Voice: — Exactly like Snow Goose.
Range: — Very rare or accidental in w. U.S.

ROSS'S GOOSE. *Chen rossi.* (Illus. p. 24.)
Descr. 23. Two sizes of white Geese are often found together in winter in the interior valleys of Calif. The Ross's Goose can be told from the Lesser Snow Goose by its *smaller size* (near size of Mallard) and *decidedly smaller bill,* which at very close range is seen to lack the black 'lips' of the larger bird. Young birds are somewhat paler than young Snow Geese.
Voice: — 'No loud notes like Snow Goose; a simple grunt-like *kug,* or weak *kek, kek* or *ke-gak, ke-gak,* usually uttered twice. No other California Goose utters a similar note' (J. Moffitt).
Range: — Winters in Calif. (Sacramento and San Joaquin Valleys); migrates ne. through Mont. (Great Falls).

TREE DUCKS: DENDROCYGNINÆ

BLACK-BELLIED TREE DUCK. *Dendrocygna autumnalis autumnalis.* (Illus. pp. 33, 40.)
Descr. 22. A large Duck with a short tail and long heavy legs; largely rusty with a black belly, black wings with *great white patches,* and a bright *coral-pink* bill. No other Duck resembles it. It has a slightly Goose-like aspect.
Voice: — A squealing whistle.
Range: — S. Tex.; accidental in Ariz. and s. Calif.

FULVOUS TREE DUCK. *Dendrocygna bicolor helva.* (Illus. pp. 33, 40.)
Descr. 20–21. A long-legged, Goose-like Duck, blackish above, pale cinnamon below; does not ordinarily frequent trees. In flight, long legs extending beyond tail, slightly drooped neck, and slow wing-beats (for a duck) are distinctive. On the wing the bird looks dark, with blackish wing-linings and a white ring at the base of the tail. The Cinnamon Teal is smaller, not Goose-like in shape, and of a deeper reddish color.
Voice: — A squealing double-noted whistle.
Range: — Cent. and s. Calif., cent. Nev., sw. Ariz., and s. Tex.

SURFACE–FEEDING DUCKS: ANATINÆ

Ducks of this group, although not always confined to small bodies of water, are most characteristic of creeks, ponds, and marshes. They obtain their food by dabbling and tipping up rather than by diving. When frightened, they spring directly into the air instead of pattering before getting under way. They swim as a rule with the tail held quite clear of the water. Most birds of this group have a metallic *speculum*, or '*mirror*,' a rectangular patch situated at the hind edge of the wing.

MALLARD. *Anas platyrhynchos platyrhynchos.* (Illus. pp. 25, 28.)
Descr. 20–28. *Male:* — Similar to, but smaller than, domesticated Mallard of barnyard; grayish with green head, narrow white ring around neck, ruddy breast, and white tail. A few other Ducks have heads glossed with greenish and are, because of that, frequently mistaken for Mallards, but the white ring around the neck and the dark ruddy breast are diagnostic. *Female:* — A mottled brown Duck with whitish tail and conspicuous white borders *on each side* of metallic wing-patch. Female Pintails appear more stream-lined and have a white border on only one side of the wing-patch or speculum. The bill of the Mallard is *yellowish*. In sustained flight Mallards have a characteristic wing-stroke; it is slower than in most Ducks, and the downward sweep does not carry the wings much below the level of the body. The 'silvery' appearance of the under wings in flight is also a good field-mark.
Voice: — Female quacks like a barnyard Duck (so does female Gadwall). Male, a reedy *yeeb-yeeb*.
Range: — Breeds from Can. s. to Calif. and N.M.; winters n. to n. border of U.S.

NEW MEXICAN DUCK. *Anas diazi novimexicana.* (Illus. p. 25.)
Descr. 22. Like a very dark female Mallard, but male's bill greenish rather than yellow (female's bill indistinguishable); resembles closely the Black Duck and the Mottled Duck, but with a narrow white stripe on each side of the metallic speculum in the wing. (Black and Mottled Ducks do not occur in N.M.) Sexes alike.
Range: — N.M., chiefly along Rio Grande from El Paso to Albuquerque.

BLACK DUCK. *Anas rubripes.* (Illus. p. 28.)
Descr. 20–24. *Both sexes:* — Dark sooty brown with lighter

yellowish-brown head; feet brown or red; bill dull greenish or yellowish; metallic blue speculum on wing; under surface of wing silvery white. The Black Duck in flight, with its uniform dark coloration and flashing white wing-linings, is unmistakable. It resembles a very dark female Mallard but lacks the whitish tail and the white borders on the speculum.

Range: — E. U.S., w. rarely to e. Colo. and e. Wyo. Examples occasionally seen in Calif. might be liberated stock.

GADWALL. *Chaulelasmus streperus.* (Illus. pp. 25, 28.)
Descr. 19–21. *Male:* — A slender *gray* Duck with a white belly and a white patch on the *hind* edge of the wing. This white speculum is diagnostic. On the water the gray feathers of the flanks often conceal the white wing-patch; then the best mark is the black tail-coverts, which contrast sharply with the pale gray of the wing-coverts (see plate). *Female:* — Similar to male but browner; resembles in shape and general color female Pintail, but has white speculum. On the water it is likely to be confused with the female Baldpate, but that bird is more ruddy-colored, with a blue bill. The location of the white wing-patch is the best mark; that of the Baldpate is on the *fore* edge of the wing. Some females and young Baldpates in the fall show so little white in the wing that they might be easily confused with the Gadwall. Female Mallards and female Gadwalls are somewhat similar. Both have yellow in the bill, but the square white speculum and white belly identify the Gadwall.
Voice: — Female quacks similarly to female Mallard.
Range: — Breeds from e. Wash. and Mont. s. to ne. Calif., n. Nev., n. Ut., and Colo.; winters from Wash. and Colo. s. to Mex.

EUROPEAN WIDGEON. *Mareca penelope.* (Illus. p. 28.)
Descr. 18–20. This European bird is not so scarce in North America as was formerly supposed. *Male:* — Similar to following species, but is a *gray* Widgeon with *reddish-brown head* and buffy crown, instead of a brown Widgeon with gray head and white crown. It suggests, upon first acquaintance, a Redhead Duck. In bad light, or when too distant to show color, head appears much darker than rest of bird, quite unlike Baldpate, and sides are much lighter, with less contrast with rear white patch. *Female:* — Very similar to female Baldpate, but in very typical individuals under favorable light conditions head is distinctly tinged with reddish, whereas that of Baldpate is gray. The surest point, but one that can be noted only when the bird is in the hand, or very rarely in the field when the bird flaps its wings, is the appearance of the axillars — dusky in this species, white in the Baldpate.
Range: — Occasional visitor to Calif., Ore., Wash., and perhaps other W. States.

BALDPATE. *Mareca americana.* (Illus. pp. 25, 28.)
Descr. 18–22. The shining white crown of the male, which gives it its name, is the character by which most beginners learn this bird. *Male:* — Mainly brownish with gray head and white crown; patch on side of head glossy green, visible only in good light; patch on fore part of wing white; bill blue with a black tip. *Female:* — Ruddy brown with gray head and neck; belly and fore part of wing white. The Baldpate in flight can be recognized at a good distance by the large white patch on the *fore edge* of the wing; in other Ducks possessing white patches they are placed on the hind edge. The similarly placed blue wing-patches of the Blue-winged Teal, Cinnamon Teal, and Shoveller often appear whitish at a distance, however. Immature birds that have not acquired the white wing-patch are nondescript brownish Ducks with a paler gray head and neck, and a white belly which contrasts sharply with the brown breast.
Voice: — A whistled *whee whee whew* (male). A hoarse growl *grurrr* or *urrrr* (female).
Range: — Breeds from e. Wash. and Mont. s. to ne. Calif., n. Ut., and n. Colo.; winters along Pacific Coast and from s. Nev., cent. Ut., and ne. Colo. s. into Mex.

PINTAIL. *Dafila acuta tzitzihoa.* (Illus. pp. 25, 28.)
Descr. 26–30. Male Pintails in flight are white-bellied Ducks with long, slim necks and long, *pointed* tails, quite different in cut and appearance from the other surface-feeding Ducks. *Male:* — A slender white-breasted Duck, with long, pointed central tail-feathers and conspicuous white line running up side of neck and head. *Female:* — A slender, streaked brown Duck, similar to female Mallard, but more slender and without white-bordered blue speculum in wing. The bill is blue-gray. In flight the light border on the rear of the wings is a good character.
Voice: — Male utters a characteristic double-toned whistle, often in flight; female a hoarse quack.
Range: — Breeds from Can. s. to n.-cent. Calif., w. Nev., n. Ut., and n. Colo. Winters in Pacific States and from ne. Colo. s. to Mex.

GREEN-WINGED TEAL. *Nettion carolinense.* (Illus. pp. 25, 28.)
Descr. 13–15½. *Male:* — Small gray Duck with brown head and conspicuous *white mark* in front of wing. In sunlight, shows an iridescent green speculum in wing and green patch on side of head. *Female:* — A little speckled Duck with an iridescent green speculum. When Ducks fly up from the marsh, Teal are conspicuous by their half-size proportions. If they show no large light-colored patches on the wings, they are this species.

Voice: — Male utters a very characteristic single-noted whistle, sometimes repeated two or three times; female, a crisp quack.
Range: — Breeds from Can. s. to e. Ore., cent. Calif. (formerly), n. Nev., n. Ut., and n. N.M.; winters from Wash. and Mont. s. to Mex.

BLUE-WINGED TEAL. *Querquedula discors.* (Illus. pp. 25, 28.)
Descr. 15–16. *Male:* — Small, dull-colored, with large *white crescent in front of eye*, and large *chalky-blue patch on fore edge of wing.* The blue, at a distance in some lights, looks whitish. *Female:* — Mottled, with large blue patch on fore part of wing. Little half-sized marsh Ducks with large light-colored patches on the front of the wing are either Cinnamon Teal or this species. The white facial crescent identifies the male Blue-wing. It is rare in the Pacific States; the Cinnamon Teal is common. Farther east, the Blue-wing becomes more common. The somewhat larger Shoveller has pale-blue wing-patches, too, but can immediately be recognized by its tremendous bill.
Range: — Breeds from e. Wash. and Mont. s. to ne. Calif., Nev., n. Ut., and N.M.; migrates into Mex.; rare in Pacific States w. of Cascades and Sierras; winters rarely in Calif.

CINNAMON TEAL. *Querquedula cyanoptera.* (Illus. pp. 25, 28.)
Descr. 15½–17. *Male:* — Small, dark *cinnamon-red* Duck with large chalky-blue patches on front edges of wings. *Female:* — Almost identical with female Blue-winged Teal, but a bit rustier and more coarsely marked (see Blue-winged Teal).
Range: — Breeds from Wash. and Mont. s. to n. Calif., Nev., Ut., and N.M.; winters from Calif., Ariz., and N.M. s.

SHOVELLER. *Spatula clypeata.* (Illus. pp. 25, 28.)
Descr. 17–20. *Male:* — Largely black and white; belly and sides rufous-red; head blackish glossed with green; breast white; pale blue patch on fore edge of wing. *Female:* — Mottled brownish, with large blue wing-patch as in male. The Shoveller is a small Duck, somewhat larger than a Teal; best identified by its tremendous long and flattened bill, which in flight gives the bird a long appearance to the fore of the wings. On the water the bird sits very squatty and low, with the bill pointed downward, presenting a distinctive appearance. Broadside on the water, or flying overhead, the pattern of the Drake is totally unlike that of any other Duck. It consists of five alternating areas of light and dark, thus: dark, white, dark, white, dark.
Voice: — Male utters a low musical quack; female, a Mallard-like quack.
Range: — Breeds from e. Wash. and Mont. s. to s. Calif., nw. Nev., Ut., and N.M.; winters in Pacific States and from Ariz. and N.M. s.

CACKLING, LESSER CANADA and COMMON CANADA GEESE

SNOW GOOSE

ROSS'S GOOSE

WHITE-FRONTED GOOSE

ADULT

IMMATURE

BLACK BRANT

EMPEROR GOOSE

TRUMPETER SWAN

WHISTLING SWAN

CINNAMON TEAL

B'LUE-WINGED TEAL

GREEN-WINGED TEAL

SHOVELLER

WOOD DUCK

PINTAIL

MALLARD

NEW MEXICAN DUCK

BALDPATE

GADWALL

AMERICAN MERGANSER

RED-BREASTED MERGANSER

HOODED MERGANSER

WOOD DUCK. *Aix sponsa.* (Illus. pp. 25, 40.)
Descr. 17–20. Chiefly a bird of woodland ponds and streams.
The male is the most highly colored North American Duck.
Male in winter and spring plumage: — Highly iridescent;
descriptive words fail; the pattern diagram explains it much better. *Female:* — Dark brown with lighter flanks, white belly,
dark crested head, and white area about eye. *Male in eclipse
plumage (summer):* — Similar to female, but with the white
face-markings and red-and-white bill of the spring male.
On the wing, the white belly of the Wood Duck contrasts very
strikingly with the dark back. This, and the short neck, the
fairly long tail, and the angle at which the bill is pointed downward are all good aids to identification.
Voice: — A shrill raucous *whoo-eek* (female) or a wheezy *jeee*
(male).
Range: — Breeds in n. Calif., e. Ore., and e. Wash., and,
locally or formerly, elsewhere in Pacific States, Ida., Mont.,
and Wyo.; winters in Pacific States; occasional elsewhere in
migration.

DIVING DUCKS: NYROCINÆ

ALTHOUGH birds of this group are often called 'Sea Ducks' or
'Bay Ducks' for convenience, many are found more commonly
on the lakes and rivers of the interior; primarily, they are birds of
the more open bodies of water, although they breed in marshes.
They all dive for food, whereas the Surface-feeding Ducks rarely
dive. In taking wing, they do not spring directly upward from
the water, but find it necessary to patter along the surface
while getting under way.

REDHEAD. *Nyroca americana.* (Illus. pp. 29, 33.)
Descr. 18–23. *Male:* — Mostly gray, with black upper and
under tail-coverts, black neck and breast, red-brown head, and
blue bill. The male resembles the Canvas-back, but is much
grayer; the Canvas-back is very white. The Redhead has a high,
abrupt forehead and a blue bill, in contrast to the Canvas-back's
long sloping forehead and blackish bill. Redheads flock in much
the same formation as Canvas-backs, but are apt to shift about
more in the flock. They are shorter and chunkier than the latter,
much more like the Scaup in general contour. In flight, at a
distance, the gray wing-stripe distinguishes the more uniformly
colored Redhead from the contrastingly patterned Scaup.
Female: — A brownish Duck with a broad gray wing-stripe and
a blue bill. The female differs from the female Scaup in having
a gray wing-stripe and an indistinct buffy area about the base
of the bill, instead of a white wing-stripe and a well-defined

white face-patch. The only other female Ducks with broad
gray wing-stripes are the Canvas-back and the Ring-neck. The
Canvas-back is larger and paler, with the long profile; the Ring-
neck is smaller, darker, and has a conspicuous white eye-ring
and a ring on the bill.
Range: — Breeds from e. Wash. and Mont. s. to ne. Calif.,
Nev., nw. N.M., and s. Colo.; winters in Pacific States, chiefly
Calif., and from ne Colo. s.

RING-NECKED DUCK. *Nyroca collaris.* (Illus. pp. 29, 33.)
Descr. 16–18. *Male:* — A black-backed Scaup. Head, fore parts,
and back, black; sides, light gray with conspicuous white mark
in front of wing; bill crossed by two white rings. In flight, the
only black-backed Duck having a broad *gray* wing-stripe. The
name Ring-billed Duck would be much more appropriate, as
an examination at very close range is necessary to be aware of
the dull chestnut ring that encircles the neck. The rather triangular head-shape is distinctive in both sexes. *Female:* —
Brown, darkest on crown of head and back; wing-stripe gray;
whitish area about base of bill; white eye-ring, and ring on bill;
belly, white. Differs from female Scaup in possessing a *gray*
wing-stripe, white eye-ring, and a ring on the bill; from female
Redhead in its smaller size, darker back, and the conspicuous
rings about the eye and on the bill. Females are a little difficult
to tell from the Scaup which they so often associate with, but
the males can be picked out at a great distance, as no other
species of this distinctive genus has a black back.
Range: — Breeds chiefly in Canada, but occasionally in W.
States ('colonies' in sw. Mont. and White Mts. of e. Ariz.); migrates s. to Mex.; winters in Pacific States.

CANVAS-BACK. *Nyroca valisineria.* (Illus. pp. 29, 33.)
Descr. 20–24. *Male:* — White, with rusty-red head and neck,
black breast and tail, and blackish bill. *Female:* — Grayish,
with a suggestion of the male's general pattern. The long, sloping profile will distinguish either sex from any of the other species
which they superficially resemble. In flight, Canvas-backs
string out in lines or in V-formation. The long head, neck, and
bill give the bird a front-heavy appearance, as if the wings were
set far back.
Range: — Breeds chiefly in Can., and locally or occasionally s.
to e. Ore., n. Ut., and Colo.; winters along Pacific Coast and
from nw. Mont. and n. Colo. s.

GREATER SCAUP DUCK. *Nyroca marila.* (Illus. pp. 27, 29, 33.)
Descr. 17–20½. *Male:* — The two Scaups are the Ducks that at
a distance on the water appear to be 'black at both ends and
white in the middle.' The flanks and back are finely barred with

WINGS OF SCAUP DUCKS

A. Greater Scaup; long white wing-stripe
B. Lesser Scaup; short white wing-stripe

gray, but at any distance those parts appear quite white. The bill is blue; hence the gunner's nickname, 'Blue-bill.' Close at hand, in sunlight, the black head of the male Greater Scaup is glossed with green; that of the Lesser with dull purple. At a great distance, on the water, drake Golden-eyes and Scaup look somewhat alike, but where the Golden-eye has only a black head, the Scaup is black to the waterline. *Female:* — Brown, with broad white wing-stripe and a well-defined white area at the base of the bill. The two Scaups are our only Ducks possessing a broad white wing-stripe. The white in the Lesser extends about halfway along the hind edge of the wing, while in the present species this stripe extends considerably farther toward the wing-tip (see diagram). This character does not always hold, as the birds sometimes seem to intergrade, but typical individuals can be told in this way.

Range: — Winters along Pacific Coast; chiefly a migrant elsewhere. Much scarcer inland than Lesser Scaup.

LESSER SCAUP DUCK. *Nyroca affinis.* (Illus. pp. 27, 29.)
Descr. 15–18. *Male:* — Similar to Scaup, but slightly smaller, comparatively large-headed, and grayer on flanks; head glossed with dark purple instead of green. These differences are slight

and can be made out only when the bird is near-by in good light. The length of the wing-stripe is the easiest way to separate typical individuals in the field (see Greater Scaup Duck). The Greater is the winter Scaup of deep, open salt-water bays along the Pacific Coast, while the Lesser prefers more sheltered waters, and is much more often found on fresh water than is the Greater. It is the commonest species of the genus and should be used as a standard of comparison for the others.

Range: — A few breed locally in e. Ore., Ida., Mont., Wyo., and n. Colo. Winters in Pacific States and from ne. Colo. s.; a migrant elsewhere. The commonest Scaup in inland localities.

AMERICAN GOLDEN-EYE. *Glaucionetta clangula americana.* (Illus. pp. 29, 33.)

Descr. 17–23. *Male:* — Largely white, with a black back and a black green-glossed head. A large round white spot between the eye and the bill is the best identification mark. In flight the wings show large white patches. The *male*, at a distance, bears a superficial resemblance to the male Merganser, but is stocky and short-necked, with a large, round head, quite unlike the 'long-geared' Merganser. *Female:* — Gray with a white collar and a dark-brown head; wings with large square white patches. The immature male resembles the female but lacks the white collar. The whistling sound produced by the Golden-eye's wings, which has earned for the bird the name 'Whistler,' is often useful in identification.

Range: — Breeds from Can. s. to nw. Mont.; winters along Pacific Coast and irregularly from Mont. to Nev. and Colo., rarely farther.

BARROW'S GOLDEN-EYE. *Glaucionetta islandica.* (Illus. p. 29.)

Descr. 20–23. *Male:* — Similar to drake Golden-eye, but with a greater amount of black on sides of body, a row of *white* spots on black scapulars, black of head glossed with purple instead of green, and a *crescent-shaped* white patch in front of eye, instead of a round white spot. *Female:* — Very difficult to tell in field from female Golden-eye, but bill more yellow, shorter, and deeper. Forehead more abrupt.

Range: — Breeds from Can. s. in mts. to Ore. and Colo.; winters along coast s. to cent. Calif. (rarely) and inland irregularly to s. Colo.

BUFFLE-HEAD. *Charitonetta albeola.* (Illus. pp. 33, 40.)

Descr. 13–15. One of the smallest Ducks. *Male:* — Mostly white, with black back and large, puffy head marked with great white patch that extends from eye around back of head; large white wing-patches in flight. Because of the large triangular

BLACK DUCK GADWALL ♂

♂ MALLARD ♀

♂ PINTAIL ♀

EUROPEAN WIDGEON ♂ ♀ BALDPATE ♂

SHOVELLER ♂ ♀ BLUE WINGED TEAL ♂

GREEN-WINGED TEAL ♂ CINNAMON TEAL ♂

♂ CANVASBACK ♀

♂ REDHEAD ♀

♂ RING·NECKED DUCK ♀

♂ LESSER SCAUP ♀

GREATER SCAUP ♂

BARROW'S GOLDEN·EYE ♂

♂ AMERICAN GOLDEN·EYE ♀

white area on the head, it is sometimes mistaken for the scarcer Hooded Merganser, which is very dark instead of very white. *Female:* — Dark little Duck with large head, white cheek-spot, and white wing-patch.
Range: — Breeds in n. Mont. and Can.; migrates s. to Mex.; winters along Pacific Coast and on open bodies of water inland.

OLD-SQUAW. *Clangula hyemalis.* (Illus. pp. 32, 33.)
Descr. ♂ 21, ♀ 17. *Male in winter:* — Patchily patterned with dark brown and white. Head, neck, belly, and scapulars white; breast, back, and wings dusky brown; dark patch on side of head; bill banded with black and pink. The long, pointed central tail-feathers of the male Old-Squaw are different from those of any other Duck except the Pintail, which is a Duck of the marshes, ponds, and rivers, rather than a bird of the ocean. *Male in summer:* — Mostly dark with white flanks and belly, and white patch surrounding eye. *Female in winter:* — Lacks long, pointed tail-feathers of male. Dark above and white below; head white with black crown and cheek-spot. *Female in summer:* — Similar but darker. The Old-Squaw is the only Sea Duck combining white on the body and unpatterned dark wings. In flight it presents a pied appearance with dark, pointed wings that dip low with each beat. The Old-Squaws bunch in irregular flocks rather than in long, stringy lines like the Scoters.
Voice: — Noisy musical cries, *onk-a-lik.*
Range: — Winters along Pacific Coast; rare inland.

(WESTERN) HARLEQUIN DUCK. *Histrionicus histrionicus pacificus.* (Illus. pp. 32, 33.)
Descr. 15–17½. *Male:* — A rather small dark blue-gray Duck (blackish at a distance) with reddish-brown sides and odd white patches and spots. A glance at the diagram best explains the bird's appearance. In flight it has the shape, short neck, and manner of a Golden-eye but at a great distance stands out as a uniformly dark bird. Often cocks tail like Ruddy Duck. *Female:* — Dusky brown with two or three round white spots on side of head; may be distinguished from female Buffle-head — which has only one white face-spot — by absence of white in wing; from female Scoters, which it also resembles by its smaller size and shorter bill. In brief, it is a Duck with the pattern of a female Surf Scoter and the shape of a Buffle-head.
Range: — Breeds from Can. s. in mts. to Calif. (occasional in Sierras) and Colo.; winters mostly along rocky shores on coast s. to cent. Calif.

KING EIDER. *Somateria spectabilis.*
Descr. 21–24. *Male:* — A large, heavy Duck; back and belly black; wings black with large white patches; breast and fore

parts whitish; top of head pearl-gray; cheeks tinged with green-ish; bill and large frontal processes orange. At a distance the fore parts appear white, the rear parts black. No other Duck gives this effect. *Female:* — A large, chunky brown Duck, heavily barred with black. The heavy barrings and lack of light spots on face distinguish her from female Scoters. *Immature male:* — A dusky, Scoter-like bird with light breast and dark chocolate-brown head. Shows no square white wing-patch, as does the female Golden-eye Duck, a bird with which it might be confused. The amount of white varies in birds changing to adult plumage.
Range: — Casual on coast of Calif.

WHITE-WINGED SCOTER. *Melanitta deglandi.* (Illus. pp. 32, 33.)
Descr. 20–23. The Scoters are the large, chunky, blackish Ducks commonly seen coastwise, flying in stringy formation low over the waves. The White-wing is the largest of the three species. *Male:* — Black with white wing-patches. *Female:* — Dusky-brown with white wing-patch and two white patches on side of head.
Range: — Breeds in Can.; winters along Pacific Coast; rare inland. Non-breeding birds found along coast in summer.

SURF SCOTER. *Melanitta perspicillata.* (Illus. pp. 32, 33.)
Descr. 18–22. *Male:* — Black, with one or two white patches on crown of head — hence nickname 'Skunk-head.' *Female:* — Dusky-brown with two white patches on side of head. The smaller size and lack of white wing-patches distinguish it from similarly marked female White-wing. This species is the only Duck that invariably holds its wings elevated upon alighting, a fine field character.
Range: — Winters along Pacific Coast; non-breeders found all summer. Very rare inland.

AMERICAN SCOTER. *Oidemia americana.* (Illus. pp. 32, 33.)
Descr. 17–21. *Male:* — The only American Duck with *entirely* black plumage. This, and the bright yellow-orange base of the bill, are diagnostic. *Female:* — Dusky brown, with light cheeks contrasting with a darker crown. Females of the other two Scoters have two distinct white patches on each side of the head. At a distance in flight, the female American Scoter shows more light color on the under parts than the females of the other two species of Scoters.
Range: — Winters along Pacific Coast; a few non-breeders summer. Very rare inland.

RUDDY AND MASKED DUCKS: ERISMATURINÆ

RUDDY DUCK. *Erismatura jamaicensis rubida.* (Illus. pp. 32, 33.)
Descr. 14–17. *Male in breeding plumage:* — Largely rusty-red with *white cheeks*, black crown, and large blue bill. *Male in winter:* — Gray with white cheeks, blackish crown, and bluish bill. *Female:* — Similar to winter male, but with light cheeks crossed by dark line. In the air, in any plumage, the Ruddy appears as a small, chunky Duck, quite dark, and unpatterned in color except for the conspicuous white cheeks. On the water it often cocks its tail vertically, like a Wren. It is possible to mis-identify a female American Scoter as a winter Ruddy Duck — both are unpatterned except for light cheeks. Occasionally, the Scoter even cocks its tail. The Ruddy Duck is very much smaller, with a definitely shovel-shaped blue bill. The flight of the Ruddy is close to the water, and is extremely fast and buzzy, the short small wings beating very rapidly.
Range: — Breeds locally from Can. s. to s. Calif., n. Ariz., and N.M.; winters in Pacific States and from Ariz. and N.M. s.

MASKED DUCK. *Nomonyx dominicus.* (Illus. p. 32.)
Descr. 12–14. Smaller than any other Duck; somewhat like Ruddy Duck. *Male:* — Rusty with blackish stripes on back, white wing-patches, and black mask on front of face. *Female:* — Like a small female Ruddy, but with *two* black stripes crossing each cheek instead of one.
Range: — Occasional near Brownsville, Tex.

MERGANSERS: MERGINÆ

OUR three Mergansers, or fish-eating Ducks, lack the broad and flattened bills so characteristic of most Ducks; the mandibles are slender, equipped with toothed edges, well adapted for seiz-ing their slippery prey. Most species have crests and are long-geared, slender-bodied birds. In flight, the bill, head, neck, and body are held perfectly horizontal; at a distance, this gives them an unmistakable long-drawn appearance, quite unlike other Ducks.

HOODED MERGANSER. *Lophodytes cucullatus.* (Illus. pp. 25, 40.)
Descr. 16–19. *Male:* — Black and white, with *fan-shaped white* crest on head; breast white with two black bars in front of wing; wing dark with white patch; flanks brownish. The male, dis-tinctive as it is, is often confused with the male Buffle-head.

The Buffle-head is smaller, chubbier, and whiter with white flanks; the flanks of the Hooded Merganser are dark. The white head-patch of the Merganser is outlined with a narrow dark border. *Female:* — Recognized as a Merganser when close at hand by the narrow, spike-like bill, and in flight by the long-drawn appearance, with bill, head, neck, and body held in a horizontal line. Differentiated from the other two female Mergansers by the small size, dark coloration, *dark head and neck,* and buffy crest. The female Wood Duck is also dark and has a crest, but the square white wing-patch and different flight will identify the Merganser. Like the Wood Duck it often frequents woodland pools.

Range: — Breeds locally from Can. s. to Ore. and Wyo.; winters in B.C. and Pacific States and from Ut. and Colo. s.

AMERICAN MERGANSER. *Mergus merganser americanus.* (Illus. pp. 25, 40.)

Descr. 22–27. In line formation, low over the water, the American Mergansers follow the winding course of the creeks and rivers which they frequent. Like the others of the group, they are rakish, long-bodied birds. The large, white, black-headed males are unmistakable. *Male:* — White, with a black back and a green-black head; bill and feet orange; breast tinged with a delicate peach-colored bloom. The whiteness of the bird and the Merganser shape, with bill, head, neck, and body all held horizontal, will identify it in flight a long way off. The Merganser and Golden-eye resemble each other at a distance, but the Golden-eye, aside from having the conspicuous white spot in front of the eye, is smaller, chubbier, shorter-necked, and rounder-headed. *Female:* — Largely gray with a *crested* rufous-red head, red bill, orange feet, and a large square white patch on the wing (see female Red-breasted Merganser).

Range: — Breeds from Can. s. to cent. Calif., n. Ariz., and n. N.M. (rarely); winters along most of coast and on open water inland.

RED-BREASTED MERGANSER. *Mergus serrator.* (Illus. pp. 25, 40.)

Descr. 20–25. *Male:* — Not so white as American Merganser; black head glossed with green and *conspicuously crested*; area on breast at waterline brownish, whereas same area in American Merganser appears white; bill red, feet orange. *Female:* — Largely gray, with crested rufous-red head and large square white patch on wing; bill and feet orange-red. Very similar to female American Merganser, but head less bushy, with rufous blending into white of throat and neck instead of being sharply defined as in that bird. Both sexes are smaller and slimmer in build than the American Merganser. The Red-breasted Mer-

♂ AMERICAN SCOTER ♀

♂ WHITE-WINGED SCOTER ♀

♂ SURF SCOTER ♀

♂ HARLEQUIN DUCK ♀

♂ SUMMER   ♂ WINTER   ♀ WINTER

OLD-SQUAW

♂ RUDDY DUCK ♀

♂ MASKED DUCK ♀

REDHEAD

GREATER SCAUP

RING-NECKED DUCK

CANVAS-BACK

BUFFLEHEAD

AMERICAN GOLDEN-EYE

HARLEQUIN DUCK

OLD-SQUAW WINTER

RUDDY DUCK

BLACK-BELLIED TREE-DUCK

FULVOUS TREE-DUCK

SURF SCOTER

AMERICAN SCOTER

WHITE-WINGED SCOTER

ganser is more characteristic of the ocean than is the American,
which is chiefly a fresh-water species. Both birds may, at times,
be found on the same bodies of water.
Range: — Winters on Pacific Coast; local or rare in Great Basin
and Rocky Mt. region.

VULTURES: CATHARTIDÆ

VULTURES are great blackish Eagle-like birds, usually seen soaring in wide circles high in the heavens. Their naked heads are
so small for the size of the bird that at a great distance they
sometimes appear to be almost headless. Hawks and Eagles
have large, well-proportioned heads.

TURKEY VULTURE. *Cathartes aura.* (Illus. p. 41.)
Descr. 30. Wing-spread 6 ft. This species, the only Vulture
found in most parts of w. U.S., is nearly Eagle-size with great
'two-toned' blackish wings (the flight feathers are noticeably
lighter than the rest of the bird). It is usually to be seen high
in the air, soaring on motionless wings in wide circles. The
diminutive head and slimmer tail at once distinguish it from the
Eagles. At close range the red color of the head can be seen. A
Turkey Vulture soars with its wings held perceptibly above the
horizontal and rocks unsteadily as it floats along. Eagles and
Ravens soar with wings perfectly horizontal. Where all three
are common this comparison helps.
Range: — Throughout most of w. U.S.; winters from Calif.
and s. Ariz. s. The Turkey Vulture of the West has recently
been described as the Western Turkey Vulture (*C. a. teter*), but
the name has not yet been adopted.

BLACK VULTURE. *Coragyps atratus atratus.* (Illus. p. 41.)
Descr. 24. Wing-spread under 5 ft. One of the best points of
difference between this black-headed species and the Turkey
Vulture is the comparatively short tail which barely projects
from the hind edge of the wings. The tail of the Turkey Vulture
is longer and slimmer. A whitish patch on the under surface of
the Black Vulture's wing is also a sure mark. The wings are
shorter than the Turkey Vulture's, and the bird flaps more frequently and soars less. Young Turkey Vultures have black
heads and are sometimes mistaken for Black Vultures.
Range: — W. Tex. and s. Ariz. (a few).

CALIFORNIA CONDOR. *Gymnogyps californianus.* (Illus.
p. 34.)
Descr. 45–55. Wing-spread 8½–10½ ft. Much larger than the

CALIFORNIA CONDOR

Turkey Vulture; adults with extensive *pure white wing-linings* toward the front edges of the wings. Head yellow or orange. Young birds are dusky-headed and lack the white linings, but are twice the size of Turkey Vultures and have much broader proportions. Many Golden Eagles have some white under the wing, but it is placed differently and the shape of the bird is somewhat different (see diagram).

Range: — Now very rare, a small number living in mts. of s. Calif.

KITES: ELANINÆ

WHITE-TAILED KITE. *Elanus leucurus majusculus.* (Illus. p. 45.)

Descr. 15½. This rare species is Falcon-shaped, with long, pointed wings and a long tail, but the flight lacks the dash of Falcons. The bird frequently hovers in one spot like a Sparrow Hawk. *Adult:* — Pale gray with white head, *tail*, and under parts, and a *large black patch* toward fore edge of wing. No other Falcon-like bird (except White Gyrfalcon) has a white tail. Beginners often mistake this species for a Gull. *Immature:* — Broad rusty band on breast; tail tipped with gray.

Range: — Calif., chiefly from San Francisco Bay region to Ventura Co.; rather rare. Straggler in Ore. Also occurs around Brownsville, Tex.

ACCIPITERS, OR SHORT–WINGED HAWKS: ACCIPITRINÆ

LONG-TAILED Hawks with short, rounded wings; woodland birds that do not often soar about high in the air as do the Buteos. The typical flight is several short quick beats and a sail. The Goshawk is not properly an Accipiter, but it belongs to the same subfamily.

GOSHAWK. *Astur atricapillus.* Subsp. (Illus. p. 45.)
Descr. 20–26. A large, long-tailed, short-winged Hawk with a pearly-gray breast and a blue-gray back; of a lighter gray than the Cooper's or Sharp-shin. It is easily told from the Cooper's Hawk, which it resembles in shape, by its much larger size — considerably larger than a Crow; Cooper's is smaller than a Crow. The gray-backed adult Cooper's is reddish below; the Goshawk, pale gray. The white line over the Goshawk's eye is also distinctive. Young accipitrine Hawks are brown above

IMMATURE COOPER'S HAWK

The Hawks shown in overhead flight in the plates are adults. Immature birds have the same shapes, but in many instances are streaked below as in this bird.

and heavily streaked below. They all have much the same pattern. Size, although sometimes deceptive, is a reasonable point of difference between this species and the Cooper's. A well-pronounced light stripe over the eye in the young Goshawk is about the only definite point of distinction. Some immature birds are generally paler throughout and identifiable on this basis.

Range: — Breeds from Can. s. in mts. to cent. Calif., Ariz., and N.M.; wanders to lowlands in winter.

Subsp. (No apparent field differences): (1) Eastern Goshawk, *A. a. atricapillus*; (2) Western Goshawk, *A. a. striatulus*.

SHARP-SHINNED HAWK. *Accipiter velox.* (Illus. pp. 45, 49.)
Descr. 10–14. A small Hawk with a long tail and short, rounded wings. Flies with several quick beats and a sail. Size near that of Sparrow and Pigeon Hawks, but those two species have pointed wings. Large females are often near the size of small male Cooper's. The two are almost identical in pattern, but generally the Cooper's has a rounded tail and the Sharp-shin a *square-tipped* tail (slightly forked when folded).
Range: — Breeds from Can. s. to Calif., Ariz., and N.M.; winters through most of w. U.S.

COOPER'S HAWK. *Accipiter cooperi.* (Illus. pp. 35, 45, 49.)
Descr. 14–20. A short-winged, long-tailed Hawk; not quite so large as a Crow. Keeps to the woods and does not soar high in the open as often as many other Hawks. Can be known from the Sharp-shin by its *rounded tail*, and from the Goshawk by its much smaller size. Immature birds are usually more sharply and narrowly streaked below than immature Sharp-shins
Range: — Breeds from Can. to Mex.; winters from Wash. and Wyo. s.

BUTEOS, OR BUZZARD HAWKS: BUTEONINÆ (IN PART)

Large Hawks with *broad wings* and *broad, rounded tails*, which habitually soar in wide circles, high in the air.

Black or melanistic phases occur in most species, and one must indeed be an expert to tell some of them apart. There is considerable variation in individuals within most of the species. This may cause confusion among beginners. The Hawks figured in the pattern-diagrams are in the most characteristic plumages. Young birds are similar to the adults in shape, but in most species are *streaked lengthwise* below.

RED-TAILED HAWK. *Buteo borealis.* Subsp. (Illus. pp. 41, 44, 49.)
Descr. 19–24. The tyro usually finds it necessary to wait till this large broad-winged, round-tailed Hawk veers in its soaring so that the rufous-red of the upper side of the tail can be seen. From beneath, adults have light-colored tails with little or no apparent banding. Young birds have grayish tails, which might or might not show banding. The under parts of the Red-tail are more or less zoned (light breast, broad band of dark streakings across belly). With much practice one can easily identify the various Buteos by shape alone. The Red-tail is chunkier, with wider wings and a shorter tail than most of others. There is considerable color variation. Some individuals are very dark, almost black, but *black adults usually show red tails*, a point of distinction from black Swainson's or black Rough-legs.
Voice: — A squealing whistle, *keeer-r-r*.
Subsp. WESTERN RED-TAILED HAWK. *B. b. calurus.*
    Resident through most of w. U.S.
    KRIDER'S HAWK. *B. b. krideri.*
    In appearance, a partially albinistic Red-tail with much white mixed in the plumage, especially about the head. The tail may range from pale red to white, and is crossed by a number of narrow bars. Sask. and s. Man. s. to Wyo. and N.D.

RED-BELLIED HAWK. *Buteo lineatus elegans.* (Illus. pp. 41, 49.)
Descr. 18–24. A race of the Eastern Red-shouldered Hawk; resident of valleys in central and s. Calif. Recognized as a Buteo by the ample tail and broad wings; distinguished in any plumage from the Red-tail, which is chunkier, wider-winged, and shorter-tailed, by the *heavy banding* across both sides of the tail. The Swainson's Hawk has *fine* banding. Adults are marked with rich chestnut shoulders and bright rusty-red under parts and wing-linings. These barred rusty under parts set it apart from any other Western Buteo. The adult Cooper's Hawk also has rusty under parts but has proportionately shorter wings and a longer tail. Immature birds lack the rusty under parts, and are streaked below as are most other young Hawks. They can be best identified by the tail-banding, proportions, and, in flight overhead, by a light-colored patch or 'window' toward the tip of the wings at the base of the primaries. This is a good mark in any plumage.
Voice: — A piercing *kee-yer* (Red-tail's more like a squeal).
Range: — Valleys and lowlands of cent. and s. Calif.

SWAINSON'S HAWK. *Buteo swainsoni.* (Illus. pp. 41, 44, 49.)
Descr. 19½–22. · A Buteo similar in size to a Red-tail but with wings longer and more pointed. The wings when soaring are

held somewhat above the horizontal, giving a slightly Vulture-like or Marsh-Hawk-like impression. In typical adults the wide dark breast-band is a good mark. There are confusing lighter individuals where the breast-band nearly disappears and blackish birds which are hard to tell from other melanistic Buteos. Most individuals can be told very readily in flight overhead by the *unmarked light buffy wing-linings which contrast with the darker-toned flight feathers* (see diagram). From above, the tail is gray, often shading to white at the base. (Do not confuse with Rough-leg.) Black Swainson's Hawks lack the rusty tail of the black Red-tail, and lack the snowy-white primaries and secondaries on the under wing-surface which are such a distinctive feature of black Rough-legs. These wing areas are often quite pale, but *clouded*, not clear white. (See diagram.) When perched, facing the observer, the bird's tail is pale, crossed by narrow black bars. This species migrates in flocks, a habit not common in Hawks.
Range: — Breeds and migrates in dry open country through all of West except the coastal belt (w. of Cascades and Calif. coast ranges).

ZONE-TAILED HAWK. *Buteo albonotatus.* (Illus. pp. 44, 49.)
Descr. 18½–21½. A *black* Buteo, with somewhat more slender wings than the others of its genus. Upon first acquaintance is likely to be mistaken for a Turkey Vulture because of the proportions and '*two-toned*' *wing effect* (see diagram), but the Hawk head and *white tail-bands* identify it. The Mexican Black Hawk, which also occurs along the Mexican border of the U.S., is much chunkier, has evenly colored wings and much wider tail-banding. The Mexican Black Hawk prefers cottonwood stream-bottoms; the Zone-tail is often seen in mountainous country.
Range: — Chiefly near Mex. border of Tex., N.M., and Ariz.

SENNETT'S WHITE-TAILED HAWK. *Buteo albicaudatus hypospodius.* (Illus. pp. 41, 44, 49.)
Descr. 23–24. A long-winged, short-tailed Buteo with *clear white under parts* and *white tail* with a black band near its tip. The upper parts are dark (gray, shoulders rusty-red). The white tail is the best mark. The Ferruginous Rough-leg has whitish under parts and a whitish tail, but lacks the well-defined black band near the tip of the tail. (See Ferruginous Rough-leg.) Immature White-tails are quite blackish, and in flight overhead have whitish tails and blackish wing-linings which contrast with light primaries. The black Ferruginous Rough-leg has the under surface of the primaries and secondaries snowy-white (not clouded). The black Swainson's has a noticeably barred tail and is more evenly black below. The immature White-tail is usually somewhat spotted with white on the breast.
Range: — Southern Tex.

AMERICAN ROUGH-LEGGED HAWK. *Buteo lagopus s.-johannis.* (Illus. pp. 41, 44, 49.)
Descr. 20–23½. A Buteo by shape, but with longer wings and a longer, more rounded tail than most of the others. As it usually flies low in open country, it might easily be taken for a Swainson's Hawk, especially because of the white base of the tail, but the Swainson's tail is not so contrasting (gray, often blending with white at base). The best marks by which to distinguish the normal or light phase from below are the *well-defined black belly* and the *conspicuous black patch at the wrist of the wing.* Light-bellied birds sometimes are seen. The black phase does not have the large amount of white at the base of the tail. It can be told from the black Red-tail by the lack of rusty on the tail and from the black Swainson's by the snowy-white primaries and secondaries on the under surface of the wings (see diagram).
Range: — Winters from n. edge of U.S. s. to s. Calif. and s. N.M.

FERRUGINOUS ROUGH-LEG. *Buteo regalis.* (Illus. pp. 41, 44, 49.)
Descr. 23–24. A large Buteo of the plains and prairies, distinguished from the American Rough-leg by its coloration, ruddy above and whitish below, and the lack of a contrasting black terminal band on the whitish tail. Shows two light-colored areas on upper surface of wings. A very good mark in typical light-bellied birds when flying overhead is a dark V formed by the dark chestnut-colored feathers on the legs. First-year birds lack these dark 'leggings' and are pure white below. In the dark phase the Ferruginous Rough-leg resembles the black American Rough-leg but usually is more tinged with rusty. The long tail is paler, often whitish, without any suggestion of a broad black band at the tip, as in the other species. The snowy-white under surface of the primaries and secondaries, and the pale unbanded tail identify the bird in this confusing plumage.
Range: — Breeds in arid country from e. Wash. and Mont. s. to ne. Calif., Nev., and n. N.M.; winters from Mont., e. Ore., and interior Calif., s. to Mex.; occasional on coast.

HARRIS'S HAWK. *Parabuteo unicinctus harrisi.* (Illus. p. 44.)
Descr. 22. A black Buteo with a flashy white rump and a white band at the tip of the tail; like a Marsh Hawk in habits, but looks more dumpy when perched on yucca, etc. The Harris's Hawk perched close to would show chestnut-colored areas on the body and wings — a mark of distinction from the other black or melanistic Buteos. In flight at a distance, from the side, the white on the Harris's Hawk completely encircles the base of the tail, whereas in the female or young Marsh Hawk it is visible only above, on the rump.
Range: — Se. Calif., s. Ariz., s. N.M., and s. Tex.

MEXICAN GOSHAWK. *Asturina plagiata plagiata.* (Illus. p. 41.)
Descr. 16–18. Not a Goshawk at all, but more like a small Buteo. Adults are distinguished by their Buteo proportions, gray back, gray and white barred under parts, and widely banded black-and-white tail. (Tail-banding will remind Easterners of Broad-winged Hawk.)
Range: — Streams locally along Mex. border of Ariz., N.M., and Tex.

MEXICAN BLACK HAWK. *Urubitinga anthracina.* (Illus. p. 44.)
Descr. 20–23. A black Buteonine Hawk with exceptionally broad wings. Identified by its chunky shape and the broad white band crossing the center of the tail. A white spot near the tip of the wing at the base of the primaries can be seen under favorable circumstances, but is inconspicuous at a distance.
Range: — Along streams near Mex. border of Ariz., N.M., and Tex.

EAGLES: BUTEONINÆ (IN PART)

EAGLES are at once recognizable from the 'Buzzard Hawks,' or Buteos, which they somewhat resemble, by their immense size and proportionately longer wings. The powerful bill of an Eagle is nearly as long as the head, a point of distinct difference from the lesser Hawks.

GOLDEN EAGLE. *Aquila chrysaëtos canadensis.* (Illus. p. 48.)
Descr. 30–40. Wing-spread 6½–7½ ft. The Eagle of the mountainous country. *Adult:* — Evenly black below or with white at the base of the tail. When the bird wheels, showing the upper surface, the white tail, with its contrasting dark terminal band, identifies it. The amount of white varies. The light 'gold' on the hind neck is of occasional importance as a field-mark. *Immature:* — From above and below, typical individuals show a *white flash in the wing* at the base of the primaries, and a white tail with a *broad, dark terminal band*. All manner of variation exists between this typical plumage of the immature and the plumage of the adult described above. The Golden Eagle has a more graceful, Vulture-like flight, flapping less and soaring more than the Bald. Even the general contour is different; the wings are shorter and wider, the tail more ample. Perched at a distance the bird appears flat-headed with a much smaller and less massive bill than the Bald Eagle.
Range: — Mountainous regions of w. U.S.

♂ AMERICAN MERGANSER ♀

♂ RED-BREASTED MERGANSER ♀

♂ HOODED MERGANSER ♀

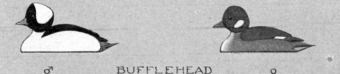

♂ BUFFLEHEAD ♀

♂ WOOD DUCK ♀

BLACK-BELLIED
TREE-DUCK

FULVOUS
TREE-DUCK

TURKEY VULTURE

BLACK VULTURE

AM.
R. LEG
ABOVE

AMERICAN
ROUGH-LEGGED
HAWK

FERRUGINOUS
ROUGH-LEG

SENNETT'S
WHITE-TAILED
HAWK

RED-TAILED
HAWK

RED-BELLIED
HAWK

SWAINSON'S
HAWK

MEXICAN GOSHAWK

BALD EAGLE. *Haliæetus leucocephalus.* Subsp. (Illus. p. 48.)
Descr. 30–31. Wing-spread 6–7½ ft. The Eagle of the ocean,
rivers, and lakes. The adult, with its great size and *snowy-white*
head and tail, needs little description. The immature bird is
dusky all over. Melanistic Buteos (black Rough-legs, Swainson's, etc.) are much smaller. Immatures are frequently mistaken for Golden Eagles. Although in some individuals there
may be some white on the under surface of the wings, it is usually in the linings rather than at the base of the primaries. A
young Bald Eagle going into adult plumage may have a tail that
is whitish at the base, but never with a contrasting dark band.
Range: — Local from Can. to Mex. chiefly near water; absent
in arid sections.
Subsp. (No apparent field differences): (1) Northern Bald
Eagle, *H. l. alascanus*; (2) Southern Bald Eagle, *H. l. leucocephalus.*

HARRIERS: CIRCINÆ

MARSH HAWK. *Circus hudsonius.* (Illus. p. 45.)
Descr. 18–24. The *white* rump-patch is the badge of the species.
Adult males are pale gray; *females*, brown. In ordinary flight,
the bird glides low over the ground with the wings held perceptibly above the horizontal, in a manner suggestive of the Vultures.
The white rump is always conspicuous. The American Rough-
leg and the Swainson's often have white at the base of the tail,
but are much more heavily proportioned than the slim Marsh
Hawk. When the bird is flying high, the long tail might suggest
a Falcon, but the wings are not pointed. The Accipiters have
much shorter wings.
Range: — Breeds in marshy country from Can. s. to s. Calif.
and N.M. (a few), except in nw. coast belt. Winters from Ore.
and Mont. to Mex.

OSPREYS: PANDIONINÆ

OSPREY. *Pandion haliaëtus carolinensis.* (Illus. p. 48.)
Descr. 21–24. Wing-spread 4½–6 ft. A large Eagle-like Hawk —
blackish above and *clear white* below; only *large* bird of prey so
patterned. Head largely white, suggestive of Bald Eagle. Flies
with decided kink or crook in wings. The Eagles and lesser
Hawks are all quite straight-winged. The habits of hovering,
and of plunging feet first for fish, are characteristic.
Range: — Migrant or summer resident along coast and about
large streams and lakes locally from Can. to Mex.

CARACARAS: POLYBORINÆ

AUDUBON'S CARACARA. *Polyborus cheriway auduboni.*
(Illus. p. 44.)
Descr. 22. A large, long-legged, long-necked black Hawk. The
under surface presents three alternating areas of light and dark
— whitish throat and breast, black belly, and white, dark-
tipped tail. In flight the *pale-colored patches* at the wing-tips are
conspicuous from above or below. These are determinative,
especially when seen in conjunction with the white breast area.
Range: — Mexican border of Tex., N.M. (rare), and Ariz.
(uncommon).

FALCONS: FALCONINÆ

HAWKS with long, *pointed* wings and comparatively long tails.
The wing-strokes are rapid; the slim wings are not built for
soaring in the manner of the Buteos.

GYRFALCON. *Falco rusticolus obsoletus.* (Illus. pp. 45, 49.)
Descr. 20–24½. A very large Falcon, usually much larger than
the Duck Hawk. It was formerly assumed that three or four
races of this bird occur in North America, with a distinction
made between black, gray, and white types. Recent studies
have led to the conclusion that there is only one Gyrfalcon in
North America (Friedmann). White birds are distinguished
from the Snowy Owl at a distance by the smaller head, pointed
wings, and quicker flight. Black birds are much larger and
blacker-breasted than the Duck Hawk. Gray birds are more
uniformly colored above and below than the Duck Hawk, without such marked contrast between dark upper parts and light
under parts.
Range: — Arctic America; casual in migration, and winter to
Mont., Wyo., Wash., and Ore.

PRAIRIE FALCON. *Falco mexicanus.* (Illus. pp. 45, 49.)
Descr. 17. A pointed-winged Hawk, very much like the Duck
Hawk in size and appearance, but whereas the back of that bird
is slaty-gray, almost blackish, this species is a paler, sandy
color. In flight overhead the Prairie Falcon shows blackish
patches (formed by the dark flanks and axillars) where the
wings join the body. These patches contrast noticeably with
the light tone of the rest of the under surface. Female Sparrow
Hawks are smaller and darker.
Range: — Chiefly arid sections from Can. to Mex.

DUCK HAWK. *Falco peregrinus.* Subsp. (Illus. pp. 45, 49.)
Descr. 15–20. Recognized as a Falcon by its long, pointed wings and long, narrow tail, and its *quick*, deep wing-beats that carry the wings far below the level of the body. Its size, near that of a Crow, and its dark coloration identify it as this species. (Sparrow and Pigeon Hawks are not much larger than a Robin.) On perching birds of this species the heavy dark 'moustachios' are distinctive. (See Prairie Falcon.)
Subsp. DUCK HAWK. *F. p. anatum.*
> Breeds locally, on cliffs, usually near water, from Can. to Mex.; winters in Pacific States and from Colo. s.
> PEALE'S FALCON. *F. p. pealei.*
> A dark race, recognizable. Chiefly migrant, and winter visitor to coast of Wash. and Ore.

APLOMADO FALCON. *Falco fusco-cœrulescens septentrionalis.* (Illus. pp. 45, 49.)
Descr. 15–18. A handsome medium-sized Falcon of the desert and dry plains; now very rare in the U.S. Somewhat larger than the Sparrow Hawk or a little smaller than the Duck Hawk or Prairie Falcon. Identified readily by its dark wing-linings and *black belly* contrasting markedly with its white breast. Thighs and under tail-coverts orange-brown.
Range: — Formerly deserts along Mex. border of Ariz., N.M., and Tex. Now practically gone.

PIGEON HAWK. *Falco columbarius.* Subsp. (Illus. pp. 45, 49.)
Descr. 10–13½. A small Falcon, hardly larger than a Robin. The male is bluish-gray above, with broad bands on the tail. Female and young are dusky brown. One subspecies, the Black Pigeon Hawk, is nearly black above and more heavily marked below. The long, pointed wings and Falcon-like wing-action distinguish it from the little Sharp-shinned Hawk, which has rounded wings. The lack of any rufous-red on the tail or upper plumage distinguishes it at once from the Sparrow Hawk. In flight the Pigeon Hawk cuts the air speedily, sailing less between strokes than the other bird. During migration the Pigeon Hawk is looked for to best advantage in open country, coastal marshes, etc.
Subsp. BLACK PIGEON HAWK. *F. c. suckleyi.*
> Decidedly darker than Western Pigeon Hawk, especially on the cheeks; belly more heavily marked. Sometimes recognizable if the student knows the common bird well. Winters along coast from Wash. to n. Calif.
> RICHARDSON'S PIGEON HAWK. *F. c. richardsoni.*
> Males are often recognizable because they are so pale above, especially on the tail and crown (the male West-

ern Pigeon Hawk has a very dark crown).   Breeds in
Great Plains region from Can. s. to n. Mont. Winters s.
through Colo., N.M., and w. Tex.
WESTERN PIGEON HAWK. *F. c. bendirei.*
Breeds from Can. s. in mts. to n. Calif. and Colo.; win-
ters s. into Mex.

SPARROW HAWK. *Falco sparverius.* Subsp. (Illus. pp. 45,
49.)
Descr. 9–12. A small Falcon, not much larger than a Robin.
No other *small* Hawk has a rufous-red tail. At a distance, in
flight, the narrow, pointed wings eliminate the Sharp-shin,
which has short, round wings. It is the only common *small*
Hawk that habitually hovers, Kingfisher-like, in one spot. The
Sparrow Hawk almost always pumps its tail on alighting, then
sits fairly erect with an occasional, but characteristic, jerk of
the tail. (See Pigeon Hawk.)
Voice: — A rapid, high-pitched *killy, killy, killy.*
Range: — Breeds from Can. to Mex.; winters from Wash. and
Wyo. s.
Subsp. (No apparent field differences): (1) Eastern Sparrow
Hawk, *F. s. sparverius*; (2) Desert Sparrow Hawk, *F. s. phalæna.*

CURASSOWS AND GUANS: CRACIDÆ

CHACHALACA. *Ortalis vetula vetula.* (Illus. p. 44.)
Descr. 20–24. A large brown bird shaped like a half-grown Tur-

CHACHALACA

AUDUBON'S CARACARA

AMERICAN ROUGH-LEGGED HAWK

DARK PHASE

DARK PHASE

FERRUGINOUS ROUGH-LEG

SWAINSON'S HAWK

DARK PHASE

DARK PHASE

RED-TAILED HAWK

SENNETT'S WHITE-TAILED HAWK
IMMATURE

ZONE-TAILED HAWK

HARRIS'S HAWK

MEXICAN BLACK HAWK

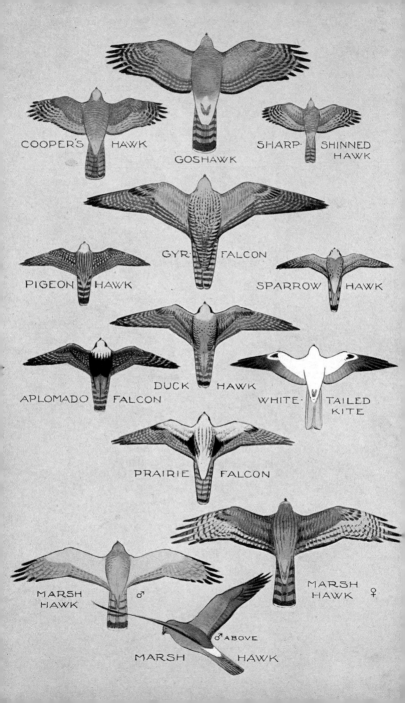

COOPER'S HAWK

GOSHAWK

SHARP-SHINNED HAWK

GYR-FALCON

PIGEON HAWK

SPARROW HAWK

APLOMADO FALCON

DUCK HAWK

WHITE-TAILED KITE

PRAIRIE FALCON

MARSH HAWK ♂

MARSH HAWK ♀

MARSH HAWK ♂ ABOVE

key, with a small head and a long rounded tail. Very shy and difficult to observe, a skulking denizen of dense woods and thickets in the lower Rio Grande Valley, where it is best found at daybreak when it calls raucously from the tree-tops.

Voice: — A loud raucous three-syllabled cackling call, *cha'-cha-lac*, repeated in chorus from tree-tops in early morning and evening and sometimes before rain. Dr. Arthur A. Allen describes the harsh chorus of a pair of these birds as *keep'-it-up*, *keep'-it-up, keep'-it-up*, etc., answered by a lower-pitched *cut'-it-out, cut'-it-out, cut'-it-out*, etc.

Range: — Lower Rio Grande Valley, Tex.

GROUSE: TETRAONIDÆ

LARGE Chicken-like birds, larger than Quail. Some are almost restricted to woods; others inhabit prairies and deserts. Peculiar courting antics of males are spectacular and distinctive.

DUSKY GROUSE. *Dendragapus obscurus.* Subsp. (Illus. p. 56.)
Descr. ♂ 21, ♀ 18. Three dusky gray or blackish Grouse occur in the evergreen forests of the West. Two, the Dusky and the Franklin's Grouse, are found in the Rocky Mt. section. The Dusky Grouse is the larger and grayer of the two. The best marks by which to tell the male Franklin's Grouse are the blacker under parts and the *black and white banding on the sides of the rump.* At close range male Franklin's Grouse show *orange-red* or *red* patches over the eyes; Dusky Grouse *yellow or orange.* Female Franklin's Grouse are *blackish* above; female Dusky Grouse, brownish.
Voice: — Male in courtship gives a series of five or six 'hoots' similar to those of the next species but with only fraction of their carrying power.
Subsp. DUSKY GROUSE. *D. o. obscurus.*
　　　Similar in field to next species. Rockies from n. Ut., se. Ida., and n. Colo. s. to cent. N.M. and cent. Ariz., w. to cent. Nev.
　　　RICHARDSON'S GROUSE. *D. o. richardsoni.*
　　　Lacks pale band at tip of tail. N. Rockies from Can. s. to Wyo. and s.-cent. Ida., w. to e. Wash. and e. Ore.

SOOTY GROUSE. *Dendragapus fuliginosus.* Subsp.
Descr. 16–19. A dark gray or blackish Grouse with a light band at the tip of the tail. The only dark gray Grouse found in the fir forests of the Pacific States (except in section east of Cascades in Wash. and Ore.). The range of this species nowhere overlaps those of the Dusky and Franklin's Grouse. Females

are browner than males, but have a gray cast rather than the rusty-red of the female Oregon Ruffed Grouse.

Voice: — Male in courtship gives a series of six or seven low muffled booming or hooting notes about one octave lower than notes of Horned Owl; ventriloquial.

Range: — Evergreen forests in high mts. of Pacific States from Wash. to s. Calif. (Mt. Pinos), except in section e. of Cascades in Wash. and Ore.

Subsp. (No apparent field differences): (1) Sooty Grouse, *D. f. fuliginosus*; (2) Sierra Grouse, *D. f. sierræ*; (3) Mount Pinos Grouse, *D. f. howardi*.

FRANKLIN'S GROUSE. *Canachites franklini.* (Illus. p. 56.)
Descr. 15–16. Very similar to the Spruce Grouse of e. and n. Can. See Dusky Grouse for description.
Range: — Mt. regions e. of Cascades from Can. s. to ne. Ore., cent. Ida., and w. Mont.

RUFFED GROUSE. *Bonasa umbellus.* Subsp. (Illus. p. 56.)
Descr. 16–19. A large, *red-brown*, or *gray-brown* Chicken-like bird of brushy woodlands, usually not seen until it springs into the air with a startling whir. Female Pheasants are somewhat similar, but have pointed instead of fan-shaped tails, usually prefer more open country, and they flush with less of a whir, generally croaking as they go. The black band near the tip of the tail distinguishes this species from the other woodland Grouse. The Oregon subspecies (coastal belt) is especially distinctive because of its red-brown color.
Voice: — The drumming of the male might be overlooked as a distant 'flivver' starting up, or an outboard motor on some far-distant lake. Their drumming (not a vocal sound, but made by the wings) starts off slowly, gaining speed until it ends in a whir: — *bup ... bup ... bup ... bup .. bup . bup . up . r . rrr*. At a distance the thumping is so hollow that sometimes it hardly registers as an exterior sound, but seems rather to be a disturbing series of vibrations within the ear itself.
Subsp. OREGON RUFFED GROUSE. *B. u. sabini.*
　　Distinguished from next race by rustier color. Coastal belt from w. Wash. to nw. Calif.
　　GRAY RUFFED GROUSE. *B. u. umbelloides.*
　　Like the preceding but with more gray and less rufous on the upper parts. E. of Cascades, from Can. s. to n. Colo. (formerly), n. Ut., and e. Ore.

WHITE-TAILED PTARMIGAN. *Lagopus leucurus.* Subsp. (Illus. p. 56.)
Descr. 12–13. Ptarmigan are small Arctic or Alpine Grouse that change their brown summer plumage for white feathers

when winter sets in. They frequent bleak, barren wastes above timber line on high mountains where few other birds would long survive. This is the only species found in w. U.S. In summer it is brown with a white belly and white wings and tail, conspicuous in flight. In winter the bird is pure white except for black eyes and bill.

Range: — Cascade Mts. of Wash., and Rockies from Mont. to n. N.M.

Subsp. (No apparent field differences): (1) Rainier White-tailed Ptarmigan, *L. l. rainierensis*; (2) Southern White-tailed Ptarmigan, *L. l. altipetens*.

GREATER PRAIRIE CHICKEN. *Tympanuchus cupido americanus.*

Descr. 18. A large brown Hen-like bird of the prairies and brushy grasslands known from the Sharp-tailed Grouse and female Sage Hen by the *short rounded black tail* and, when close, by the heavy transverse barrings on the under parts.

Range: — Great Plains w. to e. Colo. and ne. Mont.; occasional in e. Wyo.

LESSER PRAIRIE CHICKEN. *Tympanuchus pallidicinctus.*

Descr. 16. Similar to Greater Prairie Chicken but much paler.

Range: — Southern Great Plains w. to se. Colo. and e. N.M.

SHARP-TAILED GROUSE. *Pediœcetes phasianellus.* Subsp. (Illus. p. 56.)

Descr. 17½. A *pale* speckled brown Grouse of the prairies with a *short pointed tail.* Female Pheasants have *long* pointed tails; Sage Hens, which also inhabit prairies, are much larger and have black bellies. The various woodland Grouse have wide fanlike tails.

Voice: — In courtship, a hollow 'booming' sound.

Range: — Great Plains w. to foothills in Mont., Wyo., and cent. Colo. Also Great Basin region (e. Wash., e. Ore., Ida., Nev., Ut., w. Mont., sw. Colo., and n. N.M.).

Subsp. (No apparent field differences): (1) Columbian Sharp-tailed Grouse, *P. p. columbianus*; (2) Prairie Sharp-tailed Grouse, *P. p. campestris*.

SAGE HEN. *Centrocercus urophasianus.* (Illus. p. 56.)

Descr. ♂ 28, ♀ 22. Large gray-brown Grouse-like birds of the open sage country, as large as small Turkeys; identified by the contrasting *black belly* and spike-like tail-feathers. Males are considerably larger than females.

Range: — Sagebrush plains e. of Cascades and Sierras from se. Wash. and Mont. s. to e. Calif., Nev., Ut., and n. Colo.

OLD WORLD PARTRIDGES:
PERDICINÆ

EUROPEAN PARTRIDGE. *Perdix perdix perdix*.
Descr. 12–14. A grayish Partridge with chestnut-colored markings; smaller than any of the Grouse and larger than a Quail; found locally in farming country where it has been introduced. In flight, the short, chestnut-colored tail is a good mark.
Range: — Has been introduced locally in several W. States.

QUAIL: ODONTOPHORINÆ

SMALL, scratching, Chicken-like birds, smaller than Grouse or Pheasants.

BOB-WHITE. *Colinus virginianus texanus*. (Illus. p. 57.)
Descr. 8½–10½. A small, ruddy, Chicken-like bird, much smaller than a Grouse, or near the size of a Meadowlark. It is distinguished from the Grouse by its smaller size and short round tail; from other Quail by its rusty color; and from the Meadowlark in flight by the lack of white outer tail-feathers. On the ground or perched the male shows a conspicuous white throat and stripe over the eye, the female buffy.
Voice: — A clearly enunciated whistle *Bob-white*, or *Poor Bob-white*.
Range: — Has been introduced locally in several of the W. States.

SCALED QUAIL. *Callipepla squamata*. Subsp. (Illus. p. 57.)
Descr. 10–12. Often called 'Blue Quail.' A pale grayish Quail of open arid country recognized by the scaly markings on the breast and a *bushy white crest* or 'cotton top.'
Voice: — A two-noted, Guinea-hen-like *chek-ah*.
Range: — Arid country in cent. and s. Ariz., s. Colo., N.M., and w., cent., and s. Tex.
Subsp. (No apparent field differences): (1) Arizona Scaled Quail, *C. s. pallida*; (2) Chestnut-bellied Scaled Quail, *C. s. castanogastris*.

CALIFORNIA QUAIL. *Lophortyx californica*. Subsp. (Illus. p. 57.)
Descr. 9½–10½. A small, plump, grayish Chicken-like bird with a *short plume that curves forward* from its crown. Males have an interesting black-and-white face pattern; females are duller. This species frequents open brush country and cultivated areas.
Voice: — Both sexes, a three-syllabled call, *qua-quer-go*, vari-

BALD EAGLE   ADULT

BALD EAGLE   IMMATURE

GOLDEN EAGLE   ADULT

GOLDEN EAGLE   IMMATURE

OSPREY

BUTEOS
BROAD WINGS
BROAD ROUNDED TAIL

RED-TAILED HAWK
SWAINSON'S HAWK
AM. ROUGH-LEGGED H.
FERRUGINOUS ROUGH-LEG

Local or Rare Species:
RED-BELLIED HAWK
SENNETT'S WHITE-TAILED H.
ZONE-TAILED HAWK
HARRIS'S HAWK (PARABUTEO)
MEXICAN GOSHAWK (ASTURINA)
MEXICAN BLACK H.(URUBITINGA)

ACCIPITERS
LONG TAIL
SHORT ROUNDED WINGS

GOSHAWK (ASTUR)
COOPER'S HAWK
SHARP-SHINNED HAWK

FALCONS
LONG TAIL
LONG POINTED WINGS

DUCK HAWK
PRAIRIE FALCON
SPARROW HAWK
PIGEON HAWK
Local or Rare Species
GYRFALCON
APLOMADO FALCON

SILHOUETTES OF THREE COMMON TYPES OF HAWKS

ously interpreted as *where are you? you go way, chi-ca-go, tuc-a-hoe*, etc. Note of male on territory a loud *kurk* or *twerk*.
Range: — Native in s. Ore. and Calif. (except in e. parts of Mohave and Colorado deserts, where replaced by Gambel's Quail. Both California Quail and Gambel's Quail occur together in spots on the w. edge of the Colorado and Mohave deserts and sometimes hybridize). Widely introduced elsewhere in W. States.
Subsp. (No apparent field differences): (1) California Quail, *L. c. californica*; (2) Valley Quail, *L. c. vallicola*; (3) Catalina Quail, *L. c. catalinensis.*

GAMBEL'S QUAIL. *Lophortyx gambeli.* Subsp. (Illus. p. 57.)
Descr. 10–11. Replaces the California Quail in the desert regions of the Sw. Similar, but male with a large black patch on a light belly; flanks and top of head more russet, latter giving rise to local name 'Redhead.'
Voice: — A loud *kway-o* and a querulous three-noted call, *chiquer-go*, somewhat more drawling than California Quail.
Range: — Deserts of s. Calif., sw. Ut., Ariz., cent. and sw. N.M., and extreme w. Tex.; introduced locally elsewhere.
Subsp. (No apparent field differences): (1) Gambel's Quail, *L. g. gambeli*; (2) Olathe Quail, *L. g. sanus.*

MOUNTAIN QUAIL. *Oreortyx picta.* Subsp. (Illus. p. 57.)
Descr. 11. A Quail of the mountains of the Pacific States. Distinguished from the California Quail by the long *straight* head plume and the *chestnut throat*. The flank pattern is also distinctive.
Voice: — A loud mellow cry, *wook?* or *to-wook?* repeated at infrequent intervals by male in breeding season. Both sexes utter rapid, tremulous whistling sounds when alarmed.
Range: — Mts. of sw. Wash., Ore., s. Ida., w. Nev., and Calif. (to s. part).
Subsp. (No apparent field differences): (1) Mountain Quail, *O. p. palmeri*; (2) Plumed Quail, *O. p. picta.*

MEARNS'S QUAIL. *Cyrtonyx montezumæ mearnsi.* (Illus. p. 57.)
Descr. 8. A small Quail of the brushy slopes of desert mountains. The oddly striped face and speckled body of the male are best shown in the drawing. Females are duller without the facial stripings.
Voice: — A soft whinnying or rolling cry.
Range: — Arid regions from cent. Ariz., cent. N.M., and w. Tex. s.

PHEASANTS: PHASIANIDÆ

RING-NECKED PHEASANT. *Phasianus colchicus torquatus.*
(Illus. p. 56.)
Descr. ♂ 33–36, ♀ 20½. A large Chicken-like or Gamecock-like bird with a long, sweeping pointed tail. The male is quite highly colored with a white neck-ring; the female is brown and more Grouse-like. Its pointed tail is much longer than that of the Sharp-tailed Grouse, which lives in grassy country.
Voice: — Males in spring utter a loud double squawk followed by a whir of wings.
Range: — Introduced in many parts of w. U.S.

TURKEYS: MELEAGRIDIDÆ

MERRIAM'S TURKEY. *Meleagris gallopavo merriami.*
Descr. ♂ 48, ♀ 36. Very similar to the familiar Domestic Turkey of the barnyard. Differs from the Eastern Wild Turkey in having whitish tips to the tail-feathers instead of chestnut.
Voice: — Similar to 'gobbling' of Domestic Turkey.
Range: — Mts. of s. Colo., Ariz., N.M., and w. Tex.

CRANES: GRUIDÆ

LONG-LEGGED, long-necked birds, superficially a little like large Herons, but with long feathers on the back, which curl down over the ends of the wings. They also have shorter bills, and bare red skin about the face. Their blaring trumpet-like calls, once heard, dispel any doubt as to their identity. In flight, the wing-motion of Cranes is quite unlike that of either Herons or Ibises. The wings are less bowed and they beat with a very characteristic deft upward flap. Cranes fly with their necks extended (Herons 'tuck' them in). They do not stand as stiff and erect as Herons.

WHOOPING CRANE. *Grus americana.*
Descr. 50. Larger than Sandhill Crane or Great Blue Heron. A large *white* Crane with a red face; neck outstretched in flight, primary wing-feathers black. (See Wood Ibis.)
Range: — Now an extremely rare migrant in Great Plains; w. occasionally to Mont., Wyo., and probably Colo. and N.M. Winters on coastal prairies of s. Tex.

SANDHILL CRANE. *Grus canadensis.* Subsp. (Illus. pp. 12, 17.)
Descr. A long-legged, long-necked, gray bird with a bald red

forehead. The Great Blue Heron is often called a 'Crane,' but the Heron in sustained flight carries its head drawn back to its shoulders, while the Crane flies with neck extended and legs trailing, like a 'flying cross.' The deft upward flap of the wings in flight is typical.

Voice: — A deep, trumpet-like rolling *k-r-r-r-oo* repeated several times.

Subsp. LITTLE BROWN CRANE. *G. c. canadensis.*
>   34–39. Difficult to distinguish from the Sandhill Crane except when both birds are together, when the smaller size and shorter bill of this race is evident. In California the Little Brown Crane is the commoner race. Breeds in Arctic; migrates through interior of U.S. to Calif., Tex., and Mex.
>   SANDHILL CRANE. *G. c. tabida.*
>   40–48. Breeds in ne. Calif., e. Ore., n. Nev., s. Ida., n. Vt., sw. Mont., w. Wyo., and nw. Colo. Winters from Calif. and Tex. s. to Mex.

RAILS, GALLINULES, AND COOTS: RALLIDÆ

RAILS are somewhat Chicken-like marsh-birds of secretive habits, shy rather than wary, and much more often heard than seen. When flushed, they rise from the reeds close at hand, fly feebly with legs dangling for a short distance, and drop back again suddenly into the marsh.

Gallinules and Coots resemble Ducks except for their smaller heads and rather Chicken-like bills.

CALIFORNIA CLAPPER RAIL. *Rallus obsoletus.* Subsp. (Illus. p. 60.)
Descr. 16. A large brown Rail of the *salt marshes.* Its Hen-like appearance, strong legs, long bill, and white patch under the short tail identify it. The only other Western Rail with a long, slender bill, the Virginia, is much smaller (see Virginia Rail).
Voice: — A clattering *kek-kek-kek-kek*, etc.
Range: — Salt marshes from San Diego to San Francisco, Calif. (casually farther n.), also lower Colo. R. from Yuma to Laguna Dam, and Imperial Valley marshes s. of Salton Sea.
Subsp. (No apparent field differences): (1) California Clapper Rail, *R. o. obsoletus*; (2) Light-footed Rail, *R. o. levipes*; (3) Yuma Clapper Rail, *R. o. yumanensis.*

VIRGINIA RAIL. *Rallus limicola limicola.* (Illus. p. 60.)
Descr. 9–10½. A small reddish Rail, less than ten inches in

length, with *gray cheeks* and a long, slightly decurved bill, the only small Rail, smaller than a Quail, with a *slender* bill. The only fresh-water Rail with a slender bill. When in salt marshes it might be confused with the California Clapper Rail, which is larger (as large as a small Hen), but the ruddier color and gray cheeks are good marks.

Voice: — *Cut-cutta-cutta*, etc., *wak-wak-wak*, etc., and *kidick-kidick-kidick*, besides various 'kicking' and grunting sounds.

Range: — Breeds from Can. s. to s. Calif., Ut., and Colo.; winters from Mex. n. to n. Calif., Ut., and Colo., casually farther.

SORA. *Porzana carolina.* (Illus. p. 60.)
Descr. 8–9¾. The adult Sora is a small gray-brown Rail with a black patch on its face and throat, and a short, Chicken-like *yellow* bill. This short yellow bill will distinguish the bird readily in any plumage from the only other similar-sized Rail of the fresh-water marshes it inhabits, the reddish Virginia Rail, which has a long, slender bill. The immature bird lacks the black throat-patch, and is buffy-brown below, not gray. It can be confused with the smaller and rarer Yellow Rail.
Voice: — 'Song,' a whinnying series of notes, descending. In the spring, a plaintive whistled *ker-wee*. In the fall, a sharp *keek* is the usual note of response when a stone is tossed into the marsh.
Range: — Breeds from Can. s. to s. Calif., Ut., and n. N.M.; winters from Calif. and Ariz. s.

YELLOW RAIL. *Coturnicops noveboracensis.* (Illus. p. 60.)
Descr. 6–7½. Rare. A small yellowish Rail, showing a conspicuous *white* wing-patch in flight — the only Rail so marked. Yellow Rails are so extremely secretive that it requires the services of a bird dog to hunt for them successfully. They prefer grassy marshes to the reedy swamps frequented by their larger relatives. The immature Sora might be taken for a Yellow Rail but is larger, not so yellow, and lacks the white wing-patch.
Voice: — Clicking or ticking notes, often in long series; usually in this sequence: *tic-tic, tic-tic-tic; tic-tic, tic-tic-tic; tic-tic*, etc. (groups of two and three). Some observers describe another call: *kĭ kĭ kĭ kĭ kĭ kreeah*, the last note with a rolling quality (Francis H. Allen).
Range: — Winters in w.-cent. Calif.; casual in other W. States. Breeds in e.-cent. Calif. (Mono Co.).

CALIFORNIA BLACK RAIL. *Creciscus jamaicensis coturniculus.* (Illus. p. 60.)
Descr. 5–6. A very tiny slaty or blackish Rail with white specks on the back and a black bill; about the size of a young Song Sparrow with a bobbed tail. All young Rails in the downy plum-

age are glossy black, and thus are sometimes called Black Rails by the inexperienced. This species inhabits salt meadows where salicornia grows, and is very difficult to flush, or even get a glimpse of.
Range: — Calif., locally in coastal marshes and occasionally inland.

PURPLE GALLINULE. *Ionornis martinica.*
Descr. 12–14. Accidental in Arizona. Distinguished from the Florida Gallinule by its *deep purple* under parts, *pale blue* frontal shield on bill, and, in flight, the bright *yellow* legs.

FLORIDA GALLINULE. *Gallinula chloropus cachinnans.* (Illus. p. 60.)
Descr. 12–14½. Gallinules are Hen-like birds with stout, rather Chicken-like bills, equally at home swimming like Ducks in the open water or wading like Rails in the shallows and among the reeds, or even perching in the bushes along the margin. This is the only one that ordinarily occurs in the West. A slate-gray Duck-like or Rail-like bird with a *red* bill is certainly this species. A white stripe along the flanks is also distinctive. A Gallinule in the company of Coots is smaller, with a somewhat smaller head.
Voice: — Some notes have whining quality, others Chicken-like.
Range: — Marshes from cent. Calif. and Ariz. s. Casual or accidental elsewhere in West.

COOT. *Fulica americana.* (Illus. p. 60.)
Descr. 13–16. Largely gray with a blackish head and neck, white under tail-coverts, and a whitish Chicken-like bill. In flight a white border shows on the hind edge of the wing. It is the only slate-gray Duck-like bird with a whitish bill. Like the Gallinule, when swimming it pumps its neck and head back and forth to facilitate its progress. The dabbing motion while feeding is also quite characteristic. In deep water it dives expertly. When it takes wing, it patters its feet over the water for a considerable distance.
Voice: — Various cackling and croaking notes.
Range: — Breeds from Can. s. to Mex.; winters in Pacific States and from Colo. s.

JACANAS: JACANIDÆ

MEXICAN JACANA. *Jacana spinosa gymnostoma.* (Illus. p. 60.)
Descr. 8½. Occasional near Brownsville, Tex. Frequents ponds and marshes with dense vegetation where Gallinules are found.

Built somewhat like a shore-bird, with *extremely long toes*. Head and neck blackish, rest of body deep rusty. The best field-marks are the conspicuous yellow *frontal shield* on the forehead and *large pale-yellow wing-patches* (primaries and secondaries). Immature birds which wander north across the Mexican boundary in the fall are entirely unlike adults and slightly suggest Wilson's Phalaropes. They are gray-brown above, with white under parts and a broad white stripe over the eye. The upper breast is tinged with buffy. The extremely long toes, short, rounded wings, and Rail-like flight, notes, and habitat will distinguish them from any shore-bird.

OYSTER–CATCHERS:
HÆMATOPODIDÆ

FRAZAR'S OYSTER-CATCHER. *Hæmatopus palliatus frazari.*
Descr. No longer found in Calif. but might occur as a straggler from Mex. Resembles Black Oyster-catcher but has a *white belly* and *white wing-patches*. A race of the American Oyster-catcher of the eastern United States.

BLACK OYSTER-CATCHER. *Hæmatopus bachmani.* (Illus. p. 73.)
Descr. 17. A large heavily built, *all-dark* shore-bird with a heavy *red bill* and pale legs. Unmistakable. Frequents rocky shores along the ocean.
Voice: — A piercing, sharply repeated whistled note.
Range: — Rocky shores and islands along Pacific Coast.

PLOVERS: CHARADRIINÆ

WADING birds, more compactly built, more contrastingly patterned, and with shorter, stouter bills than Sandpipers.

(WESTERN) SNOWY PLOVER. *Charadrius nivosus nivosus.* (Illus. pp. 65, 72.)
Descr. 6. Slightly smaller and very much paler than the Semipalmated Plover, from which it can be distinguished by its slim, black bill, dusky legs, and *incomplete* black neck-ring. The 'ring' is reduced to a black patch on each side of the breast. The Semipalmated Plover is the brown color of wet sand; the Snowy, the color of the sun-bleached dry sand or alkali flats it inhabits.
Voice: — A whistled *too-leep.*
Range: — Breeds along coast and locally inland in Pacific

States, also locally in Ut. and N.M.; winters from cent. Calif. s.

SEMIPALMATED PLOVER. *Charadrius semipalmatus.* (Illus. pp. 65, 72.)
Descr. 6½–8. A small ring-necked shore-bird, brown above and white below; half the size of the Killdeer, from which it may also be distinguished by the short tail and the *single* ring about the neck instead of two. The legs are yellowish and the base of the bill orange (in adults). The Snowy Plover is somewhat similar, but is much paler and whiter, with blackish bill and legs.
Voice: — A plaintive slurred *chi-we,* second note higher.
Range: — Migrates along Pacific Coast; rare inland; winters from cent. Calif. s.

BELDING'S PLOVER. *Pagolla wilsonia beldingi.*
Descr. 7½. A race of the Wilson's Plover, an accidental straggler from Lower Calif. to w. U.S., which might be looked for on s. Calif. beaches. A ring-necked Plover, larger than either the Semipalmated or Snowy Plovers, from which it can be distinguished by its *longer and heavier black bill* and *flesh-colored* legs.
Voice: — A whistled *wheep!*

MOUNTAIN PLOVER. *Eupoda montana.* (Illus. pp. 65, 72.)
Descr. 8–9½. Like a small Killdeer, but with *no breast-rings.* In the breeding season a black mark extends from the bill through the eye. In winter plumage the bird lacks this, but may be told from the winter Black-bellied Plover, which it resembles a little, by its smaller size and the even coloration of its back, *devoid of mottling.* Its habitat is not the shore-line or mud-flat, but prairies, open fields, and alkali-flats.
Voice: — A low whistle; variable.
Range: — Breeds in high plains e. of Continental Divide from Mont. s. to N.M. and w. Tex.; winters from Calif. and s. Ariz. s.

KILLDEER. *Oxyechus vociferus vociferus.* (Illus. pp. 65, 72.)
Descr. 9–11. The Killdeer is the common breeding Plover of the plowed fields, prairies, farm country, lake-shores, and golf-courses. It is larger than the *two* other 'ringed' Plovers, has two breast-bands instead of one, and, in flight, shows an ample, golden-red tail.
Voice: — Noisy; a loud, insistent *kill-deer,* or *kill-dee* or *dee-ee,* oft repeated.
Range: — Breeds from Can. to Mex.; winters in Pacific States and from Colo. s.

GOLDEN PLOVER. *Pluvialis dominica.* Subsp. (Illus. pp. 65, 72.)

Descr. 10–11. A trifle larger than a Killdeer. Spring adults are brown above and black below, with a broad white line extending over the eye down the side of the head. The only other similar bird is the Black-bellied Plover, which is pale gray above, not golden brown, and has a white rump and tail. The Golden Plover has a brown tail. Young birds and winter adults are brown, darker above than below. They are distinguished from the Black-bellied Plover by the lack of white in the wings and tail, and the lack of black axillary feathers beneath the wings (where the wings join the body). In flight, in mixed flocks, they can be picked out by their lack of conspicuous pattern. They prefer prairies, dunes, and burned marshes to the mud-flats.

Voice: — The harsh, whistled *queedle* or *quee* is quite unlike the plaintive *whee-er-ee* of the Black-belly.

Range: — Rare migrant along edge of Great Plains, in Ut., and on Pacific Coast.

Subsp. (No apparent field differences): (1) American Golden Plover, *P. d. dominica*; (2) Pacific Golden Plover, *P. d. fulva*.

BLACK-BELLIED PLOVER. *Squatarola squatarola.* (Illus. pp. 65, 72.)

Descr. 10½–13½. In summer dress the Black-bellied Plover, with its black under parts, resembles no other shore-bird except the rare Golden Plover, which is somewhat smaller and much browner-backed. White-breasted winter birds and immatures are gray-looking and are recognized as Plovers by their stocky proportions and short, stout bills. In any plumage the black axillary feathers under the wing, and the white rump and tail, are determinative.

Voice: — A plaintive slurred whistle, *whee-er-eee*.

Range: — Migrates along Pacific Coast and locally inland; winters along Calif. coast.

SURF–BIRDS: APHRIZINÆ

SURF-BIRD. *Aphriza virgata.* (Illus. pp. 65, 73.)

Descr. 10. A stocky Sandpiper-like shore-bird that inhabits the wave-washed rocks along the ocean where Black Turnstones are found. In flight, it shows a conspicuous *white tail tipped with a broad black band*. It can be told from the Black Turnstone by its somewhat larger size, grayer color, *yellowish* legs, and different flight pattern (see diagram).

Voice: — A sharp *pee-weet* or *key-a-weet*.

Range: — Migrates and winters along Pacific Coast.

RING·NECKED
PHEASANT ♂

RING·NECKED
PHEASANT ♀

SHARP·TAILED
GROUSE

DUSKY
GROUSE ♂

RUFFED
GROUSE ♂

FRANKLIN'S
GROUSE ♂

SAGE
HEN ♂

WHITE·
TAILED
PTARMIGAN SUMMER

WHITE
TAILED
PTARMIGAN WINTER

GROUSE AND
PHEASANTS

MOUNTAIN QUAIL - CALIFORNIA QUAIL - GAMBEL'S QUAIL

SCALED QUAIL - MEARNS'S QUAIL - BOB-WHITE

QUAIL

TURNSTONES: ARENARIINÆ

RUDDY TURNSTONE. *Arenaria interpres morinella.* (Illus. pp. 65, 73.)
Descr. 8–9½. A squat, robust, *orange-legged* shore-bird, larger than a Spotted Sandpiper. In breeding plumage with its *russet-red* back and fantastic black face and breast markings, the bird is handsome enough, but when it flies the real revelation occurs. This harlequin pattern is best explained by the diagram. Young birds and winter adults are more sober in color but easily recognized. The much commoner Black Turnstone has a similar flight pattern but does not have the orange legs, rusty-colored areas, and odd breast-pattern.
Voice: — A rough *chut-a-chut.*
Range: — Migrates along Pacific Coast; very rare inland. Winters from cent. Calif. s.

BLACK TURNSTONE. *Arenaria melanocephala.* (Illus. pp. 65, 73.)
Descr. 9. A squat black shore-bird with blackish breast and white belly. Frequents rocks and ledges along the ocean. Its wing-pattern, shown in the diagram, is very distinctive.
Voice: — A shrill rattling note higher than the Ruddy Turnstone.
Range: — Migrant and winter visitant along coast.

SNIPE, SANDPIPERS, ETC.: SCOLOPACIDÆ

IN GENERAL, small or medium-sized waders with more slender bills than Plovers. Most species are of plain or sober coloration.

WILSON'S SNIPE. *Capella delicata.* (Illus. p. 72.)
Descr. 10½–11½. A striped brown bird, larger than a Spotted Sandpiper, with a short orange tail and an extremely long, slender bill. When flushed, it makes off in a zigzag manner, uttering a sharp, rasping note. Its preferred habitat is wet meadows and the boggy margins of little streams and marshes.
Voice: — Nasal, rasping note when flushed. Nuptial 'song,' uttered in flight, a melodious, winnowing whistle (not vocal).
Range: — Breeds locally from Can. s. to e. Calif., n. Nev., n. Ut., and n. Colo.; winters from w. Wash. and Mont. s. to Mex.

LONG-BILLED CURLEW. *Numenius americanus.* Subsp. (Illus. pp. 58, 73.)
Descr. 20–26, bill 5–7. Curlews are very large brown shore-

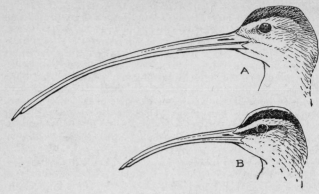

HEADS OF CURLEWS

A. Long-billed Curlew   B. Hudsonian Curlew

birds with long *down-curved* bills. The bills of Godwits turn up.
In flight they appear as large as some Ducks, and when in flocks
often fly in line or wedge formation, with sickle bills extended
and legs trailing. Of the two Western species, the Long-bill is
the one chiefly encountered in the interior. On the coast, both
it and the Hudsonian Curlew occur. The points of distinction
are the much larger size of the Long-bill, the more *buffy* coloration, and the lack of contrasting head-striping (i.e., dark line
through eye, stripes on crown, etc.). In flight overhead, its
bright cinnamon wing-linings make a sure means of identification. In many individuals, the bill is seven inches long, or *twice
as long* as that of the average Hudsonian, but in a few birds bill-
lengths approach each other. Then the other identification
marks must be used.

Voice: — A harsh *cur-lee!* with rising inflection. Also a rapid,
whistled *kli-li-li-li*.

Range: — Great Basin and Great Plains regions (e. Wash., e.
Ore., ne. Calif., s. Ida., Ut., Nev., Mont., Wyo., Colo., and n.
N.M.). Winters in cent. and s. Calif. and along coast of Tex.

Subsp. (No apparent field differences): (1) Long-billed Curlew,
N. a. americanus; (2) Northern Curlew, *N. a. occidentalis*.

HUDSONIAN CURLEW. *Phæopus hudsonicus*. (Illus. pp. 58,
64.)

Descr. 15–18, bill 3–4. (See Long-billed Curlew.)

Voice: — Four or five rapidly repeated short whistles, softer and
lower than those of Greater Yellow-legs, *whi-whi-whi-whi-whi*.

Range: — Migrates along Pacific Coast and in interior valleys
of Calif.; occasional along Great Plains; winters from s. Calif. s.

UPLAND PLOVER. *Bartramia longicauda.* (Illus. p. 64.)
Descr. 11–12½. A large streaked buffy-brown shore-bird, larger than a Killdeer but with no really distinctive markings; inhabits extensive fields, prairies, burnt meadows, etc. It habitually perches on posts. The general brown coloration, the rather short bill, the comparatively small-headed, long-necked, long-tailed appearance, and the habit of holding the wings elevated upon alighting are all helpful points. It can hardly be confused with any other large brown Sandpiper-like bird in the grass country where it is found. Curlews and Godwits are very much larger and have much longer bills.
Voice: — *Kip-ip-ip-ip.* Also a rolling note in flight. 'Song,' a long-drawn melodious wind-like whistle.
Range: — Breeds sparingly from Can. s. in Plains country to e. Ore. (rare), ne. Ut., Colo. (rare), and N.M. (rare). Casual in migration in ne. Calif. and Ariz.

SPOTTED SANDPIPER. *Actitis macularia.* (Illus. pp. 65, 72.)
Descr. 7–8. The common breeding Sandpiper near lakes and streams through much of the W. It runs along the margin, teetering up and down between steps as if it were a little too delicately balanced on its slim legs. In the breeding plumage the breast is covered with *large round spots*; many Sandpipers are streaked, but this is the only one that is definitely spotted. Juvenile birds and fall and winter adults lack this distinctive spotting. They are olive-brown above and whitish below, with a white line over the eye. A white mark on the shoulder is a good aid. The constant teetering is as good a characteristic as any. The wing-stroke is very short, below the horizontal, the wings maintaining a stiff, bowed appearance, entirely unlike the more deep-sweeping flight of the other small shore-birds. This is the most useful distinction of all when Sandpipers rise from the margin. A white wing-stripe, more broken than that of the other small shore-birds having similar stripes, shows in flight.
Voice: — A well enunciated *peet-weet!* — first note higher. (See Solitary Sandpiper.)
Range: — Breeds from Can. s. to s. Calif., n. Ariz., and N.M.; migrates into Mex.; winters along Pacific Coast.

(WESTERN) SOLITARY SANDPIPER. *Tringa solitaria cinnamomea.* (Illus. pp. 64, 73.)
Descr. 7½–9. A dark Sandpiper, blackish above and whitish below, with a white eye-ring. Resembles a Lesser Yellow-legs, and nods like one, but has a dark rump instead of white, and dark legs instead of yellow. The Spotted Sandpiper *teeters* more than it nods and has a white stripe in the wing, which the Solitary lacks; the Spotted has a narrow wing-arc; the Solitary, deep. Both haunt similar places (margins of pools, lakes,

streams). The Solitary may best be described as a *dark-winged Sandpiper with white sides to the tail, which are very conspicuous in flight.*
Voice: — *Peet-weet weet* (higher-pitched than Spotted).
Range: — Migrates throughout w. U.S.

WANDERING TATTLER. *Heteroscelus incanus.* (Illus. pp. 65, 73.)
Descr. 11. A medium-sized shore-bird of the rocky ocean shores where Black Turnstones and Surf-birds are found. It is solid grayish above, with a white line over the eye; legs yellowish. In breeding plumage, the under parts are white, narrowly barred with black. In fall and winter the under parts are unbarred. It can be told at any time from the three shore-birds that inhabit similar haunts (Black Turnstone, Surf-bird, and Spotted Sandpiper) by its *lack of pattern* in flight (see diagram).
Voice: — A clear *whee-we-we-we*, less sharp than that of Greater Yellow-legs, or *tweet-tweet-tweet*, similar to Spotted Sandpiper's.
Range: — Migrates along Pacific Coast; winters from Calif. s.

(WESTERN) WILLET. *Catoptrophorus semipalmatus inornatus.* (Illus. pp. 64, 73.)
Descr. 14–17. A large gray and white shore-bird, with an unmistakable flashy *black-and-white wing-pattern* (see diagram). At rest, when the banded wings cannot be seen, the bird is of a rather uniform gray appearance and quite nondescript. It is large and slender, smaller than the brown Godwits and Curlews and a little larger and more heavily built than the Yellow-legs, which shows much more contrast between the tones of the upper and under parts. The legs are bluish.
Voice: — In breeding season, an oft-repeated *pill-will-willet*; in migration, a loud *kay-tee* or *kā-eh.*
Range: — Breeds in e.-cent. Ore., ne. Calif., n. Nev. (probably), Ut., e. Mont., Wyo., and Colo. (occasionally); migrates through sw. States; winters along Calif. coast.

GREATER YELLOW-LEGS. *Totanus melanoleucus.* (Illus. p. 64.)
Descr. 13–15. A rather large, slim, gray and white Sandpiper with *bright yellow legs.* Flying, it appears as a dark-winged shore-bird with a whitish rump and tail.
Voice: — The three- or four-syllabled whistle, *whew-whew-whew,* is distinctive. Also in spring, a fast-repeated *whee-oodle, whee-oodle,* etc.
Range: — Migrates through w. U.S.; winters from Ore. and N.M. s.

LESSER YELLOW-LEGS. *Totanus flavipes.* (Illus. p. 73.)
Descr. 9½–11. Exactly like the much commoner Greater Yel-

RAILS, GALLINULE,
COOT and JACANA

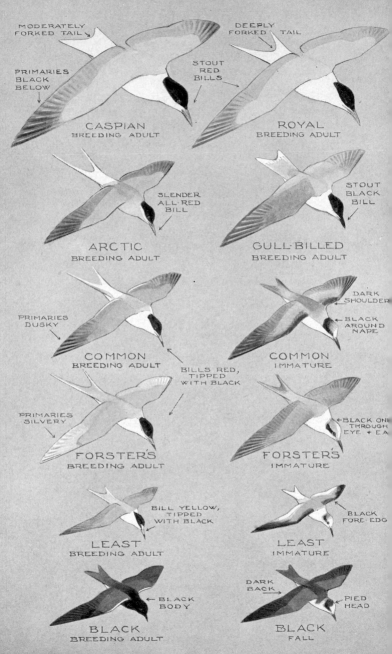

MODERATELY FORKED TAIL

DEEPLY FORKED TAIL

PRIMARIES BLACK BELOW

STOUT RED BILLS

CASPIAN BREEDING ADULT

ROYAL BREEDING ADULT

SLENDER ALL-RED BILL

STOUT BLACK BILL

ARCTIC BREEDING ADULT

GULL-BILLED BREEDING ADULT

PRIMARIES DUSKY

DARK SHOULDER

BLACK AROUND NAPE

COMMON BREEDING ADULT

COMMON IMMATURE

BILLS RED, TIPPED WITH BLACK

PRIMARIES SILVERY

BLACK ON THROUGH EYE + EA

FORSTER'S BREEDING ADULT

FORSTER'S IMMATURE

BILL YELLOW, TIPPED WITH BLACK

BLACK FORE-EDG

LEAST BREEDING ADULT

LEAST IMMATURE

BLACK BODY

DARK BACK

PIED HEAD

BLACK BREEDING ADULT

BLACK FALL

TERNS

low-legs in color, but considerably smaller. The shorter, slimmer bill of the Lesser is perfectly straight; that of the Greater, *slightly upturned*. The fall Wilson's Phalarope might be mistaken for this species but is smaller and paler, immaculately white below, has a more needle-like bill, and duller legs (greenish-yellow or straw-colored).

Voice: — The call most often given by the Greater is a clear, three-syllabled *whew-whew-whew*. That of the Lesser is a flatter, less penetrating cry of one or two notes, *cu* or *cu-cu*. The spring song, corresponding to the *whee-oodle* of the Greater Yellowlegs, is *wheedle-oory*, *wheedle-oory*, etc.

Range: — Migrates through w. U.S.; commonest along edge of Great Plains; uncommon in Pacific States.

KNOT. *Calidris canutus rufus.* (Illus. pp. 64, 72.)
Descr. 10–11. Stout and chunky; larger than a Spotted Sandpiper, or about the size of a Dowitcher. *Spring:* Breast light Robin-red, back mottled gray and black. The short bill, about as long as the head, will distinguish it from the spring Dowitcher, which is also red-breasted. *Fall:* More nondescript, breast whitish. A dumpy light-grayish shore-bird with short legs, a short bill, and a whitish rump. In flight the rump does not show so conspicuously as that of the Yellow-legs, nor does it extend up the back as in the Dowitcher.
Voice: — A soft two-syllabled note.
Range: — Migrates along Pacific Coast; seems to skip Ore.; occasional in Ut.

ALEUTIAN SANDPIPER. *Arquatella ptilocnemis couesi.* (Illus. pp. 64, 73.)
Descr. 8–9. A Sandpiper of irregular occurrence in winter on rocky shores along the Nw. Coast. It is stocky and bluish-gray or slaty colored, resembling somewhat the two other rock-feeding species with which it is sometimes found, the Black Turnstone and the Surf-bird. Both those birds in flight show a broad white band across the base of the tail, *lacking in this species*. It has a white wing-stripe. Very similar to the Purple Sandpiper of the Atlantic Coast.
Voice: — A Flicker-like *clu-clu-clu*.
Range: — Winter visitant to coast of Wash., Ore., and casually Calif.

SHARP-TAILED SANDPIPER. *Pisobia acuminata.*
Descr. 8½. Of rare occurrence along coast of Wash. Like the Pectoral Sandpiper, but in winter plumage, breast rich buffy, *spotted* instead of streaked, with no sharp contrast between white belly and brown of throat and breast (Ludlow Griscom).

PECTORAL SANDPIPER. *Pisobia melanotos.* (Illus. pp. 65, 72.)
Descr. 8–9½. A streaked, brown Sandpiper, larger than a
Spotted; prefers grassy mud-flats and short-grass marshes. The
rusty-brown back is striped with black and lined with white.
The most characteristic thing about the bird is the brownish
streaked breast, which is *defined sharply* against the white belly.
The Least Sandpiper is colored similarly, but is half the size.
The top of the head is darker and the neck longer than that of
the other shore-birds with which it might be confused. Small
individuals might be confused with the less richly marked
Baird's Sandpiper, but the greenish or yellowish legs are a good
mark (Baird's, black).
Voice: — A reedy *krrik, krrik,* heavier than note of Western
Sandpiper.
Range: — Rare coastal migrant; uncommon migrant e. of
Cascades in e. Wash., e. Ore., and Ut.; also along edge of Great
Plains.

WHITE-RUMPED SANDPIPER. *Pisobia fuscicollis.* (Illus.
p. 72.)
Descr. 7½. Somewhat larger than the Western Sandpiper, from
which it is distinguished by its *white rump,* conspicuous in flight.
Other small streaked Sandpipers have only the sides of the
rump white. At rest this species has a more attenuated or
pointed-tailed appearance than other similar shore-birds.
Voice: — A thin, mouse-like *jeet* resembling *jee-jeet* note of
Pipit.
Range: — Migrates through e. U.S.; occurs w. in Great Plains
uncommonly to Mont., Wyo., Colo., and N.M.

BAIRD'S SANDPIPER. *Pisobia bairdi.* (Illus. pp. 65, 72.)
Descr. 7–7½. Resembles a large Least or Western Sandpiper,

TYPICAL BILLS OF 'PEEP'

a. Least Sandpiper   *b.* Semipalmated Sandpiper
                c. Western Sandpiper

but paler, with *a very buffy head and breast*. Those two similar species, and the larger Pectoral are more or less *striped* on the back; the Baird's has a more *scaly* appearance, and the predominating color is buff-brown. A 'Peep' Sandpiper, a little larger than a Western, with a buffy wash across the breast, is quite certainly this species.

Voice: — A husky *kree*.

Range: — Migrates along Pacific Coast and through Great Plains and Great Basin.

LEAST SANDPIPER. *Pisobia minutilla.* (Illus. pp. 62, 72.)
Descr. 5–6½. Collectively we call the small Sparrow-sized Sandpipers 'Peep.' These include the Least, Western, and Baird's. All have a characteristic streaked, brown pattern. The Least is the smallest of the three. It may be known at all seasons from the somewhat larger Western Sandpiper by the *yellowish*, or *greenish*, instead of blackish or greenish-black, legs and the *thinner* and shorter bill. In the fall it is browner than the Western and has a more streaked breast.

Voice: — A sharp thin *kree-eet* more drawn out than note of Western.

Range: — Migrates through w. U.S.; winters from cent. Calif. s.

RED-BACKED SANDPIPER. *Pelidna alpina sakhalina.* (Illus. pp. 64, 72.)
Descr. 8–9. Slightly larger than a Spotted Sandpiper. *Spring plumage:* Rusty-red above, with a black patch across the belly and a white breast. No other *Sandpiper* has a black belly. (Black-bellied and Golden Plovers are black below.) *Winter plumage:* Plain, unpatterned gray above, with a gray suffusion across the breast; much darker than a Sanderling. The Western Sandpiper is smaller and shorter-billed. The best mark in the Red-back is the long stout bill for a bird of that size, which has a marked *downward droop* at the tip.

Voice: — A harsh, rasping *cheezp*.

Range: — Migrates through w. U.S., chiefly along coast. Winters along coast.

DOWITCHER. *Limnodromus griseus.* Subsp. (Illus. pp. 64, 72.)
Descr. 11–12½. In any plumage recognized by the very long Snipe-like bill and *white* lower back, rump, and tail. The Wilson's Snipe, the only other bird with similar proportions, is rarely found on the beaches and flats where the Dowitcher commonly feeds, but the two are often found together on grassy 'snipe ground.' In spring plumage the breast is tinged with cinnamon-red; in fall, with light gray.

Voice: — (See Long-billed Dowitcher, below.)

Subsp. EASTERN DOWITCHER. *L. g. griseus.*
Dowitchers of two races migrate through w. U.S. and winter from Calif. s. It was only recently pointed out that the Eastern Dowitcher outnumbers the Long-bill on the West Coast. Formerly it was believed that the Long-bill was the only one that occurred.

LONG-BILLED DOWITCHER. *L. g. scolopaceus.*
The bill measurements of the two Dowitchers overlap, but extreme long-billed birds of this race are easily recognized; the length of the bill, by comparison, dwarfs the head, giving the bird a small-headed appearance. The rusty tinge on the under parts of Long-bills in breeding plumage extends farther down on the belly than in the other bird, often even to the under tail-coverts. The sides of the breast are barred rather than spotted, and the back is darker, with the buffy feather-edgings more restricted. The notes are quite different. That of the Eastern Dowitcher is a trebled *tu-tu-tu* metallic and slightly Yellow-legs-like. The most common note of the Long-bill is a single thin *keek*, occasionally trebled.

STILT SANDPIPER. *Micropalama himantopus.* (Illus. pp. 64, 73.)
Descr. 7½–9. *Fall plumage:* Resembles a Lesser Yellow-legs and has a *similar flight pattern* but is smaller, with a conspicuous white stripe over the eye and *greenish*, not yellow, legs. The bill, which is proportionately longer and heavier, tapering markedly and with a slight droop at the tip, gives the bird a somewhat Dowitcher-like look. Its feeding habits are also similar to that species. *Spring plumage:* Dark gray, heavily marked with *transverse* bars beneath, and having a heavy rusty mark through the eye.
Voice: — A soft *quirt.*
Range: — Migrates through e. U.S., w. uncommonly in Great Plains to Colo. and Wyo.

SEMIPALMATED SANDPIPER. *Ereunetes pusillus.* (Illus. p. 62.)
Descr. 6⅓. Very similar to the Western Sandpiper and difficult to distinguish in the field. Usually a trifle smaller, and with a noticeably *shorter bill.* Late summer Westerns usually have some rusty on the scapulars, which this species lacks. Least Sandpipers are even smaller, are browner, thinner-billed, and have yellowish legs.
Voice: — Commonest note, a simple *cher* or *cheh.*
Range: — Eastern N.A.; w. uncommonly in migration through Great Plains to Mont., Wyo., and Colo. Occasional in Ut. and Wash.

BLACK-NECKED
STILT

AVOCET

LONG-BILLED
CURLEW

BLACK
OYSTER-CATCHER

MARBLED
GODWIT

SOLITARY
SANDPIPER

WILLET

WANDERING
TATTLER
FALL

RUDDY
TURNSTONE
BREEDING

LESSER
YELLOW-LEGS

SURF-BIRD

STILT
SANDPIPER
FALL

ALEUTIAN
SANDPIPER

BLACK
TURNSTONE

WILSON'S
PHALAROPE
FALL

SHOREBIRDS   I

DOWITCHER
FALL

WILSON'S
SNIPE

KNOT
FALL

SANDERLING
FALL

SPOTTED
SANDPIPER
FALL

RED-BACKED
SANDPIPER
FALL

NORTHERN
PHALAROPE
FALL

PECTORAL
SANDPIPER

WHITE-
RUMPED
SANDPIPER
FALL

RED
PHALAROPE
FALL

LEAST
SANDPIPER

BAIRD'S
SANDPIPER

BLACK-BELLIED
PLOVER
FALL

ABOVE

BELOW

KILLDEER

MOUNTAIN
PLOVER

GOLDEN
PLOVER
FALL

SNOWY
PLOVER

SEMI-PALMATED
PLOVER

SHOREBIRDS II

WESTERN SANDPIPER. *Ereunetes mauri.* (Illus. pp. 62, 65.)
Descr. 6–7. This and the Least Sandpiper are the two common streaked Sparrow-sized Sandpipers which are nicknamed 'Peeps.' The Western is larger, has blackish legs (Least, yellow or yellow-green) and a longer, heavier bill. In the fall, the Western lacks the suffusion of dusky across the upper breast which the Least has, and is grayer above, not so brown.
Voice: — A thin *jeet*, shorter and not so drawn out as note of Least Sandpiper.
Range: — Migrates through w. N.A.; winters from cent. Calif. s.

MARBLED GODWIT. *Limosa fedoa.* (Illus. pp. 64, 73.)
Descr. 16–20. A large shore-bird with a long, straight or perceptibly *upturned bill.* The large size and rich *buff-brown* coloration distinguish this species from all other shore-birds except the Curlews, whose bills turn *down.*
Voice: — A harsh *kret, kret.*
Range: — Formerly bred in Ut. Migrates through Calif., Ut., and Great Plains. Rare in Wash. and Ore. Winters from cent. Calif. s.

SANDERLING. *Crocethia alba.* (Illus. pp. 65, 72.)
Descr. 7–8½. A small, plump Sandpiper with a flashing white stripe in the wing. Other small shore-birds have more or less evident wing-stripes, but in none does the stripe contrast so boldly or extend so far along the wing. It is a little larger than a Spotted Sandpiper; usually rusty in the spring; the whitest of the Sandpipers in the fall; bill and legs stout and black; prefers the outer beaches and sand-flats.
Voice: — A short *kip*, distinctive.
Range: — Migrates along coast and Great Plains and through Ut.; winters along coast.

AVOCETS AND STILTS:
RECURVIROSTRIDÆ

AVOCET. *Recurvirostra americana.* (Illus. pp. 64, 73.)
Descr. 16–20. A very large shore-bird with a slender *upturned*, somewhat Godwit-like bill. This and the striking coloration, black and white (pinkish head and neck in breeding season), set it quite apart from anything else.
Voice: — A sharp *wheek* or *kleek*, oft-repeated in excited tones.
Range: — Breeds from e. Wash. and Mont. to s. Calif., N.M., and s. Tex.; winters from cent. Calif. and s. Tex. s.

BLACK-NECKED STILT. *Himantopus mexicanus.* (Illus. pp. 64, 73.)
Descr. 13½–15½. A large, slim wader, black above and white below, with *extremely long red legs*. In flight it is white beneath, with black, *unpatterned* wings.
Voice: — A sharp yipping.
Range: — Breeds from s.-cent. Ore., n. Ut., and s. Colo. to s. Calif., s. N.M., and s. Tex.

PHALAROPES: PHALAROPODIDÆ

SMALL Sandpiper-like birds with longer necks than most small waders; equally at home wading or swimming.

Two species, the Northern and the Red Phalarope, are most commonly seen along the coast or out at sea, where, especially in the fall, they much resemble Sanderlings except for their swimming habits. When feeding, they often spin around like tops, rapidly dabbing their thin bills into the roiled water. The females wear the bright colors, the males the dull — a reversal of the usual order of things.

RED PHALAROPE. *Phalaropus fulicarius.* (Illus. pp. 66, 72.)
Descr. 7½–9. The Red Phalarope is the most maritime species of the family in migration, rarely occurring inland. The sea-going habits distinguish it as a Phalarope; in the breeding plumage, the *reddish under parts* (blackish at a distance in poor

PHALAROPES

1. Wilson's Phalarope: *a*, breeding female; *b*, winter
2. Red Phalarope: *a*, breeding female; *b*, winter
3. Northern Phalarope: *a*, breeding female; *b*, winter

light) separate it from the Northern. In fall and winter plumage, it resembles a winter Sanderling, gray and white, but with
a characteristic dark '*Phalarope-mark*' through the eye. In
this plumage it is very similar to the Northern Phalarope, but
is a little larger and paler (more solid 'Gull-gray'). The white
wing-stripe can, in the Northern, be compared to that of a
Sanderling, but in the Red, it does not contrast so much with
the gray of the wing. At close range, the *heavier* bill of the Red
and the *yellowish* legs will identify it positively (the Northern
has *black* legs and a more *needle-like* bill). Another good mark
in the gray plumage is the greater amount of gray on the sides
of the breast, forming a partial breast-band.
Voice: — Similar to Northern Phalarope.
Range: — Migrates offshore along Pacific Coast; casual inland.

WILSON'S PHALAROPE. *Steganopus tricolor.* (Illus. pp.
66, 73.)
Descr. 8½–10. This is the common Phalarope of lakes and ponds
of the interior. In breeding plumage the broad neck-stripes of
cinnamon blending into black are the most conspicuous mark.
In flight the bird bears a striking resemblance to a small Yellow-
legs; it is dark-winged (no wing-stripe as in the other Phalaropes) with a white rump. In fall, the Wilson's Phalarope is
gray-backed and immaculately white below, and has a thin
needle-like bill, and greenish or straw-colored legs. The manner
when feeding along the margin is very nervous. The swimming
and spinning habit, when indulged in, is quite conclusive.
Voice: — A grunting note, also a nasal *wurk*.
Range: — Breeds from e. Wash. and Mont. s. to cent. Calif.,
Nev., Ut., and Colo. Migrates to S.A.

NORTHERN PHALAROPE. *Lobipes lobatus.* (Illus. pp. 66,
72.)
Descr. 6½–8. Should a 'Sanderling' be observed at sea, and
should it light upon the water, then it is a Phalarope. The
present species occurs at times on inland lakes as well as along
the coast. In the breeding plumage, it is gray above with a
patch of *rufous-red on the side of the neck* (the Red Phalarope is
completely rufous below). In winter plumage, the way we often
see them (even in late summer), the two are much more similar
(see Red Phalarope). The Phalarope has a shorter wing-
stripe than the Sanderling, which it resembles in flight, and it
flies with a deeper stroke.
Voice: — A sharp *kit*, similar to note of Sanderling.
Range: — Migrates through w. U.S., chiefly off coast, but
common locally inland.

JAEGERS: STERCORARIIDÆ

THE Jaegers are dark Hawk-like, or rather Falcon-like, sea-birds that may occasionally be seen chasing and plundering Gulls and Terns. Their plumages vary considerably; so we have light phases, birds with dark backs and light under parts; dark phases, birds of uniform dark coloration; and intermediates. One noticeable field character is the *flash of white* displayed in the wing across the base of the primary feathers. This feature and the two *elongated central tail-feathers* will immediately distinguish these birds as Jaegers. Immature birds of the three species do not show the distinctive differences in the central tail-feathers and are difficult to identify in the field.

The rare Skua belongs to this group, but lacks the long central tail-feathers of the Jaegers. The British call all Jaegers 'Skuas.'

POMARINE JAEGER. *Stercorarius pomarinus*. (Illus. pp. 13, 68.)
Descr. 20–23. Distinguished from the other Jaegers by the shape of the central tail-feathers, which are broad and twisted. It is larger and heavier than the following species (a little smaller

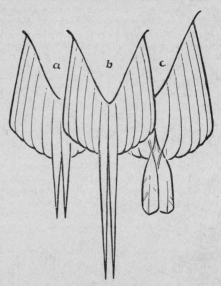

TAILS OF JAEGERS

a. Parasitic   *b*. Long-tailed   *c*. Pomarine

than a California Gull). Immatures lacking the broad central
tail-feathers can be told from immatures of the other two Jaegers
by their larger size and much heavier bill.
Range: — Migrates off Pacific Coast.

PARASITIC JAEGER. *Stercorarius parasiticus.* (Illus. pp. 13,
68.)
Descr. 16–21. The most frequently seen Jaeger of the three.
The pointed central tail-feathers, usually short compared with
those of the other Jaegers, provide the best specific character.
(Immatures of the other two species often have the central tail-
feathers short or lacking, however.)
Range: — Migrates along Pacific Coast.

LONG-TAILED JAEGER. *Stercorarius longicaudus.* (Illus.
pp. 13, 68.)
Descr. 20–23. The Long-tail is much less often seen than the
other two Jaegers. As the central tail-feathers of the Parasitic
Jaeger vary greatly in length, only typical birds with extremely
attenuated central tail-feathers with points extending eight to
ten inches can be safely identified as this species on this character alone. White-bellied Long-tails are usually much whiter on
the breast than the same plumage of the Parasitic, and have a
more clean-cut black cap, sharply defined against a broad white
collar (breast and face of Parasitic are usually somewhat dingy
or clouded).
Range: — Migrates off Pacific Coast, but observed much less
often than other two Jaegers.

SKUA. *Catharacta skua.* (Illus. p. 13.)
Descr. 20–22. A rare sea-bird, about the size of a California
Gull. A large dark-brown Hawk-like bird with a short *square-
cut slightly uptilted tail* and *conspicuous white patches at the base
of the primaries.* Resembles a dark Jaeger, but the wings are
wider and rounded at the tips, not long and pointed. Flight
suggests Hawk (Buteo).
Range: — Casual off coast of Calif. and Wash. These Pacific
Coast Skuas have been designated as the Chilean Skua (*C. s.
chilensis*) in the literature, but Dr. Robert Cushman Murphy
says they are not typical and either represent a little-known
dark-brown phase of the Chilean Skua or an undescribed race.

GULLS: LARINÆ

Long-winged swimming birds with superb powers of flight.
Gulls differ from the Terns in averaging larger, having the bill,
which is proportionately shorter, slightly hooked, and the tail

square-cut or rounded, rarely forked. Gulls are more robust in form and wider of wing than the Terns. In Gull terminology the word *mantle* is frequently used, meaning the upper surface of the wings and the broad strip of back separating them.

The three Gulls most frequently found on inland bodies of water in the West are the California, Ring-billed, and Bona-parte's. The Franklin's Gull occurs exclusively inland but is local (Great Plains and Great Salt Lake).

In identifying adult Gulls the most important marks lie in the feet, bills, and wing-tips. In studying them, notice carefully the following:

(1) Feet (whether pinkish, yellowish, greenish, red, or black)

(2) Bills (whether yellowish, greenish, red, or black, and whether distinctively marked)

(3) Wing-tips (whether solid black, black with white spots or 'mirrors,' gray, or white. The wing-patterns of most species are quite distinctive. See diagram.)

At the end of this brief discussion is a simplified analysis of the above points in the adults of the fourteen species of Gulls known to occur in the West.

Immature birds are more difficult. They are usually darkest in plumage the first year, lighter the second. The leg and bill color of the more confusing species (Glaucous-winged, Western, Herring, California, Ring-bill, and Short-bill) is not helpful, as the majority of individuals of them have *pinkish* legs (at least at first). The bills of first-year Glaucous-wings, West-erns, and Herrings are usually *blackish*, while those of Cali-fornias, Ring-bills, and Short-bills are more or less pinkish at the base. The bills of second-year birds of all six species are basically pinkish or flesh-colored. For the most part, plumage and size must be depended upon for the analysis of these six confusing species.

ANALYSIS OF ADULT GULLS

Species	Bill	Legs	Wing-tips
Glaucous	Yellow with red spot on lower mandible	Flesh-colored	White primaries, unmarked
Glaucous-winged	Yellow with red spot on lower mandible	Flesh-colored	Gray spots
Western	Yellow with red spot on lower mandible	Flesh-colored	Black (with small white tips) blending into *dark* mantle

ANALYSIS OF ADULT GULLS (*Cont.*)

Species	Bill	Legs	Wing-tips
Herring	Yellow with red spot on lower mandible	Flesh-colored	Contrasty black tips with white spots or 'mirrors' within the black
California	Yellow with red or red and black spot on lower mandible	Greenish	Contrasty black tips with white spots or 'mirrors' within the black
Ring-billed	Yellow with complete black ring	Yellowish or yellow-green	Contrasty black tips with white spots or 'mirrors' within the black
Short-billed	Yellow-green, unmarked	Yellow-green	Contrasty black tips with white spots or 'mirrors' within the black
Laughing	Dark red or dusky	Dark red or dusky	Blackish, blending into dark mantle
Franklin's	Dark red	Dark red-brown	Irregular black bar crossing white ground
Bonaparte's	Black	Red	Long white triangle, tipped black
Heermann's	Red	Black	Black, unmarked
Kittiwake	Yellow, unmarked	Black	Solid black, cut straight across
Red-legged Kittiwake	Yellow, unmarked	Red	Solid black, cut straight across
Sabine's	Black with yellow tip	Black	Long, clear-cut black triangle

GLAUCOUS GULL. *Larus hyperboreus.* (Illus. pp. 76, 77.)
Descr. 26–32. A large chalky-white Gull *without dark wing-tips*; usually a little larger than the Western or Glaucous-winged Gull. Immature birds in the first winter are pale cream-colored or very pale buffy, but are recognizable as this species by the extremely pale coloration and the 'frosty' primaries or wing-tips, which are even a shade lighter than the rest of the wing. Second-year birds are often extremely white throughout. Adults, which occur less frequently, have a pale-gray mantle, but the unmarked white primaries are still con-

spicuous. The adult Glaucous-winged Gull, which is the only Western species which at all resembles it, always has some dusky gray in the primaries. Immature Glaucous-winged Gulls are much darker than this species and resemble it but little.
Range: — Rare winter visitor along Pacific Coast; straggler to Colo.

GLAUCOUS-WINGED GULL. *Larus glaucescens.* (Illus. pp. 76, 77.)
Descr. 24–27. *Adult:* — A *pink-footed* Gull with a pale-gray mantle and *gray* markings toward the tips of the wings, the only Western Gull so marked. *First year:* Gray-brown throughout; similar to first-year Western Gull but lighter and browner, less dusky, and *primaries the same gray-brown as the rest of the bird,* not darker or black, as in that species or the other Gulls with which it might be confused. *Second year:* Paler and grayer, primaries gray. *Gray wing-tips in any plumage.*
Range: — Breeds along coast of Wash.; found along entire coast in migration and winter.

WESTERN GULL. *Larus occidentalis.* Subsp. (Illus. pp. 76, 77.)
Descr. 24–27. A *pink-footed* Gull with a *very dark mantle.* At a great distance the dark gray of the mantle often stands out as a dark or blackish spot superimposed on the white of the under parts, making identification simple. The northern race of the Western Gull, found from central Calif. to Wash., has a paler mantle, which, however, is still noticeably darker than that of the California Gull. The pink feet are also a helpful point. *First year:* A large dark gray-brown Gull distinguished from the first-year California Gull by the larger size and much heavier and darker bill, and from first-year Glaucous-winged Gull by the blackish primaries. *Second year:* Head and under parts whitish; bird has 'saddlebacked' appearance of adult. The stout bill and black primaries are good aids to identification.
Subsp. WESTERN GULL. *L. o. occidentalis.*
Paler-backed. Breeds along coast from Wash. to n. Calif. and Farallons; winters s. to s. Calif.
WYMAN'S GULL. *L. o. wymani.*
Noticeably darker-backed. Easterners will be somewhat reminded of Great Black-backed Gull. Breeds along coast of Calif. from Monterey Co. s.

HERRING GULL. *Larus argentatus.* Subsp. (Illus. p. 76.)
Descr. 23–26. *Adult:* — The only large Gull with a *pearly gray* mantle that combines the characteristics of *black wing-tips* and *flesh-colored legs.* The Western Gull has a much darker mantle and a dark eye (Herring Gull, whitish eye). The California Gull has greenish legs. *First year:* Dusky gray-brown throughout,

UPLAND PLOVER

WILLET
FALL

GREATER
YELLOWLEGS

HUDSONIAN
CURLEW

SOLITARY
SANDPIPER

MARBLED
GODWIT

AVOCET

BLACK-
NECKED
STILT

KNOT
SPRING

DOWITCHER
SPRING

STILT SANDPIPER
SPRING

RED-
BACKED SANDPIPER
SPRING

ALEUTIAN SANDPIPER

SHOREBIRDS III

BLACK-BELLIED PLOVER

FALL

SPRING

GOLDEN PLOVER
SPRING

KILLDEER

SEMIPALMATED PLOVER

SNOWY PLOVER

MOUNTAIN PLOVER
SPRING

BAIRD'S SANDPIPER

PECTORAL SANDPIPER

WESTERN SANDPIPER

SPOTTED SANDPIPER
SPRING

SANDER-LING
FALL

RUDDY TURNSTONE
SPRING

WANDERING TATTLER
SPRING

SURF-BIRD
FALL

BLACK TURNSTONE
FALL

SHOREBIRDS IV

not easily distinguishable in the field from first-year Western Gull, but bill usually longer without such a deep angle on the lower mandible. The brown coloration is a shade tawnier, not so gray, and the forehead and front of face is much paler, perhaps a good field-mark (first-year Western has much duskier face). *Second year:* Whiter. The tail is broadly tipped with dark which blends into the white of the rump. Easily told from the second-year Western Gull, which has a more 'saddlebacked' appearance. Much more similar to the second-year California Gull, but much larger with larger and heavier bill.
Range: — Migrates and winters along Pacific Coast and Great Plains.
Subsp. (No very apparent field differences): (1) Herring Gull, *L. a. smithsonianus*; (2) Thayer's Gull, *L. a. thayeri.*

CALIFORNIA GULL. *Larus californicus.* (Illus. pp. 76, 77.)
Descr. 20–23. *Adult:* — Several species of Western Gulls have gray 'mantles' and black wing-tips which give them a similar pattern. This is one of the commonest, and might be used as a basis of comparison. It resembles the smaller Ring-billed Gull, which also has greenish legs, but this species has a *red or red and black spot* on the lower mandible of bill, not a complete black ring as in adult Ring-bill. It shows more white in wing-tips than Ring-bill. The distribution of the black on the under side of the tip of the wing of the adult will identify it at almost any distance. It is cut straight across 'as if dipped in ink.' The other black-wing-tipped Gulls also have their characteristic under-wing patterns, though they are not quite as useful as that of the California Gull. *First year:* Dusky brown throughout; bill flesh-colored with black end. Most second-year immature Gulls have bills like this, but in no other dusky brown first-year bird is there so much light flesh-color. Distinguished from the first-year Western Gull by its lighter coloration, smaller size, and smaller bill; from young Ring-bills by the darker coloration and lack of a contrasting tail-pattern. *Second year:* Paler; whiter below and with more white at base of tail. The different tail-pattern still distinguishes it from the Ring-bill; the small size, small bill, and lighter back from the second-year Western.
Range: — Breeds locally on inland lakes from Can. s. to Mono Lake, Calif., Great Salt Lake, Ut., and Yellowstone Lake, Wyo. Winters along Pacific Coast and inland in Ut., Ore., and Calif.

RING-BILLED GULL. *Larus delawarensis.* (Illus. pp. 76, 77.)
Descr. 18–20. *Adult:* — Very similar in pattern to the California Gull, but may be distinguished by smaller size, lighter mantle, *complete black ring* on bill, and *more yellowish-green legs. Immature:* — Whitish below, gray-brown above; similar to second-year California Gull, which has semblance of ring on

bill. One of the best distinguishing features, aside from the slightly smaller size, is the pattern of the tail. In the California Gull the tail terminates in a broad dark band that blends into the whitish color of the rump. The band near the tip of the tail of the Ring-bill is narrower (a little over an inch wide) and sharply defined. (See immature Short-billed Gull.)

Range: — Breeds on lakes in interior from Can. s. to s. Ore., Ut., and Colo. Migrates along Pacific Coast and inland (perhaps commonest Gull inland); winters from Ore. and Colo. s.

SHORT-BILLED GULL. *Larus canus brachyrhynchus.* (Illus. pp. 76, 77.)
Descr. 16–18. *Adult:* — Has *greenish legs.* Is smaller than the Ring-billed Gull with a small, *unmarked greenish-yellow bill.* Shows more white in the wing-tips than either the California or the Ring-billed Gull. *Immature:* — First year, uniform sooty grayish-brown, making it look like a half-pint-sized first-year Western or Herring Gull with a tiny bill. Differs from young Ring-billed Gull in having a brownish instead of a whitish belly. The second-year plumage is even more like the young Ring-bill. but the bird is smaller, with a *smaller, more Plover-like bill* and a less contrasting tail-pattern. (The rump is duskier and the blackish of the tail wider, not confined to a clean-cut band.)
Range: — Migrates and winters along Pacific Coast.

LAUGHING GULL. *Larus atricilla.* (Illus. p. 76.)
Descr. 15½–17. A little smaller than a Ring-billed Gull; larger than a Bonaparte's. Distinguished in any plumage from other small Gulls by its *dark mantle* and the conspicuous *white border* that lines the hind edge of the wings. In the breeding season, the head is black; in winter, white with dark markings. The immature bird is a very dark small Gull with a *white rump.* The white border on the rear edge of the wing and the dark breast are also good marks.
Range: — Occurs in w. U.S. only at Salton Sea, Calif., where it has recently bred.

FRANKLIN'S GULL. *Larus pipixcan.* (Illus. pp. 76, 77.)
Descr. 13½–15. A bird of the Great Plains and Great Salt Lake. Bears some resemblance to Bonaparte's Gull. In summer the breast has a pale rosy 'bloom,' and the head is black. In fall and winter, the bloom is gone, and the head is white, with a dark patch extending from the eye around the back of the head. The best mark is the very sharply defined black markings which form an *uneven band across the white tips of the wings.* The diagram explains it. There is a long triangle of white in the front edge of the Bonaparte's wing, giving a very different effect.

The only other small Gull found in the prairies which is apt to be confused with this species is the Ring-bill, which has white spots, or 'mirrors,' in the black wing-tips, and pale legs (Franklin's Gulls are dark reddish). Immatures are quite different from young Bonaparte's or young Ring-bills, *small dark-backed Gulls with conspicuous white rumps.* Young Bonaparte's are pale, with whitish primaries; young Ring-bills are paler, with a narrow tail-band.

Range: — Breeds and migrates in Ut.; migrant along w. edge of Great Plains and in N.M.

BONAPARTE'S GULL. *Larus philadelphia.* (Illus. pp. 76, 77.)
Descr. 12–14. The smallest of the Western Gulls. Can be identified at a great distance by the characteristic wing-pattern created by the *white outer primaries*, which contrast strikingly with the gray of the mantle. In the breeding plumage this species has a black head. In winter adults and immature birds the head is white with a conspicuous black spot behind the eye. Immature birds have a narrow black band on the tip of the tail.
Range: — Migrates and winters along coast; local migrant inland, especially in Pacific States and Ut. and on Great Plains.

HEERMANN'S GULL. *Larus heermanni.* (Illus. pp. 76, 77.)
Descr. 18–21. The easiest of Western Gulls to identify. *Adult:* — Dark gray with a *whitish head*, *red bill*, and black tail. *Immature.* — Lacks white head; very dark, with bill brown or partly red.
Range: — Summer and fall visitor along Pacific Coast; winters in Calif.

PACIFIC KITTIWAKE. *Rissa tridactyla pollicaris.* (Illus. pp. 76, 77.)
Descr. 16–18. An 'offshore' Gull of the ocean, smaller than either the California or the Ring-billed, which it resembles in coloration. The legs of the Kittiwake are *black.* Another good point is the appearance of the black wing-tips, which are solid black, and cut *straight across* as if they had been dipped in ink. The immature bird is most likely to be confused with the Bonaparte's Gull in the same plumage, but the Kittiwake has a dark bar on the back of the neck, instead of a dark spot behind the eye, and has more black in the outer primaries and the *fore border* of the wing. Belongs to the same species as the Atlantic Kittiwake.
Range: — Migrates and winters along Pacific Coast, offshore.

RED-LEGGED KITTIWAKE. *Rissa brevirostris.*
Descr. 14–15¾. Wing-pattern similar to Kittiwake, but bird

smaller, *legs bright red*. (Bonaparte's Gull also has bright-red legs.)
Range: — Accidental on coast of Ore.

SABINE'S GULL. *Xema sabini.* (Illus. pp. 76, 77.)
Descr. 13–14. An offshore Gull, the only species with a *forked* tail. The jet-black outer primaries and the conspicuous triangular white patch on the hind edge of the wing create a distinctive wing-pattern that renders this little Gull unmistakable. The head is dark only in the breeding plumage.
Range: — Migrates along Pacific Coast, offshore; occasional inland.

TERNS: STERNINÆ

The Terns are Gull-like water-birds, differing from the Gulls in being more slender in build, narrower of wing, and more graceful in flight. The bill is considerably more slender and sharper-pointed, usually held pointed downward toward the water. The tail is forked. Most Terns are white, or whitish, with black caps. Six species have red or orange bills. In fall and winter the black cap is more or less imperfect or absent, the black of the forehead being largely replaced by white. At this season the red bills of the three similar small species (Forster's, Common, and Arctic) become clouded with dusky, rendering them useless as aids in identification. Immature birds are similar to winter adults but usually are marked with dusky on the upper plumage. A typical Tern habit is to plunge head first into the water King-fisher-fashion.

GULL-BILLED TERN. *Gelochelidon nilotica aranea.* (Illus. p. 61.)
Descr. 13–14½. Somewhat larger and paler and with tail less forked than the Common or Forster's Terns; feet black. The *stout*, almost Gull-like, *black* bill is, perhaps, the best field-mark.
Voice: — A rasping, three-syllabled *ză-ză-ză* (has Magpie-like quality).
Range: — Breeds at Salton Sea, in s. Calif.; does not occur elsewhere in West.

FORSTER'S TERN. *Sterna forsteri.* (Illus. p. 61.)
Descr. 14–15. This is the small black-capped Gull-like bird with the red bill which is so familiar along the ocean and around other large bodies of water. The Forster's is the commonest of the White Terns in the W. *Adult in breeding plumage:* — White with a light-gray mantle and black cap; bill orange-red with a black tip; feet orange-red; tail deeply forked. *Immature*

GLAUCOUS-WINGED   GLAUCOUS

HERRING   WESTERN

CALIFORNIA   HEERMAN'S

RING-BILLED   LAUGHING

SHORT-BILLED   KITTIWAKE

FRANKLIN'S   SABINE'S   BONAPARTE'S

GULLS - ADULTS

GLAUCOUS-WINGED — 1st yr.

GLAUCOUS — 1st yr.

WESTERN — 1st yr.

WESTERN — 2nd yr.

CALIFORNIA — 1st yr.

CALIFORNIA — 2nd yr.

HEERMAN'S — 1st yr.

RING-BILLED — 1st yr.

FRANKLIN'S

SHORT-BILLED — 1st yr.

KITTIWAKE

SABINE'S

BONAPARTE'S

GULLS - Immatures

and winter adult: — Similar, without the black cap; instead, a heavy black patch like an ear-cap on the side of the whitish head. (See Common Tern.) Bill largely dusky at this season instead of bright red.

Voice: — A harsh nasal *za-a-ap* or a nasal *keer*, not so drawn out as note of Common Tern.

Range: — Breeds inland from e. Wash. and Wyo. s. to e. Calif., Nev., Ut., and Colo.; migrates and winters along coast of cent. and s. Calif.

COMMON TERN. *Sterna hirundo hirundo.* (Illus. p. 61.)
Descr. 13–16. Very similar to the much commoner Forster's Tern in size and appearance. White, with pale-gray mantle and black cap; bill and feet orange-red; tail deeply forked. *Winter plumage:* — Similar, but without the black cap; instead, a heavy black patch extending from the eye around the back of the head. Red of bill obscured with dusky. This species in adult plumage is generally considered very difficult to identify in the field because of its close resemblance to the Forster's Tern, but with a little practice it actually becomes an easy matter. The tail of the Forster's is of nearly the same tone of gray as the back and wings; that of the Common is a clear white that contrasts strikingly with the gray of the back. Then, too, the primaries of the Forster's are *silvery* (lighter than rest of wing), in direct contrast to those of the Common, which are *dusky* (darker than rest of wing). Immature Forster's Terns have a black patch through the eye and ear, while in the Common Tern this same dark area extends from the eye clear around the back of the head. The dusky patch on the fore part of the wing in the immature Common Tern is absent in the Forster's.

Voice: — A drawling *kee-arr* more drawn out than corresponding note of Forster's.

Range: — Migrant along coast and in Ut. Breeds locally or occasionally in Wash. and Mont.

ARCTIC TERN. *Sterna paradisæa.* (Illus. p. 61.)
Descr. 14–17. *Adult:* — Grayer than Forster's Tern. Very difficult to distinguish from the Common Tern. Grayish-white with a darker gray mantle, black cap, and *blood-red* feet and bill; tail deeply forked. A good mark is the *white streak below the black cap.* In the Common the whole face seems clear white. The Arctic Tern is *grayer* than any of the other species which it closely resembles. In summer plumage the bill is blood-red *to the tip,* whereas those of the Common and Forster's are orange-red, *usually* (but not always) tipped with black. The tarsi of the Arctic Tern are shorter than those of the others, so when the bird is at rest, it stands lower. The tail is longer and more streaming than that of the Common (projecting slightly be-

yond the wing-tips when at rest), and the flight is more willowy. Immature birds, so far as we know, are quite indistinguishable. Fall adults probably are also, as the red bill becomes quite dusky.

Voice: — Note shriller than Common Tern's, often ending in rising inflection.

Range: — In migration along Pacific Coast, usually well off-shore; seldom seen on beaches.

LEAST TERN. *Sterna antillarum.* Subsp. (Illus. p. 61.)
Descr. 8½–9½. The smallest of the Terns. *Adult:* — White, with a pale-gray mantle and black cap; white patch cutting into black cap on forehead; bill and feet *yellow.* The extremely small size and the yellowish bill and feet render identification certain. *Immature:* — Bill darker; dark patch from eye around back of head, large dark areas on fore edge of wings. May be mistaken for the fall Black Tern, but is smaller, paler above, and with a *whitish,* instead of dark, tail.

Voice: — A harsh squealing *zeek* or *zree-eek.*
Range: — Breeds on coast n. to cent. Calif.; also along North Platte R. in Wyo.; occasional in Colo.
Subsp. (No apparent field differences): (1) Least Tern, *S. a. antillarum;* (2) Brown's Tern, *S. a. browni.*

ROYAL TERN. *Thalasseus maximus maximus.* (Illus. p. 61.)
Descr. 18–21. A large Tern, slightly smaller than the California Gull or the Caspian Tern, which it closely resembles. The more deeply forked tail and more slender bill are the best field-marks by which to differentiate the bird from the Caspian Tern. At rest, the wing-tips of the Caspian extend well beyond the end of the tail; those of the Royal barely reach the tail-tip. (See Caspian Tern.)

Voice: — A harsh *keer,* higher than note of Caspian.
Range: — Coast of Calif. from San Francisco Bay s.

ELEGANT TERN. *Thalasseus elegans.*
Descr. 16–17. This rare species should be looked for in the early fall along the coast from San Francisco Bay south. It most likely will be with Royal Terns, from which it can be picked out by its smaller size, about halfway between that of the Royal and the Forster's. The student should not attempt to identify this species until he first knows those two commoner species from A to Z.

CASPIAN TERN. *Hydroprogne caspia imperator.* (Illus. p. 61.)
Descr. 19–23. About the size of a California Gull, from which it may be distinguished by its black cap, red bill, and forked

tail. The great size and large red bill will set this species apart from all others of this group except the Royal. The tail of the Caspian is forked for only a quarter of its length; that of the Royal for fully half its length. The Caspian Tern occurs inland on many bodies of water as well as on the coast, but the Royal is confined to the coast from San Francisco south. When both species are together this species may be distinguished readily at long range from the Royal Tern by the greater amount of dark in the primaries, especially below.

Voice: — A deep raucous *ka-arr*, deeper than note of Royal.

Range: — Breeds locally inland from Can. s. to s. Ore., e. Calif., Ut., and Wyo.; migrates through Pacific States.

BLACK TERN. *Chlidonias nigra surinamensis.* (Illus. p. 61.) **Descr.** 9–10. *Breeding plumage:* — Head and under parts black; back and wings gray; under tail-coverts white. In this plumage it is the only *black-bodied Tern. Immature and adult in winter:* — Head and under parts white; back and wings gray; dark markings on head, about eye, ear, and back of neck. The winter plumage comes very early; mottled, changing birds appear in midsummer. In this pied plumage the short tail and deeply swooping wing-beats are good points.

Voice: — A sharp *keek* or *klea.*

Range: — Breeds locally inland from Can. s. to Calif., Nev., and Colo. Migrates through interior and on coast from Monterey, Calif., s.

AUKS, MURRES, AND PUFFINS: ALCIDÆ

BIRDS of this group frequent salt water and are quite accidental elsewhere. Most of them prefer the open ocean or rocky shores. They are Duck-like in appearance, but may be distinguished by their short necks, and pointed, stubby or deep and compressed bills. When flying, they beat their wings very rapidly on account of the narrow wing-arc, and are given to much circling and veering, seldom holding the straight course of a Duck. On the water most species appear chubby and neckless (except California Murre and Pigeon Guillemot).

CALIFORNIA MURRE. *Uria aalge californica.* (Illus. p. 92.) **Descr.** 16–17. Size of a small Duck, identified by its black-and-white pattern and slender pointed bill. *Breeding plumage:* Head, neck, back, and wings *dark*; under parts and line on the hind edge of the wing *white*; bill *pointed. Winter plumage:* Similar, but white on the throat and side of face, and a *short black mark extending from eye into white of face.* Larger and with

a longer, more pointed bill than any other Western 'Alcid.' A race of the Common Murre.
Range: — Coastal; breeding chiefly on islands from Wash. to cent. Calif.; winters along coast to s. Calif.

PIGEON GUILLEMOT. *Cepphus columba.* (Illus. p. 92.)
Descr. 12–14. About the size of our smallest Ducks. *Breeding plumage:* A small black Duck-like bird with large *white shoulder patches, red feet,* and a pointed bill. The White-winged Scoter, with which it might be confused, is much larger, with white patches placed on the rear edge of the wing, not on the fore edge, and which show less plainly as the bird rides the water. *Winter plumage:* Pale with white under parts and blackish wings with large white patches as in summer. *No other Western 'Alcid' has white wing-patches* (although others have white linings on the under sides of the wings). Very similar to the Black Guillemot of the Atlantic.
Range: — Coastal, resident along rocky shores and islands from Santa Barbara Ids., Calif., n. to Wash.

MARBLED MURRELET. *Brachyramphus marmoratus.* (Illus. p. 92.)
Descr. 9½–10. Three Murrelets occur more or less commonly in the winter along the Pacific Coast. They are chubby, neckless-looking little sea-birds, dark above and white below, with conspicuous white throats. This species seems to be the commonest, and can be told from others in winter plumage by the *strip of white between the back and wing.* *Breeding plumage: Dark brown* above; heavily *barred* on the under parts. The only Alcid so colored.
Range: — Coastal. Summers along coast of Wash. and Ore.; winters s. to s. Calif.

XANTUS'S MURRELET (SCRIPPS'S MURRELET). *Endomychura hypoleuca.* (Illus. p. 92.)
Descr. 10. Does not show as much white in the sides as the other two Murrelets, and white of under parts does not run so far up on sides of neck (see diagram); upper parts without distinctive pattern (other two species distinctively patterned above). Summer and winter plumages similar. It was pointed out recently that the original Xantus's Murrelet came from Guadalupe Island, Mexico, and that the birds off the California Coast were quite different, so it was proposed that the California bird be designated by the name Scripps's Murrelet and the other one retain the name Xantus.
Range: — Oceanic. Breeds on ids. off s. Calif.; winters n. to cent. Calif.

CRAVERI'S MURRELET. *Endomychura craverii.*
Descr. Probably indistinguishable in the field from Xantus's
Murrelet, but identifiable under exceptional circumstances or in
the hand by the *clouded wing-linings.* (Wing-linings of Xantus's
are usually *immaculate white*, not spotted or clouded.) Thought
by some to be just a race of the preceding species.
Range: — Breeds in Gulf of Calif.; occurs after breeding season
n. to Monterey, Calif.

ANCIENT MURRELET. *Synthliboramphus antiquus.* (Illus.
p. 92.)
Descr. 10. *Winter plumage:* Like the Marbled Murrelet but
without the white strip on the back. *Back paler, contrasting with
the black cap.* Throat often dusky, but white extending up sides
of neck as in Marbled Murrelet. *Breeding plumage:* The sharply
cut black throat-patch and white stripe over the eye make identification certain.
Range: — Winters along Pacific Coast.

CASSIN'S AUKLET. *Ptychoramphus aleuticus.* (Illus. p. 92.)
Descr. 9. A small chubby neckless sea-bird, the smallest of the
Alcidæ; smaller than any of the Murrelets, from which it can
be told at any season by its obscure coloration and dusky throat.
In winter all the other *small* Alcidæ have white either on the
throat or on the sides of the neck.
Range: — Resident offshore along entire coast.

PAROQUET AUKLET. *Cyclorrhynchus psittacula.* (Illus. p.
92.)
Descr. 10. A small 'Alcid' with black upper parts and white
under parts, characterized by a *stubby, upturned red bill.* Puffins,
the only other 'Alcids' with red bills, have much larger bills.
Range: — Coastal, offshore. Winters s. to cent. Calif.

RHINOCEROS AUKLET. *Cerorhinca monocerata.* (Illus. p.
92.)
Descr. 15. A dark neckless-looking sea-bird, larger than the
Murrelets, smaller than a Murre. *Winter plumage:* Resting on
the water, the size, *uniform dark coloration*, and lack of a white
throat and breast distinguish it from all other Alcids, except the
immature Tufted Puffin. The smaller, more slender brownish-
yellow bill and the tendency to occur closer inshore identify this
Auklet. The Cassin's Auklet is also dusky with a dark throat,
but is very much smaller (9 inches). *Breeding plumage:* Acquired
in late winter. Characterized by conspicuous *white mustaches*
and *white eye plume.*
Range: — Coastal. Breeds on ids. off coast of Wash.; winters
s. along entire coast.

HORNED PUFFIN. *Fratercula corniculata.* (Illus. p. 92.)
Descr. 14½. A Puffin with *clear white under parts* and a black band across its breast would be this uncommon species. Immature Tufted Puffins have pale under parts but not clear white.
Range: — Occasional in winter, offshore s. to Calif.

TUFTED PUFFIN. *Lunda cirrhata.* (Illus. p. 92.)
Descr. 15. A chunky sea-bird, with an amazing *triangular* bill. *Breeding plumage:* Blackish with white cheeks, *large triangular red bill,* and *long curved buffy-yellow ear-tufts.* Nothing else like it. *Winter adult:* — White cheeks and yellow ear-tufts gone; a chunky *all-black* bird with a deep-*red bill. Immature:* — Whitish below, bill smaller and dark. Resembles the immature Rhinoceros Auklet, but the bill is considerably stouter.
Range: — Coastal. Resident offshore from Wash. to Santa Barbara Ids., Calif.

PIGEONS AND DOVES: COLUMBIDÆ

Two types of Pigeons occur in N.A.; those with fanlike tails, of which the Domestic Pigeon is the most familiar, and the slimmer, brownish type with rounded or long pointed tails. The Mourning Dove is the most characteristic of the latter group. The notes of the various species are very distinctive, once learned.

BAND-TAILED PIGEON. *Columba fasciata fasciata.* (Illus. p. 120.)
Descr. 15½. A heavily built Pigeon, with a broad rounded tail. Readily distinguished from the Mourning Dove, which has a pointed tail. More easily mistaken for the Domestic Pigeon, except for its woodland or mountain habitat and the tendency to alight in trees. Under favorable circumstances the pale broad tail-band can be seen as the bird flies. At close range, a white crescent is visible on the nape of the neck. The rump is not conspicuously pale as in the domestic species, and the legs are *yellow,* not red.
Voice: — A hollow Owl-like *oo-whoo* or *whoo-oo-whoo,* repeated several times.
Range: — Breeds in Pacific States from Cascades and Sierras to coast; also in se. Ariz., N.M., Colo., and w. Tex.; winters in sw. U.S.

RED-BILLED PIGEON. *Columba flavirostris flavirostris.* (Illus. p. 120.)
Descr. 13. A rather large dark Pigeon, with a broad rounded tail. In favorable light shows much deep maroon on the fore

parts. Distinguished from all other Pigeons in the lower Rio Grande Valley by its size and uniform dark appearance.
Voice: — Cooing similar in quality to that of White-winged Dove but more drawn out: *who who wooooooo*, the long note almost rising to a wail. Dr. G. M. Sutton describes the song of the ardent male as *Ooooooo, up-cup-a-coo, up-cup-a-coo, up-cup-a-coo*.
Range: — Lower Rio Grande Valley, Tex.

ROCK DOVE *or* DOMESTIC PIGEON. *Columba livia.*
Descr. This bird has become feral, and in places is as firmly established as a wild species as the House Sparrow. It needs no description. (See Band-tailed Pigeon.)

(WESTERN) MOURNING DOVE. *Zenaidura macroura marginella.* (Illus. p. 120.)
Descr. 11–13. The common Wild Dove of much of the West. A small *brown* Pigeon, smaller and slimmer than a Domestic Dove, with a *pointed*, not fan-shaped, tail, which shows large white spots when the bird flies. This pointed tail distinguishes it from any other Dove.
Voice: — A mournful *coah-cooo-cooo-coo.* At a distance only the last three *coos* are audible.
Range: — Breeds throughout w. U.S.; winters from Ore. and s. Colo. s.

CHINESE SPOTTED DOVE. *Spilopelia chinensis chinensis.* (Illus. p. 120.)
Descr. Larger than Mourning Dove, with a moderately long rounded or square-tipped tail which has much white in the corners. *A broad collar of black and white spots* encircling the back of the neck is the most distinctive mark.
Voice: — A typical Dove-like cooing, *coo-who-coo*; resembles somewhat voice of White-winged Dove.
Range: — Found commonly around Los Angeles, Calif., where it has been introduced.

RINGED TURTLE DOVE. *Streptopelia risoria.*
Descr. Slightly larger than the Mourning Dove with moderately long *rounded* tail which has much white in the corners. Much *paler* than Mourning Dove, with a *narrow black ring encircling the back of the neck.* In flight the dark primaries contrast boldly with the pale coloration of the rest of the bird.
Range: — Has been introduced around Los Angeles, Calif.

WHITE-WINGED DOVE. *Melopelia asiatica.* Subsp. (Illus. p. 120.)
Descr. 11–12½. Like a Mourning Dove but heavier, with a

rounded tail, which is tipped with a broad white band. The best field-mark is a large *white patch* on the wing. No other Dove has this.

Voice: — A harsh cooing, *coo-uh-cuck'-oo* or *who cooks' for you'?* Sounds vaguely like crowing of a young Rooster.

Range: — Se. Calif. (deserts), s. Ariz., sw. N.M., and s. Tex.

Subsp. (No apparent field differences): (1) Eastern White-winged Dove, *M. a. asiatica*; (2) Western White-winged Dove, *M. a. mearnsi.*

MEXICAN GROUND DOVE. *Columbigallina passerina pallescens.* (Illus. p. 120.)

Descr. 6¾. A very small short-tailed Dove, *not much larger than a Sparrow*, with wings that flash rufous-red in flight. (See Inca Dove.)

Voice: — A series of soft coos, sounding double at close range *coo-oo, coo-oo, coo-oo*, etc.

Range: — Se. Calif., s. Ariz., N.M., and w. Tex.

INCA DOVE. *Scardafella inca inca.* (Illus. p. 120.)

Descr. 8. A very small Dove. May be told from the Mexican Ground Dove by the *comparatively long* square-ended tail, which has conspicuous white sides. The Ground Dove's tail is dark and stubby. Like the Ground Dove it shows some rufous in wing in flight. Perched, the back has a scaly appearance.

Voice: — Usually two notes of nearly even emphasis *coh-coo*, or, as heat-hating residents of Arizona interpret it, '*no hope.*'

Range: — Ariz., s. N.M. (rare), and sw. and s. Tex.

WHITE-FRONTED DOVE. *Leptotila fulviventris angelica.* (Illus. p. 120.)

Descr. 12. A dark-winged, ground-inhabiting Dove with a rounded white-tipped tail. Best identified from all other Doves by its whitish under parts. In flight, shows reddish wing-linings.

Voice: — A low, soft, ghostly *oo-whoooooo*, lower in pitch and softer than the notes of any other Dove; at a distance, only the hollow long-drawn *whooooooo* is audible.

Range: — Lower Rio Grande Valley, Tex.

PARROTS: PSITTACIDÆ

THICK-BILLED PARROT. *Rhynchopsitta pachyrhyncha.*

Descr. 16½. A heavily built green Parrot, with a very heavy black bill and red forehead. Young with white bill and less red. The only Parrot that occurs in w. U.S.

Range: — Occasional in mts. of se. Ariz., especially Chiricahua Mts. Has also occurred in sw. N.M.

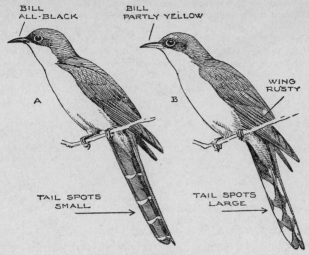

A. BLACK-BILLED CUCKOO

B. YELLOW-BILLED CUCKOO

ANIS, ROAD–RUNNERS, CUCKOOS, ETC.: CUCULIDÆ

YELLOW-BILLED CUCKOO. *Coccyzus americanus.* Subsp.
(Illus. p. 85.)
Descr. 11–13½. Known as a Cuckoo by the slim proportions and
coloration, dull brown above and whitish below; further distinguished by the presence of *rufous* in the wings, *large* white
spots at the tips of the tail-feathers and, at close range, the
yellow lower mandible of the bill. In flight the slim look and the
flash of rufous in the wings are the best marks.
Voice: — A rapid throaty *ka ka ka ka ka ka ka ka ka ka ka ka
ka ka kow kow kowp kowp kowp kowp.*
Range: — Breeds from Wash. and Colo. s. to Mex.
Subsp. (No apparent field differences): (1) Yellow-billed
Cuckoo, *C. a. americanus*; (2) California Cuckoo, *C. a. occidentalis.*

BLACK-BILLED CUCKOO. *Coccyzus erythropthalmus.* (Illus.
p. 85.)
Descr. 11–12. Brown above, white below; similar to preceding
species, but without rufous wings and yellow lower mandible.

ROAD-RUNNER

White tail-spots smaller; usually a narrow red ring around eye.
Range: — Breeds in e. Mont., e. Wyo., and ne. Colo.

ROAD-RUNNER. *Geococcyx californianus.* (Illus. p. 86.)
Descr. 20–24. The 'Chaparral Cock' is quite unique. It is long
and slender, heavily streaked, with a long expressive tail, a
shaggy crest, and strong legs for running. In flight the short,
rounded wing shows a white crescent. The bird is more likely to
run than fly.
Voice: — Song, a series of six or eight Dove-like *coos* descending
in pitch (last note about pitch of Mourning Dove's call). Dr.
George M. Sutton describes the most characteristic note as 'an
incisive note made by rolling mandibles sharply.'
Range: — Chiefly arid or semi-arid regions from n.-cent. Calif.,
Ut., and Colo., s. to Mex.

GROOVE-BILLED ANI. *Crotophaga sulcirostris sulcirostris.*
(Illus. p. 87.)
Descr. 12½. A coal-black Cuckoo-like bird, with loose-jointed
tail, short wings (hence a weak flight), and a deep bill with a
high, curved ridge on the upper mandible. The peculiar bill formation gives the bird a decidedly Parrot-like or Puffin-like profile. Except for the bill, the bird might easily be mistaken on
first acquaintance for a Great-tailed Grackle.
Voice: — A repeated *pee-oh*, or *tee-ho*, the first note higher and
thin, the second guttural; also Cuckoo-like calls and wailing
notes.
Range: — Lower Rio Grande Valley, Tex.; occasional in Ariz.

GROOVE-BILLED ANI

OWLS: TYTONIDÆ AND STRIGIDÆ

NOCTURNAL birds of prey, characterized by the large head, large eyes, *facial disks*, and soft, moth-like, noiseless flight. They seem quite neckless. Some species have conspicuous feather-tufts, or 'horns'; others are round-headed, devoid of such orna-mentation.

BARN OWL. *Tyto alba pratincola.* (Illus. p. 93.)
Descr. 15–20. A long-legged, light-colored Owl with a *white heart-shaped face.* Distinguished in flight at a distance as an Owl by the large head and light, moth-like flight; as this species, by the whitish or pale-cinnamon under parts and buffy or rusty upper plumage (Short-ear does not have such pale under parts).
Voice: — A rasping hiss or 'snore.'
Range: — From Wash. and Colo. s. to Mex.

SCREECH OWL. *Otus asio.* Subsp. (Illus. p. 93.)
Descr. 8–10. A small gray Owl with conspicuous ear-tufts, the only common *small* Western Owl so adorned. Screech Owls in w. U.S. are invariably gray except for two races, the Macfar-lane's Screech Owl (e. Wash., e. Ore., ne. Calif., Ida., and w. Mont.), which has two color-phases, gray and brown, and the

Kennicott's Screech Owl of w. Wash., which is *usually* dark brown.

Voice: — A series of several hollow whistles on the same pitch, distinctly separated at first, and running into a tremolo at the end; often likened to the rhythm of a small ball bouncing faster and faster to a standstill; sometimes preceded by two prolonged opening notes. Usual call very different from descending whinny of eastern Screech Owls.

Range: — Can. to Mex.

Subsp. (No apparent field differences except in Nos. 3 and 4 — see above): (1) Aiken's Screech Owl, *O. a. aikeni*; (2) Rocky Mountain Screech Owl, *O. a. maxwelliæ*; (3) Macfarlane's Screech Owl, *O. a. macfarlanei*; (4) Kennicott's Screech Owl, *O. a. kennicotti*; (5) Brewster's Screech Owl, *O. a. brewsteri*; (6) California Screech Owl, *O. a. bendirei*; (7) Pasadena Screech Owl, *O. a. quercinus*; (8) Mexican Screech Owl, *O. a. cineraceus*; (9) Sahuaro Screech Owl, *O. a. gilmani*.

FLAMMULATED SCREECH OWL. *Otus flammeolus.* (Illus. p. 93.)

Descr. 6½–7. A rare little Owl, much smaller than the Screech Owl, largely gray (and a touch of tawny), with inconspicuous rounded ear-tufts. *The only small Western Owl with brown eyes.*

Voice: — A single soft mellow *hoot*, low in pitch for so small an Owl, repeated steadily at intervals of two or more seconds; sometimes two notes, *hoo-hoot*.

Range: — Locally distributed or rare in high mts. from Mex. to e. Wash. and Ida.

SPOTTED SCREECH OWL. *Otus trichopsis.*

Descr. Often found living in same localities as the Mexican race of the Screech Owl (*Otus asio cineraceus*). U.S. individuals of the Spotted Screech Owl are gray like *Otus asio*, and very similar in appearance, but may be distinguished by the large white spots on the lower hind neck and scapulars, larger black spots on the under parts, and much longer facial bristles. They are more easily identified at night by voice.

Voice: — Four notes given thus: *boobooboo-boo, boobooboo-boo*, etc. (three notes, a pause and a fourth note). At times, a repeated four-syllabled *chooyoo-coocoo*, vaguely reminiscent of call of White-winged Dove; also a series of four to seven rapid, evenly spaced notes: *boo boo boo boo boo boo boo*.

Range: — Found chiefly among oaks in canyons between 4000 and 6500 feet in mts. of s. Ariz.

HORNED OWL. *Bubo virginianus.* Subsp. (Illus. p. 93.)

Descr. 18–25. The only *large* Owl (nearly two feet in length) with ear-tufts, or 'horns.' The Long-eared Owl is much smaller (fifteen inches; Crow-sized in flight), with lengthwise streakings, rather than crosswise barrings, beneath. In flight this Owl is larger than our large Buteo Hawks (Red-tail, etc.); is darker, looks neckless, and is larger-headed. The race of this bird known as the Arctic Horned Owl, *B. v. subarcticus*, which occasionally wanders s. to Ida. and Ore., is quite recognizable by its extreme paleness. Some individuals are almost as white as Snowy Owls.

Voice: — A deep resonant hooting of three to eight hoots; males usually four or five, in this rhythm: *hoo, hoo-oo, hoo, hoo*; females six or eight: *hoo, hoo-hoo-hoo, hoo-oo, hoo-oo*.

Range: — Can. to Mex.

Subsp. (No apparent field differences except in No. 1 — see above): (1) Arctic Horned Owl, *B. v. subarcticus*; (2) Montana Horned Owl, *B. v. occidentalis*; (3) Northwestern Horned Owl, *B. v. lagophonus*; (4) Dusky Horned Owl, *B. v. saturatus*; (5) Pacific Horned Owl, *B. v. pacificus*; (6) Western Horned Owl, *B. v. pallescens*.

SNOWY OWL. *Nyctea nyctea*. (Illus. p. 93.)
Descr. 20–26. A large *white* Owl with a round head. More or less flecked or barred with dusky. The Barn Owl is whitish on the under parts only. Young Owls of all species are white or whitish before the feathers replace the down, and are often dubbed 'Snowy' Owls. Even in callow youngsters of this sort, the resemblance to their parents is already visible; stubby ear-tufts adorn the fuzzy heads of baby Horned Owls, while the heart-shaped faces of Barn Owls reflect their parentage.
Range: — Arctic, s. irregularly in winter to Wyo. and Ore., rarely farther (San Francisco Bay, Calif.).

HAWK OWL. *Surnia ulula caparoch*. (Illus. p. 93.)
Descr. 15–17. A medium-sized, diurnal Owl, with a long Falcon-like tail; smaller than a Crow; maintains a more inclined body-posture at rest, not so upright as other Owls; often perches at the tip-top of a tree or in some other exposed situation and bobs its tail in the manner of a Sparrow Hawk.
Range: — Casual in winter in Mont., Wyo., and Wash.

PYGMY OWL. *Glaucidium gnoma*. Subsp. (Illus. p. 93.)
Descr. 7–7½. A very small 'earless' Owl of the woodlands, smaller than a Screech; rusty-brown or gray-brown with a striped breast. The most widely distributed small earless Owl in forested areas of the West. It is frequently heard calling or seen flying in the daytime. Has a proportionately smaller head and longer tail than most other small Owls. When perched, tail is held at a perky angle from body. A black patch on each side of hind neck is a good mark when seen.

Voice: — A rolling series of mellow Owl-like whistled notes ending with two or three slow deliberate notes thus: *too-too-too-too-too-too-too-too — took — took — took.* Commonest note a single *took* uttered every two or three seconds.
Range: — Can. s. to s. Calif., s. Ariz., and N.M.
Subsp. (No apparent field differences): (1) Rocky Mountain Pygmy Owl, *G. g. pinicola*; (2) Coast Pygmy Owl, *G. g. grinnelli*; (3) California Pygmy Owl, *G. g. californicum.*

FERRUGINOUS PYGMY OWL. *Glaucidium brasilianum.*
Descr. 6½. Very similar to the Pygmy Owl, and perhaps best recognized by its habitat, woodlands along low river-bottoms within the range outlined below. The breast streakings are *brownish* rather than black. In southern Arizona the other Pygmy Owl is a bird of the mountains. This little Owl has a habit of jerking or flipping its tail.
Voice: — *Chu, chu, chu,* a number of times repeated (Bendire); *chook* or *took,* sometimes repeated thirty or forty times at rate of about once per second, suggesting exhaust of a small distant engine (Sutton).
Range: — Rio Grande Delta, Tex., and low river valleys of s. Ariz.

ELF OWL. *Micropallas whitneyi whitneyi.* (Illus. p. 93.)
Descr. 6. A very tiny earless Owl about the size of a Sparrow, under parts largely reddish-brown, 'eyebrows' white. Found chiefly in deserts where Sahuaro cactus grows, but also in wooded canyons up to 5000 feet or more. Sits in hole in cactus or tree in daytime, but most frequently heard at night, when it may be seen with a flashlight.
Voice: — A series of rapid high-pitched notes, *whi-whi-whi-whi-whi-whi,* often becoming higher and more excited and chattering in the middle of the series; or *chew-chew-chew-chew-chew* or *teook-teook-teook-teook,* etc., rapidly uttered and descending slightly.
Range: — Se. Calif., s. Ariz., sw. N.M., and sw. Tex. (Chisos Mts.).

(WESTERN) BURROWING OWL. *Speotyto cunicularia hypugæa.* (Illus. p. 91.)
Descr. 9. A small brown *ground* Owl often seen in daytime; about the size of a Screech Owl, earless and with *very long legs* (for an Owl); resident of deserts, prairies, and open barren country.
Voice: — Commonest note, a tremulous chuckling or chattering call: at night a high mellow *coo-co-hoo,* or *coo-hoo,* like Roadrunner or Dove in quality, but higher.

BURROWING OWL

Range: — Open country of most of w. U.S. from Pacific e. through Great Plains; migratory in nw. States.

SPOTTED OWL. *Strix occidentalis.* Subsp. (Illus. p. 93.)
Descr. 19. Large dark-brown earless Owl of the woodlands, with a puffy round head. The large dark eyes (all other large Owls except the Barn Owl have yellow eyes) and the heavily spotted and barred under parts will identify the bird. Rare throughout most of its range.
Voice: — A high-pitched hooting, like barking of a small dog; much higher than that of the Horned Owl. Usually given in groups of three: *hoo, hoo-hoo,* or four: *hoo — whoowhoo — whooo.*
Range: — Mts. from Mex. n. to s. Colo., Ariz., and Cascades of cent. Calif. (Mariposa Co.); also coast belt from Marin Co., Calif., to Wash.
Subsp. (No apparent field differences): (1) California Spotted Owl, *S. o. occidentalis*; (2) Northern Spotted Owl, *S. o. caurina*; (3) Mexican Spotted Owl, *S. o. lucida.*

GREAT GRAY OWL. *Scotiaptex nebulosa nebulosa.* (Illus. p. 93.)
Descr. 24–33. Larger even than the Horned Owl; resembles somewhat the much smaller Spotted Owl; like that bird, it is earless, but *gray,* not brown. The eyes are *yellow,* and the under parts are heavily striped lengthwise. The facial disks are especially large, and come to the top of the head as the bird sits, and are outlined against the sky.

Range: — Rare resident from tree-limit in Can. s. to n. Mont., n. Ida., and probably Yellowstone Park, Wyo.; also in Cascades and Sierras to Yosemite region of Calif. (rarely); occurs more frequently in winter in nw. States.

LONG-EARED OWL. *Asio wilsonianus.* (Illus. p. 93.)
Descr. 13–16. A medium-sized Owl of the woodlands, with long ear-tufts; much smaller than the Horned Owl, streaked lengthwise, rather than barred crosswise, beneath. The 'ears' are situated close together toward the center of the forehead, giving the bird an entirely different aspect. The rusty face distinguishes it from the smaller Screech Owl. In flight the ear-tufts are pressed flat against the head; then the large amount of gray separates it from the much buffier Short-eared Owl.
Voice: — A low mellow Dove-like call of three or four notes: *hoo, hoo, hoo* or *who-hoo, hoo, hoo.* Also 'a cat-like whine, and a high-pitched whistled *whee'-you*' (Ludlow Griscom).
Range: — Breeds from Can. s. nearly to Mexican boundary; winters from Wash. and Wyo. s.

SHORT-EARED OWL. *Asio flammeus flammeus.* (Illus. p. 93.)
Descr. 13–17. Nearly the size of a Crow; a diurnal Owl of the marshes. The buffy-brown color and the irregular flopping flight, suggesting that of a Nighthawk, identify it. It might possibly be mistaken for one of the Hawks, but the Owl has a somewhat slovenly flight, and appears quite big-headed and neckless. Large buffy wing-patches show in flight. (See Barn Owl.)
Voice: — An emphatic sneezy *keee-yow!* 'like a hurt cat' (C. W. Lockerbie).
Range: — Breeds in marshy or open country from Can. s. to Colo. and ne. Calif. (occasionally farther); winters from Wash. and Mont. s. to Mex.

RICHARDSON'S OWL. *Cryptoglaux funerea richardsoni.* (Illus. p. 93.)
Descr. 9–12. Near the size of a Screech Owl, but *earless.* The even smaller Saw-whet is the species that most closely resembles it. The facial disks of the Richardson's Owl are *framed with black,* and the bill is *yellowish* (Saw-whet, black). The forehead is heavily spotted with white. The Pygmy Owl is much smaller and redder, with well-defined *black* breast-streaks.
Range: — Breeds in Can.; casual in winter s. to Ore. and Colo.

SAW-WHET OWL. *Cryptoglaux acadica acadica.* (Illus. p. 93.)
Descr. 7–8½. A very small, ridiculously tame little Owl; smaller than Screech Owl, *without* ear-tufts. It can be told from the Pygmy Owl by the wide *soft-brown stripes* on the under parts,

XANTUS'S MURRELET
(SCRIPPS'S MURRELET)

ANCIENT MURRELET
WINTER   SUMMER

CASSIN'S AUKLET

MARBLED MURRELET
WINTER   SUMMER

PAROQUET AUKLET

WINTER

RHINOCEROS AUKLET
                    SUMMER

HORNED PUFFIN
WINTER

IMMATURE

TUFTED PUFFIN
                    SUMMER

PIGEON GUILLEMOT
WINTER   SUMMER

CALIFORNIA MURRE
WINTER   SUMMER
ALCIDAE

SCREECH

GREAT HORNED

LONG·EARED

FLAMMULATED
SCREECH

SNOWY

BARN

SPOTTED

SHORT-
EARED

GREAT GRAY

RICHARDSON'S

HAWK

ELF

SAW·WHET

OWLS

PYGMY

the proportionately larger head and shorter tail (see Pygmy Owl). The young Saw-whet is very different, chocolate-brown with a *blackish* face and conspicuous white patches or 'eyebrows' forming a broad V between the eyes.

Voice: — A mellow whistled note repeated mechanically in endless succession, often between one hundred and one hundred and thirty times per minute, *too, too, too, too, too, too,* etc.; has bell-like quality in distance. Also a rasping double note.

Range: — Breeds from Can. s. in evergreen forests to mts. of N.M., Ariz., and Sierra Nevada of Calif.; in winter s. to s. Calif.

GOATSUCKERS: CAPRIMULGIDÆ

THE Goatsuckers are ample-tailed nocturnal birds with small bills and weak, tiny feet. During the day they rest horizontally on some limb, or on the ground, where their mottled brown pattern blends with the surroundings.

STEPHENS'S WHIP-POOR-WILL. *Antrostomus vociferus arizonæ.* (Illus. p. 93.)

Descr. 9–10. Best known by its call, oft-repeated at night in mountain woodlands. When discovered during the day, the

GOATSUCKERS
A. Merrill's Pauraque   B. Stephens's Whip-poor-will
C. Poor-will

bird springs from its hiding-place and flits away like a large dusky moth. If it is a male, large white tail-patches flash out; if it is a female, it appears largely brown; never does it show the white wing-patches characteristic of the Nighthawk. It is considerably larger and duskier than a Poor-will, and the white tail-patches of the male are much more conspicuous (tipped for 1½ inches). The Poor-will's tail is only tipped with white for ½ inch. The latter bird also shows much more white on the throat. Female Whip-poor-wills have only a small amount of white or buff in the tail, but can be told from the Poor-will by the buffy-brown appearance around the head and breast.

Voice: — At night a loud oft-repeated *prrrip-purr-rill* or *whip-poor-will*, more rolling than cry of Eastern bird.

Range: — Breeds in mts. of s. Ariz., s. N.M., and w. Tex.

POOR-WILL. *Phalænoptilus nuttalli.* Subsp. (Illus. p. 93.)
Descr. 7–8. Best known by its call heard at night. When flushed during the day it flutters up like a large gray-brown moth. It appears smaller than a Nighthawk, has more rounded wings (with no white bars). Its tail is tipped with white. Prefers arid or semi-arid country.

Voice: — At night a loud, oft-repeated *Poor-will* or more exactly, *Poor-jill*; when close, *Poor-jill-ip*.

Range: — Breeds chiefly in arid country from Can. to Mex. (e. of Cascades and Sierras); and from Rogue River Valley in s. Ore. to Lower Calif. (w. of Cascades and Sierras).

Subsp. (No apparent field differences): (1) Nuttall's Poor-will, *P. n. nuttalli*; (2) Dusky Poor-will, *P. n. californicus*; (3) Desert Poor-will, *P. n. hueyi*.

MERRILL'S PAURAQUE. *Nyctidromus albicollis merrilli.* (Illus. p. 93.)
Descr. 12. A large Goatsucker of the Whip-poor-will type, best identified at night by voice. The Whip-poor-will and the Chuck-will's-widow migrate through its range, but it can be told from those species when accidentally discovered in the daytime by the bold black triangular marks on the scapulars, and the *white band across the primary wing-feathers*. It can be told from the Night-hawk, which also has white in the wing, by the *large amount of white in the tail*. Note the tail's shape (see diagram).

Voice: — At night a hoarse whistle, *pur-we'eeeeer*, repeated. The accent is in the middle of the call. At a distance only the *we'eeeeer*, which is rolled out emphatically, can be heard. By no stretch of the imagination does it seem to say '*Pau-ra-que.*'

Range: — Gulf coast of Tex. and Lower Rio Grande Valley.

NIGHTHAWK. *Chordeiles minor.* Subsp. (Illus. p. 95.)
Descr. 8½–10. The Nighthawk is the slender, slim-winged bird

NIGHTHAWKS

A. Nighthawk   B. Texas, or Lesser, Nighthawk

we see flying erratically about after insects high in the air. In courtship the male occasionally folds his wings and dives earthward, zooming up sharply at the end of the drop. The *broad white patch* across the wing is the Nighthawk's mark.

Voice: — A nasal *peent* or *pee-ik*.

Range: — Breeds from Can. s. to Tex., N.M., Ariz., mts. of s. Calif., and coast of n. Calif.

Subsp. (No apparent field differences): (1) Eastern Nighthawk, *C. m. minor*; (2) Howell's Nighthawk, *C. m. howelli*; (3) Western Nighthawk, *C. m. henryi*; (4) Pacific Nighthawk, *C. m. hesperis*; (5) Sennett's Nighthawk, *C. m. sennetti*.

TEXAS, *or* LESSER, NIGHTHAWK. *Chordeiles acutipennis texensis.* (Illus. p. 95.)

Descr. 8–9. Smaller and browner than the other Nighthawks, with *white bar closer to tip of wing.* This species is most easily identified by its odd calls (below) and its manner of flight, *very low over the ground*, never high like other Nighthawks. In the breeding season it is a bird of the lowlands, whereas other Nighthawks, breeding within its range, prefer the mountains.

Voice: — Does not have the characteristic *spee-ik* or *peent* of other Nighthawks; instead a low *chuck chuck* and a soft purring or whinnying sound very like the trilling of a toad.

Range: — Breeds in lowlands of sw. U.S. n. to n.-cent. Calif., s. Nev., s. Ut., and cent. Tex.

SWIFTS: MICROPODIDÆ

Swallow-like birds with long, stiff wings, more slender than those of Swallows. Unlike most other birds, they often appear to beat their wings alternately, not in unison; such is often the *illusion*, at least, although slow-motion pictures seem to disprove this. The effect is somewhat bat-like. Their wings fairly twinkle as they fly and they frequently sail between spurts, holding the wings *bowed* in a very characteristic manner.

BLACK SWIFT. *Nephœcetes niger borealis.* (Illus. p. 96.)
Descr. 7¼. Rare. A large *black* Swift with a slightly forked tail which it sometimes fans wide in flight. Known from the Purple Martin, the only other Swallow-like bird of similar size, with black under parts, by its longer, slimmer wings and different flight (see Swifts, above). Has a more leisurely flight than other Swifts. The Vaux's Swift is much smaller, with a paler throat and under parts and a rounded tail. At close range the Black Swift shows a touch of white around the face.
Voice: — A light twitter.
Range: — Migrates and breeds at scattered points along Pacific Coast, and inland in mts.

CHIMNEY SWIFT. *Chætura pelagica.*
Descr. 5–5½. Very similar to Vaux's Swift, but somewhat larger and darker. Probably not easily distinguishable in the field, but any small dark Swift occurring on the Plains in e. Wyo. and e. Mont. would most likely be this species.
Range: — E. U.S., rarely to e. Mont. and e. Wyo.

SWIFTS
A. White-throated   B. Black   C. Vaux's

VAUX'S SWIFT. *Chœtura vauxi.* (Illus. p. 96.)
Descr. 4½. A small dark Swallow-like bird, with no apparent tail (except when tail is spread). A good metaphor that can be applied to it is a 'cigar with wings.' The long slightly curved, stiff wings and twinkling flight mark it as a Swift; the small size and dingy under parts as this species.
Voice: — A feeble chipping call.
Range: — Breeds chiefly near coast from Santa Cruz, Calif., n. to Alaska; casual e. to Mont. and Nev.; migrates through s. Calif. and Ariz.

WHITE-THROATED SWIFT. *Aëronautes saxatalis.* Subsp. (Illus. p. 96.)
Descr. 6½–7. Known as a Swift by its long, narrow, stiff wings and characteristic twinkling and gliding flight; and from other Swifts by the contrasting black-and-white pattern. The Violet Green Swallow, which is often found in the same places, has pure white under parts but lacks the black patches.
Voice: — A shrill, excited *je je je je je je*, etc., in descending scale.
Subsp. WHITE-THROATED SWIFT. *A. s. saxatalis.* Breeds locally from s. Can. s. through W. States to Mex., chiefly in mts.; winters from Santa Barbara, Calif., s.

HUMMINGBIRDS: TROCHILIDÆ

THE smallest of all birds; iridescent, with long needle-like bills for sipping honey from flowers. The wing-motion is so rapid that the wings look like blurry gauze. The brilliant throat feathers or 'gorgets' are the best aid in identifying the males. Females lack these, and are mostly greenish above and whitish below, often presenting a very difficult identification problem. Some females are not safely distinguishable in the field. In a few cases certain sounds made by the males are very distinctive. These are mentioned, but only when they are especially outstanding. It might conceivably be possible to tell nearly every species by the sounds it produces. At certain seasons the countryside is full of young Hummers that are just about impossible for even crack field experts to identify. It is important to realize this and not worry too much about them.

LUCIFER HUMMINGBIRD. *Calothorax lucifer.* (Illus. p. 98.)
Descr. 3½. Very rare or accidental in U.S. Male has purple throat and *rusty* sides. The rusty sides and lack of purple on the forehead would distinguish it from the Costa's. The slightly decurved bill is also a fair field-mark.
Range: — Occasional in s. Ariz. and w. Tex. (Brewster Co.).

BLACK-CHINNED HUMMINGBIRD. *Archilochus alexandri.*
(Illus. p. 98.)
Descr. 3¾. *Male:* — Identified by the *black throat* and the con-
spicuous white collar below it. The brilliant blue-purple patch
on the lower part of the throat shows only in certain lights.
Female: — Greenish above, whitish below. Cannot be told in
field from female Costa's. (See Costa's Hummingbird.)
Range: — W. U.S.; breeds from Mex. n. to e. Wash. (rare) and
nw. Mont. (rare); commonest in s. parts of Calif., Ariz., and
N.M., and in w. Tex.; winters in s. Calif. and to the southward.

COSTA'S HUMMINGBIRD. *Calypte costæ.* (Illus. p. 98.)
Descr. 3¼. *Male:* — Throat and forehead *purple* or *amethyst.*
The feathers of the 'gorget' are longer and stand out more from
the sides of the throat than in any other Hummer. The male
can possibly be confused with the male Anna's, which is larger
and has the throat and forehead *rose-red*, not purple. The Black-
chin has blue-purple on the throat, but it is very restricted and
there is none on the forehead. The sound made by the male
Costa's as it dives through the air during its mating performance is distinctive — a high, shrill hissing sound, ventriloquial
in effect, growing louder and dying away. This species has a
habit of *soaring* from one flower clump to another. *Female:* —
Greenish above, whitish below; impossible to distinguish in the
field from the female Black-chin, but although the two are often
found together, the Costa's usually prefers more arid conditions.
Females on the nest might be identified by the difference in nest
construction. That of this species is usually thatched on the
outside with lichens or bits of dead leaves; that of the Black-
chinned is a felt-like or cocoon-like structure, usually made of
the yellowish down of the sycamore, devoid of exterior decora-
tion (occasional nests have a few lichens).
Range: — Breeds in low country of sw. U.S. (s. Calif., s. Ut., s.
Nev., and Ariz.).

ANNA'S HUMMINGBIRD. *Calypte anna.* (Illus. p. 98.)
Descr. 4. *Male:* — Somewhat larger than other California Hummingbirds, with a red throat and *red forehead.* The male is the
only California Hummingbird that seems to 'sing.' From a
perch, it utters a long series of squeaking and grating notes. The
sound made by the male as it dives through the air in its mating
performance or 'pendulum dance' is also distinctive, a *sharp
explosive or popping sound* as it reaches the bottom of the dive.
Female: — Similar to females of other California Hummingbirds, but with practice can be told by its larger size and darker
green color above. As a rule it has grayer under parts and a
more heavily spotted throat than the female Costa's or Black-
chin. There is often a central patch or scattering of red spots.

HUMMINGBIRDS

1. BLACK-CHINNED HUMMINGBIRD, ♂ MALE; ♀ FEMALE
2. BUFF-BELLIED HUMMINGBIRD, ♂ MALE
3. WHITE-EARED HUMMINGBIRD, ♂ MALE; ♀ FEMALE
4. BROAD-BILLED HUMMINGBIRD, ♂ MALE; ♀ FEMALE
5. COSTA'S HUMMINGBIRD, ♂ MALE
6. LUCIFER HUMMINGBIRD, ♂ MALE
7. RIVOLI'S HUMMINGBIRD, ♂ MALE; ♀ FEMALE
8. BLUE-THROATED HUMMINGBIRD, ♂ MALE; ♀ FEMALE
9. ANNA'S HUMMINGBIRD, ♂ MALE; ♀ FEMALE
10. BROAD-TAILED HUMMINGBIRD, ♂ MALE; ♀ FEMALE
11. CALLIOPE HUMMINGBIRD, ♂ MALE; ♀ FEMALE
12. ALLEN'S HUMMINGBIRD, ♂ MALE
13. RUFOUS HUMMINGBIRD, ♂ MALE; ♀ FEMALE

ROGER
TORY
PETERSON

1♂ 2♂ 3♂ 4♂

5♂ 6♂ 7♂ 8♂

9♂ 10♂ 11♂ 12♂ 13♂

1♀ 9♀ 10♀ 11♀ 13♀

4♀ 7♀ 8♀ 3♀

This is the only Hummingbird commonly found in California in midwinter.

Range: — Calif. w. of Sierras; resident at low altitudes n. to San Francisco Bay region and head of Sacramento Valley; in autumn farther north; casual in Ariz.

BROAD-TAILED HUMMINGBIRD. *Selasphorus platycercus platycercus.* (Illus. p. 98.)

Descr. 4½. This Rocky Mt. species can be identified at once by the sound of its wings, a *shrill trilling* as the bird flies from place to place. The female produces scarcely any sound. *Male:* — Back green, throat-patch bright *rose-red*; resembles Ruby-throat of East. The only other Hummer with a solid-red throat-patch normally occurring in its range, the Rufous Hummingbird, has a rufous back. *Female:* — Similar to female Black-chin and Costa's, but sides tinged with buffy, and touch of rufous at sides of tail (near base when tail is spread). Resembles female Calliope even more closely except for its considerably larger size.

Range: — Rocky Mt. region; breeds from Mont. and s. Ida. s. to Mex. and w. to e. Wash. (rare), e. Ore. (rare), and w. Ariz.

RUFOUS HUMMINGBIRD. *Selasphorus rufus.* (Illus. p. 98.)

Descr. 3½. *Male:* — Upper parts bright red-brown in full breeding plumage, throat flame-red. *No other Hummingbird has a rufous back.* The male Allen's Hummingbird has a rufous *rump* and rufous cheeks and, when perched at a distance or overhead, looks very much like a Rufous Hummingbird, but *be sure to see the middle of the back. Female:* — Similar to other female Hummingbirds but has some rufous on the rump or tail-feathers. Cannot be told from the female Allen's Hummingbird in the field (in the hand, female Allen's has narrower tail-feathers). In migration in the Rockies, the female Rufous might be mistaken for the female Broad-tailed Hummingbird, which shows just a touch of rufous at the base of the tail-feathers (but not in the center of the rump).

Range: — Breeds from Ore. and sw. Mont. n. into Can.; migrates through valleys of Pacific States in spring and throughout mts. of entire w. U.S. in autumn.

ALLEN'S HUMMINGBIRD. *Selasphorus alleni.* (Illus. p. 98.)

Descr. 3⅛. *Male:* — Green back, *rufous rump,* and red throat. The only similar Hummingbird, the male Rufous, has the entire back rufous. The two species can easily be confused if not scrutinized carefully. (See Rufous Hummingbird.) *Female:* — Not distinguishable in field from female Rufous.

Range: — Calif.; breeds along coast from Ventura Co. n. to Humboldt Co.; migrates farther inland, casually through Ariz.; some winter in Santa Barbara Ids.

CALLIOPE HUMMINGBIRD. *Stellula calliope.* (Illus. p. 98.)
Descr. 3. The smallest U.S. Hummer; seldom found away from
mountains. *Male:* — Throat with *red rays on a white ground*,
the only Hummingbird with this effect. *Female:* — Can be told
from female Rufous, which occurs in high mountains in late
summer, by lack of rusty on center of rump (has a touch of
rusty at base of all tail-feathers except central pair). Distinguishable from female Broad-tail of Rockies, which closely resembles it, by the smaller size when comparison is possible.
Range: — Breeds in high mts. of w. U.S. from Can. s. to s.
Calif. and n. N.M., and from Rockies w. to e. Wash., e. Ore.,
and Sierras of Calif.

RIVOLI'S HUMMINGBIRD. *Eugenes fulgens.* (Illus. p. 98.)
Descr. 5. *Male:* — A large Hummingbird with *blackish belly*,
bright green throat, and *purple crown*. Looks all black when seen
at distance. Wing-beats discernible, not buzzy as in smaller
Hummers; sometimes scales on set wings like a Swift. *Female:* —
A large Hummingbird, greenish above, heavily washed with
greenish or dusky below. Can be told from female Blue-throated
by more mottled under parts, heavily spotted throat, dark
greenish tail, and smaller grayish tail-corners (Blue-throated
has uniformly gray under parts and a blue-black tail with exceptionally large white spots at corners); wings of Rivoli project back
of its tail, noticeable when bird is perched.
Range: — Mts. of se. Ariz. and sw. N.M.

BLUE-THROATED HUMMINGBIRD. *Lampornis clemenciæ.*
Subsp. (Illus. p. 98.)
Descr. 5. *Male:* — A large Hummingbird with black and white
streaks through the eye and a *blue throat*. The only Hummer in
which the *male* has *white spots* in the tail. *Female:* — A large
Hummingbird, with *evenly gray* under parts, white marks on the
face, and a large blue-black tail which has *exceptionally large
white spots* at the corners. This long, broad tail with its promi-
nent white patches is the best field-mark in all plumages. (See
female Rivoli's Hummingbird.)
Range: — Sw. Tex. (Chisos Mts.), sw. N.M. (San Luis Mts.),
and mts. of s. Ariz. (s. and e. of Tucson).
Subsp. (No apparent field differences): (1) Texas Blue-throated
Hummingbird, *L. c. clemenciæ*; (2) Arizona Blue-throated
Hummingbird, *L. c. bessophilus.*

BUFF-BELLIED HUMMINGBIRD. *Amazilia yucatanensis
chalconota.* (Illus. p. 98.)
Descr. 4½. *Male:* — Under parts *buffy*, throat *green*, bill coral-
red or pink with black tip. The only coral-billed Hummingbird

in the Brownsville region of Tex., and the only one with a green throat. *Female:* — Similar to male.
Range: — Rio Grande Delta, Tex.

WHITE-EARED HUMMINGBIRD. *Hylocharis leucotis leucotis.* (Illus. p. 98.)
Descr. 3¼. *Male:* — Under parts greenish, throat blue and green, forehead purple, bill pink with black tip, *broad white stripe behind eye.* *Female:* — Lacks the metallic forehead and throat-patches but is easily identified by the pink bill and bold white eye-stripe similar to those of the male.
Range: — Mts. of se. Ariz. (Huachuca, Chiricahua, Santa Rita).

BROAD-BILLED HUMMINGBIRD. *Cynanthus latirostris* (Illus. p. 98.)
Descr. 3¼. *Male:* — Greenish above and below with a metallic *blue throat.* The bill, *bright pink or red* with a black tip, is the best mark. The bird that resembles it most is the White-eared Hummingbird, which also has a pink bill. The White-ear has a broad white head-stripe, while the present species has only a tiny spot of white behind the eye. *Female:* — Identified by pink at base of bill and distinguished from female White-eared Hummingbird, the only other pink-billed species found in its range, by the *lack* of the white eye-stripe. The unmarked pearly-gray throat and under parts furnish a good mark. The females of the White-ear and of most other species have some spotting on the throat.

COPPERY-TAILED TROGON, *male*

Range: — Mts. of s. Ariz. and sw. N.M., also sw. Tex. (Brewster Co. — rare).

TROGONS: TROGONIDÆ

COPPERY-TAILED TROGON. *Trogon ambiguus ambiguus.* (Illus. p. 101.)
Descr. 11½. *Male:* — Head and upper parts dark glossy green (blackish at a distance), *under parts bright rose-red,* separated by a white band from the dark head; tail square-tipped and moderately long; bill stout and pale. The posture as shown in the picture, the slightly Parrot-like profile, and the bright-red under parts identify this unusual bird. *Female:* — Similar, but head and upper parts brown and with much less red on under parts.
Voice: — A rapid series of low, coarse notes, sounding like a Hen Turkey: *kowm kowm kowm kowm kowm kowm kowm* (slightly dissyllabic); Sutton describes it as *cory cory cory,* etc.
Range: — Mts. of s. Ariz.

KINGFISHERS: ALCEDINIDÆ

BELTED KINGFISHER. *Megaceryle alcyon.* Subsp. (Illus. p. 102.)
Descr. 11–14. Hovering above the water in readiness for the plunge, or flying with peculiar uneven wing-beats, rattling as it

A. BELTED KINGFISHER, *male*
B. TEXAS KINGFISHER, *male*

goes, the Kingfisher is easily learned by the novice. Perched, it is big-headed, larger than a Robin, blue-gray above, with a ragged crest and one (male) or two (female) broad breast-bands.
Voice: — A loud rattle.
Range: — Breeds from Can. s. to s. Calif. and N.M.; winters from Mex. n. to Wyo. and n.-cent. Calif., and along coast to Wash.
Subsp. (No apparent field differences): (1) Eastern Belted Kingfisher, *M. a. alcyon*; (2) Western Belted Kingfisher, *M. a. caurina*.

TEXAS KINGFISHER. *Chloroceryle americana septentrionalis.* (Illus. p. 102.)
Descr. 7¼. A very small Kingfisher, not much larger than a large Sparrow; upper parts greenish-black, with white spots; collar and under parts white. The male has a broad rusty breast-band. (In the Belted Kingfisher the female wears the rusty band.) The long bill, large head, and the shape when perched over the water identify it as a Kingfisher; the small size as this species.
Voice: — A clicking note; also a sharp squeak.
Range: — S. Tex. n. to Mason, Kerr, Bexar, and Comal Cos., and westward along Rio Grande Valley to Valverde Co. Casual in s. Ariz.

WOODPECKERS: PICIDÆ

TREE-CLIMBING birds, with stiff, spiny tails which act as props in their upward progress. The flight of most species is undulating, produced by several quick beats and a pause. The males of most species have some amount of red on the head.

NORTHERN, *or* **YELLOW-SHAFTED, FLICKER.** *Colaptes auratus luteus.*
Descr. 12–13. Differs from the following species, which is the common Flicker of the W., by having *yellow* wing- and tail-linings, and a *red crescent* on the back of the head. The male has a black *mustache mark* instead of red. Hybrids or intermediates between the two species are more frequently seen than typical examples of this species in the W. States. Some of these have orange-yellow wing-linings and spotted 'whiskers,' or one whisker black, the other red.
Voice: — Similar to Red-shafted Flicker.
Range: — E. U.S. w. to e. Mont., e. Wyo., and e. Colo.; occasional in Pacific States, especially in Wash.

RED-SHAFTED FLICKER. *Colaptes cafer.* Subsp. (Illus. p. 112.)
Descr. 13–14. Flickers are brown-backed Woodpeckers; flight

HEAD OF PILEATED WOODPECKER, *male*

deeply undulating: overhead this species shows considerable *salmon-red* under the wings and tail. The brown back and conspicuous *white rump*, visible as the bird flies up, is the best field-mark at a distance. Close up, a black crescent shows across the breast.

Voice: — Song, a loud *wick-wick-wick-wick-wick*, etc.; notes, a loud *kew* or *kee-yer* and a *flick-a, flick-a*.

Range: — Breeds throughout w. U.S.; winters throughout most of range.

Subsp. (No apparent field differences): (1) Northwestern Flicker, *C. c. cafer*; (2) Red-shafted Flicker, *C. c. collaris*.

MEARNS'S GILDED FLICKER. *Colaptes chrysoides mearnsi.* (Illus. p. 112.)

Descr. 13. A desert Flicker. Similar to the Red-shafted Flicker but with wing- and tail-linings *yellow* instead of red. Differs from the Northern, or Yellow-shafted, Flicker, which would never occur in the desert, in lacking the red crescent on the back of the head and in having a red mustache mark in the males. In short, this species has the head of the Red-shafted Flicker and the body of the Yellow-shaft.

Voice: — Similar to Flicker's.

Range: — Resident in deserts of se. Calif. and s. Ariz., mainly in Sahuaro belt along Colo. R. and tributaries.

(WESTERN) PILEATED WOODPECKER. *Ceophlœus pileatus picinus.* (Illus. p. 104.)

Descr. 17–18. A very large, *Crow-sized* Woodpecker of the deep woodlands with a conspicuous red *crest*. It is the only Western

Woodpecker with a crest. The great size, bounding flight, and flashing black-and-white coloration identify it at a distance. The diggings, large *oval* or *oblong* holes, are certain evidence of its presence.

Voice: — One common call resembles that of a Flicker, but is louder, and more hesitant — *kuk* — *kuk kukkuk* — *kuk* — *kuk*, etc. Another call is more ringing and hurried than that of a Flicker, and often rises in pitch at the beginning.

Range: — Heavy timber from Wash. s. along coast to Marin Co., Calif., and in Sierra Nevada to Yosemite; e. to Ida. and w. Mont.

GOLDEN-FRONTED WOODPECKER. *Centurus aurifrons.* (Illus. p. 112.)

Descr. 9½. *Male:* — A 'zebra-backed' Woodpecker with drab-colored under parts and a white rump. Shows a small white wing-patch in flight. The head is marked by three separated patches of bright color: yellow on the forehead, red on the crown, and orange on the nape of the neck. The only other common Woodpecker in southern Texas, the Ladder-backed Woodpecker, also has a 'ladder' or 'zebra' back, but is much smaller with a striped black-and-white face. In central Texas this species occurs with the similar Red-bellied Woodpecker. The bright red crown of the latter species is all in one piece, not broken into patches. *Female:* — Similar to male, but lacking the red patch. Has the conspicuous yellow hind-neck patch.

Voice: — A rolling *churr.*

Range: — S. Tex. n. to n.-cent. part and w. to the Big Bend (Brewster Co.).

GILA WOODPECKER. *Centurus uropygialis uropygialis.* (Illus. p. 112.)

Descr. 8–10. *Male:* — A 'zebra-backed' Woodpecker of the desert, showing a white patch in each wing in flight; head and under parts dull gray-brown; round red patch on top of head. *Female:* — Similar, without the red crown. The only other Woodpeckers occurring in the low desert country where this species is found are the Flickers and the Ladder-backed Woodpecker. Flickers are brown, and the Ladder-backed Woodpecker has a striped face. Neither shows a white wing-patch in flight, so characteristic of this species.

Voice: — A rolling *churr* and a sharp *pit.*

Range: — Low desert regions along Colo. R. in se. Calif. and extreme se. Nev.; and e. through s. Ariz. to sw. N.M.

RED-HEADED WOODPECKER. *Melanerpes erythrocephalus.* (Illus. p. 112.)

Descr. 8½–9½ This and the Red-breasted Sapsucker are the

only Woodpeckers with the *entire* head red. Many other species
have a *patch* of red somewhere or other on the head. At a distance in flight it appears as a black-and-white Woodpecker with
large square white patches on the rear edge of the wing. The
immature bird is brown-headed; the large white wing-patches
identify it. Perched, these patches make the lower back look
white. As the Red-breasted Sapsucker is a bird of the Pacific
States, the two species would never occur in the same locality.
Voice: — A loud *chur-chur.*
Range: — E. U.S. w. to cent. Mont., cent. Wyo., cent. Colo.,
and e. N.M.

CALIFORNIA, *or* **ACORN, WOODPECKER.** *Balanosphyra
formicivora.* Subsp. (Illus. p. 112.)
Descr. 9½. A bird of the oaks and yellow pines. A black-backed
Woodpecker with a white rump and a small white patch in each
wing in flight. The clownish black, white, and red head-pattern,
shown in the diagram, is unmistakable. Both male and female
have red crowns.
Voice: — Most characteristic note, *whack-up, whack-up, whack-
up,* or *ja-cob, ja-cob, ja-cob.*
Range: — Sw. Ore., Calif., Ariz., N.M., and w. Tex. (se. to Kerr
Co. and Chisos Mts.).
Subsp. (No apparent field differences): (1) California Woodpecker, *B. f. bairdi;* (2) Mearns's Woodpecker, *B. f. aculeata;*
(3) Ant-eating Woodpecker, *B. f. formicivora.*

LEWIS'S WOODPECKER. *Asyndesmus lewis.* (Illus. p. 112.)
Descr. 11. A large dark, black-backed Woodpecker, with a
rosy-red belly (the only Woodpecker so marked), a wide gray
collar around the breast and back of neck, and a red face-patch.
The reddish under parts and the flight, somewhat like that of a
small Crow, are the best marks. Sexes alike.
Voice: — Usually silent. A harsh *churr* in breeding season.
Range: — Timbered country in transition zone from Can. s. to
cent. Calif., Ariz., and N.M.; more widely distributed in winter.

RED-NAPED SAPSUCKER. *Sphyrapicus varius nuchalis.*
(Illus. p. 112.)
Descr. 8–8½. Best identified in all plumages by the combination
of *red forehead patch* and *longitudinal white patch* on the black
wing. Males are the only Western Woodpeckers with both a
red forehead and red throat-patch. Females have white throats.
Very similar to the Yellow-breasted Sapsucker of the E.
Voice: — A nasal note, *cheerrrr,* slurring downward. On the
nesting grounds the drumming of the Sapsucker is very distinctive, several rapid thumps followed by several slow rhythmic
ones.

WHITE
BELLY

EASTERN KINGBIRD

STRIPED
YELLOW
BREAST

SULPHUR-BELLIED
FLYCATCHER

WHITE RIM

BLACKISH
TAIL

YELLOWISH
BELLY

WESTERN KINGBIRD

*Two other Kingbirds
are similar to
this species:*

CASSIN'S KINGBIRD
COUCH'S KINGBIRD

YELLOWISH
BELLY

RUSTY
TAIL

ASH·THROATED
FLYCATCHER

*Two other Flycatchers
are similar to
this species:*

MEXICAN CRESTED FLYCATCHER
OLIVACEOUS FLYCATCHER

EASTERN   WESTERN   CASSIN'S   COUCH'S

TAILS of KINGBIRDS

FLYCATCHERS I

RUSTY UNDERPARTS

SAY'S PHOEBE

STREAKED BREAST

PINKISH SIDES

♀

BRIGHT RED AND BLACK

♂

VERMILION FLYCATCHER

BLACK BREAST

BLACK PHOEBE

EYE-RING

BROWNISH WING-BARS

SMALL SIZE

BEARDLESS FLYCATCHER

WING BARS

WESTERN FLYCATCHER

↑

Five other Flycatchers are very similar to this species:

TRAILL'S
WRIGHT'S
HAMMOND'S
GRAY
LEAST

NO EYE-RING

WING BARS

WESTERN WOOD PEWEE

GRAY THROAT

COUES'S FLYCATCHER

WHITE THROAT

WHITE STRIP SEPARATING DARK SIDES

WHITE TUFTS (NOT ALWAYS VISIBLE)

OLIVE-SIDED FLYCATCHER

FLYCATCHERS II

Range: — Chiefly mts. e. of Cascades and Sierras from e. Wash. and Mont. s. to ne. Calif., Ariz., cent. N.M., and w. Tex.; winters s. into Mex.

RED-BREASTED SAPSUCKER. *Sphyrapicus varius*. Subsp. (Illus. p. 112.)

Descr. 8½–9. Although the Red-breasted Sapsucker and the Red-naped Sapsucker are considered to be races of the same species, they are so absolutely different in appearance that it is better to describe them under separate headings. In the Red-breasted Sapsucker the *entire head and breast are bright red*. The long white wing-patch and the rest of the markings are somewhat like those of the Red-naped Sapsucker. Immature birds are duller. (See Red-headed Woodpecker.)

Voice: — Similar to Red-naped Sapsucker.

Range: — Breeds in higher mts. of Calif., s. Ore. (Klamath, Jackson, and Josephine Cos.), w. Ore. (w. slope of Cascades), and w. Wash. Winters in adjacent lowlands and s. along Calif. Coast to Monterey.

Subsp. (No apparent field differences): (1) Northern Red-breasted Sapsucker, *S. v. ruber*; (2) Southern Red-breasted Sapsucker, *S. v. daggetti*.

WILLIAMSON'S SAPSUCKER. *Sphyrapicus thyroideus*. Subsp. (Illus. p. 112.)

Descr. 9½. *Male:* — Identified by the black crown, black back, and long white shoulder-patch. The white face-stripes and narrow red throat-patch are also distinctive. The belly is yellow. Flying, the male looks black with a white rump and white wing-patches, the only Woodpecker of the evergreens so patterned. The Red-naped Sapsucker is not so dark. *Female:* — Very different, a *zebra-backed* Woodpecker with a white rump, barred sides, and a *brown head*. No other Woodpecker of the evergreens resembles it.

Voice: — A nasal *cheeer* or *que-yer*, similar to notes of other Sapsuckers or suggestive of squeal of Red-tailed Hawk. Drumming distinctive; broken, several rapid thumps followed by three or four slow, accented ones, usually thus: - - - - - -, -, -, -, -.

Range: — Breeds chiefly in high Cascades, Sierras, and Rockies and adjacent high mt. ranges from Can. s. to s. Calif., cent. Ariz., and N.M. Winters at lower altitudes in Pacific States and from s. N.M. and w. Tex. into Mex.

Subsp. (No apparent field differences): (1) Williamson's Sapsucker, *S. t. thyroideus*; (2) Natalie's Sapsucker, *S. t. naturaliæ*.

HAIRY WOODPECKER. *Dryobates villosus*. Subsp. (Illus. p. 112.)

Descr. 8½–10½. Many other Woodpeckers have white rumps

or white bars or stripes on the back, but the Downy and the Hairy are our only common *white-backed* Woodpeckers. They are almost identical in pattern, checkered and spotted with black and white; the *males* with a small red patch on the back of the head; the *females*, without. The Hairy is like a magnified Downy; it is much larger; the bill is especially large, all out of size-relation to the Downy's little 'bark-sticker.' The Three-toed Woodpecker (*Picoides tridactylus*) of the high mountains often has a white back and resembles the Hairy (see Three-toed Woodpecker). The Hairy Woodpecker of the humid coastal belt in Wash. and Ore. which is known as the Harris's Woodpecker is recognizably different from the other races. There is very little white spotting on the wings, and the under parts are tinged with smoky or brownish.

Voice: — A Kingfisher-like rattle, run together more than call of Downy Woodpecker. Note, a sharp *pleek!*

Range: — Forested regions from Can. s. in mts. to Mex.

Subsp. (No apparent field differences except in No. 2 — see above): (1) Eastern Hairy Woodpecker, *D. v. villosus*; (2) Harris's Woodpecker, *D. v. harrisi*; (3) Cabanis's Woodpecker, *D. v. hyloscopus*; (4) Modoc Woodpecker, *D. v. orius*; (5) Rocky Mountain Hairy Woodpecker, *D. v. monticola*; (6) White-breasted Woodpecker, *D. v. leucothorectis*; (7) Chihuahua Woodpecker, *D. v. icastus.*

DOWNY WOODPECKER. *Dryobates pubescens.* Subsp. (Illus. p. 112.)

Descr. 6½–7. Identified by white back, small size, and small bill. (See Hairy Woodpecker and Nuttall's Woodpecker.) The Downy Woodpecker of the humid coastal belt in Wash. and Ore., which is known as the Gairdner's Woodpecker, is recognizably different from the other races. There is very little white spotting on the wings, and the under parts are tinged with smoky or brownish.

Voice: — A rapid series of notes, descending in pitch at the end of the series, less run together than those of Hairy Woodpecker. Note, a flat *pick*, not as sharp as Hairy's note.

Range: — Forested regions from Can. s. to s. Calif., n. Ariz., and n. N.M.

Subsp. (No apparent field differences except in No. 2 — see above): (1) Batchelder's Woodpecker, *D. p. leucurus*; (2) Gaird-ner's Woodpecker, *D. p. gairdneri*; (3) Willow Woodpecker, *P. p. turatii.*

LADDER-BACKED WOODPECKER. *Dryobates scalaris.* Subsp. (Illus. p. 112.)

Descr. 7¼. A small black-and-white Woodpecker of the desert. Males have red caps. It is the only '*ladder-backed*' Woodpecker *with a striped face* in the range outlined below. The similar Nuttall's Woodpecker is found only in Calif., and never occurs in the desert, so the ranges do not overlap.

Voice: — A rattling series of notes, descending in pitch toward the end (similar to Downy's). Note, a sharp *pick.*

Range: — Arid country in se. Calif., Ariz., N.M., se. Colo., w. Okla., and Tex. (e. to 97th meridian).

Subsp. (No apparent field differences): (1) Texas Woodpecker, *D. s. symplectus*; (2) Cactus Woodpecker, *D. s. cactophilus.*

NUTTALL'S WOODPECKER. *Dryobates nuttalli.* (Illus. p. 112.)

Descr. 7. A small black and white Woodpecker. Males have red caps. It is the only '*ladder-backed*' Woodpecker with a *striped face* found in Calif. w. of the Sierras. (See Ladder-backed Woodpecker.) The only similar Woodpecker found in its range is the Downy, which has a white, *unbarred* back.

Voice: — A high-pitched rattling cry and a loud *prrit.*

Range: — Foothills of Calif. w. of Cascades and Sierras (except along nw. coast belt).

ARIZONA WOODPECKER. *Dryobates arizonæ arizonæ.* (Illus. p. 112.)

Descr. 8. A dark, brown-backed Woodpecker with a *striped face* and heavily barred sides. Males have a red patch on the nape. It is the only brown-backed Woodpecker with the exception of the Flickers.

Voice: — A sharp *spik* or *tseek*, sharper than notes of Downy and Ladder-backed Woodpeckers.

Range: — Oak belt of mts. in se. Ariz. and sw. N.M.

WHITE-HEADED WOODPECKER. *Dryobates albolarvatus.* Subsp. (Illus. p. 112.)

Descr. 9. A black Woodpecker with a *white head.* No other Woodpecker resembles it. A large white wing-patch shows in flight. Males have a red patch on the nape.

Voice: — A sharp *chick*, sometimes rapidly multiplied, *chick-ik-ik-ik*; also a rattle similar to Downy Woodpecker's.

Range: — Cascades and Sierras from Wash. to s.-cent. Calif., also mts. of s. Calif. (San Gabriel, San Bernardino, San Jacinto, Santa Rosa, and Cuyamaca Mts.); e. to Ida. and w. Nev.

Subsp. (No apparent field differences): (1) Northern White-headed Woodpecker, *D. a. albolarvatus*; (2) Southern White-headed Woodpecker, *D. a. gravirostris.*

ARCTIC THREE-TOED WOODPECKER. *Picoides arcticus.* (Illus. p. 112.)

Descr. 9-10. A Woodpecker with a white breast, heavily barred sides, and a *solid black* back. The male has a yellow crown-patch which the female lacks. She can be told by the combination of solid black back and heavily barred sides. The two Three-toed Woodpeckers inhabit the evergreen forests of the higher mts.; there their presence can often be detected by large patches scaled from the trunks of dead conifers.

Voice: — A sharp *chick* or *chuck*.

Range: — High mts. from Can. s. to cent. Calif. (Sierras), Mont., and n. Wyo.

THREE-TOED WOODPECKER. *Picoides tridactylus.* Subsp. (Illus. p. 112.)

Descr. 9–9½. The males of the two Three-toed Woodpeckers are the only species of the family with *yellow* caps. The '*ladder-back*' or *white-back* will separate this species from the black-backed Arctic Three-toed. The female lacks the yellow cap and resembles the Hairy Woodpecker, but the *barred* flanks identify it. (In many specimens the white of the back is crossed by bars, which make an additional mark.) White-backed individuals resemble the Hairy Woodpecker more closely. Occasional male Hairy Woodpeckers have yellow or orange head-patches and are called Three-toed Woodpeckers, but they lack the barrings on the flanks.

Voice: — Similar to that of Arctic Three-toed Woodpecker.

Range: — High mts. from Can. s. to Ore., Ariz., and N.M.

Subsp. (No apparent field differences): (1) Alpine Three-toed Woodpecker, *P. t. dorsalis*; (2) Alaska Three-toed Woodpecker, *P. t. fasciatus.*

COTINGAS: COTINGIDÆ

XANTUS'S BECARD. *Platypsaris aglaiæ albiventris.*

Descr. 6½. Accidental in U.S. but to be looked for along Mexican border. *Male:* — A big-headed, thick-billed bird, somewhat resembling a Flycatcher. Gray with blackish *cap and cheeks* and a *lovely rose-colored throat. Female:* — Brown with a rusty tail, a *dark gray cap*, and a *light buffy collar* around nape. Under parts whitish washed with buffy.

Range: — Accidental. Recorded from Lower Rio Grande Valley, Tex., and mts. of se. Ariz.

FLYCATCHERS: TYRANNIDÆ

BIRDS of this family usually perch in an upright attitude on exposed twigs or branches, from which, at intervals, they sally forth to snap up passing insects. They are not so restless as most birds, but sit quite motionless save for an occasional jerk of the tail.

EASTERN KINGBIRD. *Tyrannus tyrannus.* (Illus. p. 106.)

Descr. 8½–9. When this large slaty-black and white Flycatcher flies from one perch to another, the white band at the tip of its fanlike tail leaves no doubt as to its identity. The red crown-mark, invariably emphasized in color plates, is usually concealed and seldom noticed.

Voice: — A series of high rasping notes.

Range: — Breeds from e. N.A. w. to e. Wash., e. Ore., n. Nev., Ut., and e. N.M.; a straggler in Calif.

COUCH'S KINGBIRD. *Tyrannus melancholicus.* Subsp. (Illus. p. 106.)

Descr. 9½. Back olive, head gray, belly yellowish. Very similar to the Western and Cassin's Kingbirds, but tail more deeply forked, *brownish*, without hint of black, and *without white edgings*. The common Kingbird of the Lower Rio Grande.

Voice: — A high nasal *queer* or *chi-queer*, resembling notes of Cassin's Kingbird but higher; also a scolding series of notes.

Range: — Tex. (Lower Rio Grande Valley) and s. Ariz. (rare and local).

Subsp. (No apparent field differences): (1) Couch's Kingbird, *T. m. couchi*; (2) West Mexican Kingbird, *T. m. occidentalis.*

WESTERN, *or* ARKANSAS, KINGBIRD. *Tyrannus verticalis.* (Illus. p. 106.)

Descr. 8–9½. Smaller than a Robin, with a pale-gray head and back, yellowish under parts, and a dark mark through the eye. The best index to the identity of the four Kingbirds is their tails. In this species, the black tail is bordered on each side with white as in a Junco or Vesper Sparrow, but the borders are much narrower. Immature Arkansas Kingbirds do not always have the white on the sides of the tail, and may be mistaken for the Cassin's Kingbird, but the paler and grayer back will identify them.

Voice: — A shrill bickering call; various shrill twittering notes; also a sharp *whit*.

Range: — Breeds at low altitudes throughout W. States except in w. Wash. and along coast of Ore. and n. and cent. Calif. Winters in Mex.

CASSIN'S KINGBIRD. *Tyrannus vociferans.* (Illus. p. 106.)

Descr. 9. Like the Western, or Arkansas, Kingbird but darker, with an *olive-gray* rather than pearly-gray back, and *no white sides on the tail*. Immature Western Kingbirds sometimes lack these white edges, but the paler and grayer backs identify them. This species appears to have a whiter throat than the two simi-

SCISSOR-TAILED FLYCATCHER

lar Kingbirds, owing to the darker chest coloration. Although
in many places this species prefers somewhat higher altitudes,
the Western and Cassin's are often found together. Then their
strikingly different calls are often a help.
Voice: — A low nasal *queer*, or *chi-queer*, or *chi-bew*; also an
excited *ki-dear, ki-dear, ki-dear*, etc.
Range: — Breeds from cent. Calif., Ut., and s. Wyo. s. to Mex.;
winters from cent. Calif. into Mex.

SCISSOR-TAILED FLYCATCHER. *Muscivora forficata.* (Illus.
p. 112.)
Descr. 11½–15. A beautiful bird, pale pearly-gray, white, and
pink, with an extremely long scissor-like tail. The sides and
wing-linings are salmon-pink. No other land bird in its range
has such streaming tail-feathers. Perched, the 'scissors' are
folded. Immature birds with short tails resemble the Western,
or Arkansas, Kingbird, but have a touch of *pinkish* on the lower
belly instead of yellowish. The breast is whiter, and there is
more white in the sides of the tail.
Voice: — A harsh *keck*, or *kew*; also shrill, excited twitterings
and chatterings.
Range: — S. Great Plains w. to se. N.M. and w. Tex.

WOODPECKERS

1. GILDED FLICKER, MALE
2. RED-SHAFTED FLICKER, MALE
3. ARIZONA WOODPECKER, MALE
4. DOWNY WOODPECKER, MALE
5. GOLDEN-FRONTED WOODPECKER, MALE
6. LADDER-BACKED WOODPECKER, MALE
7. NUTTALL'S WOODPECKER, MALE
8. HAIRY WOODPECKER, MALE
9. GILA WOODPECKER, MALE
10. RED-BREASTED SAPSUCKER, MALE
11. RED-NAPED SAPSUCKER, MALE
12. THREE-TOED WOODPECKER
13. WILLIAMSON'S SAPSUCKER, FEMALE
14. RED-HEADED WOODPECKER, MALE
15. ARCTIC THREE-TOED WOODPECKER, MALE
16. WILLIAMSON'S SAPSUCKER, MALE
17. CALIFORNIA, OR ACORN, WOODPECKER, MALE
18. LEWIS'S WOODPECKER, MALE
19. WHITE-HEADED WOODPECKER, MALE

HEAD OF DERBY FLYCATCHER

DERBY FLYCATCHER. *Pitangus sulphuratus derbianus.* (Illus. p. 113.)

Descr. 10½. A very large short-tailed Flycatcher, near the size of the Belted Kingfisher, and somewhat like that bird in actions, often catching small fish. It has rufous wings and tail, bright yellow under parts and crown-patch, and a *strikingly patterned black-and-white face*. The yellow under parts and black and white face identify it at once.

Voice: — A loud *git-a-hear!* also *wheep!*

Range: — Lower Rio Grande Valley, Tex.

SULPHUR-BELLIED FLYCATCHER. *Myiodynastes luteiventris swarthi.* (Illus. p. 106.)

Descr. 8. A large *streaked* Flycatcher with a rufous tail, white stripe over the eye, and narrow yellow crown-patch; under parts yellowish with black streakings, back also streaked. *No other Flycatcher has a streaked yellow breast.*

Voice: — 'A high penetrating *kee-zee'-ick!* given by both male and female, often in duet' (G. M. Sutton); has also been likened to creaking of wheelbarrow.

Range: — Higher mts. of se. Ariz., chiefly where there are sycamores.

MEXICAN CRESTED FLYCATCHER. *Myiarchus tyrannulus.* Subsp.

Descr. 9–9½. Like the Ash-throated Flycatcher, but an inch or more longer, with a proportionately larger bill; breast deeper yellow and back more olive. These are all differences of degree only. To tell the two species apart the field student must have a keen ear or be very sure of size and color differences. The Crested Flycatcher (*M. crinitus*), which migrates through the range of the Mexican Crested in s. Tex., can be distinguished by the *brown* lower mandible of the bill and the different call-notes (most characteristic note a loud whistled *wheeeep!* with rising inflection).

Voice: — A sharp *pwit*, and a rolling throaty *purreeet*. Voice much more vigorous and raucous than Ash-throated Flycatcher.

Range: — Lower Rio Grande Valley, Tex., and deserts of s. Ariz. (Sahuaro belt).

Subsp. (No apparent field differences): (1) Mexican Crested Flycatcher, *M. t. nelsoni*; (2) Arizona Crested Flycatcher, *M. t. magister*.

ASH-THROATED FLYCATCHER. *Myiarchus cinerascens cinerascens.* (Illus. p. 106.)

Descr. 8–8½. A medium-sized Flycatcher, smaller than a Kingbird, with two white wing-bars, white throat, *pale yellowish belly, and rufous tail.* The Kingbirds have pale yellow bellies, but dusky or *blackish* tails. Except in s. Ariz. and along the lower Rio Grande in Tex., no other Flycatcher in the West has a rufous tail. (See Mexican Crested Flycatcher and Olivaceous Flycatcher.)

Voice: — *Pwit*; also a rolling *prrrit* and *ke-wherr*.

Range: — Breeds from e. Ore., e. Wash., n. Ut. (occasionally), and s. Wyo. (occasionally), s. into Mex.; prefers low altitudes and foothills, especially in arid or semi-arid country.

OLIVACEOUS FLYCATCHER. *Myiarchus tuberculifer olivascens.*

Descr. 7¼. Of the same type as the Ash-throated Flycatcher, rufous-tailed and yellow-bellied, but considerably *smaller*, with a gray instead of white throat.

Voice: — A mournful drawling whistle, slurring downward, *peeur*; very characteristic.

Range: — Breeds in mts. of se. Ariz.; casual in sw. Tex. (Chisos Mts.).

EASTERN PHOEBE. *Sayornis phœbe.*

Descr. 6½–7. Similar to the Western Wood Pewee, but with a whiter breast and *without* conspicuous wing-bars. Its lack of wing-bars and persistent tail-wagging habit are good points. The bill is black, those of the Wood Pewee and the other small Flycatchers are pale or yellowish on the lower mandible.

Voice: — A well-enunciated *fee-bee*.

Range: — Breeds locally in se. Colo. and e. N.M.

BLACK PHOEBE. *Sayornis nigricans nigricans.* (Illus. p. 107.)

Descr. 6½. Upper parts, head, and breast *black*; belly *white*. in sharp contrast to black of sides and breast. The only black-breasted Flycatcher.

Voice: — Song, a thin, strident *fĭ-bee, fĭ-bee*, the first two notes rising, the last two dropping; note, a sharp *kip*.

Range: — Resident in w. Tex., s. N.M., Ariz., s. Ut., s. Nev., and n. through Calif. (chiefly w. of Sierras).

SAY'S PHOEBE. *Sayornis saya saya.* (Illus. p. 107.)

Descr. 7–8. A Bluebird-sized Flycatcher with pale-*rusty* under parts. The brownish back, black tail, and rusty breast give the bird the look of a small Robin, but its Flycatcher habits identify it. The only Flycatcher that might be confused with it is the female Vermilion Flycatcher.

Voice: — A plaintive *pee-ur*.

Range: — Breeds in open or arid country from Can. s. to Mex. except in humid coastal sections; winters chiefly from N.M., Ariz., and cent. Calif. s.

TRAILL'S FLYCATCHER. *Empidonax trailli.* Subsp.

Descr. 5¼–6. A small Flycatcher with a dark back, and light breast, conspicuous light *eye-ring* and two white *wing-bars*. Four other common Western Flycatchers, the Hammond's, Wright's, Gray, and Western, fit this description exactly. They are all much more easily identified by their breeding habitats and their songs than by the almost imperceptible differences in coloration. This species is the brownest of the genus, and lives in thickets of willow and alder along streams, especially in low country but also in mt. meadows.

Voice: — *Fay-be'-o*, or *weep-a-dee'-ar*, with accent on next to last syllable; some birds contract this into a sneezy *fitz-be'-o* or *fitz-bew*. The other similar Western Empidonaces have songs made up of two or three separate elements, not uttered as a single emphatic phrase as in this species. Note, a low *pit*.

Range: — Breeds from Can. s. to Mex. (from Rockies w.) and to ne. Colo. (e. of Rockies).

Subsp. (No apparent field differences): (1) Alder Flycatcher, *E. t. trailli*; (2) Little Flycatcher, *E. t. brewsteri*.

LEAST FLYCATCHER. *Empidonax minimus.*

Descr. 5–5¾. A small Eastern Empidonax that gets into Wyo. and Mont. in those sections that lie east of the Rockies. Grayer above and whiter below than the other small Flycatchers of this group occurring in those two States. Its voice and the open groves of trees which it inhabits identify it.

Voice: — A sharply snapped *che-bec'* with the accent on the second syllable.

Range: — Breeds in e. N.A., w. to cent. Mont. and e. Wyo.; migrant in e. Colo.

HAMMOND'S FLYCATCHER. *Empidonax hammondi.*

Descr. 5–5½. Of the five similar Western Empidonax Flycatchers, the Wright's and the Hammond's have given field students the most headaches. It is considered a standing joke among Western ornithologists that no one seems to have an infallible way of telling them apart in the field. The Wright's and the Hammond's both breed in the transition and Canadian zones of the mts. higher up than the Western Flycatcher breeds. The habitats of the two hardly overlap, the Hammond's on the whole occurring higher up in the taller firs, while the Wright's prefers the chaparral or a mixture of chaparral and firs. As a rule, this species is more olive above, not so gray; the under parts are more yellowish, contrasting with a grayer chest-band. These points are so intangible and variable as to be of almost no use in the field.

Voice: — Voice descriptions by different writers vary greatly. Personally the author can see no great difference in the songs of the Wright's and the Hammond's. Birds which he was assured were *hammondi* sang a thin colorless song as follows:

Se-lip   twur   tree-ip

This order sometimes varies. Hoffmann ventured the opinion that the low *twur* or '*tsurp*' note is always typical of *hammondi*. The birds which the author was told were Wright's sang similarly, but with perhaps less emphasis. His transcription is as follows:

See-pit   serzel   pee-ee

The arrangement is very similar to that of *hammondi*, especially the first and third elements. The low note, *serzel* or *se-wer*, is double-noted rather than a single *twur* and does not drop quite so much in pitch.

Range: — Breeds in coniferous forests of mts. from Can. s. to cent. Calif. (Yosemite) and Colo.; usually at higher altitudes than next species.

WRIGHT'S FLYCATCHER. *Empidonax wrighti.*
Descr. 5¼–6. See Hammond's Flycatcher.
Voice: — See Hammond's Flycatcher.
Range: — Breeds in high chaparral or deciduous growths on mts. from Can. s. to s. Calif., n. Ariz., n. N.M., and w. Tex.

GRAY FLYCATCHER. *Empidonax griseus.*
Descr. 5½. Very similar to the Wright's Flycatcher, but slightly larger, and grayer on the back, and with the base of the lower mandible more flesh-colored, points seldom seen in the field. This, like most of the other Empidonax Flycatchers, can hardly be safely identified in the field except on the breeding grounds, when it is identified by its habitat. In e. Ore. this is sagebrush country. In Ut., according to Dr. Woodbury, the bird's habitat is arid pinyon and juniper country ('Pygmy Forest'). In neither habitat would one expect to find the Wright's or Hammond's Flycatcher.
Voice: — Notes said by Swarth to be identical to Wright's Flycatcher. Hoffmann differs with this, stating that the song is less varied than Wright's or Hammond's, with only two elements, a vigorous *chiwip* and a fainter *cheep* in a higher pitch (used in a variety of combinations).
Range: — Breeds in Great Basin from w. Colo. to extreme e. Calif. and e. Ore.; winters from s. Calif. and s. Ariz. s.

WESTERN FLYCATCHER. *Empidonax difficilis difficilis.*
(Illus. p. 107.)
Descr. 5½–6. Upper parts olive-brown, under parts washed with yellowish, wing-bars whitish, eye-ring white. Very similar to the other small Flycatchers of this group, but under parts usually more yellowish, *including the throat.* Some individuals of the other species have a faint wash of yellow on the under parts and closely resemble it, but their throats are white. Its breeding habitat is canyons, and shady groves of trees near streams or around dwellings. It is the most widely distributed Empidonax.
Voice: — A sharp lisping *ps-seet*, with rising inflection. The song, heard chiefly at daybreak, is composed of three thin colorless notes:

Bz-zeek trip Seet!

Range: — Breeds from Can. s. to Mex. border.

BUFF-BREASTED FLYCATCHER. *Empidonax fulvifrons pygmæus.*
Descr. 5. A very small Flycatcher of the Empidonax group with a *white eye-ring* and *white wing-bars,* but easily distinguished from its confusing relatives by its rich *buffy* breast.
Voice: — *Chicky-whew* (Lusk).
Range: — Breeds in mts. of se. Ariz. and sw. N.M.

COUES'S FLYCATCHER. *Myiochanes pertinax pallidiventris.* (Illus. p. 107.)
Descr. 7¾. In the high mts. along the Mexican border of Ariz. and N.M. a large gray Flycatcher is seen which looks like a large Wood Pewee but has a larger head, slight triangular crest, and less conspicuous wing-barring. The lower mandible of the bill is conspicuously yellow. It resembles even more closely the Olive-sided Flycatcher in size and shape, but the under parts are more uniformly gray, the throat is *grayer,* and there is no white strip up the middle of the breast separating the dusky sides.
Voice: — A plaintive whistled *ho-say, re-ah,* or *ho-say, ma-re-ah,* hence the bird's nickname, 'José Maria'; suggests call of Olive-sided Flycatcher. Note, a low *pip.*
Range: — Breeds in mts. of cent. and se. Ariz. and sw. N.M.

WESTERN WOOD PEWEE. *Myiochanes richardsoni richardsoni.* (Illus. p. 107.) ·
Descr. 6–6½. A Sparrow-sized Flycatcher, dusky gray-brown above and lighter gray on the breast and sides. It has two narrow white wing-bars but no white eye-ring. The slightly larger size, much darker back, grayer under parts, and lack of an eye-ring distinguish it from any of the smaller Flycatchers. When perched, the long wings extend two-thirds to three-fourths the length of the tail instead of one-third the way as in the Empidonax group.
Voice: — A nasal whistle *peeyee* or *peeeer.*
Range: — Breeds from Can. to Mex.

OLIVE-SIDED FLYCATCHER. *Nuttallornis mesoleucus.* (Illus. p. 107.)
Descr. 7¼–8. A rather large, bull-headed Flycatcher, usually seen perched at the extreme tip of a dead tree or exposed branch. It resembles the smaller Wood Pewee but the distinctive points are its large bill, white throat, and *dark chest-patches* separated or nearly separated by a narrow strip of white down the center from the throat to the belly. It also has two tufts of white which sometimes poke out from behind the wings near the back.
Voice: — Note, a trebled *pip-pip-pip.* Song, a spirited whistle,

hip-three'-cheers! or *whip whee' wheer!* the middle note highest, the last slurring down.

Range: — Breeds in coniferous forests from Can. s. to s. Calif., cent. Ariz., N.M., and w. Tex.; also in eucalyptus groves in cent. Calif.; migrates into Mex.

VERMILION FLYCATCHER. *Pyrocephalus rubinus mexicanus.* (Illus. p. 107.)

Descr. 5½–6½. *Male:* — Unmistakable. *Head and under parts, flaming vermilion-red*; tail and upper parts *blackish*. *Female:* — Much plainer, upper parts dark brown, breast white, belly and under tail-coverts *tinged with pinkish or salmon*. The only other Flycatcher that might be mistaken for the female is the Say's Phoebe, which is longer-tailed and more extensively buffy or 'pinkish' below. The white breast of the female Vermilion is *narrowly streaked* with dusky. Immature females have yellowish bellies.

Voice: — A twittering Phoebe-like *zi-breee* or *p-p-pit-zeee*; note, *zeep.*

Range: — Resident in arid regions of s. and w. Tex., s. N.M., s. and w. Ariz., sw. Ut., s. Nev., and se. Calif.; winters occasionally along coast of sw. Calif.

BEARDLESS FLYCATCHER. *Camptostoma imberbe.* (Illus. p. 107.)

Descr. 4½. A very small, nondescript Flycatcher whose general appearance and behavior suggest a Kinglet, a Vireo, or an immature Verdin. Upper parts olive-gray; under parts dingy white; indistinct wing-bars and eye-ring; bill small and dark. Distinguished from the *Empidonax* Flycatchers by its smaller size, smaller head, different behavior, and very small bill. The Vireo most apt to be confused with it is the Bell's Vireo, which is somewhat larger, with a slightly more yellowish wash on the sides. In many individuals of this Flycatcher the wing-bars are distinctly buffy or even brownish; those of the Vireo are whitish or grayish. The immature Verdin is probably the bird that resembles the Beardless Flycatcher most closely, but the young Verdin's bill is strongly yellow at the base.

Voice: — Call-note a thin *peeee-yuk.* Song a series of fine rather gentle notes, *ee, ee, ee, ee, ee,* increasing in volume toward the middle of the series (G. M. Sutton).

Range: — Low woodlands along streams in se. Ariz. and Rio Grande Delta in Tex.

HORNED LARK

LARKS: ALAUDIDÆ

HORNED LARK. *Otocoris alpestris.* Subsp. (Illus. p. 120.)
Descr. 7–8. A streaked brown terrestrial bird, larger than a
Sparrow, with two small erectile black *horns* (not always noticeable), and a black collar, or ring, below the yellow throat; *walks*,
does not hop; frequents plains, prairies, extensive fields, and
shores; flying overhead, looks light-bellied with a contrasting
black tail. The contrasting face pattern, shown in the diagram,
is distinctive.
Voice: — Song, a long tinkling twitter, irregular and high-
pitched. Note, *tee* or *tee titi.*
Range: — Breeds and winters from Can. to Mex.
Subsp. (No apparent field differences): (1) Pallid Horned Lark,
O. a. arcticola; (2) Desert Horned Lark, *O. a. leucolæma*; (3)
Streaked Horned Lark, *O. a. strigata*; (4) Dusky Horned Lark,
O. a. merrilli; (5) Island Horned Lark, *O. a. insularis*; (6) Cali-
fornia Horned Lark, *O. a. actia*; (7) Ruddy Horned Lark, *O. a.
rubea*; (8) Montezuma Horned Lark, *O. a. occidentalis*; (9)
Scorched Horned Lark, *O. a. adusta*; (10) Mohave Horned Lark,
O. a. ammophila; (11) Sonora Horned Lark, *O. a. leucansiptila.*

SWALLOWS: HIRUNDINIDÆ

Sparrow-sized birds with long, slim wings and extremely graceful flight. Although the voices of Swallows are very distinctive,
once learned, they do not adapt themselves well to verbal
description, hence are omitted in the following accounts. (See.
Swifts.)

MOURNING DOVE

POINTED TAIL

WHITE WING-PATCHES

WHITE-WINGED DOVE

WHITE CRESCENT

LIGHT TAIL-BAND

BAND-TAILED PIGEON

UNIFORMLY DARK COLORATION

RED-BILLED PIGEON

SPOTTED NECK

CHINESE SPOTTED DOVE

WHITISH UNDERPARTS

WHITE FRONTED DOVE

← REDDISH WINGS →

SLENDER TAIL WITH WHITE SIDES

SHORT BLACK TAIL

INCA DOVE

GROUND DOVE

PIGEONS and DOVES

BLUE-BLACK BREAST   GRAYISH BREAST

PURPLE MARTIN

DEEPLY-FORKED TAIL   LIGHT RUMP

BARN SWALLOW   CLIFF SWALLOW

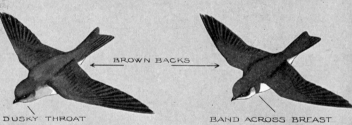

BROWN BACKS

DUSKY THROAT   BAND ACROSS BREAST

ROUGH-WINGED SWALLOW   BANK SWALLOW

BLUE BLACK BACK   WHITE PATCHES

CLEAR WHITE
UNDERPARTS

TREE SWALLOW   VIOLET-GREEN SWALLOW

SWALLOWS

VIOLET-GREEN SWALLOW. *Tachycineta thalassina lepida.*
(Illus. p. 121.)
Descr. 5½. Dark above, adults glossed with green and purple;
clear white below. Separated from the Tree Swallow, which
also has immaculate white under parts by the greener back
coloration and the *white patches* that almost meet over the base
of the tail. When the bird is perched, it will be seen that the
white of the face is more extensive, *partially encircling the eye.*
Range: — Breeds from Can. s. to Mex., chiefly in mts. s.

TREE SWALLOW. *Iridoprocne bicolor.* (Illus. p. 121.)
Descr. 5–6. Steely blue-black or green-black above and *clear
white* below. The only other Swallow possessing such immaculate white under parts is the Violet Green, which shows conspicuous white rump-patches. (See Rough-winged Swallow.)
Range: — Breeds from Can. s. to s. Calif. and Colo.; winters
from cent. Calif. s.

BANK SWALLOW. *Riparia riparia riparia.* (Illus. p. 121.)
Descr. 5–5½. A small *brown-backed* Swallow with a distinct
dark *band* across the white breast. The only other brown-
backed Swallow, the Rough-wing, lacks this band.
Range: — Breeds from Can. s. to s. Calif., Ariz. and N.M.

ROUGH-WINGED SWALLOW. *Stelgidopteryx ruficollis.*
(Illus. p. 121.)
Descr. 5–5¾. A *brown-backed* Swallow, larger and lighter brown
than the Bank Swallow, with the dark breast-band absent. The
light under parts shade into a dingy color toward the throat.
Immature Tree Swallows in late summer are rather brownish
above and might be mistaken for this species, except for their
white throats and more snowy-white under parts. The breast
of the Rough-wing is dingier; the back browner, not so sooty.
Range: — Breeds from Wash. and Mont. s. to s. Calif., Ariz.,
and n. N.M.; winters occasionally in s. Ariz.

BARN SWALLOW. *Hirundo erythrogaster.* (Illus. p. 121.)
Descr. 6–7½. Pinkish or cinnamon-buff below, with a blue-black
back and a *very deeply forked* tail; the only native Swallow that
is really 'Swallow-tailed.' It is also the only one with white
spots in the tail.
Range: — Breeds from Can. s. to Mex.; a few winter in se. Calif.

CLIFF SWALLOW. *Petrochelidon albifrons.* Subsp. (Illus.
p. 121.)
Descr. 5–6. In flight the pale rusty or *buffy* rump quickly distinguishes the bird; perched overhead with other Swallows, it
appears *square-tailed* with a *dark* throat-patch. Cliff Swallows

nest in gourd-like nests plastered against cliffs, under bridges, or beneath the eaves on the *outside* of barns. Barn Swallows build open nests, *usually* but not always on the *inside* of barns. The race of this bird known as the Mexican Cliff Swallow (s. Ariz., sw. N.M., and Brewster Co., Tex.) can be told from other Cliff Swallows, with which it sometimes associates, by its dark *chestnut* forehead, nearly as dark as the throat. The foreheads of other Cliff Swallows are *pale buff*, the throat dark.
Range: — Breeds from Can. to Mex.; a few winter in se. Calif.
Subsp. (No apparent field differences except in No. 3; see above): (1) Northern Cliff Swallow, *P. a. albifrons*; (2) Lesser Cliff Swallow, *P. a. tachina*; (3) Mexican Cliff Swallow, *P. a. melanogaster*.

COAHUILA CLIFF SWALLOW. *Petrochelidon fulva pallida.*
Descr. Like Cliff Swallow but throat *pale rusty* or *buffy* not dark chestnut. Quite distinctive in field.
Range: — Occurs in s.-cent. Tex. (Kerr Co.).

PURPLE MARTIN. *Progne subis subis.* (Illus. p. 121.)
Descr. 7½–8½. Our largest Swallow. The male is uniformly blue-black *above and below*. No other Swallow is black-bellied. (See Black Swift.) The female is whitish-bellied, often with a pale collar around the back of the neck; she may be known by her size, and from the much smaller Tree Swallow by the dingy grayness of the throat and breast.
Range: — Breeds from Can. s. to Mex.

JAYS, MAGPIES, AND CROWS: CORVIDÆ

CANADA JAY. *Perisoreus canadensis.* Subsp. (See Frontis.)
Descr. 11–13. A large *gray* bird of the cool forests of high mountains; larger than a Robin, with a *dark patch* on back of head, and a *white crown*; suggests a huge, overgrown Chickadee. This species is very similar to the next, but the under parts are grayer, the crown is more extensively white, and the tail is tipped with white. Their ranges do not overlap. Young birds are dark slate-colored, lightening out toward the tail.
Voice: — A soft whistled *whee-ah*; also many other notes, some harsh, some pleasant.
Subsp. ROCKY MOUNTAIN JAY. *P. c. capitalis.*
    White of crown much more extensive, going back to nape (dusky collar on nape only about one-half inch wide). High forests of Rocky Mt. region from Can., s. to n. N.M. and cent.-e. Ariz.; w. to e. Wash. and e. Ore.

CANADA JAY. *P. c. canadensis.*
White of crown confined chiefly to forehead, seldom
extending much behind eye (blackish collar on nape
much more conspicuous than in preceding race, 1 to 1½
inches wide). Head-pattern suggests Oregon Jay. Said
to be the race inhabiting the Black Hills in ne. Wyo.

OREGON JAY. *Perisoreus obscurus.* Subsp.
Descr. 9½–11. Similar to the preceding species but smaller and
with whiter under parts (see Canada Jay). Confined to Pacific
States.
Voice: — Similar to Canada Jay.
Range: — Cascades and Pacific slope from Wash. to n. Calif.
(Mendocino Co., Mt. Shasta, and Warner Mts.).
Subsp. (No apparent field differences): (1) Oregon Jay, *P. o.*
obscurus; (2) Gray Jay, *P. o. griseus.*

BLUE JAY. *Cyanocitta cristata.* (See Frontis.)
Descr. 11–12. A *large* blue bird, larger than a Robin; blue above,
whitish below, and *crested.* The Steller's Jay which does not occur so far east, is darker, without the whitish areas on the wings,
tail, and under parts.
Voice: — A harsh slurring *jeeah* or '*jay*'; also many other notes,
some musical.
Range: — E. N.A. w. to e. Colo. and e. Wyo.

STELLER'S JAY. *Cyanocitta stelleri.* Subsp. (See Frontis.)
Descr. 12–13½. *A large dark black and blue bird with a long*
crest. Fore parts blackish or brownish black; wings, tail, and
under parts deep blue. It is the only Jay with a crest and the
only *blue* bird of any sort with a crest found between the Pacific
and the Rockies. East of the Rockies the Blue Jay occurs.
This is the Jay of the pines and other conifers. The California
Jay is the Jay of the oaks and scrub.
Voice: — A loud *shook-shook-shook* or *shack-shack-shack* or
wheck — wek — wek — wek — wek or *kwesh kwesh kwesh*; also
many other notes.
Range: — Coniferous forests from Can. s. to Mex. (in mts.) and
to Monterey Co., Calif. (on coast).
Subsp. (No apparent field differences): (1) Steller's Jay, *C. s.*
stelleri; (2) Coast Jay, *C. s. carbonacea*; (3) Blue-fronted Jay,
C. s. frontalis; (4) Black-headed Jay, *C. s. annectens*; (5) Long-
crested Jay, *C. s. diademata.*

CALIFORNIA JAY. *Aphelocoma californica.* Subsp. (See
Frontis.)
Descr. 11½–12. Larger than a Robin. *A blue Jay without a*
crest. Head, wings, and tail blue; back brownish; under parts

pale gray; dark band across breast. The pale under parts and lack of a crest distinguish it readily from the Steller's Jay. The Steller's Jay prefers pines; this species, oaks.

Voice: — A harsh *check-check-check-check* higher than Steller's Jay; also *kwesh kwesh kwesh kwesh*. One of the commonest calls is a *shreek* with a rising inflection.

Range: — Chiefly oaks from extreme s. Wash., s. Idaho, and s. Wyo. s. to Mex., and from Rockies and cent. Tex. w. to coast.

Subsp. (No apparent field differences): (1) Long-tailed Jay, *A. c. immanis*; (2) Nicasio Jay, *A. c. oöcleptica*; (3) California Jay, *A. c. californica*; (4) Woodhouse's Jay, *A. c. woodhousei*; (5) Texas Jay, *A. c. texana*.

SANTA CRUZ JAY. *Aphelocoma insularis.*
Descr. 12. The Jay found on Santa Cruz Island off the Calif. Coast is regarded as a distinct species. It is almost identical with the California Jay but is somewhat larger and more richly colored.

Range: — Santa Cruz Id. off Santa Barbara, Calif.

ARIZONA JAY. *Aphelocoma sieberi.* Subsp. (See Frontis.)
Descr. 11½–13. A blue Jay without a crest. Resembles somewhat the California (Woodhouse's and Texas) Jay but *under parts more uniform in color*, lacking the whitish throat and the dusky band across the breast. The blue is paler and dustier, the back grayer. The voice is very different.

Voice: — A rough querulous *drenk* or *jenk*.

Range: — Live-oak regions of se. Ariz., sw. N.M., and cent.-w. Tex. (Chisos Mts., Brewster Co.).

Subsp. (No apparent field differences): (1) Arizona Jay, *A. s. arizonæ*; (2) Couch's Jay, *A. s. couchi*.

GREEN JAY. *Xanthoura luxuosa glaucescens.* (See Frontis.)
Descr. 11–12. The only *green* Jay. Throat-patch, *black*; top of head, bright blue; sides of tail, yellow. It is absolutely unmistakable, as the color plate shows.

Voice: — *Cheh cheh cheh cheh*; also a dry throaty rattle like a cricket frog and other calls.

Range: — Lower Rio Grande Valley, Tex.

AMERICAN MAGPIE. *Pica pica hudsonia.* (Illus. p. 125.)
Descr. 17½–21½, tail 9½–12. Larger than Jays, the Magpies are the only large *black-and-white* land birds with *long, sweeping* tails. In flight the iridescent tail streams out behind and large white patches flash in the wing. This species has a black bill.

Voice: — A rapid *cheg cheg cheg cheg*. Also a nasal querulous *maaag* or *maa — maa*.

GRAYISH BACK

WHITE EYE-BROW STRIPE

CHICKADEES HAVE BLACK CAPS AND BIBS

BLACK-CAPPED CHICKADEE

MOUNTAIN CHICKADEE

CHESTNUT BACK

LONG GRAY TAIL

BROWNISH CAP

CHESTNUT-BACKED CHICKADEE

BUSH-TIT

YELLOW HEAD

GRAYISH CREST

VERDIN

PLAIN TITMOUSE

"BRIDLED" FACE

BLACK CREST

♂

BRIDLED TITMOUSE

BLACK-CRESTED TITMOUSE

CHICKADEES and TITMICE

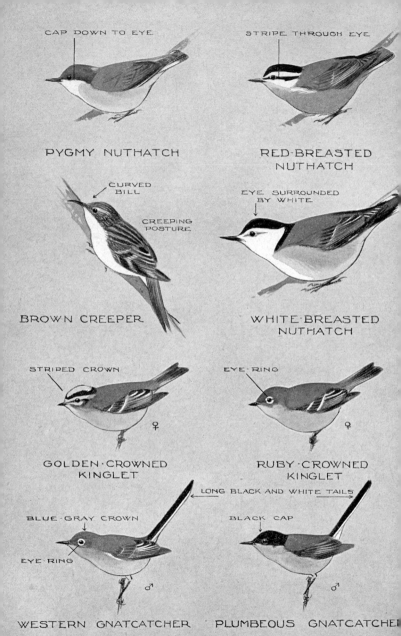

CAP DOWN TO EYE

STRIPE THROUGH EYE

PYGMY NUTHATCH

RED-BREASTED
NUTHATCH

CURVED
BILL

CREEPING
POSTURE

EYE SURROUNDED
BY WHITE

BROWN CREEPER

WHITE-BREASTED
NUTHATCH

STRIPED CROWN

EYE-RING

GOLDEN-CROWNED
KINGLET

RUBY-CROWNED
KINGLET

LONG BLACK AND WHITE TAILS

BLUE-GRAY CROWN

BLACK CAP

EYE-RING

WESTERN GNATCATCHER   PLUMBEOUS GNATCATCHER

NUTHATCHES, CREEPER
KINGLETS AND GNATCATCHERS

AMERICAN MAGPIE

Range: — Rocky Mt. region from Can. s. to n. Ariz. and n. N.M. and w. to e. Wash., e. Ore., and e. Calif. (e. slope of Sierras).

YELLOW-BILLED MAGPIE. *Pica nuttalli.*
Descr. 16–18, tail 9½–10¼. Similar to the American Magpie, but bill *yellow.*
Voice: — Similar to American, or Black-billed, Magpie. Bird quieter.
Range: — Valleys of cent. Calif., chiefly Sacramento and San Joaquin Valleys.

RAVEN. *Corvus corax.* Subsp.
Descr. 21½–26½. Although a Raven is nearly twice the bulk of a Crow, when comparison is not possible this difference does not always help. The flight, however, is distinctive. Hawk-like, the Raven alternates flapping with soaring. It soars on horizontal wings; the Crow and the Turkey Vulture with wings bent upward. The ample tail, seen from below, is distinctly *wedge-shaped.* Perched, at not too great a distance, the shaggy throat feathers are evident. On the whole, the Raven replaces the Crow in arid country or along rocky coasts.
Voice: — A Raven croaks: *cr-r-ruck.* (A Crow caws.)
Range: — Most of w. U.S., especially in arid or dry regions.
Subsp. (No apparent field differences): (1) American Raven, *C. c. sinuatus*; (2) Northern Raven, *C. c. principalis.*

WHITE-NECKED RAVEN. *Corvus cryptoleucus.*
Descr. 19–21. A small Raven, nearer the size of the Crow.
The typical Raven of the low desert country from s. Tex. to se.
Ariz. In this range the larger American Raven is most commonly seen in the mts., while the White-neck prefers the yucca
deserts. The Crow does not occur in the range of the White-
neck (except in sw. Oklahoma). The base of the feathers on the
neck and breast of this species are *white*. This often shows when
the bird's feathers are ruffled by the desert wind.
Voice: — A hoarse *kraak*, flatter than croak of American Raven.
Range: — Deserts of se. Ariz., s. N.M., se. Colo., sw. Okla., and
w. and s. Tex.

CROW. *Corvus brachyrhynchos.* Subsp.
Descr. 17–21. Much larger than any of the Blackbirds, and
smaller than the Raven, the Crow needs no description. (See
Raven.)
Voice: — A loud *caw* or *cah*, easily imitated by the human
voice.
Subsp. WESTERN CROW. *C. b. hesperis.*
W. U.S. from Can. s. to s. Calif., cent. Ariz., and cent.
N.M.
NORTHWESTERN CROW. *C. b. caurinus.*
Puget Sound area of w. Wash. Although the A.O.U.
Check-List (1931) calls this bird a race of the Crow,
C. brachyrhynchos, some authorities insist it is more
closely related to the Fish Crow, *C. ossifragus*, of the
Atlantic Coast (Ludlow Griscom). Certainly it is true
that this bird differs from the Western Crow in the
same way that the Fish Crow differs from the Eastern
Crow. Its habitat is the salt water; it is smaller, has a
noticeably quicker wing-beat, and, most important of
all, its voice is more nasal (a short, nasal *car* or *că*, instead of an honest-to-goodness *caw*).

PIÑON JAY. *Cyanocephalus cyanocephalus.* (See Frontis.)
Descr. 10–11½. In appearance and actions like a small *dull blue*
Crow, hardly larger than a Robin, with a long sharp bill. It
can be easily told from the California Jay by its short tail
and uniform coloration, and from the Steller's Jay by lack of a
crest (Steller's Jay depresses crest when flying). It is often seen
in large noisy flocks, especially in arid country where Piñon
pines and junipers grow. Often seen walking about on ground
like Crows.
Voice: — A high nasal cawing, *kaa-eh*, or *karn-eh*, with descending inflection; has mewing effect. Also Jay-like notes and chattering sounds.
Range: — Rocky Mt. area and e. slope of Cascades and Sierras

from Wash., Ida., and cent. Mont., s. to s. Calif., Ariz., s. N.M., and w. Tex.

CLARK'S NUTCRACKER. *Nucifraga columbiana.* (See Frontis.)
Descr. 12–13. Built like a small Crow, with a *light gray body* and conspicuous *white patches* in black wings and tail. Can be confused with no other bird of the high mts. (Canada Jays and Oregon Jays do not have white patches.)
Voice: — A harsh grating caw, *khaaa* or *khraa.*
Range: — High mts. from Can. s. to s. Calif., Ariz., and N.M.

TITMICE, VERDINS, AND BUSH–TITS: PARIDÆ

SMALL birds, smaller than most Sparrows, with proportionately longer tails and small stubby bills; extremely active, hanging upside down as well as right side up in their busy search for insects.

BLACK-CAPPED CHICKADEE. *Penthestes atricapillus.* Subsp. (Illus. p. 124.)
Descr. 4¾–5½. A small gray, black and white bird, smaller than a Sparrow. Chickadees are the only small birds with the combination of *black cap*, *black bib*, and *white cheeks.* This species can be told from the Mountain Chickadee by its *solid* black cap, and from the Chestnut-backed Chickadee by its *gray* back.
Voice: — A clearly enunciated *chick-a-dee-dee-dee* or *dee dee dee.* In spring a clear two-noted or three-noted whistle, *fee-bee*; or *fee-bee-ee,* the first note higher.
Range: — Can. s. to nw. Calif. (Siskiyou Co.), e. Ore., ne. Nev., and n. N.M.
Subsp. (No apparent field differences): (1) Long-tailed Chickadee, *P. a. septentrionalis*; (2) Oregon Chickadee, *P. a. occidentalis.*

MEXICAN CHICKADEE. *Penthestes sclateri eidos.*
Descr. 5. Similar to Black-capped Chickadee, but *black of throat more extensive,* spreading across upper breast; sides *dark gray* (other Chickadees have buffy or rusty sides).
Range: — Chiricahua Mts. of se. Ariz. (7000–10,000 ft.), and mts. of extreme sw. N.M.

MOUNTAIN CHICKADEE. *Penthestes gambeli.* Subsp. (Illus. p. 124.)
Descr. 5–5¼. Similar to Black-capped Chickadee but black of cap broken by *white line over each eye.*

Voice: — Song, three high clear whistled notes *fee-bee-bee*, first note highest, second two on same pitch and more distinctly separated than in call of Black-capped Chickadee. Some races utter three or four thin whistled notes going slightly down the scale in half-notes. 'Chickadee' notes huskier than those of Black-capped Chickadee; *chuck-a-zee-zee-zee*.

Range: — Mts. from Can. to w. Tex., N.M., Ariz., and s. Calif. (except along humid coast belt).

Subsp. (No apparent field differences): (1) Grinnell's Chickadee, *P. g. grinnelli*; (2) Short-tailed Chickadee, *P. g. abbreviatus*; (3) Bailey's Chickadee, *P. g. baileyæ*; (4) Mountain Chickadee, *P. g. gambeli*; (5) Inyo Chickadee, *P. g. inyoënsis*.

COLUMBIAN CHICKADEE. *Penthestes hudsonicus columbianus.*

Descr. 5–5½. The small size and black bib proclaim it a Chickadee; the general color of the upper parts is dull *brown* rather than gray or rufous, and the cheeks are duller than those of other Chickadees, and the cap is duller and *browner*. A race of the Hudsonian, or Brown-capped, Chickadee of eastern Canada.

Voice: — The notes are slower and more drawling than those of the Black-cap; instead of a lively *chick-a-dee-dee-dee*, it utters a wheezy *chick—che—day—day*.

Range: — In U.S. only nw. Mont. (rare).

CHESTNUT-BACKED CHICKADEE. *Penthestes rufescens.*
Subsp. (Illus. p. 124.)

Descr. 4½–5. The dusky cap, black bib, and white cheeks identify it as a Chickadee; the *rufous back* as this species. The sides also have some chestnut.

Voice: — Hoarser and more rasping than Black-cap, *tsick-tsick-a-dee-dee*. This species has no whistled call as do most other Chickadees.

Range: — Coast belt from cent. Calif. (n. San Luis Obispo Co.) to Wash., and sparingly to e. Ore. and w. Mont.

Subsp. (No apparent field differences): (1) Chestnut-backed Chickadee, *P. r. rufescens*; (2) Nicasio Chickadee, *P. r. neglectus*; (3) Barlow's Chickadee, *P. r. barlowi*.

BLACK-CRESTED TITMOUSE. *Bæolophus atricristatus.*
Subsp. (Illus. p. 124.)

Descr. 5–6. A small gray bird with a *slender black crest*; under parts white, sides rusty. The Titmice are the only small *gray* birds with conspicuous crests. This is the only Titmouse found in s. Tex. and along the Rio Grande.

Voice: — Chickadee-like notes, also a rapidly whistled *peter peter peter peter* or *hear hear hear hear*.

Range: — Lowlands of Tex. from n. part (Young and Armstrong Cos.) s. to Rio Grande Valley; e. to Brazos R. and w. to Tom Green, Concho, and Brewster Cos.

Subsp. (No apparent field differences): (1) Black-crested Titmouse, *B. a. atricristatus*; (2) Sennett's Titmouse, *B. a. sennetti*.

PLAIN TITMOUSE. *Bæolophus inornatus.* Subsp. (Illus. p. 124.)

Descr. 5–5½. The birds bearing the name Titmouse are the only small gray-backed birds with conspicuous crests. This is the only species found in most of the W., and the only one without distinctive markings, hence its name. Has a preference for oaks or pinyon-juniper association.

Voice: — *Tchick-a-dee-dee*, similar to notes of Chickadee. In spring an accented whistled chant *weet-y weety weety* or *tee-wit tee-wit tee-wit*.

Range: — S. Ore., s. Ida., and sw. Wyo., s. to s. Calif., s. Ariz., se. N.M., and cent.-w. Tex.

Subsp. (No apparent field differences): (1) Oregon Titmouse, *B. i. sequestratus*; (2) Plain Titmouse, *B. i. inornatus*; (3) San Diego Titmouse, *B. i. transpositus*; (4) Gray Titmouse, *B. i. griseus*.

BRIDLED TITMOUSE. *Bæolophus wollweberi annexus.* (Illus. p. 124.)

Descr. 4½–5. The crest and black-and-white 'bridled' face identify this Southwestern species. (See diagram.)

Voice: — Notes similar to those of other Titmice and Chickadees but more rapid (*tsick-a-dee-dee-dee-dee*, etc.).

Range: — Oak regions of mts. of se. and cent. Ariz. and sw. N.M.

VERDIN. *Auriparus flaviceps.* (Illus. p. 124.)

Descr. 4–4½. A very small gray bird with a *yellowish head*; bend of wing *rufous*. Lives in brushy valleys in the low desert country. Immature birds lack the yellow and rusty, and might possibly be mistaken for Bush-Tits, but the latter species is much longer-tailed and does not inhabit the desert valleys, preferring mountain-slopes covered with trees.

Voice: — An insistent *see-lip* or *see*. Song, a whistled *weet*.

Range: — Deserts of se. Calif., s. Nev., sw. Ut., w. and s. Ariz., s. N.M., and s. Tex.

BUSH-TIT. *Psaltriparus minimus.* Subsp. (Illus. p. 124.)

Descr. 4–4¼. Little plain gray-backed birds that travel about in flocks, constantly conversing in high-pitched notes as they investigate the trees for food. The nondescript drab color, stubby bill, and rather long tail identify them. It is said that light-eyed birds are females, dark-eyed birds males. Birds of the race known as the Lead-colored Bush-Tit (Rocky Mt. and Great Basin regions) can be told from the Bush-Tits of the Pacific States by their *brown* cheeks. Males of the Lloyd's Bush-Tit (mts. between Pecos and Rio Grande in cent.-w. Tex.) have *blackish* cheek-patches.

Voice: — Insistent light *chips* and lisps constantly uttered as flock moves about.

Range: — W. Wash., w. and s. Ore., s. Ida., Ut., and w. Wyo., s. to Mex. and from Rockies and cent.-w. Tex. (Pecos River) w. to coast.

Subsp. (No apparent field differences except in Nos. 3 and 4; see above): (1) Coast Bush-Tit, *P. m. minimus*; (2) California Bush-Tit, *P. m. californicus*; (3) Lead-colored Bush-Tit, *P. m. plumbeus*; (4) Lloyd's Bush-Tit, *P. m. lloydi*.

NUTHATCHES: SITTIDÆ

SMALL, chubby tree-climbers; Sparrow-sized or smaller, with a long bill and a stubby tail that is never braced against the tree Woodpecker-like as an aid in climbing. No other tree-climbers habitually go down tree-trunks *head first*, as these little birds do.

WHITE-BREASTED NUTHATCH. *Sitta carolinensis.* Subsp. (Illus. p. 125.)

Descr. 5–6. Easily identified by the white breast, the blue-gray back, the black cap, and the habit of frequently traversing tree-trunks *upside down*.

Voice: — Spring song, a series of low, slightly nasal, whistled notes all on the same pitch, *whĭ whĭ whĭ whĭ whĭ whĭ whĭ whĭ* or *who who who*, etc. Note, a nasal *yank* or *hank*.

Range: — Wash. and Mont. s. to Mex.

Subsp. (No apparent field differences): (1) Rocky Mountain Nuthatch, *S. c. nelsoni*; (2) Slender-billed Nuthatch, *S. c. aculeata*; (3) Inyo Nuthatch, *S. c. tenuissima*.

RED-BREASTED NUTHATCH. *Sitta canadensis.* (Illus. p. 125.)

Descr. 4¼–4¾. Smaller than the White-breast; buffier below, with a *broad black line* through the eye.

Voice: — The call corresponding to the *yank yank* of the White-breast is higher and more nasal, *henk, henk*, like a 'baby' Nut-hatch or a 'tiny tin horn.'

Range: — Mainly evergreen forests from Can. to s. Calif., s. Ariz., and s. N.M. (chiefly a migrant in southernmost parts of range).

PYGMY NUTHATCH. *Sitta pygmæa.* Subsp. (Illus. p. 125.)
Descr. 4½. A very small Nuthatch, usually smaller than either the Red-breasted or the White-breasted with a *gray-brown cap coming down to the eye.* A whitish spot is sometimes visible on the nape of the neck. Inhabits forests of yellow pines and other similar pines. Very similar to Brown-headed Nuthatch of se. U.S.
Voice: — A metallic piping *kit — kit — kit* and a high *ki — dee,* constantly repeated, sometimes becoming an excited twitter or chatter.
Range: — From Wash. and Mont. s. to Mex. and from Rockies w. to Cascades (e. slopes) and Sierras. Also mts. of s. Calif. and coast of middle Calif. (San Luis Obispo Co. to Mendocino Co.).
Subsp. (No apparent field differences): (1) Pygmy Nuthatch, *S. p. pygmæa;* (2) Black-eared Nuthatch, *S. p. melanotis;* (3) White-naped Nuthatch, *S. p. leuconucha.*

CREEPERS: CERTHIIDÆ

CREEPER. *Certhia familiaris.* Subsp. (Illus. p. 125.)
Descr. 5–5¾. Much smaller than a Sparrow; a slim little brown bird with a rather long, stiff tail used as a prop when climbing; sometimes difficult to detect, so well does the bird blend with the bark of the trees. The name Creeper fits.
Voice: — Note, a long thin *seeee,* similar to a note of Golden-crowned Kinglet. Song, several weak, clear notes, *see-ti-wee-tu-wee,* or *see-see-see-ti-ti-see,* the *see* notes resembling the thin call-note.
Range: — Breeds in heavily forested areas from Can. s. to Monterey, Calif. (along coast) and to Mex. (in mt. areas). Spreads to adjacent lowlands in winter.
Subsp. (No apparent field differences): (1) Rocky Mountain Creeper, *C. f. montana;* (2) Mexican Creeper, *C. f. albescens;* (3) Sierra Creeper, *C. f. zelotes;* (4) California Creeper, *C. f. occidentalis.*

WREN-TITS: CHAMÆIDÆ

WREN-TIT. *Chamæa fasciata.* Subsp. (Illus. p. 132.)
Descr. 6½. Far more often heard than seen. A small Sparrow-sized brown bird with a long tail. Back dusky; under parts *cinnamon-brown* with faint dusky streaks; eye *white.* The long, rounded, slightly cocked tail and dull-cinnamon under parts are good marks if the bird can be seen as it slips through the chaparral or shrubbery. The Bush-Tit, which is smaller and

grayer, usually travels about in flocks and does not hide itself
so persistently.

Voice: — Song, heard every month in the year, a staccato
series of short ringing notes all on the same pitch, usually
starting deliberately and running into a rapid trill; sometimes
the song is double-noted, and sometimes it drops slightly in
pitch.

Range: — Coast belt and interior valleys of Calif. and coast belt
of Ore.

Subsp. (No apparent field differences): (1) Coast Wren-Tit,
C. f. phœa; (2) Ruddy Wren-Tit, *C. f. rufula*; (3) Gambel's
Wren-Tit, *C. f. fasciata*; (4) Pallid Wren-Tit, *C. f. henshawi*.

DIPPERS: CINCLIDÆ

DIPPER *or* **WATER OUZEL.**   *Cinclus mexicanus unicolor.*
(Illus. p. 132.)

Descr. 7–8½. An inhabitant of rushing mountain streams; a
dark *slate-colored* bird, shaped like a large chunky Wren (size of
a large Thrush) with a short tail. Legs pale; eyelids *white*.
Its bobbing motions, slaty coloration, and chunky shape are
distinctive.

Voice: — Note, a sharp *zeet* given singly, or rapidly repeated.
Song clear and ringing, Mockingbird-like in form (with much
triplication and quadruplication of notes), but higher and more
Wren-like. Sings throughout year.

Range: — Mt. streams of w. U.S. from Can. s. to s. Calif., n.
Ariz., and N.M.

WATER OUZEL

GRAY-BROWN ABOVE

NO FACIAL STRIPING

HOUSE WREN

DARK BREAST

HEAVILY-BARRED FLANKS

WINTER WREN

WHITE CORNERS

BEWICK'S WREN

STRIPED BACK

MARSH WREN

BUFFY TIPS

FINELY-STREAKED BREAST

ROCK WREN

WHITE THROAT

DARK BELLY

CAÑON WREN

HEAVILY-SPOTTED BREAST

CACTUS WREN

EYE WHITE

UNDERPARTS CINNAMON-BROWN

WREN-TIT

WRENS AND WREN-TIT

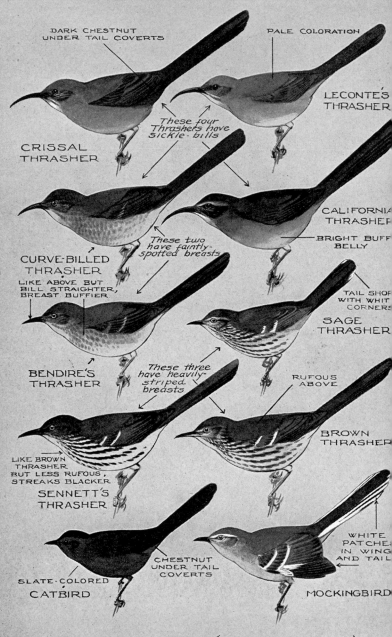

DARK CHESTNUT
UNDER TAIL COVERTS

PALE COLORATION

LECONTE'S
THRASHER

These four
Thrashers have
sickle-bills

CRISSAL
THRASHER

CALIFORNIA
THRASHER

BRIGHT BUFF
BELLY

These two
have faintly-
spotted breasts

CURVE-BILLED
THRASHER

LIKE ABOVE BUT
BILL STRAIGHTER,
BREAST BUFFER

TAIL SHORT
WITH WHIT
CORNERS

SAGE
THRASHER

BENDIRE'S
THRASHER

These three
have heavily-
striped
breasts

RUFOUS
ABOVE

BROWN
THRASHER

LIKE BROWN
THRASHER
BUT LESS RUFOUS,
STREAKS BLACKER

SENNETT'S
THRASHER

SLATE-COLORED
CATBIRD

CHESTNUT
UNDER TAIL
COVERTS

WHITE
PATCHES
IN WING
AND TAIL

MOCKINGBIRD

THRASHERS ETC. (Mimic Thrushes)

WRENS: TROGLODYTIDÆ

SMALL, energetic brown-backed birds, most species smaller than Sparrows, with slender bills; tails often cocked over the back.

(WESTERN) HOUSE WREN. *Troglodytes aëdon parkmani.* (Illus. p. 132.)

Descr. 4½-5¼. A Wren of the forests, gardens, etc.; recognized as a Wren by the small size, brown coloration, energetic actions, and habit of cocking its tail over its back; distinguished from the others by its grayer-brown color, and the lack of any evident facial stripings or white in the tail.

Voice: — A stuttering, gurgling song, rising in a musical burst, then falling at the end.

Range: — Breeds in w. U.S. from Can. s. to Mex. border and cent.-w. Tex.; winters from cent. Calif. and Tex. s. into Mex.

(WESTERN) WINTER WREN. *Nannus hiemalis pacificus.* (Illus. p. 132.)

Descr. 4. A very small dark Wren, smaller than a House Wren; has a much stubbier tail than that species, a light line over the eye, and a *brownish*, heavily barred belly; often bobs its head like Rock Wren; frequents mossy tangles, ravines, brush-piles, etc.

Voice: — Song a high rapid tinkling warble, long sustained and often ending on a high light trill. Note, a hard two-syllabled *kip-kip.*

Range: — Breeds in evergreen forests from Can. s. to cent. Calif. (Monterey Co. and Yosemite) and n. Colo. Winters from Can. s. to s. Calif. (Los Angeles Co.) and N.M. (rarely).

BEWICK'S WREN. *Thryomanes bewicki.* Subsp. (Illus. p. 132.)

Descr. 5-5½. The *white line* over the eye and the *whitish tips* of the outer tail-feathers distinguish this species from the House Wren and all other similar species except the Rock Wren. The Bewick's Wren is much darker and browner above than the Rock Wren, and has a whiter throat and breast. (See Rock Wren.)

Voice: — Song variable. Most races have a song that decidedly resembles that of the Song Sparrow, starting on two or three high notes, dropping lower, and then ending on a thin trill. Another rendering is *swee, swee, cheeeeeeee* (first two notes high, last trilled). The songs of the different subspecies and different individuals vary so much that a blanket description is not adequate.

Range: — W. Wash. and Ore. (w. of Cascades), Calif., w. and s. Nev., s. Ut., sw. Wyo., w. Colo., Ariz., N.M., and Tex.

Subsp. (No apparent field differences): (1) Baird's Wren, *T. b. eremophilus*; (2) Seattle Wren, *T. b. calophonus*; (3) Nicasio Wren, *T. b. marinensis*; (4) Vigors's Wren, *T. b. spilurus*; (5) San Joaquin Wren, *T. b. drymœcus*; (6) San Diego Wren, *T. b. correctus*; (7) Santa Cruz Wren, *T. b. nesophilus*; (8) Catalina Wren, *T. b. catalinæ*; (9) San Clemente Wren, *T. b. leucophrys*.

CACTUS WREN. *Heleodytes brunneicapillus couesi*. (Illus. p. 132.)

Descr. 7–8½. A very large Wren of the cactus country. Distinguished from the other Wrens by its much larger size and *heavily spotted* throat and breast. It also shows a white stripe over the eye and white spots in the outer tail-feathers. The only other arid-country bird with which it can be confused is the Sage Thrasher (which also has a spotted breast, white eye-line, and white spots in the tail), but the latter species is more Thrasher-like or Robin-like in appearance, grayer, *without* white stripings on the back.

Voice: — A rapid monotonous *cheh-cheh-cheh-cheh*, etc., or *chug-chug-chug-chug-chug-chug-chug*, on same pitch and gaining rapidity; unbirdlike.

Range: — Desert regions of s. Calif., s. Nev., s. Ut., Ariz., N.M., and s. Tex.

LONG-BILLED MARSH WREN. *Telmatodytes palustris*. Subsp. (Illus. p. 132.)

Descr. 4½–5½. The Wren of the Marshes; brown, with a conspicuous white line over the eye; known from the other small Wrens with white eye-stripes by the *black-and-white stripes on the back*.

Voice: — Song, a reedy, gurgling series of notes.

Range: — Breeds or occurs in marshes from Can. s. to N.M. and ne. Calif. and from Great Plains to coast.

Subsp. (No apparent field differences): (1) Western Marsh Wren, *T. p. plesius*; (2) Tule Wren, *T. p. paludicola*; (3) Suisun Marsh Wren, *T. p. œstuarinus*; (4) Prairie Marsh Wren, *T. p. dissaëptus*.

CAÑON WREN. *Catherpes mexicanus*. Subsp. (Illus. p. 132.)

Descr. 5½–5¾. A reddish-brown Wren, with a *dark reddish-brown belly*, contrasted with a *white breast and throat*. The conspicuous white throat is the best field-mark. The deep chestnut belly also distinguishes this species at once from the Rock Wren. Inhabits canyons, rocky slopes, and sometimes buildings.

Voice: — A gushing cadence of clear curved notes tripping down

the scale; sometimes picking up at the end; *te-you, te-you te-you, tew tew tew tew*, etc., or *tee tee tee tee tew tew tew*, etc.
Range: — Resident in w. U.S. from se. Wash., Ida., and Wyo. s. to s. Calif., Mex., and w. Tex.
Subsp. (No apparent field differences): (1) White-throated Cañon Wren, *C. m. albifrons*; (2) Cañon Wren, *C. m. conspersus.*

ROCK WREN. *Salpinctes obsoletus obsoletus.* (Illus. p. 132.)
Descr. 5¼–6¼. A rather *gray* Wren with a finely streaked breast (streaks visible at close range). Shows conspicuous *whitish* or *buffy* patches at the end of the tail. The finely streaked breast and pale back distinguish this species from the Bewick's Wren; the pale belly and gray color from the Cañon Wren. Inhabits rocky slopes and canyons.
Voice: — Song, a harsh mechanical chant, *tew, tew, tew, tew*, or *chr-wee, chr-wee, chr-wee*, or *che-poo che-poo che-poo*; commonest call a loud dry trill all on one pitch; also a clear *ti-keer.*
Range: — Breeds in w. U.S. from Can. s. to Mex. except in nw. coast belt; winters in Calif., Ariz., and N.M.

MOCKINGBIRDS AND THRASHERS: MIMIDÆ

THIS family of birds, sometimes called 'Mimic Thrushes' comprises a group of Robin-sized birds with strong legs and slender, more or less decurved bills. The tail is usually fairly long and expressive.

(WESTERN) MOCKINGBIRD. *Mimus polyglottos leucopterus.* (Illus. p. 133.)
Descr. 10–11. As large as a Robin, but more slender and longer-tailed; gray above and white below, with *large white patches* on the wings and tail, conspicuous in flight. Mockingbirds resemble Shrikes somewhat, but lack the black facial masks and have more white in the wings and tail. (See Townsend's Solitaire.)
Voice: — Song consists of a great variety of phrases, some clear and musical, others harsh. Each phrase is usually repeated *several* times. Note, a loud *tchack.*
Range: — Breeds from cent. Calif., se. Ore. (rare), and s. Wyo. s. to Mex.; winters from cent. Calif., s. Ariz., and s. N.M. s.

CATBIRD. *Dumetella carolinensis.* (Illus. p. 133.)
Descr. 8½–9¼. Smaller and slimmer than a Robin; *slaty gray* above and below, with a black cap and chestnut-red under tail-

coverts (these are seldom noticed in the field). Aside from the very dissimilar Dipper, the only other uniformly grayish song-birds, the female Cowbird and female Brewer's Blackbird, are shorter-tailed, not so slaty, and lack the distinctive black cap and rusty under tail-coverts.

Voice: — Catlike mewing note, distinctive. Song, a series of notes and short phrases, some musical, others harsh. Notes not repeated as in songs of Mockingbird and some Thrashers.

Range: — Breeds chiefly in e. U.S. w. through Rocky Mt. section to e. Wash., ne. Ore., n. Ut., Colo., n. N.M., and e.-cent. Ariz. (White Mts.).

BROWN THRASHER. *Toxostoma rufum.* (Illus. p. 133.)

Descr. 10½–12. Slightly larger and slimmer than a Robin, bright *rufous-red* above, *heavily striped* below. Differs from the Thrushes in possessing a much longer tail and a curved bill, and in being *streaked* rather than spotted below. The eye is yellow. No other Thrasher has a bright *rufous-red* back.

Voice: — Song, a series of deliberate notes and short phrases, resembling the Catbird's song, but each phrase quickly *repeated*. Note, a harsh *chack*.

Range: — Breeds in e. U.S. w. to base of Rocky Mts. in Mont., Wyo., and Colo.

SENNETT'S THRASHER. *Toxostoma longirostre sennetti.* (Illus. p. 133.)

Descr. 10½–12. Similar to Brown Thrasher but back less rufous and breast-streaks black rather than brown. Easily told from the other resident Thrasher in the region it occupies, the Curve-billed (Brownsville) Thrasher, by its darker color and *bold black breast-stripes.*

Voice: — Song, a series of notes and phrases similar to other Thrashers but phrases not repeated as much. Call-note, *too-ree.*

Range: — S. Tex. (Lower Rio Grande Valley and lower Gulf Coast).

BENDIRE'S THRASHER. *Toxostoma bendirei.* (Illus. p. 133.)

Descr. 9½–10½. Of the several similar species of pale clay-colored Thrashers that inhabit the sw. deserts, this is one of the easiest to identify, because it has a *shorter, straighter, more Robin-like bill* than the others (see plate). The eye is yellow and the breast faintly spotted.

Voice: — Song, a *continuous* musical warble, not broken into phrases as in other Thrashers. Note, *tirup.*

Range: — Deserts of sw. U.S. (se. Calif., Ariz., and rarely sw. N.M.).

CURVE-BILLED THRASHER. *Toxostoma curvirostre.* Subsp. (Illus. p. 133.)
Descr. $10\frac{1}{2}$–$11\frac{1}{2}$. In the sw. deserts there are several very similar Thrashers, slim Robin-sized birds with decurved bills, long tails, dull gray-brown backs, and cinnamon-tinged bellies. This species can be told from the other Thrashers that have deeply curved bills, by the *faintly spotted breast.* The Bendire's Thrasher has similar breast spotting but a short *straight* bill. Some Curve-billed Thrashers have narrow white wing-bars and white spots at the tip of the tail, but in others these are almost obsolete. The eye is pale orange.
Voice: — Note, a sharp liquid *whit-wheet!* like a human whistle of attention. Song, a series of notes and phrases, Mockingbird-like in quality but without so much repetition.
Range: — S. Ariz., N.M., w. Okla., and w. and s. Tex.
Subsp. (No apparent field differences): (1) Palmer's Thrasher, *T. c. palmeri*; (2) Curve-billed Thrasher, *T. c. curvirostre*; (3) Brownsville Thrasher, *T. c. oberholseri.*

CALIFORNIA THRASHER. *Toxostoma redivivum.* Subsp. (Illus. p. 133.)
Descr. $11\frac{1}{2}$–13. A large dull gray-brown bird, with pale-cinnamon belly and under tail-coverts; tail long, bill *sickle-shaped.* This is the only Thrasher of this type in Calif. w. of the se. desert divides except on the w. side of the San Joaquin Valley, where the pale Leconte's Thrasher is found. The eye is dark.
Voice: — Song, a long-sustained Mockingbird-like series of notes and phrases, some musical, some harsh; the phrases are often *repeated,* but not several times as in the Mockingbird's song. The song is also lower-pitched and more leisurely than the Mocker's. Note, a sharp *wheek.*
Range: — Calif., w. of deserts and Sierras, n. along coast through San Francisco Bay region and in interior to Shasta Co. in n. part of state.
Subsp. (No apparent field differences): (1) California Thrasher, *T. r. redivivum*; (2) Sonoma Thrasher, *T. r. sonomæ.*

LECONTE'S THRASHER. *Toxostoma lecontei lecontei.* (Illus. p. 133.)
Descr. $10\frac{1}{2}$–11. A very *pale* Thrasher of the desert, with a dark tail. Separated from the Crissal Thrasher by its much paler coloration, and from the Curve-billed Thrasher by its unspotted breast. Like the immature Crissal Thrasher, young birds have whitish eyes. Adults have dark eyes.
Voice: — Snatches of song infrequent, heard mostly in early morning; similar to songs of other Thrashers but more disjointed and less repetitious.
Range: — Deserts of s. and w. Ariz., extreme sw. Ut., extreme

s. Nev., and se. Calif.; also in s. San Joaquin Valley of Calif. (Kern Co. n. to s. Fresno Co.).

CRISSAL THRASHER. *Toxostoma dorsale dorsale.* (Illus. p. 133.)
Descr. 11½–12½. Distinguished from Curve-billed Thrasher by its unspotted breast and rustier under tail-coverts, from Leconte's Thrasher by its much darker color and darker and rustier under tail-coverts. The rusty under tail-patch, deeper in color than in other Thrashers, is especially characteristic. Immature birds have whitish eyes, adults dark.
Voice: — Song, similar to songs of other Thrashers but not so loud and vigorous.
Range: — Deserts of sw. U.S. (s. Nev., s. Ut., se. Calif., Ariz., s. N.M., and w. Tex.)

SAGE THRASHER. *Oreoscoptes montanus.* (Illus. p. 133.)
Descr. 8–9. Nearly size of Robin, and similar in shape. A gray-backed bird with a straight slender bill, heavily streaked breast, white spots at the tip of the tail, and pale yellow eye. The small size, shorter tail, and striped breast distinguish it from the other Western Thrashers. When perched, it frequently jerks its tail. (See Cactus Wren.)
Voice: — Song, a series of clear ecstatic warbled phrases, sometimes repeated in true Thrasher fashion, but more often continuous, suggestive of Black-headed Grosbeak; more rapid and joyous than songs of most Thrashers.
Range: — Breeds in arid sagebrush country from e. Wash. and Mont. s. to s.-cent. Calif. (chiefly e. of Sierras) and n. N.M.; winters in s. Calif., s. Ariz., and s. N.M.

THRUSHES, BLUEBIRDS, AND SOLITAIRES: TURDIDÆ

THREE Western species that bear the name 'Thrush' are brown-backed birds with *spotted* breasts. Robins, Bluebirds, Solitaires, and the Varied Thrush, although entirely unlike the other Thrushes in color, betray definite indications of their relationship to this group through their speckle-breasted young. The family as a whole have rather long legs for songbirds, and moderately slender bills.

ROBIN. *Turdus migratorius.* Subsp.
Descr. 8½–10½. One of the most familiar of all birds; easily recognized by its gray back and *brick-red* breast. In the male, the head and tail are blackish; in the female, paler. The bill is

yellow. Young Robins have speckled breasts, but the gray back and rusty under parts identify them.

Voice: — Song, a clear, whistled caroling, often long continued; made up of short phrases of two or three notes each.

Range: — Breeds in w. U.S. in Canadian and transition zones from Can. s. to Mex. and from Pacific Coast e. to Great Plains. Winters from Wash. and Wyo. s.

Subsp. (No apparent field differences): (1) Northwestern Robin, *T. m. caurinus*; (2) Western Robin, *T. m. propinquus.*

TAMAULIPAS THRUSH. *Turdus grayi tamaulipensis.*

Descr. A Mexican species accidental near Brownsville, Tex. Very much like a Robin in appearance, voice, and actions, but different in color. 'Grayish-brown above with a slight olive wash; below, pale buffy or clay-color. The chin and throat are striped with thin lines of darker color' (Irby Davis).

VARIED THRUSH. *Ixoreus nœvius.* Subsp. (See Frontis.)

Descr. 9–10. *Male:* — Similar to Robin but with an *orange eye-stripe, orange wing-bars,* and a *black band* across the rusty breast. *Female:* — Breast-band gray. *Immature:* — Breast-band imperfect or speckled with orange; under parts speckled with dusky. The rusty wing-bars and eye-stripe and shorter tail distinguish them from young Robins.

Voice: — A long, eerie, quavering whistled note, followed, after a pause, by one on a lower or higher pitch.

Range: — Breeds in evergreen forests of nw. Calif. (Humboldt Co.), Ore. (w. and ne. parts), Wash. (w. and se. parts), n. Idaho, and nw. Mont. Winters s. along coast to Monterey, Calif., and in interior Calif.

Subsp. (No apparent field differences): (1) Pacific Varied Thrush, *I. n. nœvius*; (2) Northern Varied Thrush, *I. n. meruloides.*

HERMIT THRUSH. *Hylocichla guttata.* Subsp. (See Frontis.)

Descr. 6½–7½. Larger than a Sparrow, smaller than a Robin, a brown-backed bird with a slender bill and spotted breast. The *reddish tail,* conspicuous as the bird flies away, distinguishes the Hermit Thrush from the Russet-backed Thrush and the Willow Thrush. It is the only one of the three that winters in the W. States. At rest the Hermit Thrush has a characteristic trick of *raising* the tail slowly at frequent intervals.

Voice: — Song, clear and flute-like. Four or five phrases in different pitches, each introduced by a long, pure opening note. Each phrase is given in turn after a deliberate pause. Although the phrases themselves are in different pitches, the notes of each phrase roll around on approximately the same pitch. The pure introductory note is diagnostic.

Range: — Breeds from Can. s. along coast to Monterey, Calif., and in mts. throughout w. U.S. to s. Calif., Ariz., and N.M. Migrates throughout w. U.S. and winters from Ore., Ariz., s. N.M., and w. Tex. s.

Subsp. (No apparent field differences): (1) Alaska Hermit Thrush, *H. g. guttata*; (2) Dwarf Hermit Thrush, *H. g. nanus*; (3) Monterey Hermit Thrush, *H. g. slevini*; (4) Sierra Hermit Thrush, *H. g. sequoiensis*; (5) Mono Hermit Thrush, *H. g. polionota*; (6) Audubon's Hermit Thrush, *H. g. auduboni*.

RUSSET-BACKED THRUSH. *Hylocichla ustulata.* Subsp. (See Frontis.)

Descr. 6½–7½. When we come upon a Thrush that lacks any warmth of color in its plumage and is uniformly gray-brown or olive-brown above, then we can be sure we have found this species. The bird also has a conspicuous *buffy eye-ring.* It has a more heavily spotted breast than the Willow Thrush, and lacks the rusty tail of the Hermit.

Voice: — Song, melodious, breezy flute-like phrases; distinguished from other Thrushes by tendency of each phrase to climb *upwards.*

Range: — Breeds in mts. of w. U.S. from Can. s. to Colo., Ut., Nev., and S. Calif.; also in moist woodlands in lowlands e. of Cascades and Sierras in the Pacific States.

Subsp. (No apparent field differences): (1) Russet-backed Thrush, *H. u. ustulata*; (2) Olive-backed Thrush, *H. u. swainsoni.*

WILLOW THRUSH. *Hylocichla fuscescens salicicola.* (See Frontis.)

Descr. 7–7½. A Thrush uniformly cinnamon-brown or tawny-brown above is quite certainly a Willow Thrush. (Olive-back is dull gray-brown above; Hermit reddish on the tail only.) The breast of this species is the least spotted of the three similar Thrushes; the spots are *indistinct,* not blackish. At a distance the bird sometimes looks quite clear-breasted. Inhabits woodlands along stream-bottoms. It is a race of the Eastern Veery.

Voice: — A liquid, breezy whistle, wheeling *downward*: *vee-ur, vee-ur, veer, veer.* Note, *chew* or *view.*

Range: — Breeds e. of Cascades from e. Wash. and Mont. s. to ne. Ore., Nev., Ut., and Colo. Migrates through Ariz. and N.M., but rarely observed there.

EASTERN BLUEBIRD. *Sialia sialis.* Subsp.

Descr. 6½–7½. Similar to Western Bluebird, but with throat *rusty,* not blue, and back *solid blue,* without a rusty patch (some Western Bluebirds lack this patch, however).

Voice: — Note, a simple *chur-wee* or *wee-chur-wee*. Song, a short soft warble.

Range: — Breeds in e. U.S. w. sparingly to e. Mont., e. Wyo., and e. Colo. Occasional in high mts. of se. Ariz. (Santa Ritas and Huachucas). In these mts. the following species is the common breeding Bluebird.

Subsp. (No apparent field differences): (1) Eastern Bluebird, *S. s. sialis*; (2) Azure Bluebird, *S. s. fulva*.

WESTERN, *or* **MEXICAN, BLUEBIRD.** *Sialia mexicana.*
Subsp. (See Frontis)
Descr. 6½–7. A little larger than a Sparrow; head, wings, and tail *blue*; breast and back *rusty-red*. (In some individuals the back is partially or wholly blue.) Appears round-shouldered when perched. Female paler and duller than male. Except for the Eastern Bluebird the only other blue bird with a red breast is the male Lazuli Bunting, which can be recognized by its conspicuous wing-bars. The Mountain Bluebird has a *blue* breast.
Voice: — A short *pew* or *mew*. Also a hard chattering note.
Range: — Breeds in foothills and pines throughout Pacific States and in n. Idaho and w. Mont. Also in Rocky Mt. section from Ut. and Colo. s. to Mex. Occasional in Wyo. Winters in Pacific States and in s. Ut., Ariz., N.M., and w. Tex.
Subsp. (No apparent field differences): (1) Western Bluebird, *S. m. occidentalis*; (2) Chestnut-backed Bluebird, *S. m. bairdi*.

MOUNTAIN BLUEBIRD. *Sialia currucoides.* (See Frontis.)
Descr. 6½–7¾. *Male:* — *Azure blue above and below,* belly white. Readily told from the Western Bluebird by its *blue breast.* The only other blue songbird with a blue breast found in the West is the male Blue Grosbeak, which has a short thick bill and brown wing-bars. *Female:* — Dull brownish with bluish rump, tail, and wings. Distinguished from female Western Bluebird by straighter posture, lack of rusty wash on breast, and paler, greener blue color.
Voice: — A low *chur* or *phew.* Song, a beautiful clear short warble, higher-pitched than that of Eastern Bluebird and hardly suggesting it (Francis H. Allen). Suggests caroling of Robin (W. Weydemeyer).
Range: — Breeds chiefly in mt. sections from e. slope of Cascades and Sierras to Great Plains and from Can. s. to s. Calif., cent. Ariz., and N.M. Winters from Ore., Ariz., and Colo. s. into Mex.

TOWNSEND'S SOLITAIRE. *Myadestes townsendi.* (See Frontis.)
Descr. 8–9½. A gray-bodied bird, slimmer than a Robin, with a white *eye-ring, white sides* on the tail, and a *buffy patch* in the

center of the wing. The beginner is likely to be confused by the
bird at first, imagining it to be some sort of a Thrasher, a Flycatcher, or almost anything but a Solitaire. The white in the
tail and the light wing-patches give the bird a not too remote
resemblance to a Mockingbird in flight. The eye-ring and darker
breast at once distinguish it from that species.

Voice: — Song, long and warbled, suggesting Black-headed
Grosbeak's, but more rapid.

Range: — Breeds in high mts. from Can. s. through Sierras to
San Bernardino Mts. in s. Calif. and through Rockies and adjacent high ranges to cent. Ariz. and N.M. Winters at lower
levels from Wash. and Mont. s.

GNATCATCHERS AND KINGLETS:
SYLVIIDÆ

WESTERN GNATCATCHER. *Polioptila cærulea amœnissima.*
(Illus. p. 125.)

Descr. 4½–5. Like a miniature Mockingbird in color and shape.
Western Gnatcatchers are very tiny, slender mites, smaller
even than Chickadees, blue-gray above and whitish below, with
a narrow white eye-ring, and a *long, contrastingly colored tail*
(black in the center, white on the sides, often cocked like a
Wren's tail). A race of the Blue-gray Gnatcatcher of the East.
(See Plumbeous Gnatcatcher.)

Voice: — Note, a thin complaining *peeee*; song, a thin squeaky,
wheezy series of notes.

Range: — Breeds from Colo., s. Ut., s. Nev., and n. Calif.
(Shasta Co.) s. into Mex. Winters in s. Calif. and s. Ariz.

PLUMBEOUS GNATCATCHER. *Polioptila melanura.* Subsp.
(Illus. p. 125.)

Descr. 4½. Similar to Western Gnatcatcher but with *black cap*
and much less white in tail.

Voice: — Note, a thin *chee* repeated two or three times (Western
Gnatcatcher gives single note).

Subsp. PLUMBEOUS GNATCATCHER. *P. m. melanura.*
Deserts of se. Calif., s. Nev., Ariz., N.M., and Rio
Grande Valley of w. Tex.
BLACK-TAILED GNATCATCHER. *P. m. californica.*
Under parts *dull gray* instead of whitish as in Plumbeous
Gnatcatcher; almost no white in corners of tail. San
Diegan district of sw. Calif., n. to Ventura.

(WESTERN) GOLDEN-CROWNED KINGLET. *Regulus
satrapa olivaceus.* (Illus. p. 125.)

Descr. 3½–4. Kinglets are tiny mites of birds, smaller than Warblers and hardly more than half the size of Sparrows. Their diminutive proportions and somber olive-gray backs make them difficult to discern among the thick branches of the evergreens through which they forage. The present species, except for summer juveniles, always shows a conspicuous bright crown, yellow in the female, orange in the male. Another point of distinction (if it be needed) is that the Golden-crown has a *white stripe* over the eye, the Ruby-crown a white eye-ring.

Voice: — Call-note, a high wiry *see-see-see* (similar to Creeper's single *seee*). Song, a series of thin notes (like the ordinary call-notes) rising up the scale, then dropping into a chatter.

Range: — Breeds in high mts. from Can. s. to n. N.M., Ariz., and s. Calif. and in evergreen forests along coast s. to cent. Calif. (Marin Co.). Migrates or winters in adjacent country from Can. s. to s. Calif. and Mex.

RUBY-CROWNED KINGLET. *Corthylio calendula.* Subsp. (Illus. p. 125.)

Descr. 3¾–4½. Very tiny and short-tailed; olive-gray above with two pale wing-bars; male with a scarlet crown-patch (usually concealed). The best recognition mark is the conspicuous *white eye-ring* which gives the bird a big-eyed appearance. Any King-let not showing a conspicuous crown-patch is of this species. The stubby tail distinguishes it at once from any of the War-blers. It can very easily be confused with the Hutton's Vireo (see under that species). The race known as the Sitka Kinglet, which winters south along the Pacific Coast to Monterey, Cali-fornia, is said to be distinguishable in the field from the Western Ruby-crowned Kinglet by its smaller size and darker coloration (Grinnell).

Voice: — Note, a husky two-syllabled *ji-dit.* Song, a remark-able performance for so small a bird, starting with three or four high *tees,* then several low *tews* and ending in a repetitious chant, thus: *tee tee tee tew tew tew tew,* *tee-diddle, tee-diddle, tee-diddle.* Variable.

Range: — Breeds in evergreen forests from Can. s. in high mts. to s. Calif., cent. Ariz., and cent. N.M. Migrates through low-lands, and winters along Pacific Coast and from interior Calif., Ariz., and N.M. s. into Mex.

Subsp. (No apparent field differences except possibly in No. 3 — see above): (1) Eastern Ruby-crowned Kinglet, *C. c. calen-dula*; (2) Western Ruby-crowned Kinglet, *C. c. cineraceus*; (3) Sitka Kinglet, *C. c. grinnelli.*

A. AMERICAN PIPIT   B. SPRAGUE'S PIPIT

PIPITS: MOTACILLIDÆ

AMERICAN PIPIT. *Anthus spinoletta.* (Illus. p. 144.)
Descr. 6–7. Near the size of a Sparrow, but with a *slender* bill; under parts *buffy* with streakings; *outer tail-feathers white*; frequents open country, plowed fields, shore flats, etc. It may be known from the Vesper Sparrow, which also shows white outer tail-feathers, by the buffy under parts and the habits of *constantly bobbing its tail*, of *walking* instead of hopping, and of dipping up and down when in flight.
Voice: — Note, a thin *jee jeet*, or, by a stretch of the imagination, *pĭ-pit*, thinner than note of Horned Lark.
Range: — Breeds near timber line from Can. in high mts. s. to Ore. and n. N.M. Migrates through open country of w. U.S., and winters in Calif., Ariz., and N.M. and along coast n. to Wash. The racial identity of this species in the W. is at present unsettled, as two new races have been described, whereas formerly they were regarded to be the same as the Eastern bird.

SPRAGUE'S PIPIT. *Anthus spraguei.* (Illus. p. 144.)
Descr. A buffy bird with a striped back, not solid dark upper parts like American Pipit. The breast-streakings are fine and sparse, not so heavy as in the American Pipit. The upper parts, streaked conspicuously with buff and black, make the best mark. It is the breeding Pipit of the plains region just e. of the mt.-ranges in Mont. In Mont., the other Pipit breeds in the barren parts of high mts. in the w. part of the state. The American Pipit is highly social, whereas this species often tends to occur singly or in pairs. The thin Pipit bill will help distinguish either species from obscure plumages of the Longspurs.
Range: — Breeds in prairies of Mont. ·e. of mts. Migrates through e. Wyo. to Tex.

A. BOHEMIAN WAXWING   B. CEDAR WAXWING

WAXWINGS: BOMBYCILLIDÆ

BOHEMIAN WAXWING. *Bombycilla garrula pallidiceps.* (Illus. p. 145.)
Descr. 7½–8½. Resembles the Cedar Waxwing closely, but is larger, has some *white in the wing*, is grayer, and possesses *chestnut-red* under tail-coverts instead of white.
Voice: — A low trill, longer and rougher than lisp of Cedar Waxwing.
Range: — Breeds in w. Can. Winters irregularly s. to n. Calif. and Colo.

CEDAR WAXWING. *Bombycilla cedrorum.* (Illus. p. 145.)
Descr. 6½–8. Between the size of a Sparrow and a Robin; a sleek, *crested*, brown bird with a broad *yellow* band at the tip of the tail. It is the only sleek *brown* bird with a long crest.
Voice: — A high thin lisp or *zee.*
Range: — Breeds from Can. s. to n. Calif. and Colo. Winters from Wash. and Colo. s. into Mex.

SILKY FLYCATCHERS: PTILOGONATIDÆ

PHAINOPEPLA. *Phainopepla nitens.* Subsp. (Illus. p. 146.)
Descr. 7–7¾. Size of an Oriole. *Male:* — A slim *glossy black* bird

PHAINOPEPLA, *male*

with a *slender crest* and conspicuous *white patches* in the wing. No other bird resembles it. *Female: — Dark gray*, with slender crest, but no white wing-patches. The rather uniform *gray* coloration and lack of a yellow tail-band distinguish the female from the Cedar Waxwing.

Voice: — Note, a soft, low *wurp*. Song, a weak, casual warble, wheezy and disconnected.

Range: — Breeds chiefly in arid lowlands of Calif., s. Nev., s. Ut., Ariz., and sw. N.M. and w. Tex. (Brewster Co.). Winters in s. Calif., s. Ariz., and w. Tex.

Subsp. (No apparent field differences): (1) Northern Phainopepla, *P. n. lepida*; (2) Mexican Phainopepla, *P. n. nitens*.

SHRIKES: LANIIDÆ

NORTHWESTERN SHRIKE. *Lanius borealis invictus.*
Descr. 9–10½. A race of the Northern Shrike. In the colder parts of the W. States during the winter months a Robin-sized bird, sitting quite still, *alone* in the *tip-top* of some tree, is likely to be a Northwestern Shrike. If it is this species, closer inspection shows it to be light gray above and white below, with a *black mask* through the eyes. On taking flight it drops low, and, progressing with a peculiar wing-motion on a bee-line course, rises suddenly to its tree-top perch. This species can be told

from the very similar Loggerhead Shrike by its slightly larger size and *finely barred* breast. Another very good point, at close range, is the bill: those of the other two are solid black; the basal portion of the lower mandible of the present species is *pale-colored*. The other two have a narrow strip of black above the bill. Generally speaking, however, winter Shrikes in the colder parts of the w. U.S. are Northwestern Shrikes. Young birds are browner but still recognizable as this species by the fine vermiculations on the breast, which are even more pronounced than in the adult.

Voice: — Song, a long-continued Thrasher-like succession of phrases, harsher on the whole than the Thrasher's song.

Range: — Breeds in w. Can.; winters irregularly s. to n. Calif., N.M., and n. Tex.

LOGGERHEAD SHRIKE. *Lanius ludovicianus.* Subsp. (Illus. p. 147.)

Descr. 9. Slightly smaller than a Robin; big-headed and slim-tailed; gray above and white below, with a conspicuous *black mask* through the eyes. (See Northwestern Shrike.) The species is most frequently confused with the Mockingbird because of its gray, black, and white coloration and white patches in the wing, but the Mockingbird is slimmer, longer-tailed, has larger wing-patches, and lacks the black mask through the eyes.

Voice: — Song, a few musical notes and phrases, repeated. Somewhat Thrasher-like, but more deliberate, often with long pauses between passages.

Range: — Breeds from Can. s. to Mex.; winters in Calif. and in arid sections of sw. U.S.

Subsp. (No apparent field differences): (1) White-rumped Shrike, *L. l. excubitorides*; (2) California Shrike, *L. l. gambeli*; (3) Island Shrike, *L. l. anthonyi*.

LOGGERHEAD SHRIKE

STARLINGS: STURNIDÆ

STARLING. *Sturnus vulgaris vulgaris.* (Illus. p. 148.)
Descr. 7½–8½. The Starling, introduced from Europe into the e. U.S., has now reached the Rockies and might eventually penetrate the Far West. It is a *short-tailed* 'Blackbird,' with somewhat the shape of a Meadowlark. In spring the plumage is glossed with purple and green (visible at close range), and the bill is *yellow* In winter plumage the Starling is heavily speckled, and the bill is dark, changing to yellow as spring approaches. No other 'Blackbird' has a *yellow* bill. Young birds are dark dusky gray, a little like the female Cowbird, but the tail is shorter, and the bill longer and more spike-like, not stout and conical. The flight of Starlings is swift and direct, not rising and falling as much as that of Blackbirds.
Voice: — Many of the whistled notes are extremely musical; other sounds are harsh and rasping. Frequently very good imitations of other species are given.
Range: — E. U.S., spreading westward. Has at this date (1940) reached base of Rockies and Ut. To be looked for on Pacific Coast.

STARLING, *male in spring*

VIREOS: VIREONIDÆ

SMALL olive- or gray-backed birds, slightly smaller than most Sparrows; very much like the Warblers, but with somewhat heavier bills, and less active, slowly searching for insects under the leaves instead of flitting about. Because of their white wing-bars and white eye-rings, some species might be confused with the small *Empidonax* Flycatchers, but they do not sit in the typical upright Flycatcher posture, and the eye-rings join a light spot between the eye and bill, giving more the appearance of white spectacles.

BLACK-CAPPED VIREO. *Vireo atricapillus.* (Illus. p. 190.)
Descr. 4½–4¾. The only Vireo with the *top and sides of the head black*. It has conspicuous white wing-bars and white 'spectacles' formed by the eye-ring and loral patch (between the eye and bill).
Voice: — Song, short phrases, similar to other Vireos but somewhat more varied.
Range: — Cent. and cent.-w. Tex. (to Brewster Co.) and parts of sw. Okla. and s. Kans.

HUTTON'S VIREO. *Vireo huttoni.* Subsp. (Illus. p. 190.)
Descr. 4¼–4¾. A small olive-brown Vireo with two broad white wing-bars, a *partial* eye-ring, and a large light loral spot (between eye and bill). The appearance of this large light spot and the incomplete eye-ring *interrupted by a dark spot* above eye (see diagram) distinguish it from the other Vireos with eye-rings or 'spectacles.' It can be mistaken by the beginner for one of the small *Empidonax* Flycatchers, which, however, sit in an upright posture and have complete eye-rings. The bird that most closely resembles it is the Ruby-crowned Kinglet. The Vireo has a heavier bill, is slightly larger, and is much more deliberate in its movements. (Does not flirt wings like Kinglet.) The notes are especially distinctive. In most of its range, the preferred habitat of this species is live-oaks.
Voice: — A hoarse double-noted *zu-weep* with rising inflection, sometimes continuously repeated; Vireo quality. Also 'a hoarse aspirate *Day, de'-de'-de''* (Laidlaw Williams).
Range: — Resident in Pacific States (w. of Cascades and Sierras), and oak belt of mts. of se. Ariz., sw. N.M., and w. Tex.
Subsp. (No apparent field differences): (1) Hutton's Vireo, *V. h. huttoni*; (2) Stephens's Vireo, *V. h. stephensi*.

BELL'S, *or* **LEAST, VIREO.** *Vireo belli.* Subsp. (Illus. p. 190.)
Descr. 4¾–5. A small light-gray-backed Vireo. Perhaps the most nondescript of the Vireos. Distinguished from the Warbling Vireo by the faint wing-bars and narrow light eye-ring. The other similar Vireos have much more conspicuous eye-rings. Its habitat is willows and bushes along low streams.
Voice: — Song, low husky phrases repeated at short intervals; sounds like *cheedle cheedle chee? cheedle cheedle chew!* The latter phrase, which is given the more frequently, has a downward in-

flection at the end and sounds as if the bird were answering its own question.

Range: — Breeds in Calif. (central valleys, coast from Monterey Co. s., and se. portion), s. Ariz., sw. N.M., and w. Tex.; also e. Colo.

Subsp. (No apparent field differences): (1) Bell's Vireo, *V. b. belli*; (2) Texas Vireo, *V. b. medius*; (3) Arizona Vireo, *V. b. arizonæ*; (4) Least Vireo, *V. b. pusillus*.

GRAY VIREO. *Vireo vicinior.* (Illus. p. 190.)

Descr. 5½–5¾. A gray-backed Vireo of the chaparral and juniper on the slopes of arid mts. Has a *narrow white eye-ring* but differs from other Vireos having similar eye-rings by having *no wing-bars* or one faint one. Might be confused with Bell's, or Least, Vireo because of similarity in appearance, but the latter species prefers the willows of stream-bottoms and would not be found on arid slopes. The Gray Vireo, though drab, has much character, flopping its tail like a Gnatcatcher.

Voice: — Very similar to song of Solitary Vireo (Cassin's and Plumbeous) but more rapid and 'patchy.' (Solitary would not be found in the above arid habitat.)

Range· — Breeds from s. Calif., s. Nev., sw. Colo., and extreme w. Okla. s. into Mex.

SOLITARY VIREO. *Vireo solitarius.* Subsp. (Illus. p. 190.)

Descr. 5–6. A Vireo possessing *both* conspicuous white wing-bars and conspicuous white 'spectacles.' The Bell's, or Least, Vireo has these marks indistinct; in the Warbling Vireo they are wanting. The Gray Vireo has only a conspicuous eye-ring. The present species can be told from the Hutton's Vireo by the complete eye-ring and snowy-white throat.

Voice: — A series of short whistled phrases, with a rising or falling inflection, rendered with a short wait between phrases.

Subsp. PLUMBEOUS VIREO. *V. s. plumbeus.*

Breeds in Rocky Mt. region from n. Nev., n. Ut., s. Mont., and se. Wyo. s. into Mex. Lacks the contrast of *gray* head and *olive* back of next race.

CASSIN'S VIREO. *V. s. cassini.*

Breeds in Pacific States. When at close range, in good light, easily distinguished from the Plumbeous or any other Vireo possessing wing-bars by the *gray* head contrasting with an *olive* back; almost identically like the Blue-headed Vireo of the East, which is also a race of this species. The Plumbeous race is uniformly gray above.

YELLOW-GREEN VIREO. *Vireo flavoviridis flavoviridis.*

Descr. 6¼–6¾. Of very rare occurrence near Brownsville, Tex.

WARBLERS

1. GRACE'S WARBLER
2. AUDUBON'S WARBLER, *a.* MALE IN SPRING; *b.* FEMALE IN AUTUMN
3. MYRTLE WARBLER, MALE IN SPRING
4. VIRGINIA'S WARBLER
5. BLACK-THROATED GRAY WARBLER, MALE
6. BLACK AND WHITE WARBLER, MALE
7. BLACK-POLL WARBLER, *a.* MALE IN SPRING; *b.* FEMALE; *c.* AUTUMN
8. LUCY'S WARBLER
9. TOWNSEND'S WARBLER, *a.* MALE; *b.* FEMALE
10. GOLDEN-CHEEKED WARBLER, MALE
11. HERMIT WARBLER, *a.* MALE; *b.* FEMALE
12. TENNESSEE WARBLER, MALE IN SPRING
13. PILEOLATED WARBLER, *a.* MALE; *b.* FEMALE
14. YELLOW WARBLER, *a.* MALE; *b.* FEMALE
15. SENNETT'S WARBLER, MALE
16. CALAVERAS WARBLER
17. MACGILLIVRAY'S WARBLER, *a.* MALE: *b.* FEMALE
18. ORANGE-CROWNED WARBLER
19. LONG-TAILED CHAT
20. GRINNELL'S WATER-THRUSH
21. YELLOW-THROAT, *a.* MALE; *b.* FEMALE
22. OLIVE WARBLER, *a.* MALE; *b.* FEMALE
23. RED-FACED WARBLER
24. PAINTED REDSTART
25. AMERICAN REDSTART, *a.* MALE; *b.* FEMALE

Similar to Red-eyed Vireo, both in behavior and in voice, but with strong yellow tones. Sides bright olive-green and under tail-coverts *yellow* (Red-eye, white). A Vireo similar to a Red-eye during the summer months in the lower Rio Grande Valley would probably be this species. Its preferred habitat is thick-leaved trees near water.

RED-EYED VIREO. *Vireo olivaceus.* (Illus. p. 190.)
Descr. 5½–6½. Olive-green above, white below, *no wing-bars*; best characterized by the *gray cap* and the *black-bordered white stripe* over the eye. The red eye is of little aid. The Warbling Vireo is paler, and more uniformly colored above, without such contrasting facial striping. The songs of these two birds are absolutely unlike.
Voice: — A monotonous series of short phrases of a Robin-like character, repeated sometimes as often as forty times in a minute. Resembles song of Solitary (Plumbeous) Vireo but less musical and with the phrases repeated more frequently.
Range: — Breeds chiefly in e. U.S., w. to e. Colo., e. Wyo., and, in nw., to Portland, Ore., and Seattle, Wash. Accidental in Calif.

(WESTERN) WARBLING VIREO. *Vireo gilvus swainsoni.* (Illus. p. 190.)
Descr. 5–6. Only two species of Vireos found in the W. have *no* wing-bars or eye-rings. If the head is contrastingly striped, it is a Red-eye. If the head is *indistinctly* striped, then it is the present species. Of the two, this has the wider distribution in the W.
Voice: — Song, a rather lengthy languid warble unlike the abrupt phraseology of the other Vireos; resembles slightly the Purple Finch's song, but less spirited. A characteristic call-note in the summer is a wheezy querulous *twee*.
Range: — Breeds from Can. s. to Mex. border.

WOOD WARBLERS:
COMPSOTHLYPIDÆ

THESE are the sprightly 'butterflies' of the bird world — bright-colored mites, smaller than Sparrows, with thin bills. The Vireos are similar in shape, but their colors are duller and their movements when patiently foraging among the leaves and twigs are rather sluggish, unlike the active flittings of the Warblers. The majority of Western Warblers have some yellow on them. Easterners will find that many Eastern Warblers have their Western counterparts, if not in a similar subspecies in a similar species; for example: *Nashville* — Calaveras; *Orange-crowned* — Orange-crowned; *Yellow* — Yellow; *Myrtle* — Audubon's; *Black-throated Green* — Hermit; *Mourning* — Macgillivray's; *Yellow-throated* — Grace's; *Yellow-breasted Chat* — Long-tailed Chat; *Wilson's* — Pileolated; *Yellow-throat* — Yellow-throat. At least fifteen species of purely Eastern Warblers have been recorded occasionally or accidentally in the W., especially along the edge of the Great Plains in e. Mont., e. Wyo., and e. Colo. Descriptions of these waifs will be found in the Eastern counterpart to this volume, *A Field Guide to the Birds*.

BLACK AND WHITE WARBLER. *Mniotilta varia.* (Illus. p. 150.)

Descr. 5–5¼. Occasional in w. U.S. *Striped lengthwise with black and white* — the zebra's counterpart among birds; *creeps* along tree-trunks and branches. The Black-throated Gray Warbler is the only one that at all resembles it, but that species has a *solid black cap*, the present species has a *striped* crown.

Voice: — Song, a high thin *tisi tisi tisi tisi tisi tisi tisi tisi*, all on one pitch; resembles Redstart's song but is thinner and longer (*tisi* repeated at least six times).

Range: — E. N.A.; occasional in migration w. to e. Colo., e. Wyo., and e. Mont.; occasional also in Calif.

TENNESSEE WARBLER. *Vermivora peregrina.* (Illus. p. 150.)

Descr. 4½–5. *Adult male in spring:* — Very plain; unmarked save for a *conspicuous white stripe over the eye*; head gray, contrasting with olive-green back; under parts white. The bird in this plumage, with the white eye-stripe, is much like the Red-eyed and the Warbling Vireos, but the smaller size, the Warbler actions, and the thin, fine-pointed bill identify it. *Adult female in spring:* — Similar to the male, but head less gray and under parts slightly yellowish. The eye-line is the best mark. *Adults and immatures in autumn:* — Olive-green above, yellowish below, with no streaks; yellowish line over eye. Resembles the Orange-crowned Warbler, but the under tail-coverts are *white*, not yellow.

Voice: — Song, two-parted, *teet-see, teet-see, teet-see, teet-see, de-de-de-de-de-de-de-de.* The end of the song is like that of the Chipping Sparrow but more emphatic. It is loud and repetitious, one song quickly following the preceding one.

Range: — Migrates through e. Colo., e. Wyo., and e. Mont.; said to breed in mts. of nw. Mont.

ORANGE-CROWNED WARBLER. *Vermivora celata.* Subsp. (Illus. p. 150.)

Descr. 4½–5. A dull-colored Warbler *without wing-bars or other distinctive marks*; olive-green above, *greenish-yellow below*; the 'orange crown' is seldom visible (Calaveras also has a veiled crown-patch); sexes similar. The points to remember are the greenish-yellow under parts and lack of wing-bars. (The Calaveras Warbler has brighter under parts and a white eye-ring; the Hutton's Vireo and Ruby-crowned Kinglet, which might possibly be confused with it, both have light wing-bars.) One race of this species, the Dusky Warbler, is recognizable by its dull coloration, greenish drab throughout, not much paler on the under parts. However, as dull autumn immatures of the other races are so very similar to it, it is not safe to identify this subspecies in the field except on the breeding grounds (Channel Ids., Calif., and coast near San Diego), or along the coast of Calif. during the winter months. The favorite habitat of the Orange-crowned Warbler is brush-covered slopes. In the Pacific States the racial name, Lutescent Warbler, has become quite established through usage, but for the sake of consistency we suggest instead, the use of the species name, Orange-crowned Warbler, as more than one race occurs in migration.

Voice: — Song, a weak, colorless trill, dropping in pitch and energy at the end. Often the song changes pitch twice, rising a little then dropping.

Range: — Breeds from Can. s. to s. Calif., Ariz., and N.M., and from Rockies w. to coast. Migrates throughout. Winters from cent. Calif. and s. Ariz. s. into Mex.

Subsp. (No apparent field differences except in No. 4 — see above): (1) Eastern Orange-crowned Warbler, *V. c. celata*; (2) Rocky Mountain Orange-crowned Warbler, *V. c. orestera*; (3) Lutescent Warbler, *V. c. lutescens*; (4) Dusky Warbler, *V. c. sordida.*

CALAVERAS WARBLER. *Vermivora ruficapilla ridgwayi.* (Illus. p. 150.)

Descr. 4–4¾. A small, rather plain Warbler; throat and under parts bright yellow; *head gray*, contrasting with the olive-green back; eye-ring *white*; sexes similar. The *white eye-ring* in conjunction with the bright *yellow* throat is the best mark. The Macgillivray's Warbler has a white eye-ring, but its throat is dark gray or brownish (autumn female). The Calaveras is a race of the Eastern Nashville Warbler. Preferred habitat: deciduous growth on mountain-slopes.

Voice: — Song, two-parted, *see-bit, see-bit, see-bit, chilililitititi* (first part measured, last part run together).

Range: — Breeds in Pacific States from Can. s. to cent. Sierras in Calif., also e. to Ida. Migrates through Pacific States; occasional in Rockies.

VIRGINIA'S WARBLER. *Vermivora virginiæ.* (Illus. p. 150.)

Descr. 4. A *gray-looking* Warbler with a pale breast and *yellow-*

ish rump and under tail-coverts. At close range a narrow white eye-ring, a rufous spot on top of the head, and a touch of yellow on the breast can be seen. Immature birds lack the coloration on the crown and breast but can be told by their gray color and the touch of yellow at the base of the tail. The Lucy's Warbler resembles this species but has a *chestnut* rump instead of a yellowish one. The habitat is oaks on mountain-sides and foothills.
Voice: — Song, a loose, colorless series of notes on nearly the same pitch; rises ever so slightly at end: *chip-chlip-chlip-chlip-chlip-wick wick.* Resembles song of Audubon's Warbler in quality.
Range: — Breeds in s. Rocky Mt. region from s. Ariz. and ne. N.M. n. to Nev., Ut., and n. Colo.

COLIMA WARBLER. *Vermivora crissalis.*
Descr. Very similar to the Virginia's Warbler, differing chiefly in lacking the yellowish wash on the breast; also darker in general coloration. In the Chisos Mts. in Tex., a deliberate-acting, gray-looking Warbler with yellow near the base of the tail can quite safely be called this little-known species, although the Virginia's Warbler occurs as a migrant in the vicinity.
Voice: — Song, 'a simple trill, much like that of the Chipping Sparrow but rather shor:er and more musical and ending in two lower notes' (Van Tyne).
Range: — In U.S. found only in Chisos Mts., Tex. (oaks between 6000 and 7500 ft.).

LUCY'S WARBLER. *Vermivora luciæ.* (Illus. p. 150.)
Descr. 4. A little Warbler of the desert; gray-backed, with a white breast. Its best field-mark is a *chestnut rump-patch.* It also has a small patch of chestnut on the crown. The Warbler that most closely resembles it, the Virginia's Warbler, has a *yellowish* rump-patch. Immature birds are largely gray without distinctive marks.
Voice: — Song, a high and rapid utterance, *weeta weeta weeta che che che che che,* on two pitches (sometimes ending on lower pitch, sometimes on higher). Has quality of Yellow Warbler's song when ending on higher notes. Resembles Calaveras when ending on lower pitch.
Range: — Breeds in deserts of sw. U.S. (from Santa Clara Valley, Ut., s. through Ariz., sw. N.M., and se. Calif.).

SENNETT'S WARBLER. *Compsothlypis pitiayumi nigrilora.* (Illus. p. 150.)
Descr. 4¼–4¾. A *bluish* Warbler with a *yellow* throat and breast. Two white wing-bars are also noticeable. A suffused yellowish patch on the back is a clinching point, if it can be seen. The most noticeable field-character is the yellow throat, sharply sep-

arated from the blue crown by a black line (see color plate).
Female: — Similar; face-pattern not so contrasting. The general blue and yellow color is distinctive. The Parula Warbler,
which migrates through the range of this bird, is very similar, but
males can be easily distinguished by a dark *band* crossing the
yellow of the breast and much longer wing-bars.
Voice: — Commonest song, a buzzy trill which climbs the scale
and tips over at the top; also a series of buzzy notes which ascend
the scale by short steps. Both these songs are almost identical
with those of the Parula Warbler.
Range: — Resident in lower Rio Grande Valley, Tex. Found
in woodlands where hanging moss is prevalent.

OLIVE WARBLER. *Peucedramus olivaceus.* (Illus. p. 150.)
Descr. 4½–5. *Male:* — A unique-looking Warbler, easily identified by its *orange-brown head and upper breast* set off by a
black cheek-patch. The back is dark gray, the belly white, and
the wings have much white in them. *Female:* — Less distinctive; crown and nape olive, sides of throat and breast yellowish,
back gray, wing-bars white. Has a dusky ear-patch, and might
be confused with female Townsend's Warbler, but lacks the
dark breast-streakings. Even more like female Hermit Warbler,
but with more yellow on breast, less on face; cheek-patch darker
and bill much longer.
Voice: — Song, a ringing chant with several variations: *tiddle
tiddle tiddle ter,* or *cut-year, cut-year cut-year,* or *peter peter peter
peter* (Titmouse-like).
Range: — Pine forests of high mts. of se. Ariz. and sw. N.M.

YELLOW WARBLER. *Dendroica æstiva.* Subsp. (Illus. p. 150.)
Descr. 4–5. The only small bird that in the field appears to be
all yellow. Many of the other Warblers are yellow below, but
none of them is so yellow on the back, wings, and tail. Many
Warblers have white spots in the tail; this is the only species
with *yellow* spots. At close range the male shows chestnut-red
breast-streakings. In the female these are faint or nearly lacking. Has a preference for trees and shrubbery along streams.
In some localities the Goldfinch shares the nickname 'Yellow-
bird,' but it has *black* wings and a *black* tail. The Pileolated
Warbler can be mistaken for it but has a darker back and a black
spot on the crown. The Alaska Yellow Warbler, *D. a. rubiginosa,* is darker and more greenish than the other races and is
often easily recognizable in life. The immature of this race can
be confused with the Orange-crowned Warbler by the beginner.
Voice: — A clear bright *tsee-tsee-tsee-tseetsa-wee* or *tsee-tsee-
tsee-tsee-tsee-wee-a,* given rapidly.
Range: — Breeds from Can. s. to s. Calif., s. Ariz., s. N.M., and
w. Tex.

Subsp. (No apparent field differences except sometimes in No. 2): (1) Eastern Yellow Warbler, *D. a. æstiva*; (2) Alaska Yellow Warbler, *D. a. rubiginosa*; (3) California Yellow Warbler, *D. a. brewsteri*; (4) Sonora Yellow Warbler, *D. a. sonorana*.

MYRTLE WARBLER. *Dendroica coronata.* (Illus. p. 150.)
Descr. 5-6. The Myrtle Warbler is very similar to the Audubon's in pattern, but the throat is pure *white* instead of yellow. Adult males have two narrow white wing-bars instead of a large white wing-patch.
Voice: — Song, very similar to Audubon's Warbler, a Junco-like trill, that either *rises* or *falls* in pitch at the end. Call-note recognizably different in timbre from that of Audubon's Warbler.
Range: — Breeds in Can. and Alaska; migrates through Pacific States and e. of Rockies in e. Mont., e. Wyo., and e. Colo.; also recorded from N.M. and Ariz. Winters in Calif. and Tex.

AUDUBON'S WARBLER. *Dendroica auduboni.* Subsp. (Illus. p. 150.)
Descr. 4¾-5¼. The Audubon's Warbler can be identified in any plumage by its bright *yellow rump*, in connection with its note, a loud *tchip*. *Male in spring:* — Blue-gray above, with a heavy black breast-patch shaped like an inverted U. Throat, crown, and side-patches yellow. The large white wing-patches are very distinctive. *Female in spring:* — Brown instead of gray, but pattern similar except for the conspicuous wing-patch. *Winter adults and young:* — Brownish above, whitish below, streaked with dark; throat and rump yellow. The comparatively rare Myrtle Warbler shows a similar yellow rump as it flies. (See Myrtle Warbler.)
Voice: — Song, loose and Junco-like in quality, but two-parted, either rising or dropping in pitch at the end, *seet-seet-seet-seet-seet, trrrrrrrr.* Note, a loud *tchip*.
Subsp. Audubon's Warbler. *D. a. auduboni.*
> Breeds from Can. s. to mts. of s. Calif., Ariz., and se. N.M.; winters in Pacific States and lower Rio Grande Valley, Tex.
> Black-fronted Warbler. *D. a. nigrifrons.*
> Breeding males often recognizable by the heavier, more extensive black area on the breast and sides, often greatly restricting the white area on the belly. Breeds in mts. of se. Ariz. (Huachuca and Chiricahua Mts., etc.).

BLACK-THROATED GRAY WARBLER. *Dendroica nigrescens.* (Illus. p. 150.)
Descr. 4½-5. Gray above and white below with a *black-and-white striped face.* (See diagram.) Most like the Townsend's

Warbler, which has *yellow* on face and under parts instead of white. The only other birds with *both* black cap and black bib are the Chickadees, which have *white cheeks*. *Females* lack the black throat but retain the black eye- and crown-patches. (See Black and White and Black-poll Warblers.)

Voice: — Song, a buzzy chant, *zeedle zeedle zeedle zeet' che* (next to last note higher than others). Song variable, sometimes ending on the higher note, but always recognizable by its drawly quality, which one observer characterized as 'full of z's.'

Range: — Breeds from Wash., Nev., n. Ut., and w. Colo. s. to s. Calif., s. Ariz., and s. N.M.

TOWNSEND'S WARBLER. *Dendroica townsendi.* (Illus. p. 150.)

Descr. 4¼–5. Easily distinguished by the *black-and-yellow striped head* (see diagram) and striped yellow under parts. The Hermit Warbler has a black throat but lacks the black cheek- and crown-patches. The Golden-cheeked Warbler, which resembles it even more closely, is found only in central and southern Texas. Female Townsend's Warblers have the throat largely yellow instead of black, but there is still enough of the male's yellow-and-black face and breast pattern to identify them.

Voice: — Song, similar to Black-throated Gray: '*Dzeer Dzeer Dzeer tseetsee.* The first three or four notes similar in pitch with a wheezy buzzy quality, followed by two or more quick higher-pitched sibilant notes' (H. H. Axtell).

Range: — Breeds from Can. s. to w. Ore., w. Mont., and w. Wyo. (occasionally); migrates throughout West; winters along coast from Wash. to Calif.

GOLDEN-CHEEKED WARBLER. *Dendroica chrysoparia.* (Illus. p. 150.)

Descr. 4¾. Found only in cedar-clad hills of cent. Tex. (see range below); the only Warbler with the combination of yellow cheeks and black throat found in this habitat. *Male:* — Similar to Townsend's Warbler (which is never found in cent. Tex.) but with less black on the cheeks, no yellow on the breast, and a *solid black* back. *Female:* — Similar to male but back olive-green (resembles Black-throated Green Warbler, but migrants of the latter species are always in hardwoods and shade trees of lowlands, when in cent. Tex.; Golden-cheeks are always in the cedar ridges).

Voice: — Song, 'a hurried *tweeah, tweeah, twee-sy,* with some individuals introducing an extra note or two' (H. P. Attwater). Has buzzy quality of Black-throated Green.

Range: — Breeds in a section of the Edwards Plateau of cent. Tex. from San Antonio and Austin w. to Kerr, Tom Green, and Concho Cos.

HERMIT WARBLER. *Dendroica occidentalis.* (Illus. p. 150.)
Descr. 4½–4¾. The bright *yellow face* set off by the *black throat*
and dark back is the best mark. The Townsend's Warbler has
black cheek- and crown-patches. It resembles more closely the
Eastern Black-throated Green Warbler. In the female the black
of the throat is replaced by grayish or white, but its general resemblance to the male is still evident. It can be told from the
female Townsend's by its grayer back and *white* instead of yellow
breast.
Voice: — Song, three high lisping two-syllabled notes followed
by two abrupt lower ones: *sweety, sweety, sweety, chup'-chup'*,
or *seedle, seedle, seedle, chup'-chup'*. The abrupt end notes are
very distinctive. Usually heard high in tall evergreens.
Range: — Breeds in Pacific States from w. Wash. s. through
Sierras of Calif. to Mt. Whitney. Migrates through s. Calif.,
Nev., and Ariz.

GRACE'S WARBLER. *Dendroica graciæ graciæ.* (Illus. p. 150.)
Descr. 4½. A *gray-backed Warbler with a yellow throat.* Belly
white; two white wing-bars, yellowish line over the eye, and
black stripes on the sides. Lives among pines high in sw. mts.
Easily distinguished from Audubon's Warbler by lack of black
across breast, and absence of yellow rump. Easterners will note
its close resemblance to Yellow-throated Warbler.
Voice: — A repetitious *cheedle cheedle che che che che*, ending in a
Chippy-like trill.
Range: — Breeds in pine forests on high mts. of sw. Colo., cent.
and e. Ariz., and N.M.

BLACK-POLL WARBLER. *Dendroica striata.* (Illus. p. 150.)
Descr. 5–5¾. *Male in spring:* — A striped gray Warbler with *a
solid black cap* and *white cheeks*; reminds the beginner of a Chickadee, but lacks the black throat. Might be confused with the
female Black-throated Gray Warbler, but the latter species has
black cheek-patches. The Black and White Warbler, the only
other species with which it might be confused, has a *striped*
crown, and black cheeks. *Female in spring:* — Less heavily
streaked, lacking the black crown-patch; a plain, black-streaked
Warbler, greenish-gray above, white below; may be known from
the Black and White by the lack of contrasting head-stripings,
and from the female Audubon's and Myrtle by the absence of
yellow in the plumage. *Autumn birds:* — Olive-green above,
with two white wing-bars; dingy yellow below, faintly streaked;
a drab greenish-looking Warbler with white wing-bars. (Orange-
crown lacks wing-bars.)
Voice: — Song, a high, thin, mechanical *zi — zi — zi — zi — zi
— zi — zi — zi — zi*, all on one pitch, becoming louder and more
emphatic in the middle of series.

Range: — A spring migrant e. of Rockies in e. Colo., e. Wyo., and e. Mont.

OVEN-BIRD. *Seirus aurocapillus.*

Descr. 5½–6½. A Sparrow-sized ground Warbler of the leafy woodlands; has somewhat the appearance of a small Thrush — olive-brown above, but *striped* rather than spotted beneath. A *light orange patch* on the top of the head is visible at close range. The bird is usually seen *walking* on pale *pinkish* legs over the leaves or along some log.

Voice: — The song is most graphically described as an emphatic *teach'er*, TEACH'ER, TEACH'ER, etc., repeated rapidly, louder and louder, till the air fairly rings with the vibrant accents (to be more exact, the accent is really on the *second* syllable thus: *cherte'a*, CHERTE'A, CHERTE'A, etc.).

Range: — Breeds in Black Hills section of ne. Wyo. and extreme se. Mont. and locally in cent. Colo.; migrates sparingly through se. Wyo. and e. Colo.; casual in Calif.

GRINNELL'S WATER-THRUSH. *Seiurus noveboracensis notabilis.* (Illus. p. 150.)

Descr. 5–6. The Water-Thrush is a brown-backed bird about the size of a Sparrow, with a *conspicuous light stripe over the eye, and heavily striped under parts.* Though a Warbler by anatomical structure, its life along the streams and wooded swamps has made it ridiculously like a little Sandpiper; when not running along the water's edge it is constantly *tettering* up and down in much the manner of the 'Spotty' of the shore. The light under parts are strongly tinged with yellowish or buffy. A race of the Northern Water-Thrush of e. U.S.

Voice: — A vigorous song often dropping in pitch and ending in a diagnostic *chew-chew-chew.*

Range: — Breeds from Can. s. locally to w. Mont.; an uncommon or rare migrant in Mont., Wyo., Colo., N.M., and Ariz. Casual in Calif.

MACGILLIVRAY'S WARBLER. *Oporornis tolmiei.* (Illus. p. 150.)

Descr. 4¾–5½. *Male:* — Olive above, yellow below, with a *slate-gray hood* completely encircling the head and neck, and a white *eye-ring.* The only remotely similar Warbler with a white eye-ring is the Calaveras, which has a *yellow* throat. *Female* similar, but hood much paler, and washed out on throat. Stays near the ground in brushy places.

Voice: — Song, a rolling chant, *chiddle, chiddle, chiddle, turtle-turtle,* the voice dropping on the last two notes; or *chiddle-chiddle-chiddle, wick, wick.* One popular interpretation of the song is *sweeter-sweeter-sweeter, sugar-sugar.* Some observers confuse it

with the two-parted song of the Calaveras Warbler, but it lacks
the well-measured brightness in the opening notes.
Range: — Breeds from Can. s. to cent. Calif., cent. Ariz., and
n. N.M.; migrates into Mex.

YELLOW-THROAT. *Geothlypis trichas.* Subsp. (Illus. p. 150.)
Descr. 4½–5½. The *male*, with its *black mask*, or 'domino,' needs
no detailed description. *Females and immature birds* are plain
olive-brown with a yellow throat and buffy-yellow breast. The
black mask is absent. They may be distinguished from any
other similar Warblers (female Yellow, female Pileolated, and
Orange-crown) by the *whitish* belly. The others are solid yellow
below. The habitat is swamps, stream-beds, and marshes.
Voice: — Song, very distinctive; a rapid, well-enunciated
witchity-witchity-witchity-witchity-witch. In some individuals this
is lengthened to *witchity-ta-witchity-ta-witchity-ta-witch,* or short-
ened to *witchy-witchy-witchy-witch.* The call-note, a husky *tchep,*
is also distinctive.
Range: — Breeds locally from Can. s. to s. Tex., N.M., s. Ariz.,
and s. Calif.; migrates throughout West. Winters in cent. and s.
Calif. and in s. Ariz.
Subsp. (No apparent field differences): (1) Western Yellow-
throat, *G. t. occidentalis*; (2) Salt Marsh Yellow-throat, *G. t.
sinuosa*; (3) Tule Yellow-throat, *G. t. scirpicola.*

RIO GRANDE YELLOW-THROAT. *Chamæthlypis poliocephala poliocephala.*
Descr. 5½. This Mexican species which has been authentically
recorded but a few times in the U.S. should not be confused with
the totally different Yellow-throat (*Geothlypis trichas*), a race of
which occurs in the lower Rio Grande Valley. It is a different
species, considerably larger, with a thicker, more Vireo-like bill.
The male can be immediately told by its *restricted black face-
patch between the eye and bill.* This is quite different from the extensive mask of *G. trichas.* The female lacks the black, but is
larger than the female Yellow-throat and lacks the whitish on
the belly.
Voice: — Song, cheerful and Bunting-like, not like that of *G.
trichas* (Sutton).
Range: — Occasional (formerly at least) in lower Rio Grande
Valley, Tex.

LONG-TAILED CHAT. *Icteria virens longicauda.* (Illus. p. 150.)
Descr. 6½–7½. Except for its color, the Chat seems more like a
small Thrasher or a Mocker than a Warbler. Its superior size
(considerably larger than a Sparrow), its rather long tail, its
eccentric song and actions, and its brushy habitat, all suggest
those larger birds. Both sexes are plain olive-brown above, with

white 'spectacles'; the throat and breast are *bright yellow*; the belly white. The long tail and the large size at once eliminate the possibility of its being any other Warbler. Habitat, brushy places along stream-beds, valleys, and canyons. A race of the Yellow-breasted Chat of e. U.S.

Voice: — An odd song made up of various harsh or whistled notes in repetitive series, suggestive of Mockingbird but with long deliberate pauses between series. Characteristic passages are: *chut-chut-chut-chut-chut-chut* (like Bullock's Oriole); *weck-weck-weck-weck-weck-weck*; *kook — kook — kook* (whistled), etc.

Range: — Breeds from Wash. and n. Mont. s. into Mex.

RED-FACED WARBLER. *Cardellina rubrifrons.* (Illus. p. 150.)
Descr. 5¼. A gray-backed Warbler with a *bright-red face and breast*; black patch on head, white nape, and white belly. The only other Western Warbler sporting the same shade of red is the Painted Redstart, which, however, has no red on the face.
Voice: — A clear sweet Warbler song similar to that of Yellow Warbler (Painted Redstart has a more repetitious quality).
Range: — High mts. of se. Ariz. and sw. N.M.

PILEOLATED WARBLER. *Wilsonia pusilla.* Subsp. (Illus. p. 150.)
Descr. 4¼–5. *Male:* — A yellow Warbler with a *round black cap.* *Females and immature* birds may, or may not, show traces of the black cap. If they do not, they appear as small, plain Warblers, olive-green above and bright yellow below, with *no streaks, wing-bars, or marks of any kind.* The aspect of the round, beady black eye superimposed on the yellow face is an aid. The Yellow Warbler is yellower above and shows *yellow* spots in the tail. The Orange-crown is much dingier, not so bright yellow below. The female Yellow-throat has a whitish belly. The preferred habitat is thick shrubbery in woodland openings. The Eastern Wilson's Warbler is a race of this bird.
Voice: — Song, a dry series of notes all on same pitch . . . *chi-chi-chi-chi-chit-Chit-Chit*, becoming louder and faster toward end (poco crescendo). Note, a husky *chip* or *chimp.*
Range: — Breeds from Can. s. in high mts. to w. Tex., n. N.M., n. Ariz., and s. Calif.; also in coast belt of Wash. and Ore. and along coast range s. to San Diego, Calif.; migrates throughout.
Subsp. (No apparent field differences): (1) Northern Pileolated Warbler, *W. p. pileolata*; (2) Golden Pileolated Warbler, *W. p. chryseola.*

AMERICAN REDSTART. *Setophaga ruticilla.* (Illus. p. 150.)
Descr. 4½–5½. The Redstart is one of the most butterfly-like of birds. It is constantly flitting about in sprightly fashion, drooping its wings and spreading fanwise its tail as if to make all who take notice admire. *Male:* — Largely black with *bright orange*

patches on the wings and tail; belly white. No other Warbler found in the W. is colored anything like it. *Female:* — Chiefly olive-brown above, white below, with large *yellow* flash-patches on the wings and tail. *Immature male:* — Considerable variation; much like the female; yellow often perceptibly tinged with orange. The typical Redstart pattern is obvious in any plumage. Habitat, saplings and second-growth deciduous timber.

Voice: — Two commonest songs, *tsee tsee tsee tsee tsee-o* (with drop on last syllable), and *teetsa teetsa teetsa teetsa teet* (double-noted). These two songs are commonly *alternated*, an excellent field aid.

Range: — Breeds in e. U.S. and diagonally nw. through Colo., n. Ut., Wyo., and Mont. to e. Ore. and e. Wash. Casual in migration in Calif., Ariz., and N.M.

PAINTED REDSTART. *Setophaga picta picta.* (Illus. p. 150.) **Descr.** 5. Black with *large white patches* in the wings and tail and a *large bright red patch* on the breast. The only other Warbler marked with the same shade of red is the Red-faced Warbler. The Painted Redstart has no red on the face. Sexes similar.

Voice: — Song, a repetitious *weeta weeta weeta wee* or *weeta weeta, chilp chilp chilp.* The note is a ringing Finch-like *clee-ip* or *che-ilp*, surprising in a Warbler.

Range: — High mts. of cent. and s. Ariz., sw. N.M., and w. Tex. (Chisos Mts.).

HOUSE SPARROW
A. Female   B. Male

WEAVER FINCHES: PLOCEIDÆ

HOUSE, *or* ENGLISH, SPARROW. *Passer domesticus domesticus.* (Illus. p. 162.)

1. BOBOLINK: a, *male*; b, *female*
2. LARK BUNTING: a, *male*; b, *female*

Descr. 5–6¼. A species with which everybody is familiar. Males have black throats, females whitish ones (see cut).
Range: — Distributed widely about civilization; about cities, towns, farms, and ranches throughout West.

MEADOWLARKS, BLACKBIRDS, AND ORIOLES: ICTERIDÆ

As MEMBERS of this group are so vastly different, it is difficult to make any generalizations for use in the field, except that they have conical, sharp-pointed bills and rather flat profiles. They are best characterized under their various species.

BOBOLINK. *Dolichonyx oryzivorus.* (Illus. p. 163.)
Descr. 6½–8. *Male in spring:* — A songbird that is *black below and largely white above,* a direct reversal of the normal tone-pattern of other birds, which are almost invariably lighter below. The male Lark Bunting resembles it somewhat but has its white areas *confined to the wings.* *Female and late summer and autumn male:* — Somewhat larger than Sparrows, largely *yellowish-buff* with *dark stripings* on the crown and upper parts. Frequents meadows and prairies.
Voice: — Song, long, reedy, and bubbling, starting with low melodious notes and rollicking upward in pitch.
Range: — Breeds in e. U.S. and diagonally nw. through Colo. (occasionally), Wyo., Mont., and n. Ut. to nw. Nev., ne. Calif. (rare), e. Ore., and e. Wash.; migrates through e. Colo.

RIO GRANDE MEADOWLARK. *Sturnella magna hoopesi.*
Descr. 8–9. A race of the Eastern Meadowlark. Very similar to

the Western Meadowlark but the yellow of the throat not so extensive; it does not edge into the cheeks. This is a fine point, hardly useful for field recognition. The species is most easily recognized by its song (below).

Voice: — Song, clear slurred whistles, might be rendered *tee-you*, *tee-yair*, very different from bubbly, flute-like song of Western Meadowlark.

Range: — Se. Ariz., s. N.M., and s. Tex., s. into Mex.

WESTERN MEADOWLARK. *Sturnella neglecta.* (Illus. p. 164.) **Descr.** 8–10. Our first acquaintance with the Meadowlark usually comes early in our studies. On crossing some extensive field or piece of open country, a rather large, chunky brown bird flushes from the grass, showing a conspicuous patch of *white* on each side of the short, wide tail. Several other ground-dwelling birds, the Pipit, Longspur, Vesper Sparrow, and Junco show similar white outer tail-feathers. All of these are very much smaller, with the slimmer proportions of Sparrows. Should we see a Meadowlark perched on some distant fence post, our glass will reveal a bright yellow breast crossed by a black V, or gorget. (See plate.) The Flicker is similarly sized and brown above, but with a white *rump* instead of white sides of the tail, and it flies in a very different, *bounding* manner. The Meadowlark's flight is distinctive — several short, rapid wing-beats alternated with short periods of sailing.

Voice: — A variable song of seven to ten notes, flute-like, gurgling and double-noted.

Range: — Breeds from Can. s. to Mex.; winters from Wash. and Mont. s.

YELLOW-HEADED BLACKBIRD. *Xanthocephalus xanthocephalus.* (Illus. p. 164.)

Descr. 8–11. *Male:* — A Robin-sized Blackbird with a *yellow* head; shows a conspicuous white patch in the wing in flight. Females are smaller and browner, with most of the yellow confined to the throat and upper breast. Inhabits marshes.

Voice: — Note, a low *krick* or *kack.* Song, low hoarse rasping notes produced with much effort, 'like rusty hinges on the old barn door' (Lockerbie).

Range: — Breeds from Can. s. to s. Calif., n. Ariz., and N.M., and from Great Plains w. to e. Wash., e. Ore., and interior of Calif.; winters from sw. Calif., s. Ariz., and s. N.M. s. into Mex.

COMMON RED-WING. *Agelaius phœniceus.* Subsp. (Illus. p. 164.)

Descr. 7–9½. *Male:* — Black, with *red epaulets* or patches at the bend of the wings. Absolutely unmistakable. Often, when at rest, the scarlet is concealed, only the buffy or yellowish margin

RED–WINGS, MEADOWLARKS, BLACKBIRDS, ORIOLES, GROSBEAKS BUNTINGS, TOWHEES, SPARROWS

1. RED-WING, *a.* MALE; *b.* FEMALE

2. WESTERN MEADOWLARK

3. YELLOW-HEADED BLACKBIRD, *a.* MALE; *b.* FEMALE

4. BULLOCK'S ORIOLE, *a.* MALE; *b.* FEMALE

5. AUDUBON'S ORIOLE

6. SCOTT'S ORIOLE, *a.* MALE; *b.* FEMALE

7. HOODED ORIOLE, *a.* MALE; *b.* FEMALE

8. BLACK-HEADED GROSBEAK, *a.* MALE; *b.* FEMALE

9. BLUE GROSBEAK, *a.* MALE; *b.* FEMALE

10. VARIED BUNTING, *a.* MALE; *b.* FEMALE

11. PAINTED BUNTING, *a.* MALE; *b.* FEMALE

12. LAZULI BUNTING, *a.* MALE; *b.* FEMALE

13. GREEN-TAILED TOWHEE

14. TEXAS SPARROW

15. DICKCISSEL, *a.* MALE; *b.* FEMALE

16. *a.* BROWN TOWHEE; *b.* CAÑON TOWHEE

17. ABERT'S TOWHEE

18. SPOTTED TOWHEE, *a.* MALE; *b.* FEMALE

of the red patch being visible. *Immature male:* — Dusky-brown, but with the scarlet patches of the adult male. *Female and young:* — Brownish; identified by the sharp-pointed bill, Blackbird appearance, and *well-defined stripings below.* No other female Blackbirds (except next species) have these breast-streakings. Inhabits marshes and swampy places. One race, known as the Bicolored Red-wing (San Francisco Bay region and Sacramento and San Joaquin Valleys of Calif.) differs from other Red-wings in having the 'epaulets' *solid red*, without yellow edges.

Voice: — Notes, a loud *check* and a high, slurred *tee-err.* Song, a gurgling *konk-la-reeee* or *o-ka-leee*, the last note trilled or quavered.

Range: — Nearly all parts of W., from Can. to Mex., where there are suitable marshes; winters in varying abundance over a large part of the W., but shows a tendency to migrate out of colder sections.

Subsp. (No apparent field differences except in No. 6 — see above): (1) Giant Red-wing, *A. p. arctolegus*; (2) Thick-billed Red-wing, *A. p. fortis*; (3) Nevada Red-wing, *A. p. nevadensis*; (4) Northwestern Red-wing, *A. p. caurinus*; (5) San Francisco Red-wing, *A. p. mailliardorum*; (6) Bicolored Red-wing, *A. p. californicus*; (7) Kern Red-wing, *A. p. aciculatus*; (8) San Diego Red-wing, *A. p. neutralis*; (9) Sonora Red-wing, *A. p. sonoriensis*.

TRICOLORED RED-WING. *Agelaius tricolor.*
Descr. 7½–9. *Male:* — Similar to Common Red-wing but with *white* edge on red patch instead of yellow. *Female:* — Very similar to female Common Red-wing but under parts darker. This species nests in large densely crowded colonies often numbering many thousands, whereas *A. phœniceus* is territorial.

Voice: — Notes, quite different from Red-wing's; harsher and less musical.

Range: — S. Ore. (Klamath Lake) and valleys of Calif. (w. of Sierras).

ORCHARD ORIOLE. *Icterus spurius.*
Descr. 6–7¼. *Adult male:* — A *chestnut*-and-black Oriole; all other male Orioles are either bright orange or yellow. Females are difficult to tell from other female Orioles but are decidedly *greener.* Young males have the greenish cast, and a black throat-patch.

Range: — E. U.S., breeding w. to w. Tex. (Brewster Co. and Davis Mts.); occasional in e. Colo. and e. Wyo.

AUDUBON'S ORIOLE. *Icterus melanocephalus auduboni* (Illus. p. 164.)

Descr. 8–9¼. A *yellow* Oriole with black head, wings, and tail. The *yellowish back* is absolutely distinctive. All other male Orioles have black backs. The sexes are similar. The only other black-headed, *yellow* Oriole, the Scott's, is found farther w., and not in the range of this species in s. Tex.

Voice: — Song, quite different from those of other Orioles; made up of low whistled notes of a human quality, disjointed, with half-tones; suggests a small boy learning to whistle.

Range: — Resident in lower Rio Grande Valley, Tex. (casually to San Antonio).

HOODED ORIOLE. *Icterus cucullatus.* Subsp. (Illus. p. 164.)
Descr. 7–7¾. *Male:* — Orange and black with a black throat and *orange crown* or 'hood.' It is the only Oriole with the top of the head orange. *Female:* — Back olive-gray, head and tail dull yellowish, under parts yellowish, wings with two white bars. Similar to female Bullock's Oriole, but with under parts entirely yellow (Bullock's has whitish belly). The immature male resembles the female but has a *black throat.* The extensively yellow belly will separate it from the corresponding plumage of the Bullock's. The bill of this species is slenderer, more curved than that of Bullock's.

Voice: — Song, a mixture of throaty notes and piping whistles, *chut chut chut whew whew,* the opening notes throaty. Song sometimes more musical. Note, a sharp *eek.*

Range: — Breeds in s. and s.-cent. Calif., s. Ariz., sw. N.M., and lower Rio Grande Valley, Tex.

Subsp. SENNETT'S ORIOLE. *I. c. sennetti.*
Breeds in lower Rio Grande Valley, Tex.
ARIZONA HOODED ORIOLE. *I. c. nelsoni.*
Breeds in s. and s.-cent. Calif., s. Ariz., and sw. N.M.; winters in Mex.

ALTA MIRA ORIOLE. *Icterus gularis tamaulipensis.*
Descr. 8¼–9¼. A Mexican species, accidental near Brownsville, Tex. 'Almost exactly like Sennett's Hooded Oriole, but larger, thicker-billed, and more orange (does not shade off to yellow on rump and belly). The main field-mark is the upper wing-bar, which is *yellow or orange* instead of white. Sexes similar.' (Irby Davis.)

SCOTT'S ORIOLE. *Icterus parisorum.* (Illus. p. 164.)
Descr. 7¼–8¼. *Male:* — A lemon-yellow Oriole with black head, back, wings, and tail. The *solid black head* and the *yellow* instead of orange under parts distinguish it immediately from the two other Orioles which are found in its range, the Bullock's and Hooded. *Female:* — Similar to other female Orioles but of a more greenish-yellow cast beneath. (Female Hooded has more

orange-yellow under parts; female Bullock's, a whitish belly)
The immature male has a black throat similar to that of the
young male Hooded Oriole. The dingier coloration of the under
parts and the *grayish* instead of yellow cheeks will identify it.
The preferred habitat of this species is desert country, especially
where tree yuccas or agaves predominate.
Voice: — Song made up of rich variable whistled notes; suggests
Western Meadowlark.
Range: — Breeds in desert country of s. Calif., s. Nev., sw. Ut.,
Ariz., s. and cent. N.M., and w. Tex.

BALTIMORE ORIOLE. *Icterus galbula.*
Descr. 7–8. *Male:* — Bright orange and black, known from the
male Bullock's Oriole by the *solid black head* and smaller amount
of white in the wing. Along the w. edge of the Great Plains,
where the ranges of these two species overlap, puzzling hybrids
sometimes occur. *Female:* — Similar to female Bullock's, but
much more orange-yellow below, not so whitish on the belly;
back not so gray.
Range: — Summer resident in e. U.S., rarely w. to e. Mont., e.
Wyo., and e. Colo., e. of Rocky Mts. Casual in Ut.

BULLOCK'S ORIOLE. *Icterus bullocki.* (Illus. p. 164.)
Descr. 7½–8½. Smaller than a Robin. The *male* is fiery *orange
and black*, with large *white wing-patches*. Except for the Redstart, the Orioles are the only birds colored with such intense
orange. This is the only Oriole found in most sections of w.
U.S. It can be told from the others by its black crown and
orange cheeks. *Female and young:* — Olive-gray above, yellowish on tail and under parts; two white wing-bars. Female
Orioles resemble female Tanagers somewhat, but Tanagers are
darker above and on the sides of the head, and do not have such
sharp-pointed bills. This species, which looks the least Tanager-
like, resembles the females and young of other Orioles, but is less
extensively yellow below, usually with much *whitish on the belly.*
The back is decidedly grayer. Immature males resemble females but have *black throats.* They can be told from the corresponding plumage of the Hooded Oriole by the whiteness of
the belly.
Voice: — A series of accented double notes with one or two
piping notes thrown in. Call-note, a sharp *skip*; also a chatter.
Range: — Breeds from Can. s. into Mex.; winters in Mex.

RUSTY BLACKBIRD. *Euphagus carolinus.*
Descr. 8½–9½. *Male in spring:* — Very similar to male Brewer's
Blackbird, but at close range will be seen to have dull greenish
instead of purplish head reflections. The iridescence is almost
lacking, not noticeable as in the Brewer's Blackbird or the

A. BRONZED GRACKLE   B. BREWER'S BLACKBIRD, *male*

Bronzed Grackle. *Female in spring:* — Slate-colored; resembles female Brewer's Blackbird but grayer, and with the eyes *yellowish* instead of dark. *Adults and young in autumn and winter:* — Very easy to identify; more or less tinged with *rusty*, closely barred beneath. Female Red-wings are heavily *striped* beneath, not barred. No other Blackbird gives the effect of being washed with rusty or ochre on the body.
Range: — Probably a regular migrant through e. Colo., e. Wyo., and e. Mont., but often overlooked. Casual in Calif.

BREWER'S BLACKBIRD. *Euphagus cyanocephalus.* (Illus. p. 168.)
Descr. 8–9½. *Male:* — A Blackbird with a white eye; shows *purplish* reflections on head and greenish reflections on body in strong light. Looks all black at a distance. Distinguished from Red-wing by lack of red shoulders and from Cowbird by longer tail and longer, more pointed bill. *Female:* — Brownish-gray with dark eyes. Distinguished from female Red-wing by lack of stripings, and from female Cowbird by longer bill.
Voice: — Note, a harsh *check*. Song, a harsh wheezy *que-ee* or *ksh-eee*, like the creaking of a rusty hinge.
Range: — Breeds from Can. s. to Calif., n. Ariz., and N.M.; winters from Wash. and Mont. (occasionally) s. into Mex.

GREAT-TAILED GRACKLE. *Cassidix mexicanus mexicanus.* (Illus. p. 169.)
Descr. ♂ 16–17, ♀ 12–13. The Great-tail, or 'Jackdaw,' is at once recognized by its large size, a Blackbird well over a foot long with a long, wide *keel-shaped* tail. It is smaller than a Crow

GREAT-TAILED GRACKLE

or Raven, considerably larger than a Brewer's Blackbird. The proportionately large, creased tail is the best mark. The only other Grackle, the Bronzed, would not occur in the same range in the area covered by this book. Females are brown, not black, and are *much* smaller than the males.

Voice: — A harsh *check check check*, also a variety of harsh whistles and clucks.

Range: — Occurs locally in s. and w. Tex. and s. N.M., especially along Pecos and Rio Grande; possible in se. Ariz.

BRONZED GRACKLE. *Quiscalus quiscula æneus.* (Illus. p. 168.)
Descr. 11–13. Grackles are large Blackbirds, larger than Robins, with long wedge-shaped tails. A crease in the center often gives the tail a keel-shaped appearance. The line of flight is more even, not as undulating as that of other Blackbirds. Like the male Brewer's Blackbird, this species has a pale eye and iridescent coloring, but the larger size and longer tail, *which is somewhat wedge-shaped*, are good marks. The Brewer's is about the size of a Red-wing; this species, considerably larger.

Voice: — Note, *chack*; 'song,' harsh, squeaky notes.

Range: — Breeds in e. U.S. w. to foothills of Rockies in Mont., e. Wyo., and e. Colo.; casual in Ut.

COMMON COWBIRD. *Molothrus ater.* Subsp. (Illus. p. 170.)
Descr. 7–8. A rather small Blackbird with a short, conical, Sparrow-like bill. The *male* is the only black bird with a *brown* head. The *female* is uniformly gray. She can be told from the female Red-wing by her lack of streakings and from the female

A. COWBIRD, *male* B. RED-EYED COWBIRD, *male*

Brewer's Blackbird by the shorter bill and smaller size. When mixed in with other Blackbirds, Cowbirds are obviously smaller and walk about with their tails lifted high off the ground. The Finch-like bill is always a good mark.

Voice: — Note, *chuck*. Song, bubbly and creaky, *glug — glug — gleeee*, or *klug-tseeee*, last note high-pitched.

Range: — Breeds e. of Cascades and Sierras from Can. to Mex., and also in cent. and s. Calif. Rare in w. Ore. and w. Wash. Tends to winter in s. part of range.

Subsp. (No apparent field differences): (1) Eastern Cowbird, *M. a. ater*; (2) Nevada Cowbird, *M. a. artemisiæ*; (3) California Cowbird, *M. a. californicus*; (4) Dwarf Cowbird, *M. a. obscurus*.

RED-EYED COWBIRD. *Tangavius æneus.* (Illus. p. 170.)
Descr. $6\frac{1}{2}$–$8\frac{3}{4}$. *Male:* — Larger than the Cowbird and more uniform in coloration (does not have brown head). The red eye can only be seen at close range. The most distinctive field-mark in the breeding season is a conspicuous *ruff* on the back of the neck. Females are smaller, with smaller neck ruffs. They are dull blackish, more like their mates, not gray like females of *M. ater*.
Range: — S. Tex. n. to San Antonio. A race of this bird, the status of which is still unsettled, is occasional in Ariz. (vicinity of Tucson).

TANAGERS: THRAUPIDÆ

THE males of the group are among the most brilliant-colored of birds, the three species occurring in the West possessing more or less bright red. Females are duller, green above and yellow below, a little like large Warblers or Vireos; they are somewhat larger than House Sparrows. Female Tanagers are most likely to be confused with Orioles, but are sluggish, much less active, and do not have such sharp-pointed bills. The dark color of the crown comes down over the cheeks farther — nearly to the throat.

WESTERN TANAGER. *Piranga ludoviciana.* (See Frontis.)
Descr. 6¼–7. *Male:* — Yellow and black, with a *red face.* Totally unlike any other American bird. Males in autumn lose most of the red. *Female:* — Dull greenish above and yellowish below. It is the only female Tanager with conspicuous white or yellowish wing-bars. It resembles the female Bullock's Oriole, but the tail and the sides of the face are darker. The bill is shorter and not so sharply pointed.
Voice: — Song, made up of short phrases, similar to those of Black-headed Grosbeak or Robin in form, but less sustained and hoarser ('like a Grosbeak or Robin with a sore throat'). Note, a dry *pi-tic* or *pit-i-tic.*
Range: — Breeds from Can. s. to mts. of s. Calif., s. Ariz., N.M., and w. Tex.; winters in Mex.

HEPATIC TANAGER. *Piranga flava hepatica.* (See Frontis.)
Descr. 7–7¾. *Male:* — A bright-red Tanager of the sw. mts. Can be told from Cooper's Tanager by darker coloration (orange-red or flame-red), *dark ear-patch,* and *blackish bill.* (Cooper's has yellowish-brown bill.) *Female:* — Dusky above, yellowish below; can be told from female Orioles by shorter bill and lack of wing-bars, and from female Cooper's Tanager by more orange-yellow throat and *blackish* instead of yellow lower mandible. Although the two species can be found together in places, the typical habitat of the Hepatic is mountain woodlands; that of the Cooper's, low stream-bottoms.
Voice: — Song, similar to that of Cooper's Tanager, but call-note quite different, a single *chuck.*
Range: — Breeds in mts. of Ariz., N.M., and w. Tex.

COOPER'S TANAGER. *Piranga rubra cooperi.* (See Frontis.)
Descr. 7–7½. *Male:* — Bright rose-red *all over* (does not have crest like Cardinal). *Female:* — Olive above, deep yellow below. The wings lack the conspicuous white or yellowish wing-bars possessed by the female Western Tanager and the female Orioles, which it otherwise resembles. *Immature males* acquiring the adult plumage may be patched with red and green. This species is a race of the Eastern Summer Tanager. (See Hepatic Tanager.)
Voice: — Song made up of short phrases, Robin-like in form,

not as 'burry' as Western Tanager. Has quality similar to that of the Black-headed Grosbeak's song. Note, *chick-tuk*, or *chick-i-tuck*, somewhat similar to Western Tanager.

Range: — Breeds chiefly along river-bottoms in se. Calif. (Colo. R.), s. Nev., s. and cent. Ariz., s. and cent. N.M., and w. Tex.

GROSBEAKS, FINCHES, SPARROWS, AND BUNTINGS: FRINGILLIDÆ

THE best character by which this family can be recognized is the bill, which is short and stout, adapted for seed-cracking. The birds not belonging to this group which are most apt to be mistaken for *Fringillidæ*, because of their stout, conical bills, are the Cowbirds and the Bobolinks. Three types of bills exist within the group: that of the Grosbeak, extremely large, thick, and rounded in outline; the more ordinary Canary-like bill, possessed by most of the Finches, Sparrows, and Buntings; and that of the Crossbill, the mandibles of which are crossed, somewhat like pruning shears, at the tips. Many of the Grosbeaks, Finches, and Buntings are highly colored, in contrast to the Sparrows, which are, for the most part, plain, streaked with brown.

CARDINAL. *Richmondena cardinalis.* Subsp. (Illus. p. 178.)
Descr. 8–9. Smaller than a Robin. *Male:* — All red except for black patch at base of bill; *the only all-red bird with a crest.* (The Pyrrhuloxia is red and gray.) *Female:* — Largely yellowish-brown, with some red; at once recognizable by crest and heavy red bill. The female Pyrrhuloxia is similar but gray-backed and with a yellow bill.
Voice: — Song, a series of clear slurred whistled notes; several variations; note, a short thin chip.
Range: — S. Ariz., sw. N.M., and cent., w., and s. Tex. Cardinals occurring in s. Calif. are supposedly introduced (probably Eastern birds).
Subsp. (No apparent field differences): (1) Gray-tailed Cardinal, *R. c. canicauda*; (2) Arizona Cardinal, *R. c. superba*.

PYRRHULOXIA. *Pyrrhuloxia sinuata.* (Illus. p. 178.)
Descr. 7½–8¼. *Male:* — A slender *gray and red Finch with a crest*, and a small stubby, almost Parrot-like bill. The rose-colored breast and crest suggest the male Cardinal, but the gray back at once sets it apart. Females are gray-backed and yellow-breasted with a touch of red in the wings and crest. They resemble female Cardinals but have yellow bills. The latter birds are brown-backed, and have large red bills. This species prefers arid country with a growth of mesquite and similar chaparral.

Voice: — Song, a clear *quink quink quink quink quink*, all on one note; also a slurred whistled *what-cheer, what-cheer*, etc., thinner and shorter than Cardinal's song.
Range: — S. Ariz., s. N.M., and w. and s. Tex.

BLACK-HEADED GROSBEAK. *Hedymeles melanocephalus.*
Subsp. (Illus. p. 164.)
Descr. 6½–7¾. *Male:* — The *rusty* breast, *black* head, and boldly marked black-and-white wings make it unmistakable. The only Western birds whose coloration remotely resembles it are the Robin, Varied Thrush, and Spotted Towhee, none of which would be confused with it. *Female:* — Largely brown, but easily recognized by its *rusty-brown* breast, *striped head*, and heavy pale bill.
Voice: — Song made up of rising and falling passages; resembles song of Robin, but more fluent and mellow; note, a sharp *ik* or *eek*. Easterners will note resemblance to Rose-breasted Grosbeak's voice.
Range: — Breeds from Can. s. to Mex.
Subsp. (No apparent field differences): (1) Black-headed Grosbeak, *H. m. melanocephalus*; (2) Rocky Mountain Grosbeak, *H. m. papago.*

BLUE GROSBEAK. *Guiraca cœrulea.* Subsp. (Illus. p. 164.)
Descr. 6½–7½. *Male:* — Deep dull blue; appears black at distance, then resembling Cowbird. The only other *all-blue* bird is the Mountain Bluebird. The Grosbeak has a much larger bill than the Bluebird, and shows two broad *chestnut-brown* wing-bars. *Female:* — Larger than House Sparrow, or about size of Cowbird; brown, lighter below, with two *buffy* wing-bars. The female Lazuli Bunting resembles it somewhat, but is smaller (smaller than House Sparrow), with a much smaller bill. The preferred habitat is willows or brush along low stream-bottoms.
Voice: — Song, a Finch-like warble, short phrases rising and falling. Suggests song of Purple Finch but slower in tempo. Note, a sharp *pink* slightly more musical than similar note of Brown Towhee.
Range: — Breeds in river-valleys in s. and cent. Calif., s. Nev., s. Colo., Ariz., N.M., and w. Tex.
Subsp. (No apparent field differences): (1) Western Blue Grosbeak, *G. c. interfusa*; (2) California Blue Grosbeak, *G. c. salicaria.*

LAZULI BUNTING. *Passerina amœna.* (Illus. p. 164.)
Descr. 5–5½. *Male:* — A small bright-blue Finch. Head and upper parts *turquoise blue*; band across breast and sides *cinnamon*; belly and wing-bars white. It is most likely to be mistaken by the beginner for a Western Bluebird, but the small size, short

Finch bill, and *white wing-bars* are the distinctive points.
Female: — A small nondescript Finch, *brownish* above and below, lightening on throat and belly. It has whitish wing-bars,
and at close range just a trace of gray-blue in the wings and tail.
The lack of streakings on the back or breast distinguish it from
any of the dull Sparrows. It can be told from the female Blue
Grosbeak by its smaller size, smaller bill, whiter wing-bars, and
darker coloration. Prefers dry brushy canyon-slopes and hillsides.
Voice: — A high and strident Finch song with well-measured
phrases at varying pitches. Introductory notes usually paired
— *sweet-sweet, chew-chew,* etc. Easterners will note resemblance
to Indigo Bunting's song.
Range: — Breeds from Can. s. to s. Calif., n. Ariz. (probably),
n. N.M. (a few), and w. Tex.; migrates into Mex.

VARIED BUNTING. *Passerina versicolor.* Subsp. (Illus.
p. 164.)
Descr. $4\frac{1}{2}$–$5\frac{1}{2}$. *Male:* — A small dark Finch with a plum-purple
body (looks black at distance); crown blue with a *bright red
patch on the nape,* 'colored like an Easter egg.' The nearest
thing to it is the more brightly colored Painted Bunting, which
has a bright red breast. *Female:* — A small plain *gray-brown*
Finch with a lighter breast. *No wing-bars, stripes, or distinctive
marks of any kind.* Very similar to female Indigo Bunting, but
latter species is browner with a trace of wing-bars and faint
blurry breast-streakings. Female Seedeater is smaller and
browner and has wing-bars. Immature male Varied Buntings
are tinged with bluish. This species prefers dry mesquite
thickets.
Voice: — Song, a thin bright Finch song, more distinctly
phrased and less warbled than Painted Bunting. Notes not so
distinctly paired as in song of Lazuli Bunting.
Range: — Breeds in lower Rio Grande Valley, Tex.; local or
casual in s. Ariz. and se. Calif.
Subsp. (No apparent field differences): (1) Varied Bunting,
P. v. versicolor; (2) Beautiful Bunting, *P. v. pulchra.*

PAINTED BUNTING. *Passerina ciris.* (Illus. p. 164.)
Descr. $5\frac{1}{4}$. Of all our birds undoubtedly the most gaudily colored. *Male:* — A little Chippy-sized Finch, a patchwork of
bright red, green, and indigo — blue-violet on head, green on
back, red on rump and under parts. *Female:* — Very plain;
greenish above, paling to lemon-green below; no wing-bars.
The only other small greenish Finch, the female Arkansas Goldfinch, has whitish wing-bars.
Voice: — Song, a bright, pleasing warble; resembles song of
Warbling Vireo but more wiry; note, a sharp chip.

Range: — Breeds in se. U.S. w. to w. Tex. and s. N.M. (Pecos and Rio Grande Valleys); occasional in s. Ariz.

DICKCISSEL. *Spiza americana.* (Illus. p. 164.)
Descr. 6–7. About size of House Sparrow but a bit slimmer. *Male:* — Suggestive of tiny Meadowlark, with yellow breast and black bib. *Female:* — Very much like female House Sparrow, but paler, with much whiter stripe over eye, touch of yellow on breast, and bluish bill. Chestnut bend of wing is also distinctive. The Dickcissel is a frequenter of prairie country. Males in fall have the black of throat obscured or lacking.
Voice: — Song, a staccato, mechanical-sounding rendering of its name — *Dick-ciss-ciss-ciss.*
Range: — Breeds in e. Wyo. and e. Colo. (a few); migrates through Tex.; occasional in N.M. and Ariz.

EVENING GROSBEAK. *Hesperiphona vespertina.* Subsp. (Illus. p. 178.)
Descr. 7½–8½. A large, chunky, short-tailed Finch, considerably larger than House Sparrow. The dusky, dull yellowish color, and extremely large, conical whitish bill distinguish it at once. A wing, recognized as a Finch by the characteristic undulating flight and distinguished from Pine Grosbeak, only Conifer Finch of similar size, by shorter tail. The large white wing-patches show at a great distance in flight. Snow Bunting is only other northern or winter Finch showing so much white in wing. *Male:* — Body clouded with dusky around head and breast, dull yellowish toward rear parts; wings black with large white patches, bright yellow patch on forehead. *Female:* — Gray, but with just enough of the yellow and the black and white to be recognizable. The female Pine Grosbeak is slimmer, with a smaller *dark* bill, much less white in the wing, *none in the tail.* The Eastern Evening Grosbeak, which winters s. to e. Wyo. and probably Wash., is easily distinguished from the Western bird by its less dusky coloration. The yellow is much more extensive on the back and under parts.
Voice: — Song, a short uneven warble; note, a ringing Finch-like chirp, *cleer* or *clee-ip.*
Range: — Breeds in high mts. from Can. s. to Sierra Nevada of cent. Calif. and mts. of s. Ariz. and N.M. Winters in adjacent lowlands and s. to s. Calif.
Subsp. (No apparent field differences except in No. 1 — see above): (1) Eastern Evening Grosbeak, *H. v. vespertina;* (2) Western Evening Grosbeak, *H. v. brooksi;* (3) Mexican Evening Grosbeak, *H. v. montana.*

CALIFORNIA PURPLE FINCH. *Carpodacus purpureus californicus.* (Illus. p. 178.)

Descr. 5¼–6. Purple is hardly the word; old rose is more like it. *Male:* — About size of House Sparrow or Linnet, rosy-red, brightest on head and rump ('like a Sparrow dipped in berry juice'). It resembles closely the male House Finch, or Linnet, but *lacks* the sharp dark streakings on the breast and belly. In parts of the Sierras and Cascades, the breeding ranges of the California Purple Finch and the Cassin's Purple Finch overlap. The latter species can be told by its pale breast coloration and the squarish red crown-patch, which contrasts abruptly with the brown of the neck and back. The red of the California Purple Finch blends in more smoothly. (See Pine Grosbeak and Redpoll.) *Female:* — A heavily striped brown Sparrow-like bird with a broad whitish line over the eye. The large stout bill distinguishes it from the streaked Sparrows. The best mark of distinction from the female House Finch is the *dark cheek-patch behind the eye,* bordered above and below by broad pale stripes. Immature birds resemble females. (See Cassin's Purple Finch.) **Voice:** — Song, a fast, lively warble; resembles song of House Finch but is lower in pitch, shorter in length, less disjointed; more rolling and well knit. Note, a dull metallic *tick,* or *pit,* unlike any note of the House Finch.
Range: — Breeds in Transition Zone of Pacific States from Can. to Mex. and e. to Cascades and Sierra Nevadas. Distributed more widely in winter.

CASSIN'S PURPLE FINCH. *Carpodacus cassini.* (Illus. p. 178.)
Descr. 6–6½. The Purple Finch of the Rocky Mt. region. (It occasionally wanders to the Coast.) *Male:* — Similar to the California Purple Finch (which breeds only in Pacific States) but larger, red of breast paler, and tail more deeply notched; *squarish red crown-patch contrasting abruptly with brown of neck and back.* This and the *lack* of sharply defined belly streakings distinguish it from the House Finch. See Pine Grosbeak and Redpoll. *Female:* — A streaked brown Sparrow-like bird; back olive-gray streaked with black; under parts whitish narrowly streaked with dark. The larger size and sharper dark stripings on the back and under parts distinguish it from the female House Finch. The larger size, whiter under parts, and narrow breast-streakings distinguish it from the female California Purple Finch.
Voice: — Song, a lively warble, similar to that of California Purple Finch but not so closely knit; halfway between song of House Finch and Purple Finch.
Range: — Breeds in high mts. from Can. s. to n. Ariz. and n. N.M., and from Rockies w. to Cascades and Sierras, where the California Purple Finch is also found; Cassin's prefers higher altitudes. Wanders to adjacent lowlands in winter.

HOUSE FINCH, *or* **LINNET.** *Carpodacus mexicanus.* Subsp. (Illus. p. 178.)

Descr. 5½. *Male:* — Near size of House Sparrow, brownish with *bright red* breast, forehead, stripe over eye, and rump. It resembles the male of the Purple Finches (which do not nest about buildings) but is brighter red, not so rose-colored. Some individuals are almost orange. The *narrow dark stripes* on the sides and belly are the best mark of distinction. *Female:* — A striped Sparrow-like bird, gray-brown above; under parts whitish streaked with dusky. See female California Purple Finch and female Cassin's Purple Finch.

Voice: — A bright lengthy Finch song, loose and disjointed in structure. Sometimes the song ends in a harsh nasal *wheer* or *che-urr.* Notes, Finch-like, some of them reminiscent of chirping of English Sparrow but more musical.

Range: — Resident in lowlands, deserts, open country, foot-hills, and towns from se. Wash., Ore., s. Idaho, and s. Wyo. s. into Mex.

Subsp. (No apparent field differences): (1) Common House Finch, *C. m. frontalis*; (2) San Clemente House Finch, *C. m. clementis*; (3) San Luis House Finch, *C. m. potosinus.*

SHARPE'S SEEDEATER. *Sporophila morelleti sharpei.* (Illus. p. 178.)

Descr. 3¾–4¼. *Male:* — A very small Finch with whitish or buffy under parts and blackish upper parts, wings, and tail. Much white in the wing; bill very short, stubby, and swollen. There is often a narrow, indistinct dark breast-band and a light collar around the neck. The Goldfinch (*Spinus tristis*) in winter plumage resembles this species but has a bigger, longer bill. *Female:* — A tiny brown-backed Finch with buffy under parts and light wing-bars. The small size, buffy under parts, and stubby bill are good marks. The amount of white in the wings varies (See female Varied Bunting.)

Voice: — A sweet loud song for so small a bird; begins on several high repeated notes and drops to several notes on a lower pitch; *sweet sweet sweet sweet, cheer cheer cheer cheer* (often only two *cheers*).

Range: — Lower Rio Grande Valley, Tex.

PINE GROSBEAK. *Pinicola enucleator.* Subsp. (Illus. p. 178.)

Descr. 8–9½. The largest of the Conifer Finches; near the size of a Robin. *Male:* — Large size, rosy-red color, and two white wing-bars identify it. (The White-winged Crossbill is rosy-red with white wing-bars, but is smaller, about size of House Sparrow, with slender cross-tipped bill.) *Female:* — Gray with two white wing-bars; head and rump tinged with yellow. *Immature male:* — Similar to female but with touch of red on head and rump. A Robin-sized Finch in the conifer forests of the high mountains is quite surely this species. The Evening Grosbeak is shorter-tailed, with chunkier proportions. All Finches rise and fall in their flight, but this one is a regular 'roller-coaster.' **Voice:** — Song, melodious; most characteristic call, a clear three-syllabled whistle, *tee-tee-tew*, remarkably like cry of Greater Yellow-legs.

Range: — Resident in high mts. from Can. s. to n. N.M., cent.-e. Ariz., and cent. Sierra Nevada, Calif.; winters sometimes to lower altitudes, esp. in nw.

Subsp. (No apparent field differences): (1) Alaska Pine Grosbeak, *P. e. alascensis*; (2) Kodiak Pine Grosbeak, *P. e. flammula*; (3) Rocky Mountain Pine Grosbeak, *P. e. montana*; (4) California Pine Grosbeak, *P. e. californica*.

GRAY-CROWNED ROSY FINCH, *or* **LEUCOSTICTE.** *Leucosticte tephrocotis.* Subsp. (Illus. p. 178.)
Descr. 5¾–6¾. A Sparrow-sized bird of the snow-fields of nigh mts. above timber line. *Dark brown body* with a *pinkish wash* on the wings and rump. The dark brown breast and *light gray patch* on the back of the head distinguish this species from the other rose-colored Finches (Purple Finches, Redpolls, Crossbills, etc.). Females are duller than males, with the gray crown-patch less conspicuous or almost wanting.

Voice: — High Finch-like chirping notes, suggestive of English Sparrow.

Subsp. HEPBURN'S ROSY FINCH. *L. t. littoralis.*
Distinguished in field from next race by the gray of the crown, which extends *below the eye across the cheeks, often to the throat.* Breeds above timber line on mts. from Alaska s. in Cascades to n. Calif.; winters se. in mts. to e. Calif., Nev., Idaho, Mont., Wyo., Ut., and Colo.
GRAY-CROWNED ROSY FINCH. *L. t. tephrocotis.*
Breeds from nw. Mont. n. into Can. In winter w. to Cascades and s. to Ut. and Colo.
SIERRA NEVADA ROSY FINCH. *L. t. dawsoni.*
Breeds on high peaks of cent. Sierra Nevadas, Calif. Similar to above race but somewhat darker.

BLACK ROSY FINCH. *Leucosticte atrata.* (Illus. p. 178.)
Descr. 6. Similar to Gray-crowned Rosy Finch, but with body *blackish* instead of chestnut-brown.
Voice: — Similar to preceding species; high-pitched chirping notes. 'A rather high-pitched plaintive *cheew* repeated continuously' (C. W. Lockerbie).
Range: — Breeds in Salmon R. Mts. of Idaho, mts. of n. Ut., and mts. of w. Wyo.; winters to Mont., se. Wyo., s. Ut., Colo., and N.M.

GROSBEAKS, FINCHES, SNOW BUNTING, JUNCO

1. PYRRHULOXIA, *a*. MALE; *b*. FEMALE
2. CARDINAL, *a*. MALE; *b*. FEMALE
3. WHITE-WINGED CROSSBILL, *a*. MALE; *b*. FEMALE
4. PINE GROSBEAK, *a*. MALE; *b*. FEMALE
5. RED CROSSBILL, *a*. MALE; *b*. FEMALE
6. CASSIN'S PURPLE FINCH, *a*. MALE; *b*. FEMALE
7. CALIFORNIA PURPLE FINCH, *a*. MALE; *b*. FEMALE
8. HOUSE FINCH OR LINNET, *a*. MALE; *b*. FEMALE
9. REDPOLL, *a*. MALE; *b*. FEMALE
10. BLACK ROSY FINCH, MALE
11. *a*. GRAY-CROWNED ROSY FINCH, MALE; *b*. HEPBURN'S ROSY FINCH, MALE
12. BROWN-CAPPED ROSY FINCH, MALE
13. PINE SISKIN
14. EVENING GROSBEAK, *a*. MALE; *b*. FEMALE
15. SHARPE'S SEEDEATER, *a*. MALE; *b*. FEMALE
16. LAWRENCE'S GOLDFINCH, *a*. MALE; *b*. FEMALE
17. COMMON GOLDFINCH, *a*. MALE; *b*. FEMALE
18. *a*. GREEN-BACKED GOLDFINCH, MALE; *b*. ARKANSAS GOLDFINCH, MALE
19. SNOW BUNTING, *a*. MALE IN WINTER; *b*. FEMALE
20. OREGON JUNCO, MALE

BROWN-CAPPED ROSY FINCH. *Leucosticte australis.* (Illus. p. 178.)
Descr. 5¾–6¼. Similar to Gray-crowned Rosy Finch, but with brown of body *lighter* and head *without* conspicuous light-gray patch; crown dusky or blackish. Female Gray-crowned Rosy Finches often have very little evidence of a light crown-patch but are duskier in general color, not so light a brown as this species.
Voice: — Similar to other Rosy Finches.
Range: — Breeds in high mts. of Colo. and probably in n. N.M.; winters in valleys of Colo. and s. into N.M.

HOARY REDPOLL. *Acanthis hornemanni exilipes.*
Descr. 4½–5½. Similar to Common Redpoll, but smaller and whiter. The white rump, *devoid of streakings*, is the best mark.
Range: — Subarctic; very rare winter visitor to Mont.

REDPOLL. *Acanthis linaria.* Subsp. (Illus. p. 178.)
Descr. 5–5½. In notes, size, shape, and actions, Redpolls resemble Goldfinches and Siskins; little streaked, gray-brown birds that may be known in any plumage by a *bright-red cap* on the forehead and a *black chin.* *Males* are pink-breasted. Purple Finches are larger and redder (*entire head* and much of back and under parts are reddish); Siskins are darker with more heavily striped under parts. Prefers open country, and birches.
Voice: — Most characteristic note, *chug* or *chet-chet.*
Subsp. COMMON REDPOLL. *A. l. linaria.*
Subarctic, wandering irregularly s. in winter to e. Ore. and Colo.
GREATER REDPOLL. *A. l. rostrata.*
Somewhat larger (5½–6), darker, and with larger bill than Common Redpoll. Difference can sometimes be made out when the two birds are together in same flock. Winters s. to Mont., casually to Colo.

PINE SISKIN. *Spinus pinus pinus.* (Illus. p. 178.)
Descr. 4½–5. A small *heavily streaked* brown Finch with a *flash of yellow* in wing and tail. In size and actions resembles Goldfinch. All Goldfinches are unstreaked; Redpolls are paler, without the heavy streakings across front of breast; female Purple Finches and House Finches are similar, but larger (size of House Sparrow), with larger bills. None of these (except dissimilar Lawrence's Goldfinch) shows any yellow in either wings or tail. Most Siskins are seen flying high overhead, uttering their characteristic calls.
Voice: — Song, similar to Goldfinch's, but more coarse and wheezy; commonest call, a loud *clee-ip* or *chlee-ip,* also a light

tit-i-tit and a long buzzy *shreeeee* — latter unique among bird-notes.

Range: — Breeds chiefly in evergreen forests of mts. from Can. s. to s. Calif., Ariz., and N.M.; in migration and winter throughout most of w. U.S.

COMMON GOLDFINCH. *Spinus tristis.* Subsp. (Illus. p. 178.)

Descr. 5–5½. Smaller than a House Sparrow. Flight extremely undulating. *Male in summer:* — *A small yellow bird with black wings.* The Yellow Warbler, which shares with this bird the nickname 'Yellow-bird' and 'Wild Canary,' is yellow all over. The bright yellow back distinguishes this species from other Goldfinches. *Female in summer:* — Dull olive-yellow with blackish wings; distinguished from other small olive-yellow birds (Warblers, etc.) by its stout Finch bill. (See female Arkansas Goldfinch.) *Winter males, immatures, etc.:* — Much like the summer female. The two similar small winter Finches, the Redpoll and the Siskin, are *streaked*; the Goldfinch is evenly colored above and below.

Voice: — Song, a clear, long-sustained Canary-like warble. Each dip in flight often punctuated by a simple *ti-tee-di-di.*

Range: — Breeds from Can. s. to Colo., Nev., and s. Calif.; winters from Can. to Mex.

Subsp. (No apparent field differences): (1) Eastern Goldfinch, *S. t. tristis*; (2) Pale Goldfinch, *S. t. pallidus*; (3) Willow Goldfinch, *S. t. salicamans.*

ARKANSAS GREEN-BACKED} GOLDFINCH. *Spinus psaltria.* Subsp. (Illus. p. 178.)

Descr. 4. *Male:* — A very small *yellow-breasted* Finch with a *black cap* and black-and-white wings. It can be easily told in the breeding plumage from the male Common Goldfinch, *S. tristis*, by the absence of the bright-yellow back. In the winter, males of the latter species become brownish and lose their caps. Males of the present species retain the black cap all winter. Males of the two races of this species are quite distinctive. (See *subsp.*, below.) *Female:* — Very similar to female of Common Goldfinch, *S. tristis*, but back more greenish, not so brownish.

Voice: — Sweet plaintive notes very distinctive: *tee-yee* (rising inflection) and *tee-yer* (dropping inflection). Song, Canary-like, more phrased and less sustained than that of Goldfinch (*S. tristis*).

Subsp. ARKANSAS GOLDFINCH. *S. p. psaltria.*
        Males have *black* backs. From Colo., N.M., and cent.-n. Tex. s. into Mex.
        GREEN-BACKED GOLDFINCH. *S. p. hesperophilus.*

Males have *olive-green* backs. Immature male Arkansas Goldfinches are olive-backed, but have telltale blackish streakings on the back. Breeds from Ore. and Ut. through s. Calif. and s. Ariz.; winters from n. Calif. and s. Ariz. s. into Mex.

LAWRENCE'S GOLDFINCH. *Spinus lawrencei*. (Illus. p. 178.)

Descr. 4–4½. *Male:* — A gray-headed Goldfinch with a touch of yellow on the throat and rump, and *broad yellow wing-bars.* It has a black patch on the forehead and chin. No other male Goldfinch has a *black chin.* There is no seasonal change. *Female:* — Similar to male without black face-patch. The grayer color and *broad yellow wing-bars* distinguish her from other female Goldfinches.

Voice: — Song similar to that of Common Goldfinch (*S. tristis*). Call-note, distinctive; 'can be written *tink-oo*, the syllables emphasized equally. I have almost duplicated it by striking a glass tumbler, then a small plate with a spoon.' (Frank Watson.)

Range: — Breeds in cent. and s. Calif. w. of Sierras; winters in s. Calif. and sw. Ariz. (Colo. R. Valley).

RED CROSSBILL. *Loxia curvirostra*. Subsp. (Illus. p. 178.)

Descr. 5¼–6½. Size near that of House Sparrow. The sound made by the cracking open of the cones of evergreen trees, upon which they mainly feed, often betrays their presence. The crossed, pruning-shear mandibles are distinctive; at a distance, when crossed tips are not visible, the comparative slenderness of the bill is obvious (bills of other Finches are relatively shorter and stouter). *Male:* — *Brick-red*, brighter on the rump; wings and tail dusky. Several other Finches are *rosy-red*, but this is only brick-red bird of group. *Female:* — Dull olive-gray; yellowish on the rump and under parts. The plain dark wings distinguish this species from white-winged Crossbill. Immature birds are heavily striped above and below, and look like large Pine Siskins. The larger, crossed bill and absence of yellow in the wings are the points to look for.

Voice: — Song, Finch-like warbled passages; note, a hard *pip-pip* or *pip-pip-pip*.

Range: — Breeds in evergreens in high mts. from Can. s. to cent.-w. Tex., s. Ariz., s. N.M., and s. Calif., and along coast from Wash. to n. Calif.

Subsp. (No apparent field differences): (1) Sitka Crossbill, *L. c. sitkensis*; (2) Bendire's Crossbill, *L. c. bendirei*; (3) Mexican Crossbill, *L. c. stricklandi*.

WHITE-WINGED CROSSBILL. *Loxia leucoptera*. (Illus. p. 178.)

Descr. 6–6¾. *Male:* — Size of House Sparrow; *rosy-pink* with black wings and tail and *two broad white wing-bars.* The Pine

Grosbeak is rosy, with white wing-bars, but is much larger (near size of Robin). *Female and young:* — Olive-gray with yellowish rump, like Red Crossbill, but with *two broad white wing-bars.* The wing-bars are often quite evident when the birds are in flight and help in picking out individuals of this species from mixed flocks of Crossbills. Both Crossbills are usually found in conifers.

Voice: — A comparison of the notes of the two Crossbills will help. The common notes of the White-wing are a sweet *peet* and a dry *chif-chif.* The note corresponding to the *chif-chif* in the Red Crossbill is a hard *pip* or *pip-pip.* Song of White-winged Crossbill, a succession of loud trills on different pitches.

Range: — Breeds in Can.; winters irregularly s. to Puget Sound, n. Ore. (Cascades), and Colo.

TEXAS SPARROW. *Arremonops rufivirgatus rufivirgatus.* (Illus. p. 164.)

Descr. 5½–6. About size of House Sparrow, a plain *olive-backed* Finch with two broad dull-brown stripes on the crown. Upper parts uniform in coloration, without wing-bars or stripes on the back. Under parts whitish, with buffy wash across breast and along sides. Because of its olive-green back it resembles the Green-tailed Towhee, which sometimes occurs in its range in winter, more than it does any Sparrow. The Green-tailed Towhee is larger, with a gray breast, clear-cut white throat, and solid rufous crown.

Voice: — Song, a series of dry notes all on one pitch, starting off deliberately and trailing off into a Chippy-like rattle. 'Also an insect-like buzz as the birds chase each other through the thickets' (Irby Davis).

Range: — S. Tex. n. to Corpus Christi.

GREEN-TAILED TOWHEE. *Oberholseria chlorura.* (Illus. p. 164.)

Descr. 6¼–7. Slightly larger than House Sparrow, a ground-dwelling Finch with a plain *olive-green back, rufous* crown, and conspicuous *white* throat; breast gray. The rufous cap and white throat are the best marks. Some races of the Brown Towhee have quite a rusty crown, but the throat is always buffy.

Voice: — A mewing note like a kitten, and a *chink* like Brown Towhee; song, somewhat Song-Sparrow-like in quality, opening with one or two sweet notes and ending in long burry notes: *weet-chur — cheeeeeee — churrrr.* Often confused with Fox Sparrow's song but less brilliant and musical. Has more of a dry burr in the long notes.

Range: — Breeds in mts. from cent. Ore. and s.-cent. Mont. s. to s. Calif., se. N.M., and cent.-w. Tex.; w. to Cascades and Sierras; winters from s. Calif., s. Ariz., and w. Tex. s. into Mex.

These three have single breast spots

"WHISKER-MARK" SOLID

"WHISKER-MARK" USUALLY BROKEN OR RAGGED

CHESTNUT CHEEK-PATCH

WHITE CORNERS

BELL'S

SAGE

LARK

FOX

HEAVILY-SPOTTED

TAIL TINGED WITH RUSTY

VESPER

WHITE OUTER TAIL FEATHERS

LARGE CENTRAL SPOT

SHORT BREAST STRIPES

OCHRE HEAD-STRIPINGS

BUFFY BREAST-BAND

LINCOLN'S

SONG

BAIRD'S

LIKE SAVANNAH BUT BACK-MARKINGS WASHED OUT, CROWN-STRIPE OBSCURE

RGE ILL

RESEMBLES SONG, BUT WITH WHITISH CROWN-STRIPE AND NOTCHED TAIL

LIKE SAVANNAH BUT DARKER, CROWN-STRIPE OBSCURE

LARGE-BILLED

SAVANNAH

BELDING'S

CROWN STRIPED

BACK PLAINLY MARKED

CROWN SOLID

BACK OBSCURELY MARKED

These two have clear breasts

GRASSHOPPER

CASSIN'S

SPARROWS I

These three have rufous-red caps

WHITE EYE-STRIPE

BLACK "WHISKER"

CENTRAL SPOT

TREE

CHIPPING
Spring

RUFOUS-CROWNED

STRIPED CROWN

BROWN CHEEK-PATCH

CROWN SOLID, FINELY STREAKED

CLAY-COLORED
Spring

BREWER'S

BLACK CROWN

These three have black throats

WHITE STRIPES

GRAY HEAD

HARRIS'S
ADULT

DESERT

BLACK-CHINNED

BUFFY CHEEKS

BLACK AND WHITE CROWNS

GRAY THROAT

WHITE THROAT

BLACK BLOTCH

HARRIS'S
IMM.

WHITE-CROWNED
ADULT

WHITE-THROATED
ADULT

YELLOW CROWN

BROWN AND BUFF HEAD STRIPES

GOLDEN CROWNED
ADULT

SPARROWS II

WHITE-CROWNED
IMM.

SPOTTED TOWHEE. *Pipilo maculatus.* Subsp. (Illus. p. 164.)
Descr. 7–8¼. Smaller and more slender than Robin, which it remotely resembles; *reddish confined to the sides.* Frequents brushy places; often detected by noisy rummaging among dead leaves. *Male:* — Entire head and upper parts black, with rows of numerous *white spots* on back and wings; *sides Robin-red;* belly white. In flight, bird looks black, with large white spots showing toward outer tips of long, ample tail. *Female:* — Similar, but head dusky brown instead of black.
Voice: — A drawn-out, buzzy trill, *chweeeeeee.* Some races utter two or three low short introductory notes; *chup chup chup zeeeeeeeeee.*
Range: — Breeds from Can. to Mex. and from Great Plains and w. Tex. to the Pacific; winters in Pacific States and from Ariz. and N.M. s.
Subsp. (No apparent field differences): (1) Arctic Towhee, *P. m. arcticus;* (2) Spurred Towhee, *P. m. montanus;* (3) Nevada Towhee, *P. m. curtatus;* (4) Oregon Towhee, *P. m. oregonus;* (5) Sacramento Towhee, *P. m. falcinellus;* (6) San Francisco Towhee, *P. m. falcifer;* (7) San Diego Towhee, *P. m. megalonyx;* (8) San Clemente Towhee, *P. m. clementæ.*

BROWN TOWHEE. *Pipilo fuscus.* Subsp. (Illus. p. 164.)
Descr. 8¼–9½. A rather large dull-gray-brown bird with a moderately long tail; suggests a very plain overgrown Sparrow. The only distinctive marks on this somber Finch are the pale-*rusty under tail-coverts* and the streaked buffy throat. It can be told from the Thrashers, which it somewhat resembles, by its smaller size and short Sparrow-like bill. Lives on ground and among brush. The race known as the Cañon Towhee (Ariz., N.M., s. Colo., and w. Tex.) can be told from the Brown Towhees of the Pacific States by its rufous crown and obscure central breast-spot.
Voice: — Note, a sharp metallic *chink.* Song, a rapid *chink-chink-ink-ink-ink-ink-ink-ink,* almost like a repetition of the ordinary call-note. The series often ends in a trill. In some races the song sounds more like *chilp — chilp — chilp — chilp — chilp — chilp — chilp.*
Range: — Sw. Ore. (Josephine, Jackson, and Douglas Cos.), Calif., Ariz., N.M., s. Colo., and w. Tex. The Abert's Towhee, *P. aberti,* replaces this species in the Colorado Desert of se. Calif. and the hot deserts along the Colorado R. and its tributaries in s. and w. Ariz.
Subsp (No apparent field differences except in No. 5 — see above): (1) Oregon Brown Towhee, *P. f. bullatus;* (2) Sacramento Brown Towhee, *P. f. carolæ;* (3) San Francisco Brown Towhee, *P. f. petulans;* (4) California Brown Towhee, *P. f. crissalis;* (5) Cañon Towhee, *P. f. mesoleucus*

ABERT'S TOWHEE. *Pipilo aberti.* (Illus. p. 164.)
Descr. 8¼–9. A desert species, similar to the Brown Towhee, but browner, the entire under parts buffy-brown. The best mark is a *black patch* around the base of the bill.
Voice: — Similar to Brown Towhee.
Range: — Deserts of se. Calif. (Colo. Desert w. to Palm Springs), s. Nev., sw. Ut., s. Ariz., and sw. N.M.

LARK BUNTING. *Calamospiza melanocorys.* (Illus. p. 163.)
Descr. 5½–7½. *Male in spring:* — Like a small Blackbird (about House Sparrow size) *with large white wing-patches.* (Bobolink has much white *on back* as well as on wings; both are open-country birds.) *Females, young,* and *autumn males* are brown with stripings on breast; they slightly resemble female Purple Finches except for their paler color and open-country habitat. Usually some members of the flock show white or buffy wing-patches.
Voice: — Song, sweet and trilling.
Range: — Breeds in prairie country of Mont., Wyo., Colo., e. N.M., and nw. Tex., chiefly on Great Plains, but also sparingly w. of Continental Divide. Winters in s. Tex., Ariz., and deserts of se. Calif.

SAVANNAH SPARROW. *Passerculus sandwichensis.* Subsp. (Illus. p. 182.)
Descr. 4¾–6. An open-country Sparrow; like a *short-tailed* Song Sparrow with a pale or *yellowish stripe* over the eye, a whitish stripe through the crown, and *pale pink legs.* The tail of a Savannah Sparrow is slightly forked, not rounded like that of the Song Sparrow.
Voice: — Song, a dreamy lisping *tsit-tsit-tsit-tseeee-tseee* (last note dropping). At a distance only the two long notes can be heard.
Range: — Breeds from Can. s. to cent. Calif., Nev., Colo., and n. N.M.; migrates s. into Mex.; and winters in the Pacific States, Ariz., N.M., and Tex.
Subsp. (No apparent field differences): (1) Western Savannah Sparrow, *P. s. alaudinus*; (2) Aleutian Savannah Sparrow, *P. s. sandwichensis*; (3) Nevada Savannah Sparrow, *P. s. nevadensis*; (4) Bryant's Sparrow, *P. s. bryanti.*

BELDING'S SPARROW. *Passerculus beldingi.* (Illus. p. 182.)
Descr. 4½–5½. Similar to the Savannah Sparrow, with which it is often found, but *breast-streakings heavier and blacker* and stripe through crown *indistinct.* The legs are browner, not so pinkish. An inhabitant of salt marshes of s. Calif. (See Large-billed Sparrow.)

Voice: — Song similar to Savannah Sparrow but with more emphatic ending, *tsip tsip tsip tsree, tsick-a-tsee* (Hoffmann).
Range: — Breeds in salt marshes of s. Calif., n. to Santa Barbara.

LARGE-BILLED SPARROW. *Passerculus rostratus.* Subsp.
(Illus. p. 182.)
Descr. 4¾-5¾. Similar to Belding's and Savannah Sparrows, with which it is often found, but much paler and *browner without the well-defined dark markings on the back and wings*; breast-streakings brownish, not black. One of the best marks is the bill, which is *much heavier* than that of either the Belding's or Savannah. An inhabitant of coastal marshes of s. Calif. Also likes vicinity of buildings. Easterners will be reminded of the Ipswich Sparrow.
Range: — Breeds in Mex. and Lower Calif.; winters along coast of s. Calif. n. to Santa Barbara.
Subsp. (No apparent field differences): (1) Large-billed Sparrow, *P. r. rostratus*; (2) San Lucas Sparrow, *P. r. guttatus.*

(WESTERN) GRASSHOPPER SPARROW. *Ammodramus savannarum bimaculatus.* (Illus. p. 182.)
Descr. 4¼-5. A *short-tailed,* flat-headed little Sparrow of the open fields; crown with a pale stripe through the center; back striped with chestnut and black. Differs from the Savannah Sparrow in having an *unstreaked* buffy breast. Its flight is comparatively weak. The conspicuously striped back, very short tail, and unstreaked buffy breast are the best marks.
Voice: — Two songs; well described by Guy Emerson as ' (1) an insect-like tumble of notes, (2) two short introductory notes and a long thin buzz, without change of pitch — *pit-tuck zeeeeeeeeeee.*' The second song is the more characteristic.
Range: — Breeds locally from e. Wash. and Mont. s. to s. Calif. (w. of Sierras), Colo., and s. Tex.; winters from cent. Calif. and s. Tex. s.; a few migrate through Ariz. and N.M.

BAIRD'S SPARROW. *Ammodramus bairdi.* (Illus. p. 182.)
Descr. 5-5½. An open-country Sparrow with a light breast crossed by a *narrow band of fine black streaks.* Head yellow-brown streaked with black. The best mark is the *very broad center stripe on the crown,* which is conspicuously *ochre.* The Savannah Sparrow has more extensive streakings on the under parts, not confined to a narrow band. The light stripe through the crown is much narrower. The habitat of the Baird's Sparrow is dry upland prairies where the native grass is long.
Voice: — Song often begins with three or four musical chips and ends in a trill in a lower pitch; more musical than insect-like efforts of Savannah; variable.

Range: — Breeds from Can. to cent. Mont. (rarely); migrates through e. Wyo., Colo., N.M., and se. Ariz.; winters from cent. Tex. s.

VESPER SPARROW. *Pocæcetes gramineus.* Subsp. (Illus. p. 182.)

Descr. 5½–6¼. The *white outer tail-feathers* flashing conspicuously as the bird flies make the best mark. Perched, it looks like a grayish Song Sparrow, but seems to have more of an eye-ring. A *chestnut-colored patch* at the bend of the wing, visible at close range, is determinative. Several other common open-country birds have white outer tail-feathers: the Meadowlark, which is very much larger and chunkier; the Juncos, which are slate-gray; the Longspurs; and the Pipit. The last-named bird is the most similar, but close scrutiny reveals that it is thin-billed, *walks* instead of hops, and frequently *wags its tail.* The Lark Sparrow has large white spots in the outer *corners of the tail*, in addition to the white edges.

Voice: — Song throatier and more minor in quality than that of Song Sparrow, and beginning with a pair of low, clear whistled notes (Song Sparrow begins with *three* repetitious notes on a higher pitch).

Range: — Breeds from Can. s. to Ore., ne. Calif. (e. of Sierras), n. Ariz., n. N.M., and Tex.; winters from s. and cent. Calif., s. Ariz., and cent. Tex. s. into Mex.

Subsp. (No apparent field differences): (1) Oregon Vesper Sparrow, *P. g. affinis*; (2) Western Vesper Sparrow, *P. g. confinis.*

(WESTERN) LARK SPARROW. *Chondestes grammacus strigatus.* (Illus. p. 182.)

Descr. 5½–6¼. An open-country Sparrow with *chestnut* ear-patches, striped crown, and white breast with single dark central spot. *The best mark is the rounded tail with much white in the outside corners* (somewhat as in Spotted Towhee — not as in Vesper Sparrow). Young birds are finely streaked on the breast and lack the central spot, but are otherwise quite recognizable.

Voice: — A variable song consisting of clear notes and trills, best characterized by buzzing and churring passages interspersed here and there.

Range: — Breeds from Can. to Mex. except in humid nw. coast belt; winters from n. Calif. and s. Tex. s.

RUFOUS-WINGED SPARROW. *Aimophila carpalis.*

Descr. 5–5¼. A very rare Sparrow within the limits of the U.S. Like a Chipping Sparrow but with a gray line through the rufous of the crown, somewhat as in an immature Chippy in winter.

The best mark is a *bright rufous shoulder on the wing*. The habitat is a mixture of long grass and low mesquite.
Voice: — Song suggests Song Sparrow.
Range: — Se. Ariz. (very rare and local).

RUFOUS-CROWNED SPARROW. *Aimophila ruficeps*.
Subsp. (Illus. p. 183.)
Descr. 5–5¾. A Sparrow with an unstreaked breast and *rufous red cap*. A black 'whisker' mark on each side of the throat is the best field-mark. The only other Sparrow with a solid reddish cap that normally occurs in the range of this species is the Chipping Sparrow, which has a conspicuous black line through the eye and a white line over it (see Chipping Sparrow). The breeding habitat of the present species is distinctive — dry hillsides covered with low bushes and grass.
Voice: — A stuttering and gurgling song, first part ascending slightly, last notes descending; suggestive of House Wren in general effect. Some authors liken it to a weak Lazuli Bunting's song. Most characteristic note, a nasal *chur, chur, chur, chur* or *dear, dear, dear*.
Range: — W. Tex., w. Okla. (Witchita Mts.), s. N.M., Ariz., and s. and cent. Calif. (n. to Sonoma, Solano, Sutter, and Placer Cos.); casual in se. Colo.
Subsp. (No apparent field differences): (1) Rufous-crowned Sparrow, *A. r. ruficeps*; (2) Santa Cruz Sparrow, *A. r. obscura*; (3) Ashy Sparrow, *A. r. canescens*; (4) Rock Sparrow, *A. r. eremœca*; (5) Scott's Sparrow, *A. r. scotti*.

BOTTERI'S SPARROW. *Aimophila botterii botterii*.
Descr. 5¼–6¼. A dingy plain-breasted Sparrow of the coastal prairies near Brownsville, Tex. It is very nondescript, best told by its unstreaked dingy-white or buffy-white breast. The Cassin's, the only other Sparrow breeding in the same habitat, is almost identical, but is grayer and shows more dusky in the tail. The Botteri's has a much browner tail. The simplest way to tell them is by their very different songs (see below). In migration and winter the Grasshopper Sparrow invades the same area, but can be told by the browner coloration, conspicuous light stripes on the back, and conspicuous stripe through the crown. The Botteri's Sparrow is apparently not present during the winter months.
Voice: — Song, a constant tinkling and 'pitting,' sometimes running into a dry rattle. Very different from song of Cassin's Sparrow, with which it is often found.
Range: — Lower Rio Grande Valley, Tex., and formerly se. Ariz.

CASSIN'S SPARROW. *Aimophila cassini*. (Illus. p. 182.)

Descr. 5¼-5¾. A plain grayish Sparrow of open grassy country, under parts dingy-white or buffy-white without any markings, or with a touch of streaking on the lower sides. The lack of distinctive marks makes it difficult to describe. Its dull grayish upper parts obscurely marked with brown and the unmarked breast are the best clue. As for the other obscure, clear-breasted Sparrows of the open country, the Grasshopper is browner, more contrastingly marked on the back, and has a buffier breast and a light stripe through the crown. The Brewer's is smaller-headed, more Chippy-like in appearance, and distinctly striped with buff and black above. The song of the Cassin's is very distinctive.

Voice: — Song, quite sweet; one or two short opening notes, a high sweet trill and two lower notes thus: *ti ti tseeeeeee tay tay*. Oftentimes the bird 'skylarks' or flutters into the air and sings, giving the long high trill as the climax before it drops down. The song is vaguely suggestive in quality of that of the Savannah Sparrow.

Range: — Breeds in se. Nev., se. Colo., Ariz., N.M., w. Okla., and w. and s. Tex.

DESERT SPARROW. *Amphispiza bilineata.* Subsp. (Illus. p. 183.)

Descr. 4¾-5¼. A pretty, gray-backed Sparrow with white under parts, *white face-stripes* and a *jet-black throat-patch*. The face-pattern is distinctive (see diagram). Lives in desert country. Sexes similar. The only other bird with a face-pattern resembling it is the Black-throated Gray Warbler, which has broad white wing-bars.

Voice: — Song, a sweet *cheet cheet cheeeeeeee* (two short, clear opening notes and a fine trill on a lower or higher pitch).

Range: — Breeds in desert country of Calif., Nev., Ut., w. Colo., Ariz., N.M., and w. and s. Tex.; winters from se. Calif., s. Ariz., s. N.M., and Tex. s.

Subsp. (No apparent field differences): (1) Black-throated Sparrow, *A. b. bilineata*; (2) Desert Sparrow, *A. b. deserticola*.

BELL'S SPARROW. *Amphispiza belli belli.* (Illus. p. 182.)

Descr. 5-5½. The Bell's Sparrow and the Sage Sparrow are very similar; both are gray birds, identified by the combination of a *single dark breast-spot* and *dark marks on the side of the throat*. The Sage Sparrow is paler, with the 'whisker-stripe' narrower and broken into a disconnected series of black lines on the side of the throat. In the Bell's Sparrow this mark is solid and unbroken. In winter the two species sometimes occur together in s. Calif. The breeding habitats of the two species are quite different — that of the Bell's Sparrow, hillsides covered with low brush; that of the Sage Sparrow, flat desert-like country dotted with sage and similar low bushes. The Lark Sparrow resembles these species a trifle because of the single breast-spot and 'whisker-marks,' but is easily distinguished by its rusty head-stripes and large white patches in the tail.

Voice: — Song, 'four to seven notes forming a jerky but somewhat melodic phrase which is rapidly *repeated* two or three times, the higher notes with a squeaky, sibilant tone, the lower notes tinkling.' (H. H. Axtell.)

Range: — Calif., w. of Sierras; n. in interior to Shasta Co. and on coast to Marin Co.; also on San Clemente and other coastal ids.

SAGE SPARROW. *Amphispiza nevadensis.* Subsp. (Illus. p. 182.)

Descr. 5½–6¼. (See Bell's Sparrow.)

Voice: — A simple song of set pattern, suggestive of Song Sparrow in quality, *tsit-tsoo-tseee-tsay*, third note highest.

Range: — Breeds e. of Cascades and Sierras in e. Wash., e. Ore., e. Calif., cent. and s. Ida., Nev., Ut., sw. Mont., w. Wyo., w. Colo., and nw. N.M.; also w. of Sierras in cent. and s. Calif.; from Fresno s. to Mt. Pinos, Ventura Co., w. to Carrizo Plain, San Luis Obispo Co. Winters from s. edge of breeding range to deserts of se. Calif., s. Ariz., s. N.M., and w. Tex.

Subsp. (No apparent field differences): (1) Northern Sage Sparrow, *A. n. nevadensis*; (2) California Sage Sparrow, *A. n. canescens*.

JUNCOS. *Junco.*

Before describing the various Juncos, a general discussion of the group might be of help. They are unstriped, Sparrow-like birds characterized by *conspicuous white outer tail-feathers* and gray or black heads. Some species show considerable areas of rusty-red on the back or sides. In identifying them in the field, the three points of major importance are the head (whether black or gray), the sides (whether 'pinkish' or gray), and the back (whether rusty or gray). For convenience the following simplified breakdown is given. Females are duller than the males, and somewhat more confusing.

Species with gray sides:
   White-winged (white wing-bars)
   Slate-colored (fairly uniform gray coloration)
   Gray-headed (rusty back, pale upper mandible)
   Red-backed (rusty back, black upper mandible)
Species with rusty or 'pinkish' sides:
   Oregon (rusty back, black head)
   Pink-sided (brownish back, gray head)

WHITE-WINGED JUNCO. *Junco aikeni.* (Illus. p. 191.)

Descr. 6–6¾. A gray Junco with a *gray back*. Resembles Slate-colored Junco, but larger and paler, usually with two *white wing-bars* and a greater amount of white in the tail. All specimens outside the range outlined below should be carefully examined, as sometimes aberrant examples of the Slate-colored Junco show some white in the wing. In specimens of the White-winged Junco the four outer tail-feathers on each side are white.

Voice: — Song, a loose musical trill, similar to the songs of other Juncos.

Range: — Breeds in se. Mont., Black Hills in e. Wyo. and w. S.D., and nw. Neb.; winters from Black Hills to s. Colo. and n. N.M.

SLATE-COLORED JUNCO. *Junco hyemalis hyemalis.* (Illus. p. 191.)

Descr. 6–6½. A gray Junco with a *gray back.* The *uniform coloration* of the upper parts, without red or brown areas, is distinctive. Immatures often have a touch of buff or brownish on the sides, but the color always blends into the color of the hood, and is not sharply separated, as in the Oregon or Pink-sided Juncos. The color of the back also blends into the hood.

Voice: — Song, a simple trill, suggestive of Chipping Sparrow's but more musical. Note, a hard click.

Range: — Breeds in Can. and Alaska; winters s. to Colo. and n. N.M., chiefly e. of Rockies; occasional in Pacific States, s. to s. Calif.

OREGON JUNCO. *Junco oreganus.* Subsp. (Illus. pp. 178, 191.)

Descr. 5–6. *A reddish-backed* Junco easily identified by the *black head.* The yellowish or rusty sides distinguish it from all others except the Pink-sided Junco, which has a paler, *gray head* and a *dull brown* back. (See Pink-sided Junco.) Females have grayer heads, and the rusty of the back is not so sharply defined, but the 'pink' or brownish sides are always sharply separated from the gray of the hood. This is the only common species of Junco in the Pacific States. The Slate-colored Junco is found there occasionally and the Gray-headed rarely. To search for these last two in the Pacific States, look for Juncos with *gray* sides. There are a number of subspecies of the Oregon Junco distinguished by subtle differences in color, but the best authorities conclude that they are not separable except in the hand, so field students should designate them all merely as Oregon Juncos.

Voice: — Song, a loose quavering trill all on same pitch; resembles Chipping Sparrow's song, but slower and more musical. Note, a light smack or click; also twittering notes.

Range: — Breeds in nw. Mont., n. Ida., Wash., Ore., and Calif. (s. to San Diego Co.); winters through Pacific States and over entire Rocky Mt. Tableland to Mex.

BLACK CAP

INCOMPLETE EYE-RING

These three Vireos have conspicuous wing-bars

BLACK-CAPPED

HUTTON'S

CONSPICUOUS "SPECTACLES"

SOLITARY

ONE OR TWO FAINT WING-BARS

ONE FAINT WING-BAR OR NONE

These two Vireos have inconspicuous eye-rings
They are best separated by habitat (see text)

BELL'S (LEAST)

GRAY

INCONSPICUOUS HEAD-STRIPES
UNIFORMLY COLORED ABOVE

CONSPICUOUS HEAD-STRIPES
CROWN GRAY, BACK OLIVE

These two Vireos have no wing-bars

WARBLING

RED-EYED

VIREOS

These two Juncos have buffy or rusty sides

BLACK HEAD
RUSTY BACK
♂
OREGON

GRAY HEAD
BROWNISH BACK
♂
PINK-SIDED

BLACK UPPER MANDIBLE
RUSTY BACKS
♂
RED-BACKED

PALE UPPER MANDIBLE
♂
GRAY-HEADED

These four Juncos have gray sides

FAIRLY UNIFORM GRAY COLORATION
♂
SLATE-COLORED

WHITE WING-BARS
♂
WHITE-WINGED

EYE DARK
FLESH
RED BACKED

EYE BRIGHT YELLOW
PALE YELLOW
ARIZONA

JUNCOS

Subsp. (No apparent field differences): (1) Oregon Junco, *J. o. oreganus*; (2) Shufeldt's Junco, *J. o. shufeldti*; (3) Montana Junco, *J. o. montanus*; (4) Thurber's Junco, *J. o. thurberi*; (5) Point Pinos Junco, *J. o. pinosus*.

PINK-SIDED JUNCO. *Junco mearnsi.* (Illus. p. 191.)
Descr. 5½–6. Known from the Oregon Junco by the *gray* head, duller back and more extensive 'pinkish' areas on the sides, sometimes extending across the breast. Female and Immature Oregon Juncos, with grayish heads, resemble this species more closely but have the head somewhat washed with brown, and less clearly set off from the back. A Junco with the combination of clear-gray head and bright 'pink' sides is quite certainly a Pink-sided Junco.
Voice: — Similar to notes of other Juncos.
Range: — Breeds from Can. to s. Ida., s.-cent. Mont., and n. Wyo.; winters s. through Wyo. and Colo. to Ariz. and N.M.

GRAY-HEADED JUNCO. *Junco caniceps.* (Illus. p. 191.)
Descr. 5½–6. The combination of *ashy-gray* sides and *bright rufous* back distinguish this species from all others except the Red-backed Junco. The bill of the present species is pale flesh-colored *above and below*. That of the Red-backed has a black upper mandible.
Voice: — Song, a loose Chippy-like trill similar to that of other Juncos.
Range: — Breeds in Rockies in s. Wyo., Colo., Ut., Nev., and n. N.M.; winters s. to Mex.

RED-BACKED JUNCO. *Junco phæonotus.* Subsp. (Illus. p. 191.)
Descr. 5½–6½. The combination of grayish sides and *bright rufous* back distinguish this species from all others except the Gray-headed Junco. The best point of distinction is the bill, which in the Red-back has the entire upper mandible *black*. This species does not occur north of Ariz. and N.M. The two subspecies of this bird are easily distinguished by the color of the eye (see below).
Voice: — Song (Arizona Junco), lively and musical, ending with a Chipping-Sparrow-like rattle as in other Juncos, but usually with a more complicated opening; sometimes thus: *chip chip chip, wheedle wheedle, che che che che che.*
Subsp. RED-BACKED JUNCO. *J. p. dorsalis.*
> Eye *dark*; lower mandible flesh-colored. Breeds in high mts. of N.M. and ne. Ariz.; winters s. to sw. Tex. and Mex.
> ARIZONA JUNCO. *J. p. palliatus.*
> Eye *bright yellow*; lower mandible pale yellow. Resident of mts. of se. Ariz.

(WESTERN) TREE SPARROW. *Spizella arborea ochracea.*
(Illus. p. 183.)
Descr. 6–6½. A single *round black spot* in the center of the breast
and a bright *red-brown cap* identify the 'Winter Chippy.' Two
conspicuous white wing-bars are also characteristic.
Voice: — Song, sweet and variable, beginning with one or two
high sweet clear notes; note, a distinct *tseet*; feeding-note, a musical *teeler* or *teelwit.*
Range: — Breeds in Can.; winters s. in Rocky Mt. section to
N.M. and w. Tex., and w. to e. Wash., e. Ore., and Ariz. (casually).

(WESTERN) CHIPPING SPARROW. *Spizella passerina arizonæ.* (Illus. p. 183.)
Descr. 5–5½. A very small clear gray-breasted Sparrow with a
bright *rufous cap*, a *black line* through the eye, and a *white line*
over it. *Young birds* in late summer are finely streaked below,
but are recognized by their small size and moderately long
forked tail. *Immature birds* in winter look like the adults, but
are buffier, with a striped crown. *Winter adults* are browner, not
so gray-breasted. (See Rufous-crowned Sparrow and Brewer's
Sparrow.)
Voice: — Song, a dry chipping rattle or trill, all on one pitch.
Note, a short chip.
Range: — Breeds from Can. to s. Calif., cent. Ariz., and N.M.;
winters from s. Calif., s. Ariz., and cent. Tex. s. into Mex.

CLAY-COLORED SPARROW. *Spizella pallida.* (Illus. p. 183.)
Descr. 5–5½. A small open-country Sparrow, clear-breasted like
Chippy, but with a *light stripe* through center of crown and a
sharply outlined brown *ear-patch. Fall immatures* are even more
like Chippies of the same age, but the crown is more distinctly
striped and without much hint of rufous. The surest point is the
rump, which is *buffy-brown*; that of the Chippy is gray. The
Brewer's Sparrow is also similar but lacks the well-marked head-
pattern.
Voice: — Song, a rasping, insect-like *zi-zi-zi-zi-zi.*
Range: — Breeds in prairies of n.-cent. U.S., w. to e. Mont., e.
Wyo., and e. Colo.; winters from s. N.M. and s. Tex. s.

BREWER'S SPARROW. *Spizella breweri.* Subsp. (Illus. p.
183.)
Descr. 5. A small pale Sparrow of the arid sage country and
deserts. Clear-breasted; resembles Chipping Sparrow but slimmer, sandier-colored, and with *crown finely streaked*, with no
hint of rufous. Young Chipping Sparrow in fall might be confused with it, but the crown of the latter species is browner and
often divided by a pale median line.

Voice: — Song, long musical buzzy trills on different pitches; suggests trilling and chopping of Canary, but weaker; sounds like a Chipping Sparrow trying to sing like a Canary.

Range: — Breeds in Great Basin and Rocky Mt. sections from Can. s. to N.M. and Ariz. and w. to e. Wash., e. Ore. (e. of Cascades), and Calif. (e. of Sierras, also local in s. Calif.); winters from s. Calif., s. Ariz., and cent. Tex. s.

Subsp. (No apparent field differences): (1) Brewer's Sparrow, *S. b. breweri*; (2) Timberline Sparrow, *S. b. taverneri.*

WORTHEN'S SPARROW. *Spizella wortheni.*

Descr. 5½. A Mexican species that has once been taken in southern N.M., whence it was first described. Resembles Chipping Sparrow but without the conspicuous eye-stripes, having instead a *conspicuous white eye-ring;* bill *pinkish* or rufous. Resembles very closely the Field Sparrow, which has never occurred in N.M., but rusty of crown less extensive, and eye-ring more conspicuous.

BLACK-CHINNED SPARROW. *Spizella atrogularis.* Subsp. (Illus. p. 183.)

Descr. 5–5½. A uniquely different Sparrow; has a reddish-brown back like many other species, but *head and under parts gray,* with a *black chin-patch.* The *flesh-colored bill* is set off conspicuously by the black patch that encircles it. Immatures lack the black patch, but can be told by the *unmarked gray head and breast,* which contrast with the rusty-brown back. The habitat is dry mountain-slopes covered with sage, chamise, or other low bushes.

Voice: — Song, a series of notes on about same pitch, or descending slightly; starts with several high, thin, clear notes and ends in a rough trill, *sweet, sweet, sweet, weet trrrrrrrr.*

Range: — Breeds in s. N.M., Ariz., and locally in s. Calif. (n. to Monterey Co. and Owens Valley; occasionally farther).

Subsp. (No apparent field differences): (1) Mexican Black-chinned Sparrow, *S. a. atrogularis;* (2) California Black-chinned Sparrow, *S. a. cana.*

HARRIS'S SPARROW. *Zonotrichia querula.* (Illus. p. 183.)

Descr. 7–7¾. Larger than House Sparrow, or about size of Fox Sparrow; identified by its boldly marked black-and-gray head. The *black crown- and throat-patches* join to encircle the bright pinkish bill. Sexes similar. The black bib suggests no other species except the male House Sparrow, which, of course, could hardly be confused with it. Young birds are browner about the head and might have the black incomplete or confined to a disconnected blotch across the breast.

HEADS OF WHITE-CROWNED SPARROWS

A. White-crowned   B. Gambel's   C. Nuttall's

Voice: — Song, plaintive, consisting usually of three notes, *whee whee whee*.
Range: — Breeds in Can.; in migration and winter to Great Plains, w. irregularly to Mont., Wyo., Colo., and casually to other W. States.

WHITE-CROWNED SPARROW. *Zonotrichia leucophrys.*
Subsp. (Illus. pp. 183, 194.)
Descr. 5¾–7. *Adult:* — Breast clear pearly-gray, crown high and puffy, *broadly striped with black and white.* The conspicuous striped crown makes this abundant and well-known bird one of the handsomest of all the Sparrows. *Immature:* — Buffier, with head-stripings of dark red-brown and light buffy-brown instead of black and white; *bills pinkish or yellowish.* Immatures might be mistaken for the Golden-crowned Sparrow. The different subspecies can, with practice and care, be identified in the field by plumage and song. In the Rocky Mt. section only two races, the Gambel's and White-crowned Sparrows, occur. In the Gambel's, the white eye-stripe *starts from* the bill; in the White-crown, near the eye (see diagram). In s. Calif. ordinarily the Gambel's is the only one found, so there is no problem. In cent. Calif. all four races occur. Of these, the White-crown occurs only in the Sierras. It is chiefly in the San Francisco area that students are concerned with the fine points of separating the various races by appearance and voice. The Nuttall's Sparrow, the resident race, which apparently does not migrate, is known to vary remarkably in song in different localities (see below). The advice of the author is to learn the song-pattern of the local breeding birds thoroughly, and when the migrants with strange songs arrive, see whether they have pink bills (Gambel's) or yellow bills (Puget Sound), then proceed to memorize carefully their respective song-patterns by some such method as suggested below.
Subsp. (Including *descr., voice,* and *range.*)
    WHITE-CROWNED SPARROW. *Z l. leucophrys.*

Descr. Differs from the other races in having the white eye-stripe start *from the eye* instead of from the bill.

Voice: — Song, several plaintive whistled notes followed by a husky trilled whistle. As in the other subspecies, the birds sing a bit differently in different localities. Following is a transcription made in Yosemite:

Say See Say Saw Cheeeeeeeeeer
(Clear plaintive whistles) (Husky nasal trill)

Range: — Breeds in high mts. of w. U.S. from Can. s. in Rockies to n. N.M., and in Sierras to cent. Calif.; migrates through Rocky Mt. region s. into Mex.; winters in s. Ariz., N.M., and Tex.

GAMBEL'S SPARROW. *Z. l. gambeli.*

Descr. Adult differs from White-crown by having white eye-stripe *start from bill* instead of from eye. Has cleaner, grayer-appearing neck than the two coastal races. Bill *pinkish* or *flesh-colored.* (Nuttall's and Puget Sound *yellowish.*) Immatures have lighter and rustier head-stripes than immature Nuttall's or Puget Sound Sparrows.

Voice: — Song variable, more formless than Nuttall's or White-crown. Below is one transcription:

Say Chidichi See Say Saw

Range: — Breeds from Can. s. to cent. Mont.; migrates throughout w. U.S. except nw. coast belt; winters from Calif. and Ut. s.

PUGET SOUND SPARROW. *Z. l. pugetensis.*

Descr. A dark race similar to Nuttall's but black head-stripings heavier.

Voice: — Song usually starts with long note, higher-pitched than rest of song. The transcription below is adapted from the notes of Amelia Allen.

Seeeee   See Say Saw Cheeeee

Range: — Breeds in humid nw. coast belt from Wash. s. to n. Calif. (Mendocino Co.); winters s. along coast to s. Calif.

Nuttall's Sparrow. *Z. l. nuttalli.*

Descr. Breast and neck browner than Gambel's Sparrow; bill *yellowish* (Gambel's flesh-colored or orange-brown). Head-stripes wider and blacker than Gambel's.

Voice: — Song varies greatly in different localities, although birds stick to a 'community pattern'; for example, those at Point Reyes in Marin Co., Calif., sing:

Seeeee   Chechechecheche   Cheer
(whistle) (Metallic warble) (Nasal)

In one part of Berkeley they sing:

See See Chee   Chechechechecheer
(Clear) (Burr) (Rattle with overtones)

While at Carmel they sing with a characteristic double note.

Say   See   Chidi Chidi   Cheew
(Clear) (Clear)(Double notes)(Nasal)

Range: — Permanent resident around San Francisco Bay region and along coast of cent. Calif. from Mendocino Co. to Santa Barbara Co.

GOLDEN-CROWNED SPARROW. *Zonotrichia coronata.* (Illus. p. 183.)

Descr. 6–7. *Adult:* — Like a White-crowned Sparrow with *no white line over the eye* and a *golden-yellow,* instead of white, stripe through the center of the crown. Immature White-crowns (Gambel's, etc.) have the center of the crown buffy and resemble the Golden-crown, but have broad buffy lines over the eyes, which the latter species lacks. Immature Golden-crowns look like large female House Sparrows, but are browner and sometimes have a dull yellowish suffusion on the crown. Often they lack this yellow suffusion and are very plain. These birds have little distinctive about them, unless it be the fine streaking on the otherwise unpatterned crown.

Voice: — Song, three high whistled notes of plaintive minor quality, coming down the scale.

Range: — Breeds in Can. and Alaska; winters in Ore. and Calif. w. of Sierras; migrates through Wash.; casual in Nev. and Colo.

WHITE-THROATED SPARROW. *Zonotrichia albicollis.* (Illus. p. 183.)

Descr. 6½–7. *Adult:* — Clear-breasted with *white throat-patch* and *striped black-and-white crown.* The abrupt white throat, and *yellow* on eye-line between bill and eye, distinguish it from any of the White-crowns. *Immature:* — Duller, but with all essential recognition-marks of adults.

Voice: — Song, several clear, pensive whistled notes easily imitated; starts on one or two long clear whistles and changes pitch abruptly. Note, a hard *chink*, also a slurred *tseet*.

Range: — Breeds in Can., migrates through e. U.S. w. rarely to e. Mont., e. Wyo., and e. Colo.; also a rare but regular winter visitor to the Pacific States, especially Calif.

FOX SPARROW. *Passerella iliaca.* Subsp. (Illus. p. 182.)

Descr. 6¼–7¼. Large for a Sparrow; larger than a House Sparrow; dark brown or gray with heavily streaked under parts.

The heavy spottings and streakings often cluster together
densely on the upper breast. In some birds the tail has a strong
tinge of rusty. This species, which likes ravines, slopes, and
brushy places, has many confusing subspecies. They can be
roughly divided into two types: gray-headed Fox Sparrows with
large grayish bills and brown-headed Fox Sparrows with yellowish bills. It is hopeless and misguided for the field student to
try to separate them, for often in migration and winter half a
dozen races might be represented in the same flock. The only
race that can be identified easily in the field is the Eastern Fox
Sparrow, *P. i. iliaca*, which is a rare or casual winter visitor to
the Pacific States. It shows much bright rufous, especially the
tail- and breast-streakings. There is much gray around the face.
No Western Fox Sparrow shows such bright rusty coloration.

Voice: — A brilliant musical song; usually begins with one or
two clear notes followed by a sliding note: *sweet sweet cheer
chillip chillip*, etc. The arrangement varies greatly, but the
song is easy to remember once heard. (See voice of Green-tailed
Towhee.)

Range: — Breeds in high mts. from Can. to w. Colo. (rare)
and s. Calif. (San Gabriel, San Bernardino, and San Jacinto
Mts.), and from Rockies w. to Sierras, Cascades, and ids. off
coast of nw. Wash. Migrates and winters in Pacific States. A
rare migrant to Ariz. and N.M.

Subsp. (No apparent field differences except in No. 1 — see
above): (1) Eastern Fox, *P. i. iliaca*; (2) Alberta Fox, *P. i.
altivagans*; (3) Shumagin Fox, *P. i. unalaschensis*; (4) Kodiak
Fox, *P. i. insularis*; (5) Valdez Fox, *P. i. sinuosa*; (6) Yakutat
Fox, *P. i. annectens*; (7) Townsend's Fox, *P. i. townsendi*;
(8) Thick-billed Fox, *P. i. megarhyncha*; (9) Sooty Fox, *P. i.
fuliginosa*; (10) Slate-colored Fox, *P. i. schistacea*; (11) Warner
Mountains Fox, *P. i. fulva*; (12) Trinity Fox, *P. i. brevicauda*;
(13) Inyo Fox, *P. i. canescens*; (14) Mono Fox, *P. i. monoënsis*;
(15) Yosemite Fox, *P. i. mariposæ*; (16) Stephens's Fox, *P. i.
stephensi*.

LINCOLN'S SPARROW. *Melospiza lincolni.* Subsp. (Illus. p. 182.)

Descr. 5–6. Like Song Sparrow, with shorter tail; streakings on
under parts much finer and not aggregated into as large a center
spot; best identified by broad band of pale buff across breast.
The buffy band and fine breast-streakings distinguish it from all
except the immature Song Sparrow. It is grayer-backed, with
a more contrastingly striped crown. A narrow *eye-ring* is also
quite characteristic. Likes wet brushy places and boggy spots.

Voice: — Song, sweet and gurgling, suggests both House Wren
and Purple Finch, starting with low passages, rising abruptly
in pitch, then dropping at the end.

Range: — Breeds in high mts. from Can. s. to s. Calif., cent.

Ariz., and N.M.; migrates through lowlands of w. U.S.; winters from cent. Calif., Ariz., and cent. Tex. s. into Mex.

Subsp. (No apparent field differences): (1) Lincoln's Sparrow, *M. l. lincolni*; (2) Forbush's Sparrow, *M. l. gracilis*.

SONG SPARROW. *Melospiza melodia.* Subsp. (Illus. p. 182.)
Descr. 5–6¾. Breast heavily streaked, the streaks confluent into a *large central spot*: pumps its tail as it flies. The Savannah Sparrow, though streaked similarly below, shows yellow over the eye, and has a shorter, *forked* tail. The tail of the Song Sparrow is not so noticeably notched. *Young* birds are more finely streaked, often without the central spot. (See Lincoln's Sparrow.) There are many subspecies in the West, varying in size and general coloration. Those that breed in arid sections are paler; those in humid districts, duskier. In winter different races sometimes intermingle, especially in Calif. The student should not attempt to untangle them in the field.
Voice: — Song, a variable series of notes, some musical, some buzzy, usually starting with three repetitious notes, *sweet sweet sweet*, etc. Call-note, a low nasal *tchack*.
Range: — Breeds from Can. s. to s. Calif., sw. Ariz., and n. N.M.; winters from Wash. and Mont. s. into Mex.
Subsp. (No apparent field differences): (1) Dakota Song Sparrow, *M. m. juddi*; (2) Mountain Song Sparrow, *M. m. fallax*; (3) Modoc Song Sparrow, *M. m. fisherella*; (4) Merrill's Song Sparrow, *M. m. merrilli*; (5) Sooty Song Sparrow, *M. m. rufina*; (6) Rusty Song Sparrow, *M. m. morphna*; (7) Mendocino Song Sparrow, *M. m. cleonensis*; (8) Samuels's Song Sparrow, *M. m. samuelis*; (9) Suisun Song Sparrow, *M. m. maxillaris*; (10) Modesto Song Sparrow, *M. m. mailliardi*; (11) Alameda Song Sparrow, *M. m. pusillula*; (12) Heermann's Song Sparrow, *M. m. heermanni*; (13) San Diego Song Sparrow, *M. m. cooperi*; (14) Santa Cruz Song Sparrow, *M. m. santæcrucis*; (15) Santa Barbara Song Sparrow, *M. m. graminea*; (16) San Clemente Song Sparrow, *M. m. clementæ*; (17) San Miguel Song Sparrow, *M. m. micronyx*; (18) Desert Song Sparrow, *M. m. saltonis*; (19) Yakutat Song Sparrow, *M. m. caurina*.

McCOWN'S LONGSPUR. *Rhynchophanes mccowni.* (Illus. pp. 200, 201.)
Descr. 6. *Spring male:* — Forehead and patch on breast black; tail largely white. The hind-neck is *gray*, not brown or chestnut as in other Longspurs. *Female and winter plumages:* — See Chestnut-collared Longspur.
Voice: — Song, given in flight, a variety of clear sweet warbles, 'much the same character as Lark Bunting' (R. J. Niedrach).
Range: — Breeds in Great Plains, w. to e. Mont., e. Wyo., and ne. Colo.; migrates and winters in e. Colo., e. Ariz., N.M., and w. Tex.

LONGSPURS

1. Alaska: a, *female*; b, *male in spring*
2. Chestnut-collared: a, *female*; b, *male in spring*
3. McCown's: a, *female*; b, *male in spring*

ALASKA LONGSPUR. *Calcarius lapponicus alascensis.* (Illus. pp. 200, 201.)

Descr. 6–7. Longspurs, like Horned Larks and Pipits, are birds of the fields, plains, and barren grounds; like those two they *walk or run*, seldom hop. This species often associates with Horned Larks or Snow Buntings. With Snow Buntings it appears as a smaller, House-Sparrow-like bird, with *dark wings*; when with Horned Larks it can be recognized by the short, Sparrow bill, and the lack of an outlined yellow throat, and on the wing by the *smaller tail* and more undulating flight. Alone, it appears a trifle like a House Sparrow, but *walks or creeps*. Two white wing-bars, some narrow black streakings on the sides, and a varying amount of reddish on the nape of the neck are distinctive points. It has much less white in the tail than the other Longspurs. In the spring both sexes acquire a black throat and breast (breeding Chestnut-collared Longspur has black breast but whitish throat).

Voice: — The note of this Longspur amongst a flock of Larks or Buntings is a dry rattle that can be detected immediately.

Range: — Breeds in n. Alaska; winters s. to e. Ore. (occasionally), Nev., and Colo.; chiefly e. of Rockies. Accidental in Calif.

TAIL-PATTERNS OF LONGSPURS

a. Chestnut-collared   *b.* McCown's   *c.* Alaska

CHESTNUT-COLLARED LONGSPUR. *Calcarius ornatus.*
(Illus. pp. 200, 201.)
Descr. 5½–6½. Smallest of the Longspurs — smaller than a House Sparrow. *Male in breeding plumage:* — Solid *black* below except on throat; nape of neck, *chestnut. Female and winter male:* — Sparrow-like, known from other Longspurs (except McCown's) by large amount of white on sides of tail. Vesper Sparrow and Pipit have straight white sides of tail to tip; Chestnut-collared and McCown's Longspurs have dark band on end of tail. In Chestnut-collar the dark central tail-feathers *curve* into the terminal band, fanwise; in McCown's, the band is more angular, forming a T with the dark central feathers (see diagram).
Voice: — Song, short, feeble but musical, 'suggestive of Western Meadowlark in melody' (R. J. Niedrach).
Range: — Breeds in Great Plains w. to Mont. and e. Wyo.; migrates and winters in e. Colo., e. Ariz., N.M., and w. Tex.

SNOW BUNTING. *Plectrophenax nivalis nivalis.* (Illus. p. 178.)
Descr. 6–7¼. The great amount of white distinguishes the Snow Bunting. Some individuals look quite brown as they run about on the ground, but when they spring into the air the extensive white wing-patches flash forth. As they fly overhead, they look almost entirely white; Pipits and Horned Larks are both black-tailed.
Voice: — Note, a clear whistled *teer*; also a musical purring note.
Range: — Breeds in Arctic; winters s. to Ore., Wyo., and Colo. (a few), chiefly in prairie country.

SUBSPECIES

THE problem of subspecies is a very confusing one, especially in the western United States. When the author first planned his manuscript, he listed under each species all subspecies and their ranges, in much the same manner as in his Eastern *Field Guide*. Dr. Alden Miller, who has done much work on taxonomic problems, and is a leader of ornithological thought in the West, strongly urged that subspecies be left out entirely unless they can actually be identified in the field. There are many good reasons for following such a plan. First and foremost, there still seems to be no clear-cut idea as to what a subspecies is, other than that it is a geographical race that often blends with others of the same species. To explain it simply, the Song Sparrows of the desert differ from those of the mountains in being somewhat paler, so they are called by a different name. These differences are sometimes well marked, but often they can only be determined by experts after very careful examination in the hand. There is a constant dispute raging amongst ornithologists about various local races, and it is often a matter of opinion to which subspecies a bird belongs, or even whether a certain subspecies is worthy of recognition at all.

Even the concept of species is not entirely agreed upon. It was recently stated by Dr. Ernst Mayr that at least ninety-four of the 755 full species of North American birds will be considered by some authors to be merely subspecies of other species. A few Western examples are the Large-billed, Belding's, and Savannah Sparrows; the various Juncos; the Leucostictes; the Myrtle and Audubon's Warblers, etc. However, we need not concern ourselves with this theoretical question, as most of these examples are quite distinguishable in the field.

The *A.O.U. Check-List*, which has initiated the use of vernacular names for subspecies, has got things into a mess by not always indicating in the name to which species a subspecies belongs. All Song Sparrows are called Song Sparrows; i.e., San Diego Song Sparrow, Rusty Song Sparrow, etc. This is fine, but on the other hand, the several races of the Steller's Jay are designated by such totally unrelated names as Black-headed Jay, Long-crested Jay, Blue-fronted Jay, and Coast Jay. There is little in some of these names to indicate whether the bird is a race of the Steller's Jay or the California Jay. The inference might even be drawn that they are all distinct species.

Another angle is that the various races of the Steller's Jay *intergrade* on the borders of their ranges. In the latest revisionary work on this species, it was brought out that the birds around Seattle cannot be called by any currently accepted name, as they are not quite like those on the Coast farther to the south, nor typical of the form found to the north on Vancouver Island, nor yet quite like the birds in the Cascades. They are intermediates with a blend of characters. In other words, there could just as easily be ten races of this bird as five, depending on where the lines are to be drawn or how fine the splitting is to be. The point I am driving at is that if the subject is so indefinite as all this, the problem is not one for a beginner. It is better that he use only the name Steller's Jay, which is the accepted species name. This is far more scientific than using a name that has disputed validity. Subspecies have a real meaning to the student of bird distribution and evolution, but not much to the field amateur. Dr. George Miksch Sutton writes:

'One of the worst problems of present-day field bird study, as I see it, is this desire to use trinomials. Right here, at Cornell, we face the problem. . . . I asked my students to turn in a field notebook last year, and every one of them listed trinomials wherever he possibly could, without bothering himself to discover what specimens had actually been collected and identified, what the characters of certain races were, etc. They all were willing to take someone else's word on the subspecies — to use the name that seemed to fit geographically, to employ what I call *fake* accuracy. In other words, *Turdus migratorius migratorius*, Eastern Robin, looked more thoroughgoing to them than simply *Turdus migratorius*, Robin. The use of the trinomial very often is a sort of four-flushing.'

Junea Kelly, who has taught many bird classes around San Francisco, writes similarly:

'In most cases an observer cannot identify a subspecies in the field, and only uses the subspecific name because the bird is seen in a certain locality. I have never felt that this was a very satisfactory way of making out a "list." It might be approximately accurate for the breeding season, but how about the rest of the year? How is an observer to know exactly when non-breeders have arrived?'

Before taking the plunge and following Dr. Miller's suggestion, I thought it wise to get the opinions of a few other people. After writing to about twenty-five representative Westerners and Easterners about the treatment of subspecies, I finally arrived at a plan that I believe will work for all, yet still do the job Dr. Miller had in mind. Most Westerners were insistent about leaving out subspecies entirely, or at least playing them down. Most Easterners, and a few Westerners, said they would feel cheated if the subspecies were not left in, so I finally worked out the following plan:

When subspecies are readily identifiable in the field they will be treated exactly as they are in my Eastern *Field Guide*, with considerable importance given to each subspecies. A good example of this is the Canada Goose. When there are no apparent field differences, only the range *for the species as a whole* will be given. The advantage of this is that the amateur will not have to wade laboriously through the range of each subspecies to see whether his territory falls within it. If all the subspecies ranges were outlined prominently in the body of the text, the student would be encouraged to use the vernacular subspecific names, which, as has been explained, leads to confusion.

It is necessary to include at least the *names* of subspecies, however, as failure to list them would only be misleading; for example, if a person consulted a local publication and found the name Black-eared Nuthatch (a race of the Pygmy Nuthatch), he would be very much troubled if he did not find this bird in the *Field Guide* An almost identical example is described by Clinton G. Abbott, of the Natural History Museum at San Diego:

'When there was no one else in the office, a woman came in and told my secretary that we failed to include the Pygmy Nuthatch in our identification series of San Diego birds. With no one to explain the situation to her (that the White-naped Nuthatch and the Pygmy Nuthatch are the same thing) she went out feeling very much disturbed. In the plan which you are to follow in your book, if this woman had looked up Pygmy Nuthatch, she would have seen that some of the subspecies have different names, and might then have been induced to look more carefully on the labels in our cases.'

In most cases, it is quite easy to settle on an inclusive species name. To the average Westerner, the *Willow* Woodpecker or *Batchelder's* Woodpecker is still just a Downy. There are, however, a few vernacular names of subspecies that have already gained such a foothold that it would be difficult to eradicate them now; for instance, *Lutescent* Warbler (a race of the Orange-crown) and *Farallon* Cormorant (a race of the Double-crested). Most vernacular subspecies names are of recent manufacture, and have not become well established in popular use. Yet if every bird book that came out gave them full importance, it would not take long before these names were as firmly intrenched in usage as 'Lutescent' Warbler and 'Farallon' Cormorant.

The next edition of the *A.O.U. Check-List* plans to incorporate species headings, so when I have been in doubt, I have referred to the Committee's choice of a name, except in about three instances when I have disregarded it, using instead the Western name which seemed the more appropriate; for example, *Pileolated* Warbler instead of Wilson's Warbler.

This book is primarily for the amateur who merely wishes to

attach a name or a 'handle' to the creature before him. Another group consists of those who are more or less students of the subject. They will range from those who know little to those who have spent years of study and who will wish to use the book in areas unfamiliar to them. It is in deference to some of these, who will feel the book is incomplete if the ranges of subspecies are omitted, that I have decided to include these ranges, but to de-emphasize them, and relegate them to this chapter in the back of the book. For a more extended account of these ranges, the student should refer to the 1931 edition of the *A.O.U. Check-List*.

In the ten years between publication of the last *Check-List* and the publication of this handbook about eighty new subspecies have been described. Probably not half of these will be accepted by the A.O.U. Check-List Committee, so rather than include all of these, many of which are at present of questionable status, I have adhered strictly, or very nearly so, to the last edition of the *Check-List*.

If subspecific names are used at all, it is my advice to call birds by these names only on their breeding-grounds, and not when indistinguishable migrants of other races might be present.

At Mr. Ludlow Griscom's suggestion, I have reversed or altered the treatment of several highly complex migratory species, such as the Fox Sparrow, analyzing them by States or regions. Thus, a person in the Rockies knows he has to deal only with one Fox Sparrow and will not wade through the other sixteen to be sure they do not occur in migration in his area.

COMMON LOON. *Gavia immer:* (1) Lesser Loon, *G. i. elasson*; breeds from Can. s. to Wyo., e. Ore., and ne. Calif. (formerly); migrates through w. U.S.; winters along Pacific Coast. (2) Common Loon, *G. i. immer*; some authorities say it is this race and not the preceding one that occurs in Calif.

BEAL'S PETREL. *Oceanodroma leucorhoa:* (1) Beal's Petrel, *O. l. beali*; breeds from Alaska to Farallon Ids., Calif.; winters offshore from Wash. to s. Calif. (2) Kaeding's Petrel, *O. l. kaedingi*; breeds in Lower Calif.; wanders n. to s. Calif.

DOUBLE-CRESTED CORMORANT. *Phalacrocorax auritus:* (1) Double-crested Cormorant, *P. a. auritus*; Great Plains and, according to some authorities, the breeding bird of Great Salt Lake. (2) Farallon Cormorant, *P. a. albociliatus*; Pacific Coast of Ore. and Calif.; also bodies of water inland in Calif., Ore., Ariz., and w. Nev. (3) White-crested Cormorant, *P. a. cincinatus*; coast of Wash.

GREAT BLUE HERON. *Ardea herodias:* (1) Great Blue Heron, *A. h. herodias*; e. Mont. (2) Treganza's Heron, *A. h. treganzai*; interior from e. Wash., e. Ore., s. Idaho, and Wyo. s. to se. Calif. (Salton Sea) and Mex., and e. to cent. Colo. (edge of Great Plains). (3) Northwestern Coast Heron, *A. h. fannini*; coastal Wash. (4) California Heron, *A. h. hyperonca*; Calif. and Ore. w. of Sierras and Cascades.

LEAST BITTERN. *Ixobrychus exilis:* (1) Western Least Bittern, *I. e. hesperis*; breeds in Calif. and e. Ore.; occurs occasionally in Rocky Mt. States. (2) Eastern Least Bittern, *I. e. exilis*; e. U.S. w. occasionally to e. Wyo. and e. Colo.

CANADA GOOSE. *Branta canadensis:* (1) Common Canada Goose, *B. c. canadensis*; breeds from ne. Calif., n. Nev., n. Ut., and Wyo. n. into Can.; winters from Wash. and Yellowstone Park s. into Mex. (2) White-cheeked Goose, *B. c. occidentalis*; winters along coast from Puget Sound to n. Calif. (Del Norte and Humboldt Cos.). (3) Lesser Canada Goose, *B. c. leucopareia*; winters from Wash. to Mex., especially in interior valleys of Calif. (4) Cackling Goose, *B. c. minima*; winters mainly in Sacramento and San Joaquin Valleys of Calif.

WHITE-FRONTED GOOSE. *Anser albifrons:* (1) White-fronted Goose, *A. a. albifrons*; migrates chiefly through Pacific States, rare in Rocky Mt. region; winters in Calif. (2) Tule Goose, *A. a. gambeli*; winters in Sacramento Valley, Calif.

GOSHAWK. *Astur atricapillus:* (1) Eastern Goshawk, *A. a. atricapillus*; said to be the breeding form in Colo., Wyo., Ut., and probably Mont.; also migrates through Mont. e. of Continental Divide. (2) Western Goshawk, *A. a. striatulus*; breeds from Can. s. in mts. to cent. Calif.; also a few in Ariz. and N.M.; winters more widely in w. U.S.

RED-TAILED HAWK. *Buteo borealis:* (1) Western Red-tailed Hawk, *B. b. calurus*; resident through most of w. U.S. (2) Krider's Hawk, *B. b. krideri*; Sask. and s. Man. s. to Wyo. and N.D.

BALD EAGLE. *Haliœetus leucocephalus:* (1) Northern Bald Eagle, *H. l. alascanus*; winters s. to Wash. and Mont. (2) Southern Bald Eagle, *H. l. leucocephalus*; local resident from Can. to Mex.

DUCK HAWK. *Falco peregrinus:* (1) Duck Hawk, *F. p. anatum*; breeds locally from Can. to Mex.; winters in Pacific States and from Colo. s. (2) Peale's Falcon, *F. p. pealei*; migrant and winter visitor to coast of Wash. and Ore.

PIGEON HAWK. *Falco columbarius:* (1) Black Pigeon Hawk, *F. c. suckleyi*; winters along coast from Wash. to n. Calif. (2) Richardson's Pigeon Hawk, *F. c. richardsoni*; breeds in Great Plains region from Can. s. to n. Mont.; winters s. through Colo., N.M., and w. Tex. (3) Western Pigeon Hawk, *F. c. bendirei*; breeds from Can. s. in mts. to n. Calif. and Colo.; winters s. into Mex.

SPARROW HAWK. *Falco sparverius:* (1) Eastern Sparrow Hawk, *F. s. sparverius*; breeds from Can. s. to Calif. and Colo.; winters from Wash. and Wyo. s. to Mex. (2) Desert Sparrow Hawk, *F. s. phalœna*; resident of s. Calif., Ariz., and N.M.

DUSKY GROUSE. *Dendragapus obscurus:* (1) Dusky Grouse, *D. o. obscurus*; Rocky Mts. from cent. Ariz. and cent. N.M. n. to n. Ut., se. Idaho, and Wyo. (intergrading with next race in Mont.). (2) Richardson's Grouse, *D. o. richardsoni*; mt. regions from Can. s. to cent. Idaho and Mont.

SOOTY GROUSE. *Dendragapus fuliginosus:* (1) Sooty Grouse, *D. f. fuliginosus*; coastal belt from Wash. to nw. Calif. (2) Sierra Grouse, *D. f. sierræ*; extreme s. Ore. (Warner Mts.) and s. in Sierras to Kern Co., Calif., and on inner side of coast range to Mt. Sanhedrin. (3) Mount Pinos Grouse, *D. f. howardi*; s. Calif. from Mt. Pinos to Kern Co.

RUFFED GROUSE. *Bonasa umbellus:* (1) Oregon Ruffed Grouse, *B. u.*

sabini; coastal belt from w. Wash. s. to nw. Calif. (2) Gray Ruffed Grouse, *B. u. umbelloides*; e. of Cascades from Can. s. to n. Colo. (formerly*j*, n. Ut., and e. Ore.

WHITE-TAILED PTARMIGAN. *Lagopus leucurus:* (1) Rainier White-tailed Ptarmigan, *L. l. rainierensis*; Cascade Mts. of Wash. (2) Southern White-tailed Ptarmigan, *L. l. altipetens*; Rocky Mts. from Mont. to n. N.M.

SHARP-TAILED GROUSE. *Pediœcetes phasianellus:* (1) Columbian Sharp-tailed Grouse, *P. p. columbianus*; e. Wash., e. Ore., Idaho, n. Ut., w. Mont., w. Wyo., w. Colo., and n. N.M. (2) Prairie Sharp-tailed Grouse, *P. p. campestris*; Great Plains w. to e. Mont., e. Wyo., and e. Colo.

SCALED QUAIL. *Callipepla squamata:* (1) Arizona Scaled Quail, *C. s. pallida*; from cent. Ariz., s. Colo., and w. Tex. s. (2) Chestnut-bellied Scaled Quail, *C. s. castanogastris*; cent. and s. Tex.

CALIFORNIA QUAIL. *Lophortyx californica:* (1) California Quail, *L. c. californica*; humid coastal belt of n. and cent. Calif.; introduced in Wash. (2) Valley Quail, *L. c. vallicola*; native in s. Ore. and s. through Calif. except in humid coast strip (from cent. Calif. n.). Absent also in Colo. and Mohave Deserts (except w. edge). Widely introduced elsewhere in W. States. (3) Catalina Quail, *L. c. catalinensis*; Catalina Id., Calif.

GAMBEL'S QUAIL. *Lophortyx gambeli:* (1) Gambel's Quail, *L. g. gambeli*; deserts of s. Calif., s. Nev., sw. Ut., Ariz., cent. and sw. N.M., and extreme w. Tex.; introduced locally elsewhere. (2) Olathe Quail, *L. g. sanus*; supposed to have developed in sw. Colo. from birds introduced there years ago.

MOUNTAIN QUAIL. *Oreortyx picta:* (1) Mountain Quail, *O. p. palmeri*; humid mountains near coast from w. Wash. to Monterey Co., Calif. (2) Plumed Quail, *O. p. picta*; e. of Cascades in Ore., s. Idaho, extreme w. Nev., and through Sierras to mts. of s. Calif.

SANDHILL CRANE. *Grus canadensis:* (1) Little Brown Crane, *G. c. canadensis*; breeds in Arctic; migrates through interior of U.S. to Calif., Tex., and Mex. (2) Sandhill Crane, *G. c. tabida*; breeds in ne. Calif., e. Ore., n. Nev., s. Idaho, n. Ut., sw. Mont., w. Wyo., and nw. Colo.; winters from Calif. and Tex. s. to Mex.

CALIFORNIA CLAPPER RAIL. *Rallus obsoletus:* (1) California Clapper Rail, *R. o. obsoletus*; salt marshes of Monterey and San Francisco Bays, Calif.; casual farther n. (2) Light-footed Rail, *R. o. levipes*; salt marshes from San Diego to Santa Barbara, Calif. (3) Yuma Clapper Rail, *R. o. yumanensis*; lower Colo. R. from Yuma to Laguna Dam; also marshes in Imperial Valley s. of Salton Sea.

GOLDEN PLOVER. *Pluvialis dominica:* (1) American Golden Plover, *P. d. dominica*; rare migrant on Pacific Coast, along edge of Great Plains, and in Ut. (2) Pacific Golden Plover, *P. d. fulva*; has been recorded in Calif.

LONG-BILLED CURLEW. *Numenius americanus:* (1) Long-billed Curlew, *N. a. americanus*; breeds in Ut., s. Idaho, e. Nev., Colo., and n. N.M.; winters from cent. Calif. s. (2) Northern Curlew, *N. a. occidentalis*; breeds in e. Wash., e. Ore., ne. Calif., nw. Nev., Mont., Wyo., and ne. Colo.; winters s. to s. Calif ; either this race or the preceding one migrates through s. N.M. to s. Tex.

DOWITCHER. *Limnodromus griseus:* (1) Eastern Dowitcher, *L. g. griseus*; migrates through w. U.S. and winters from Calif. s. (2) Long-billed Dowitcher, *L. g. scolopaceus*; migrates through w. U.S. and winters from Calif. s.

WESTERN GULL. *Larus occidentalis:* (1) Western Gull, *L. o. occidentalis;* breeds along coast from Wash. to n. Calif. and Farallons; winters s. to s. Calif. (2) Wyman's Gull, *L. o. wymani;* breeds along coast of Calif. from Monterey Co. s.

HERRING GULL. *Larus argentatus:* (1) Herring Gull, *L. a. smithsonianus;* migrates and winters along Pacific Coast and Great Plains. (2) Thayer's Gull, *L. a. thayeri;* occurs s. to Calif. and Colo.

LEAST TERN. *Sterna antillarum:* (1) Least Tern, *S. a. antillarum;* breeds along North Platte R. in Wyo.; occasional in Colo. (2) Brown's Tern, *S. a browni;* breeds on coast n. to cent. Calif.

WHITE-WINGED DOVE. *Melopelia asiatica:* (1) Eastern White-winged Dove, *M. a. asiatica;* s. Tex. (2) Western White-winged Dove, *M. a. mearnsi;* se. Calif., s. Ariz., and sw. N.M.

YELLOW-BILLED CUCKOO. *Coccyzus americanus:* (1) Yellow-billed Cuckoo, *C. a. americanus;* e. U.S., breeding w. to e. Colo. (2) California Cuckoo, *C. a. occidentalis;* breeds from Wash. and cent. Colo. s. to Mex.

SCREECH OWL. *Otus asio:* (1) Aiken's Screech Owl, *O. a. aikeni;* se. Colo. and n. N.M. (2) Rocky Mountain Screech Owl, *O. a. maxwellia;* foothills and plains adjacent to Rocky Mts. from e. Mont. to n.-cent. Colo. (3) Macfarlane's Screech Owl, *O. a. macfarlanei;* e. Wash., e. Ore., ne. Calif., Idaho, and w. Mont. (4) Kennicott's Screech Owl, *O. a. kennicotti;* w. Wash. (5) Brewster's Screech Owl, *O. a. brewsteri;* range starting in n.-cent. Wash., turning gradually w. through w. Ore. (6) California Screech Owl, *O. a. bendirei;* coast of Calif. from San Francisco Bay n. to sw. Ore. (s. Klamath, Jackson, Josephine, and Curry Cos.). (7) Pasadena Screech Owl, *O. a. quercinus;* s. Calif. w. of the deserts and n. along w. side of Sierra Nevada to Mt. Shasta. (8) Mexican Screech Owl, *O. a. cineraceus;* mts. of s. Ariz., s. N.M., and w.-cent. Tex. (9) Sahuaro Screech Owl, *O. a. gilmani;* deserts of se. Calif. and s. Ariz. and along Colo. R. to extreme s. Nev.

HORNED OWL. *Bubo virginianus:* (1) Arctic Horned Owl, *B. v. subarcticus;* s. in winter to Idaho and Ore. (casual). (2) Montana Horned Owl, *B. v. occidentalis;* Mont., Wyo., s. Idaho, se. Ore., and ne. Calif. (3) Northwestern Horned Owl, *B. v. lagophonus;* Idaho, ne. Ore., and e. Wash. (4) Dusky Horned Owl, *B. v. saturatus;* Pacific Coast region from nw. Calif. (Humboldt Co.) through w. Wash. (5) Pacific Horned Owl, *B. v. pacificus;* s.-cent. Ore. and Calif. (except Colo. Desert and extreme n. coast). (6) Western Horned Owl, *B. v. pallescens;* se. Calif., Colo., Ut., Ariz., N.M., and w. Tex.

PYGMY OWL. *Glaucidium gnoma:* (1) Rocky Mountain Pygmy Owl, *G. g. pinicola;* Rocky Mt. section from Mont., Idaho, and ne. Ore. s. to N.M. and s. Ariz. (2) Coast Pygmy Owl, *G. g. grinnelli;* coast belt of Pacific States s. to Monterey Co., Calif., and e. to base of Mt. Shasta and Lake Co., Calif. (3) California Pygmy Owl, *G. g. californicum;* Calif. (except range of preceding race, and desert regions of se. Calif.), also Cascade Mts. of Ore. and Wash.

SPOTTED OWL. *Strix occidentalis:* (1) California Spotted Owl, *S. o. occidentalis;* mts. of s. Calif. and along edge of Sierras to Mariposa Co. (2) Northern Spotted Owl, *S. o. caurina;* coast belt from Wash. to Marin Co., Calif. (3) Mexican Spotted Owl, *S. o. lucida;* mts. of s. Colo., Ariz., N.M., and w. Tex.

POOR-WILL. *Phalænoptilus nuttalli:* (1) Nuttall's Poor-will, *P. n. nuttalli;* breeds e. of Cascades from e. Wash. and Mont. s. to e. Calif., s. Ariz., and cent. Tex.; winters from se. Calif. and s. Tex. s. (2) Dusky Poor-will, *P. n. californicus;* Calif., breeds w. of Sierras and Mohave and Colorado

Deserts n. to head of Sacramento Valley; also sw. Ore. (Rogue R. Valley). (3) Desert Poor-will, *P. n. hueyi*; breeds in deserts of se. Calif. and sw. Ariz.

NIGHTHAWK. *Chordeiles minor:* (1) Eastern Nighthawk, *C. m. minor*; said to breed in nw. Wash. (2) Howell's Nighthawk, *C. m. howelli*; central Rocky Mt. region (Wyo., ne. Ut., Colo., and ne. N.M.). (3) Western Nighthawk, *C. m. henryi*; s. Rocky Mt. region (sw. Colo., e. Ariz., and N.M.). (4) Pacific Nighthawk, *C. m. hesperis*; breeds in Wash., Ore., Idaho, w. Mont., nw. Wyo., w. and cent. Ut., Nev., coast of n. Calif., and in mts. to s. Calif. (5) Sennett's Nighthawk, *C. m. sennetti*; breeds in n. Great Plains w. to e. Mont. and e. Wyo.

BLUE-THROATED HUMMINGBIRD. *Lampornis clemenciæ:* (1) Texas Blue-throated Hummingbird, *L. c. clemenciæ*; Chisos Mts., Tex. (2) Arizona Blue-throated Hummingbird, *L. c. bessophilus*; mts. of s. Ariz. (s. and e. of Tucson) and sw. N.M. (San Luis Mts.).

BELTED KINGFISHER. *Megaceryle alcyon:* (1) Eastern Belted Kingfisher, *M. a. alcyon*; e. N.A. w. to base of Rockies. (2) Western Belted Kingfisher, *M. a. caurina*; breeds w. of Rockies to Pacific; winters n. to s. Ariz. and n.-cent. Calif. and along coast to Wash.

RED-SHAFTED FLICKER. *Colaptes cafer:* (1) Northwestern Flicker, *C. c cafer*; Pacific Coast from n. Calif. (Humboldt Co.) through w. Ore. and Wash. (w. of Cascades). (2) Red-shafted Flicker, *C. c. collaris*; breeds throughout w. U.S. except where preceding race is found; winters throughout most of range.

CALIFORNIA, *or* **ACORN, WOODPECKER.** *Balanosphyra formicivora:* (1) California Woodpecker, *B. f. bairdi*; Calif. and sw. Ore. (2) Mearns's Woodpecker, *B. f. aculeata*; Ariz., N.M., and w. Tex. (3) Ant-eating Woodpecker, *B. f. formicivora*; s.-cent. Tex. (Kerr Co. and Chisos Mts.).

RED-BREASTED SAPSUCKER. *Sphyrapicus varius:* (1) Northern Red-breasted Sapsucker, *S. v. ruber*; breeds in w. Wash. and w. Ore. (w. of Cascades); winters s. along Calif. coast to Monterey. (2) Southern Red-breasted Sapsucker, *S. v. daggetti*; breeds in higher mts. of Calif.; also in s. Ore. (Klamath, Jackson, and Josephine Cos.); winters in adjacent lowlands.

WILLIAMSON'S SAPSUCKER. *Sphyrapicus thyroideus:* (1) Williamson's Sapsucker, *S. t. thyroideus*; high Cascades and Sierras of Pacific States; winters at lower altitudes. (2) Natalie's Sapsucker, *S. t. nataliæ*; Rocky Mt. section from Mont. to cent. Ariz. and N.M.; winters from s. N.M. and w. Tex. into Mex.

HAIRY WOODPECKER. *Dryobates villosus:* (1) Eastern Hairy Woodpecker, *D. v. villosus*; pine hills of extreme e. Mont. (2) Harris's Woodpecker, *D. v. harrisi*; nw. coast belt from w. Wash. s. to Humboldt Co., Calif. (3) Cabanis's Woodpecker, *D. v. hyloscopus*; Calif. from Mendocino Co. and cent. Sierras s. (4) Modoc Woodpecker, *D. v. orius*; Cascades and Sierras from s.-cent. Wash. to cent. Calif., e. to Nev. (5) Rocky Mountain Hairy Woodpecker, *D. v. monticola*; Rocky Mt. section from e. Wash., ne. Ore., and Mont. s. to e. Ut. and n. N.M. (6) White-breasted Woodpecker, *D. v. leucothorectis*; s. Ut., Ariz. (except s. part), N.M. (except cent.-n. and extreme sw. corners), and cent.-w. Tex. (7) Chihuahua Woodpecker, *D. v. icastus*; s. Ariz. and sw. N.M.

DOWNY WOODPECKER. *Dryobates pubescens:* (1) Batchelder's Woodpecker, *D. p. leucurus*; Rocky Mt. region from Can. s. to n. N.M. and n. Ariz.; w. to e. Wash., e. Ore., and extreme ne. Calif. (Warner Mts.). (2) Gairdner's Woodpecker, *D. p. gairdneri*; coastal belt from w. Wash. to Mendocino Co., Calif. (3) Willow Woodpecker, *D. p. turatii*; Calif. (except nw. coast and desert ranges) and s. Ore. (Klamath, Jackson, and Josephine Cos.).

LADDER-BACKED WOODPECKER. *Dryobates scalaris:* (1) Texas Wood-pecker, *D. s. symplectus;* se. Colo., w. Okla., and Tex. (e. of Pecos River to 97th meridian). (2) Cactus Woodpecker, *D. s. cactophilus;* desert country from w. Tex. (w. of Pecos R.) through N.M. and Ariz. to se. Calif.

WHITE-HEADED WOODPECKER. *Dryobates albolarvatus:* (1) Northern White-headed Woodpecker, *D. a. albolarvatus;* Cascades and Sierras from Wash. s. to s.-cent. Calif. (Kern and Ventura Cos.); e. to Ida. and w. Nev. (2) Southern White-headed Woodpecker, *D. a. gravirostris;* mts. of s. Calif. (San Gabriel, San Bernardino, San Jacinto, Santa Rosa, and Cuyamaca Mts.).

THREE-TOED WOODPECKER. *Picoides tridactylus:* (1) Alpine Three-toed Woodpecker, *P. t. dorsalis;* sw. Mont. and Wyo. s. to Ariz. and N.M. (2) Alaska Three-toed Woodpecker, *P. t. fasciatus;* Wash., Ore., Ida., and nw. Mont.

COUCH'S KINGBIRD. *Tyrannus melancholicus:* (1) Couch's Kingbird, *T. m. couchi;* Tex. (lower Rio Grande Valley). (2) West Mexican Kingbird, *T. m. occidentalis;* s. Ariz. (rare and local).

MEXICAN CRESTED FLYCATCHER. *Myiarchus tyrannulus:* (1) Mexican Crested Flycatcher, *M. t. nelsoni;* lower Rio Grande Valley, Tex. (2) Arizona Crested Flycatcher, *M. t. magister;* deserts of s. Ariz. (Sahuaro belt).

TRAILL'S FLYCATCHER. *Empidonax trailli:* (1) Alder Flycatcher, *E. t. trailli;* breeds in e. N.A., w. presumably to Mont., e. Wyo., and ne. Colo. (2) Little Flycatcher, *E. t. brewsteri;* breeds in w. U.S. from Wash., cent. Ida., and cent. Wyo. s. to s. Calif., s. N.M., and w. Tex.

HORNED LARK. *Otocoris alpestris.* Horned Larks of one race or an-other breed throughout most of West from Can. s. to Mex. Races that mi-grate into areas where they do not breed are as follows: Pallid Horned Lark (n. Great Basin and n. Rocky Mt. sections), Dusky Horned Lark (n. and cent. Calif.), Island Horned Lark (coast of s. Calif. adjacent to Santa Barbara Ids.), Desert Horned Lark (se. Calif. and Ariz.). There is probably more or less of an intermingling of other races in certain sections, such as the Great Plains, Arizona, etc., but little is known about this at present. Most races are found all year round in their breeding-ranges, which are as follows: (1) Pallid Horned Lark, *O. a. arcticola;* breeds in mts. of Wash. (Cascades s. to Rainier). (2) Desert Horned Lark, *O .a. leucolæma;* breeds in Rocky Mt., Great Basin, and Great Plain areas from Mont. and s. Ida. s. to extreme e. Calif. (White Mts.), Nev., Ut., n. N.M., and w. Tex. (3) Streaked Horned Lark, *O. a. strigata;* breeds in nw. coast belt w. of Cascades from Wash. s. to nw. Calif. (Siskiyou Co.). (4) Dusky Horned Lark, *O. a. merrilli;* breeds from e. Wash. (e. of Cascades), n. Ida., and nw. Mont. s. to ne. Calif. and nw. Nev. (5) Island Horned Lark, *O. a. insularis;* Santa Barbara Ids., Calif. (6) California Horned Lark, *O. a. actia;* Calif. from San Francisco to San Diego and e. to San Joaquin Valley and desert divide. (7) Ruddy Horned Lark, *O. a. rubea;* Sacramento Valley, Calif. (8) Montezuma Horned Lark, *O. a. occidentalis;* cent. Ariz. and N.M. (9) Scorched Horned Lark, *O. a. adusta;* cent.-s. Ariz. (10) Mohave Horned Lark, *O. a. ammophila;* Mohave Desert to Owens Valley, Calif., and sw. Nev. (11) Sonora Horned Lark, *O. a. leucansiptila;* deserts along Colorado R. in se. Calif. and sw. Ariz.

CLIFF SWALLOW. *Petrochelidon albifrons:* (1) Northern Cliff Swallow, *P. a. albifrons;* breeds from Can. to s. Calif., n. Ariz., n. N.M., and w. Tex. A few winter in se. Calif. (2) Lesser Cliff Swallow, *P. a. tachina;* breeds in w. Tex. and se. along Rio Grande Valley. (3) Mexican Cliff Swallow, *P. a. mela-nogaster;* breeds in s. Ariz. and sw. N.M., and also in Brewster Co., Tex., in proximity of preceding race.

CANADA JAY. *Perisoreus canadensis:* (1) Rocky Mountain Jay, *P. c. capitalis*; Rocky Mt. region from Can. s. to n. N.M. and cent.-e. Ariz.; w. to e. Wash. and e. Ore. (2) Canada Jay, *P. c. canadensis*; Black Hills in ne. Wyo.

OREGON JAY. *Perisoreus obscurus:* (1) Oregon Jay, *P. o. obscurus*; Pacific slope of Wash., s. through coast mts. of Ore. to nw. Calif. (Mendocino Co.). (2) Gray Jay, *P. o. griseus*; Cascades from Wash., through Ore. to n. Calif. (Mt. Shasta and Warner Mts.).

STELLER'S JAY. *Cyanocitta stelleri:* (1) Steller's Jay, *C. s. stelleri*; coast belt of Wash. (2) Coast Jay, *C. s. carbonacea*; humid coast belt of Calif. from Monterey Co., Calif., to n. Ore. (3) Blue-fronted Jay, *C. s. frontalis*; mts. of Calif. (except humid coast belt n. of Monterey Co.). (4) Black-headed Jay, *C. s. annectens*; n. Rocky Mt. and Great Basin sections from e. Wash., Ida., and Mont. s. to e. Ore. and Wyo. (5) Long-crested Jay, *C. s. diademata*; s. Rocky Mt. and Great Basin sections from Ut. and s. Wyo. s. to Mex.

CALIFORNIA JAY. *Aphelocoma californica:* (1) Long-tailed Jay, *A. c. immanis*; extreme e. Wash., Ore. (valleys between Cascades and coast ranges, also Klamath and Lake Cos., Ore.), and Calif. (Sacramento and San Joaquin Valleys and adjacent slopes). (2) Nicasio Jay, *A. c. occleptica*; coast of n. Calif. from Humboldt Bay s. to e. side of San Francisco Bay. (3) California Jay, *A. c. californica*; coast of Calif. from San Francisco Bay (s. arm) s. to Mex. (4) Woodhouse's Jay, *A. c. woodhousei*; Rocky Mt. region from se. Ore., s. Ida., and s. Wyo. s. to se. Calif. (e. of Sierras), s. Ariz., s. N.M., and sw. Tex. (5) Texas Jay, *A. c. texana*; cent. and cent.-w. Tex. (Kerr and Edwards Cos. to Davis Mts.).

ARIZONA JAY. *Aphelocoma sieberi:* (1) Arizona Jay, *A. s. arizonæ*; se. Ariz. and sw. N.M. (2) Couch's Jay, *A. s. couchi*; cent.-w. Tex. (Chisos Mts., Brewster Co.).

RAVEN. *Corvus corax:* (1) American Raven, *C. c. sinuatus*; most of w. U.S. (2) Northern Raven, *C. c. principalis*; said to be the race in w. Wash. (*A.O.U. Check-List*), but specimens do not bear this out.

CROW. *Corvus brachyrhynchos:* (1) Western Crow, *C. b. hesperis*; w. U.S. from Can. s. to s. Calif., cent. Ariz., and cent. N.M. (2) Northwestern Crow, *C. b. caurinus*; Puget Sound area of w. Wash.

BLACK-CAPPED CHICKADEE. *Penthestes atricapillus:* (1) Long-tailed Chickadee, *P. a. septentrionalis*; Rocky Mt. region from Can. s. to n. N.M., w. to e. Wash. and e. Ore. (2) Oregon Chickadee, *P. a. occidentalis*; nw. coast belt w. of Cascades from w. Wash. s. to nw. Calif. (Siskiyou Co.).

MOUNTAIN CHICKADEE. *Penthestes gambeli:* (1) Grinnell's Chickadee, *P. g. grinnelli*; e. of Cascades in ne. Ore., e. Wash., and n. Ida. (2) Short-tailed Chickadee, *P. g. abbreviatus*; Cascade region and Sierras from Ore. s. to Mt. Whitney, Calif., also nw. Nev. (3) Bailey's Chickadee, *P. g. baileyæ*; mts. of s. Calif. from s. extremity of Sierras (Tulare Co.) and Santa Lucia Mts. (Monterey Co.) s. to San Diego Co. (4) Mountain Chickadee, *P. g. gambeli*; Rocky Mt. region from Mont. and Wyo. s. to Ariz., N.M., and w. Tex. (5) Inyo Chickadee, *P. g. inyoënsis*; higher mts. of e. Calif. (e. of Sierras in Mono and Inyo Cos.).

CHESTNUT-BACKED CHICKADEE. *Penthestes rufescens:* (1) Chestnut-backed Chickadee, *P. r. rufescens*; Pacific Coast from n. Calif. (Sonoma Co.) to Wash. and sparingly e. to e. Ore. and w. Mont. (2) Nicasio Chickadee, *P. r. neglectus*; coast belt of Marin Co., Calif. (3) Barlow's Chickadee, *P. r. barlowi*; coast of middle Calif. (San Francisco Bay to n. San Luis Obispo Co.).

BLACK-CRESTED TITMOUSE. *Bæolophus atricristatus:* (1) Black-crested Titmouse, *B. a. atricristatus;* Rio Grande Valley of Tex. (2) Sennett's Titmouse, *B. a. sennetti;* lowlands of cent. Tex. from Tom Green and Concho Cos. e. to Brazos R., and from Young Co. s. to Nueces and Bee Cos.

PLAIN TITMOUSE. *Bæolophus inornatus:* (1) Oregon Titmouse, *B. i. sequestratus;* s. Ore. (Jackson and Josephine Cos.) and n. Calif. (Siskiyou Co.) between coast and Cascade ranges. (2) Plain Titmouse, *B. i. inornatus;* n. and cent. Calif. (Mendocino and Shasta Cos. s. to San Luis Obispo and Kern Cos.). (3) San Diego Titmouse, *B. i. transpositus;* sw. Calif. (w. of desert divides from San Diego Co. to Santa Barbara Co.). (4) Gray Titmouse, *B. i. griseus;* Rocky Mt. and Great Basin regions from sw. Wyo. and s. Ida. s. to cent.-w. Tex., s. N.M., s. Ariz., and e. Calif. (e. of Sierras).

BUSH-TIT. *Psaltriparus minimus:* (1) Coast Bush-Tit, *P. m. minimus;* coastal belt from Wash. s. to Mex. border. (2) California Bush-Tit, *P. m. californicus;* interior valleys from s.-cent. Calif. (Kern Co.) n. to s. Ore. (Josephine, Jackson, and Klamath Cos.). (3) Lead-colored Bush-Tit, *P. m. plumbeus;* Rocky Mt. region from w. Wyo. and se. Ore. s. to w. Tex., N.M., n. and e. Ariz., and se. Calif. (desert ranges). (4) Lloyd's Bush-Tit, *P. m. lloydi;* cent.-w. Tex. (mts. between Pecos and Rio Grande).

WHITE-BREASTED NUTHATCH. *Sitta carolinensis:* (1) Rocky Mountain Nuthatch, *S. c. nelsoni;* Rocky Mt. region (e. of Cascades and Sierras) from e. Wash. and Mont. to Mex. (2) Slender-billed Nuthatch, *S. c. aculeata;* Pacific States from w. Wash. (rare) to Mex. and from coast e. to Cascades and Sierras. (3) Inyo Nuthatch, *S. c. tenuissima;* Panamint and White Mts. of Calif. (e. of Sierras).

PYGMY NUTHATCH. *Sitta pygmæa:* (1) Pygmy Nuthatch, *S. p. pygmæa;* middle Calif. (pines near coast from San Luis Obispo Co. to Mendocino Co.). (2) Black-eared Nuthatch, *S. p. melanotis;* Cascades (e. slopes) and Rocky Mt. region from Wash. and Mont. s. to Mex.; also Sierra Nevada of Calif. s. to San Bernardino Mts. (3) White-naped Nuthatch, *S. p. leuconucha;* mts. of s. Calif. (Riverside, San Diego, and Imperial Cos.).

CREEPER. *Certhia familiaris:* (1) Rocky Mountain Creeper, *C. f. montana;* Rocky Mt. section from Mont., Ida., and ne. Ore. (Blue Mts.) s. to N.M. and cent. Ariz. (2) Mexican Creeper, *C. f. albescens;* mts. of se. Ariz. and extreme sw. N.M. (3) Sierra Creeper, *C. f. zelotes;* Cascades of Wash. and Ore. (summits and e. slope) and through Sierras to mts. of s. Calif.; spreading to adjacent lowlands in winter. (4) California Creeper, *C. f. occidentalis;* forest regions of coast belt in Pacific States from w. Wash. (including w. slope of Cascades) s. to Monterey, Calif.

WREN-TIT. *Chamæa fasciata:* (1) Coast Wren-Tit, *C. f. phæa;* Pacific Coast belt of Ore. (2) Ruddy Wren-Tit, *C. f. rufula;* Pacific Coast belt of n. Calif. s. to w. shore of San Francisco Bay and n. Santa Cruz Co. (3) Gambel's Wren-Tit, *C. f. fasciata;* cent. Calif. from San Francisco Bay (e. and s. shores) s. through Santa Clara Co. and along coast to San Luis Obispo Co. (4) Pallid Wren-Tit, *C. f. henshawi;* sw. Ore. (Rogue River Valley), interior valleys of Calif., and along coast of s. Calif. from Santa Barbara Co. s.

BEWICK'S WREN. *Thryomanes bewicki:* (1) Baird's Wren, *T. b. eremophilus;* arid regions of sw. U.S. from w. Colo., sw. Wyo., s. Ut., and s. Nev. s. through extreme w. Tex., Ariz., N.M., and se. Calif. (2) Seattle Wren, *T. b. calophonus;* Pacific slope in Wash. and Ore. (w. of Cascades). (3) Nicasio Wren, *T. b. marinensis;* coast of n. Calif. s. to San Francisco Bay. (4) Vigors's Wren, *T. b. spilurus;* coast of cent. Calif. from San Francisco Bay (Golden Gate and Berkeley) s. to n. Monterey Co. (5) San Joaquin Wren, *T. b. drymæcus;* interior Calif. (Sacramento and San Joaquin Valleys, including both slopes of Sierras), also w. Nev. (6) San Diego Wren, *T. b. correctus;*

sw. Calif. from Monterey and San Benito Cos. s. to San Diego. (7) Santa Cruz Wren, *T. b. nesophilus*; Santa Cruz Id., Calif. (8) Catalina Wren, *T. b. catalinæ*; Santa Catalina Id., Calif. (9) San Clemente Wren, *T. b. leucophrys*; San Clemente Id., Calif.

MARSH WREN. *Telmatodytes palustris:* (1) Western Marsh Wren, *T. p. plesius*; marshes in Rocky Mt. region from Can. s. to ne. Calif. and N.M., and from e. Wash. and e. Ore. e. to edge of Great Plains. Winters from s. Calif. and Tex. (occasionally farther n.) s. into Mex. (2) Tule Wren, *T. p. paludicola*; resident along Pacific Coast from w. Wash. to s. Calif. (3) Suisun Marsh Wren, *T. p. æstuarinus*; interior Calif. (Sacramento and San Joaquin Valleys from Colusa Co. to Tulare Co.), also s. Nev. (4) Prairie Marsh Wren, *T. p. dissaëptus*; breeds on Great Plains west probably to e. Mont. and e. Wyo.

CAÑON WREN. *Catherpes mexicanus:* (1) White-throated Cañon Wren, *C. m. albifrons*; cent.-w. Tex. (mouth of Pecos R. to Brewster Co.). (2) Cañon Wren, *C. m. conspersus*; resident in w. U.S. from se. Wash., Ida., and Wyo. s. to s. Calif., Mex., and w. Tex.

CURVE-BILLED THRASHER. *Toxostoma curvirostre:* (1) Palmer's Thrasher, *T. c. palmeri*; s. Ariz. (except extreme se. corner). (2) Curve-billed Thrasher, *T. c. curvirostre*; w. Tex., N.M., and extreme se. Ariz. (n. to s. parts of Chiricahua and Huachuca Mts.). (3) Brownsville Thrasher, *T. c. oberholseri*; lower Rio Grande Valley, s. Tex.

CALIFORNIA THRASHER. *Toxostoma redivivum:* (1) California Thrasher, *T. r. redivivum*; s. Calif. (w. of deserts and Sierras) n. to Monterey and Placer Cos. (2) Sonoma Thrasher, *T. r. sonomæ*; n.-cent. and cent. Calif. (Shasta Co. s. to Eldorado Co. and through San Francisco Bay region to Santa Cruz).

ROBIN. *Turdus migratorius:* (1) Northwestern Robin, *T. m. caurinus*; coast belt of Wash. and nw. Ore. (2) Western Robin, *T. m. propinquus*; breeds in w. U.S. in Canadian and transition zones from Can. s. to Mex. and from Pacific Coast e. to edge of Great Plains except in w. Wash., where previous race is found. Winters from Wash. and Wyo. s.

VARIED THRUSH. *Ixoreus nævius:* (1) Pacific Varied Thrush, *I. n. nævius*; breeds in evergreen forests of w. Wash. and w. Ore. (coast to e. edge of Cascades) and nw. Calif. (Humboldt Co.). Winters s. along coast to Monterey, Calif. (2) Northern Varied Thrush, *I. n. meruloides*; breeds in Rocky Mt. region in nw. Mont., n. Ida., se. Wash., and nw. Ore.; winters mainly in interior of Calif.

HERMIT THRUSH. *Hylocichla guttata.* Six subspecies of the Hermit Thrush migrate through w. U.S. or winter from Ore., Ariz., s. N.M., and Tex. s. Practically all six migrate se. across Sw. States into w. Tex. and Mex. Two of these races (1) Alaska Hermit Thrush, *H. g. guttata*, and (2) Dwarf Hermit Thrush, *H. g. nanus*, breed in w. Can. and Alaska and migrate throughout most of W. States. They are the wintering races of Ore. and Calif. The breeding ranges of the other four subspecies are: (3) Monterey Hermit Thrush, *H. g. slevini*; heavy forests of coast belt of Calif. (s. Monterey Co. n. to Trinity Co.); also sw. Ore. (Siskiyou Mts.). (4) Sierra Hermit Thrush, *H. g. sequoiensis*; Cascades and other high mts. in cent. and w. Wash. and cent. and w. Ore.; also Sierras and other high mts. of Calif. (except humid coast belt and White Mts.); also w. edge of Nev. (5) Mono Hermit Thrush, *H. g. polionota*; White Mts. of e. Calif. and mts. of Great Basin in Nev. (6) Audubon's Hermit Thrush, *H. g. auduboni*; Rocky Mt. region from Ida. and Mont. s. to e. Nev., Ariz., and N.M., and w. to se. Wash. and ne. Ore. (Blue and Wallowa Mts.).

RUSSET-BACKED THRUSH. *Hylocichla ustulata:* (1) Russet-backed

Thrush, *H. u. ustulata*; breeds in moist woodlands of Pacific States from Can. to s. Calif. and from coast to and including Cascades and Sierras. (2) Olive-backed Thrush, *H. u. swainsoni*; breeds in Rocky Mt. region (e. of Cascades and Sierras) from e. Wash. and Mont. s. to e.-cent. Calif., Nev., Ut., and Colo. Migrates s. into Mex.

EASTERN BLUEBIRD. *Sialia sialis:* (1) Eastern Bluebird, *S. s. sialis*; breeds in e. U.S. w. sparingly to e. Mont., e. Wyo., and e. Colo. (2) Azure Bluebird, *S. s. fulva*; occasional in summer in high mts. of s. Ariz. (Santa Ritas and Huachucas).

WESTERN BLUEBIRD. *Sialia mexicana:* (1) Western Bluebird, *S. m. oc-cidentalis*; breeds throughout the Pacific States and in n. Ida. and w. Mont.; winters in Pacific States. (2) Chestnut-backed Bluebird, *S. m. bairdi*; breeds in Rocky Mt. section from Ut. and Colo. s. to Mex.; occasional in Wyo.; winters in s. Ut., Ariz., N.M., and w. Tex.

PLUMBEOUS GNATCATCHER. *Polioptila melanura:* (1) Plumbeous Gnatcatcher, *P. m. melanura*; deserts of se. Calif., s. Nev., Ariz., N.M., and Rio Grande Valley of w. Tex. (2) Black-tailed Gnatcatcher, *P. m. californica*; San Diegan district of sw. Calif. n. to Ventura.

RUBY-CROWNED KINGLET. *Corthylio calendula:* (1) Eastern Ruby-crowned Kinglet, *C. c. calendula*; breeds in Rocky Mt. section from Can. s. to cent. Ariz. and cent. N.M. Migrates through adjacent low country and winters from Ariz. and s. N.M. s. into Mex. (2) Western Ruby-crowned Kinglet, *C. c. cineraceus*; breeds in higher mts. of Calif. and in Ore. and Wash. (chiefly e. of Cascade divide), also n. Ida.; winters in Calif. (3) Sitka Kinglet, *C. c. grinnelli*; winters chiefly along coast s. to Monterey Co., Calif.

PHAINOPEPLA. *Phainopepla nitens:* (1) Northern Phainopepla, *P. n. lepida*; breeds in sw. U.S. (Calif., s. Nev., s. Ut., Ariz., and sw. N.M.); win-ters in s. Calif., s. Ariz., and w. Tex. (2) Mexican Phainopepla, *P. n. nitens*; breeds in w. Tex. (Brewster Co.).

LOGGERHEAD SHRIKE. *Lanius ludovicianus:* (1) White-rumped Shrike, *L. l. excubitorides*; breeds e. of Cascades and Sierras from Can. s. to se. Calif., Mex., and w. Tex.; winters in sw. U.S. (2) California Shrike, *L. l. gambeli*; breeds in Calif. w. of Cascade-Sierra divide and in e. Wash. and parts of Ore.; winters in Calif. (3) Island Shrike, *L. l. anthonyi*; Santa Barbara Ids., Calif.

HUTTON'S VIREO. *Vireo huttoni:* (1) Hutton's Vireo, *V. h. huttoni*; resident in Pacific States (w. of Sierras and Cascades). (2) Stephens's Vireo, *V. h. stephensi*; oak belt of mts. of se. Ariz., sw. N.M., and w. Tex.

BELL'S, *or* **LEAST, VIREO.** *Vireo belli:* (1) Bell's Vireo, *V. b. belli*; breeds in e. Colo. (2) Texas Vireo, *V. b. medius*; breeds in sw. Tex. (Presidio, Brewster, and Kinney Cos.). (3) Arizona Vireo, *V. b. arizonæ*; breeds near streams in deserts of se. Calif., s. Ariz., sw. N.M., and cent.-w. Tex. (4) Least Vireo, *V. b. pusillus*; breeds in Calif. (interior from upper Sacramento Valley s., and coast from Monterey Co. s.).

SOLITARY VIREO. *Vireo solitarius:* (1) Plumbeous Vireo, *V. s. plumbeus*; breeds in Rocky Mt. region from n. Nev., n. Ut., s. Mont., and se. Wyo. s. into Mex. (2) Cassin's Vireo, *V. s. cassini*; breeds in Pacific States.

ORANGE-CROWNED WARBLER. *Vermivora celata:* (1) Eastern Orange-crowned Warbler, *V. c. celata*; breeds in Can. and Alaska; winters in s. Calif.; a migrant elsewhere. (2) Rocky Mountain Orange-crowned Warbler, *V. c. orestera*; breeds in Rocky Mt. region from e. Wash. (e. of Cascades) and Mont. s. to Ariz. and N.M. (3) Lutescent Warbler, *V. c. lutescens;* breeds in Pacific

States w. of Sierras and Cascades; winters in Mex. (4) Dusky Warbler, *V. c. sordida*; breeds on Channel Ids., Calif., and on coast near San Diego; winters along coast of Calif., casually n. to San Francisco.

YELLOW WARBLER *Dendroica æstiva:* (1) Eastern Yellow Warbler, *D. a. æstiva*; breeds in e. N.A. and in Rocky Mt. region s. to Nev. and n. N.M. (2) Alaska Yellow Warbler, *D. a. rubiginosa*; breeds from Vancouver Id. to Alaska; migrates through Pacific States and N.M. (3) California Yellow Warbler, *D. a. brewsteri*; breeds in Pacific States w. of Cascades and Sierras. In migration also in e. Calif. and Ariz. (4) Sonora Yellow Warbler, *D. a. sonorana*; breeds in desert regions of se. U.S. (se. Calif., sw. Ut., s. and w. Ariz., s. N.M., and w. Tex.).

AUDUBON'S WARBLER. *Dendroica auduboni:* (1) Audubon's Warbler, *D. a. auduboni*; breeds from Can. s. to mts. of s. Calif., Ariz., and se. N.M.; winters in Pacific States and lower Rio Grande Valley, Tex. (2) Black-fronted Warbler, *D. a. nigrifrons*; breeds in mts. of se. Ariz. (Huachuca and Chiricahua Mts., etc.).

YELLOW-THROAT. *Geothlypis trichas:* (1) Western Yellow-throat, *G. t. occidentalis*; breeds in w. U.S., Mont., and Wash. s. to w. Tex., N.M., s. Nev., and Calif. (except where following races are found); migrates throughout. (2) Salt Marsh Yellow-throat, *G. t. sinuosa*; resident in salt and fresh marshes in coast belt of Calif. from San Francisco Bay s. to San Luis Obispo Co. (3) Tule Yellow-throat, *G. t. scirpicola*; resident in salt marshes of s. Calif. n. to Santa Barbara and s. fork of Kern R., also along Colo. R. to s. Nev. and extreme sw. Ut., also valleys of extreme s. Ariz.

PILEOLATED WARBLER. *Wilsonia pusilla:* (1) Northern Pileolated Warbler, *W. p. pileolata*; breeds at high altitudes from Can. s. to mts. of s. Ore., ne. Calif., n. Ariz., n. N.M., and w. Tex.; migrates throughout. (2) Golden Pileolated Warbler, *W. p. chryseola*; breeds in Pacific States; w. Wash., w. Ore., and Calif. (coast ranges and Sierras); migrates throughout Calif. and casually in Ariz.

RED-WING. *Agelaius phœniceus.* Red-wings breed in suitable places from Can. to Mex. Various races usually winter somewhere within their breeding ranges, but have a tendency to migrate from the colder sections in winter. There is probably some intermingling of the races in winter, but very little is known about this. In the Rocky Mts. and Great Plains sections two races are known to be strongly migratory into the ranges occupied by other Red-wings; there are the Giant Red-wing (s. to Colo. and Tex.) and the Thick-billed Red-wing (s. to Ariz., N.M., and w. Tex.). The Pacific States birds seem to be more stationary. The breeding ranges are as follows: (1) Giant Red-wing, *A. p. arctolegus*; Can. s. to Mont. (2) Thick-billed Red-wing, *A. p. fortis*; central Rocky Mt. region (e. Ida., Wyo., and Colo.). (3) Nevada Red-wing, *A. p. nevadensis*; Great Basin region (Ida., e. Wash., e. Ore., e. Calif. e. of Sierras, Nev., Ut., n. Ariz., and N.M. except sw. corner). (4) Northwestern Red-wing, *A. p. caurinus*; nw. coast belt from w. Wash. to n. Calif. (Mendocino Co.). (5) San Francisco Red-wing, *A. p. mailliardorum*; central coast region of Calif. (Sherwood, Mendocino Co., s. to Monterey Co. and e., incl. Suisun Bay and valleys between inner coast ranges). (6) Bi-colored Red-wing, *A. p. californicus*; Sacramento and San Joaquin Valleys of Calif. and San Francisco Bay area. (7) Kern Red-wing, *A. p. aciculatus*; south Fork Valley of Kern R., Kern Co., Calif. (8) San Diego Red-wing, *A. p. neutralis*; s. Calif. (Pacific slope n. to San Luis Obispo Co.). (9) Sonora Red-wing, *A. p. sonoriensis*; se. Calif. (lower Colo. R. Valley), s. Ariz., extreme s. Nev., and sw. N.M.

HOODED ORIOLE. *Icterus cucullatus:* (1) Sennett's Oriole, *I. c. sennetti*; breeds in lower Rio Grande Valley, Tex. (2) Arizona Hooded Oriole, *I. c. nelsoni*; breeds in s. and s.-cent. Calif., s. Ariz., and sw. N.M.; winters in Mex.

COWBIRD. *Molothrus ater:* (1) Eastern Cowbird, *M. a. ater*; breeds in N.M. (except extreme sw. corner) and Colo. (2) Nevada Cowbird, *M. a. artemisiæ*; breeds in Rocky Mt. region from Can. s. to e. Calif., s. Nev., Ut., and Wyo., and from Great Plains w. to e. Wash., e. Ore., and e. Calif. (e. of Sierras); winters into Mex. (3) California Cowbird, *M. a. californicus*; San Joaquin Valley of Calif. from Merced Co. s. to Kern Co. (Not considered a good subspecies by some authorities.) (4) Dwarf Cowbird, *M. a. obscurus*; s. Calif. (from Ventura and Inyo Cos. s.), s. Ariz., extreme sw. N.M., and s. Tex.

CARDINAL. *Richmondena cardinalis:* (1) Gray-tailed Cardinal, *R. c. canicauda*; cent. and cent.-w. Tex. (2) Arizona Cardinal, *R. c. superba*; s. Ariz. and sw. N.M.

PYRRHULOXIA. *Pyrrhuloxia sinuata:* (1) Texas Pyrrhuloxia, *P. s. texana*; Tex. (Nueces, Bee, Bexar, Kendall, and Tom Green Cos. s. into Mex.). (2) Arizona Pyrrhuloxia, *P. s. sinuata*; s. Ariz., s. N.M., and cent.-w. Tex.

BLACK-HEADED GROSBEAK. *Hedymeles melanocephalus:* (1) Black-headed Grosbeak, *H. m. melanocephalus*; breeds in Pacific States from Wash. s. throughout Calif.; also w. Nev. (2) Rocky Mountain Grosbeak, *H. m. papago*; breeds in Rocky Mt. States from Can. s. to Mex.

BLUE GROSBEAK. *Guiraca cærulea:* (1) Western Blue Grosbeak, *G. c. interfusa*; breeds in river valleys in se. Calif. (Colo. R.), s. Nev., s. Colo., Ariz., N.M., and w. Tex. (2) California Blue Grosbeak, *G. c. salicaria*; breeds in s. and cent. Calif.

VARIED BUNTING. *Passerina versicolor:* (1) Varied Bunting, *P. v. versicolor*; breeds in lower Rio Grande Valley, Tex. (2) Beautiful Bunting, *P. v. pulchra*; recorded casually or locally in se. Calif. and s. Ariz.

EVENING GROSBEAK. *Hesperiphona vespertina:* (1) Eastern Evening Grosbeak, *H. v. vespertina*; breeds in Can.; winter visitant s. to e. Wyo. and probably Wash. (2) Western Evening Grosbeak, *H. v. brooksi*; breeds in high mts. from Can. s. to Sierra Nevada of cent. Calif. and mts. of n. Ariz. and N.M. Winters in adjacent lowlands and s. to s. Calif. (3) Mexican Evening Grosbeak, *H. v. montana*; high mts. of se. Ariz.

HOUSE FINCH *or* **LINNET.** *Carpodacus mexicanus:* (1) Common House Finch, *C. m. frontalis*; from se. Wash., Ore., Ida., and Wyo. s. into Mex., and from Great Plains and cent. Tex. to w. coast. (2) San Luis House Finch, *C. m. potosinus*; sw. Tex. (along Rio Grande). (3) San Clemente House Finch, *C. m. clementis*; San Clemente Id., Calif.

PINE GROSBEAK. *Pinicola enucleator:* (1) Alaska Pine Grosbeak, *P. e. alascensis*; breeds in Alaska and w. Can.; winters s. to Wash. and Mont. (2) Kodiak Pine Grosbeak, *P. e. flammula*; breeds in coastal Alaska; winters s. irregularly to Wash. (3) Rocky Mountain Pine Grosbeak, *P. e. montana*; high mts. in Rockies from Ida. and Mont. s. to n. N.M.; also in Cascades in n. Wash. (4) California Pine Grosbeak, *P. e. californica*; high summits of central Sierra Nevada, Calif.

GRAY-CROWNED ROSY FINCH *or* **LEUCOSTICTE.** *Leucosticte tephrocotis:* (1) Hepburn's Rosy Finch, *L. t. littoralis*; breeds above timber line on mts. from Alaska s. in Cascades to n. Calif.; winters s. and e. in mts. to e. Calif., Nev., Ida., Mont., Wyo., Ut., and Colo. (2) Gray-crowned Rosy Finch, *L. t. tephrocotis*; breeds from nw. Mont. n. into Can.; in winter w. to Cascades and s. to Ut., Colo. (3) Sierra Nevada Rosy Finch, *L. t. dawsoni*; high peaks of cent. Sierra Nevada, Calif.

REDPOLL. *Acanthis linaria:* (1) Common Redpoll, *A. l. linaria*; subarctic, wandering irregularly s. in winter to e. Ore. and Colo. (2) Greater Redpoll, *A. l. rostrata*; winters s. to Mont., casually to Colo.

COMMON GOLDFINCH. *Spinus tristis:* (1) Eastern Goldfinch, *S. t. tristis;* breeds in e. U.S. w. to e. Mont., e. Wyo., and e. Colo.; sometimes winters in same area. (2) Pale Goldfinch, *S. t. pallidus;* breeds e. of Cascades in Rocky Mt. section from e. Wash. and w. Mont. s. to Nev. and w. Colo.; winters to Mex. (3) Willow Goldfinch, *P. t. salicamans;* resident in Pacific States from w. Wash. through Calif., chiefly w. of Cascades and Sierras.

ARKANSAS GOLDFINCH. *Spinus psaltria:* (1) Arkansas Goldfinch, *S. p. psaltria;* Colo., N.M., and cent.-n. Tex. s. into Mex. (2) Green-backed Goldfinch, *S. p. hesperophilus;* breeds from Ore. and Ut. through s. Calif. and s. Ariz.; winters from n. Calif. and s. Ariz. s. into Mex.

RED CROSSBILL. *Loxia curvirostra:* (1) Sitka Crossbill, *L. c. sitkensis;* along coast from Wash. to n. Calif. (2) Bendire's Crossbill, *L. c. bendirei;* breeds in mts. of w. U.S. from Can. s. in Cascades and Sierras to Calif. and in Rockies to Colo. and n. N.M.; wanders to adjacent lowlands and s. to s. Calif. (3) Mexican Crossbill, *L. c. stricklandi;* higher mts. of s. Calif., Ariz., s. N.M., and cent.-w. Tex.

SPOTTED TOWHEE. *Pipilo maculatus.* The five Pacific Coast races of the Spotted Towhee are apparently non-migratory except for the Oregon Towhee, which has a tendency to move southward, sometimes invading the range of the Sacramento Towhee in s. Ore. and n. Calif. West of the Cascades and Sierras the Nevada Towhee is somewhat migratory, going s. to the lower Colo. R. Valley in se. Calif. and w. Ariz. The two Rocky Mt. races are strongly migratory, the Arctic Towhee migrating through Wyo. and ne. Ut. to Colo. and Tex., and the Spurred Towhee into the southern part of its breeding range and Mex. Breeding ranges are as follows: (1) Arctic Towhee, *P. m. arcticus;* breeds in Mont. and e. Wyo. (2) Spurred Towhee, *P. m. montanus;* Ut., w. Wyo., Colo., w. Tex., N.M., Ariz., s. Nev., and se. Calif. (Panamint Mts.). (3) Nevada Towhee, *P. m. curtatus;* e. Wash., e. Ore., Ida., n. Nev., and ne. Calif. (e. of Sierras). (4) Oregon Towhee, *P. m. oregonus;* w. Wash. and w. Ore. (Cascades to Pacific). (5) Sacramento Towhee, *P. m. falcinellus;* interior Calif. (Sacramento and San Joaquin Valleys and slopes of Sierras); also s. Ore. (Jackson and Josephine Cos.). (6) San Francisco Towhee, *P. m. falcifer;* coast region of Calif. (Monterey Co. to Humboldt Co.). (7) San Diego Towhee, *P. m. megalonyx;* coast of s. Calif. (n. to San Luis Obispo Co. and e. to s. Kern Co.). (8) San Clemente Towhee, *P. m. clementæ;* San Clemente and Santa Catalina Ids., Calif.

BROWN TOWHEE. *Pipilo fuscus:* (1) Oregon Brown Towhee, *P. f. bullatus;* sw. Ore. (Josephine, Jackson, and Douglas Cos.). (2) Sacramento Brown Towhee, *P. f. carolæ;* interior valleys of Calif. w. of Sierras from Kern Co. and n. to Shasta Co. (3) San Francisco Brown Towhee, *P. f. petulana;* coast of n. Calif. (Humboldt Bay s. to Santa Cruz). (4) California Brown Towhee, *P. f. crissalis;* coast of s. Calif. (from Monterey s. to Mex. and e. to w. edge of San Joaquin Valley and deserts). (5) Cañon Towhee, *P. f. mesoleucus;* s. Colo., Ariz., N.M., and w. Tex.

SAVANNAH SPARROW. *Passerculus sandwichensis:* (1) Western Savannah Sparrow, *P. s. alaudinus;* breeds in Can. and Alaska; migrates through Pacific States and w. Great Plains; winters in Calif. and Tex. (2) Aleutian Savannah Sparrow, *P. s. sandwichensis;* breeds in Aleutians, Alaska; winters along coast to cent. Calif. (occasionally). (3) Nevada Savannah Sparrow, *P. s. nevadensis;* breeds in Great Basin (e. Wash., e. Ore., e. Calif., Nev., Ut., Idaho, Mont., Wyo., Colo., and n. N.M.); winters s. into Mex. (4) Bryant's Sparrow, *P. s. bryanti;* San Francisco Bay area and coast of Calif. from San Luis Obispo Co. n. to Humboldt Co.

LARGE-BILLED SPARROW. *Passerculus rostratus:* (1) Large-billed Sparrow, *P. r. rostratus;* breeds in Mex. and ne. Lower Calif.; winters along coast of s. Calif. n. to Santa Barbara. (2) San Lucas Sparrow, *P. r. guttatus;* breeds on San Benito Ids., Lower Calif.; winters occasionally along coast of s. Calif. with preceding race.

VESPER SPARROW. *Pooecetes gramineus:* (1) Oregon Vesper Sparrow, *P. g. affinis*; breeds in Wash. and Ore. w. of Cascades; winters in s. and cent. Calif. (2) Western Vesper Sparrow, *P. g. confinis*; breeds from Can. s. to n. Ariz., n. N.M., and Tex., and from Great Plains w. to e. Wash., e. Ore., ne. Calif., and Nev.; winters from s. Calif. (w. of Sierras), s. Ariz., and cent. Tex. s. into Mex.

RUFOUS-CROWNED SPARROW. *Aimophila ruficeps:* (1) Rufous-crowned Sparrow, *A. r. ruficeps*; Calif. w. of Sierras from Sonoma, Solano, Sutter, and Placer Cos. s. to Kern Co. (2) Santa Cruz Sparrow, *A. r. obscura*; Santa Cruz Id. and probably adjacent ids., Calif. (3) Ashy Sparrow, *A. r. canescens*; s. Calif. (San Diegan district from Ventura Co. to Mex.). (4) Rock Sparrow, *A. r. eremoeca*; breeds in Okla. (Wichita Mts.) and Tex. (Cook Co., sw. to Pecos R. and Brewster Co.). (5) Scott's Sparrow, *A. r. scotti*; Ariz., s. N.M., and w. Tex.; casual in se. Colo.

DESERT SPARROW. *Amphispiza bilineata:* (1) Black-throated Sparrow, *A. b. bilineata*; n.-cent. Tex. s. into Mex. (2) Desert Sparrow, *A. b. deserticola*; breeds in desert country of Calif., Nev., Ut., w. Colo., Ariz., N.M., and w. Tex.; winters from se. Calif., s. Ariz., and s. N.M. s.

SAGE SPARROW. *Amphispiza nevadensis:* (1) Northern Sage Sparrow, *A. n. nevadensis*; breeds in Great Basin district (e. Wash., e. Ore., e. Calif. (e. of Sierras), cent. and s. Idaho, Nev., Ut., sw. Mont., w. Wyo., w. Colo., and nw. N.M.); winters from s. edge of breeding range to deserts of s. Calif., Ariz., N.M., and w. Tex. (2) California Sage Sparrow, *A. n. canescens*; breeds in cent. and s. Calif. w. of Sierras from Fresno south to Mt. Pinos, Ventura Co., w. to Carrizo Plain, San Luis Obispo Co., and e. to Owens Valley; winters s. to Mexican border.

OREGON JUNCO. *Junco oreganus.* Races of this species winter throughout the w. U.S. from Can. to Mex. as follows: ROCKY MT. REGION, Shufeldt's Junco and Montana Junco; GREAT BASIN REGION, mostly Shufeldt's Junco, and a few Montana Juncos in n. portion (e. Wash. and e. Ore.); COAST BELT OF WASH. AND ORE., Oregon Junco and Shufeldt's Junco; CALIFORNIA, Oregon Junco (along coast s. to San Francisco), Shufeldt's Junco (n. and cent. Calif.), Thurber's Junco (lower levels throughout State), Point Pinos Junco (winters on breeding grounds, see below). The breeding ranges are as follows: (1) Oregon Junco, *J. o. oreganus*; breeds in w. Can. and Alaska. (2) Shufeldt's Junco, *J. o. shufeldti*; breeds from Can. s. to Ore. (except s. part). (3) Montana Junco, *J. o. montanus*; breeds from Can. s. to Idaho and nw. Mont. (4) Thurber's Junco, *J. o. thurberi*; breeds from s. Ore. s. throughout mts. of Calif. except where next race is found. (5) Point Pinos Junco, *J. o. pinosus*; coast district of cent. Calif. from San Mateo and Alamedo Cos. s. to Monterey Co.

RED-BACKED JUNCO. *Junco phoeonotus:* (1) Red-backed Junco, *J. p. dorsalis*; breeds in high mts. of N.M. and ne. Ariz.; winters s. to sw. Tex. and Mex. (2) Arizona Junco, *J. p. palliatus*; resident of mts. of se. Ariz.

BREWER'S SPARROW. *Spizella breweri:* (1) Timberline Sparrow, *S. b. taverneri*; breeds in nw. British Col.; occurs in Mont. and Wash. in migration. (2) Brewer's Sparrow, *S. b. breweri*; breeds chiefly in Rocky Mt. section from Can. s. to N.M. and Ariz., and w. to e. Wash., e. Ore. (e. of Cascades), and Calif. (e. of Sierras, also local in s. Calif.); winters from s. Calif., s. Ariz., and cent. Tex. s.

BLACK-CHINNED SPARROW. *Spizella atrogularis:* (1) Mexican Black-chinned Sparrow, *S. a. atrogularis*; breeds in Ariz. and s. N.M. (2) California

Black-chinned Sparrow, *S. a. cana*; breeds locally in s. Calif. n. to Monterey Co. and Owens Valley; occasionally farther.

WHITE-CROWNED SPARROW. *Zonotrichia leucophrys:* (1) White-crowned Sparrow, *Z. l. leucophrys*; breeds in high mts. of w. U.S. from Can. s. in Rockies to n. N.M. and in Sierras to cent. Calif.; migrates through Rocky Mt. region s. into Mex.; winters in s. Ariz., N.M., and Tex. (2) Gambel's Sparrow, *Z. l. gambeli*; breeds from Can. s. to cent. Mont.; migrates throughout w. U.S. except nw. coast belt; winters from Calif. and Ut. s. (3) Puget Sound Sparrow, *Z. l. pugetensis*; breeds in humid nw. coast belt from Wash. s. to n. Calif. (Mendocino Co.); winters s. along coast to s. Calif. (4) Nuttall's Sparrow, *Z. l. nuttalli*; permanent resident around San Francisco Bay region and along coast of cent. Calif. from Mendocino Co. to Santa Barbara Co.

FOX SPARROW. *Passerella iliaca.* A highly migratory species, with numerous (16) critical subspecies. Many are known as yet from very limited areas in the breeding season, and their migration routes and wintering grounds are scarcely known. Seven subspecies breed north of the U.S. and swarm through the Pacific Coast States on migration and in winter, where they mingle with Fox Sparrows of eight other races which breed in those three States. Those from n. of the U.S. boundary are: (1) Alberta Fox, *P. i. altivagans*; (2) Shumagin Fox, *P. i. unalaschensis*; (3) Kodiak Fox, *P. i. insularis*; (4) Valdez Fox, *P. i. sinuosa*; (5) Yakutat Fox, *P. i. annectens;* (6) Townsend's Fox, *P. i. townsendi*; and (7) Thick-billed Fox, *P. i. mega-rhyncha.* Even the Eastern Fox Sparrow, *P. i. iliaca*, occurs occasionally in the Pacific States. For the sake of clarity the following form of analysis is given: WASHINGTON, the Sooty Fox, *P. i. fuliginosa*, breeds on the coast and ids. in the nw. corner of Wash. and winters s. along the coast. Several other races migrate along the coast, and at least two, Shumagin Fox and Valdez Fox, are to be expected in winter. The Slate-colored Fox, *P. i. schistacea*, breeds in e. Wash. w. to the Cascades. OREGON, three breed: (1) Slate-colored Fox, *P. i. schistacea* (e. Ore.); (2) Warner Mountains Fox, *P. i. fulva* (Steens, Hart, and Warner Mts. and e. slope of Cascades n. to cent. Ore.); (3) Yosemite Fox, *P. i. mariposæ* (Siskiyous and w. slope of Cascades in Jackson and Josephine Cos.). None of these winter. Several other races migrate along the coast from the n., and at least three, Kodiak, Valdez, and Yakutat, are known to winter. CALIFORNIA, six breed: (1) Warner Mountains Fox, *P. i. fulva* (high mts. of ne. |Calif. from Modoc and Lassen Cos. n.); (2) Trinity Fox, *P. i. brevicauda* (inner n. coast ranges of Calif. from Trinity Co. s. to Mendocino Co. and Colusa Co.); (3) Inyo Fox, *P. i. canescens* (White Mts. of Inyo and Mono Cos., also mts. of cent. Nev.); (4) Mono Fox, *P. i. monoënsis* (e. slope of Sierras in vicinity of Mono Lake); (5) Yosemite Fox, *P. i. mariposæ* (n. and cent. Sierras s. to Inyo Co.); (6) Stephens's Fox, *P. i. stephensi* (San Gabriel, San Bernardino, and San Jacinto Mts., Mt. Pinos, and s. Sierras n. to Fresno Co.). These six races winter together westward toward the coast, where they are joined by eight other races. ROCKY MT. REGION, only one race occurs, the Slate-colored Fox, *P. i. schistacea*; breeds in Idaho, Mont., n. Nev., Ut., Wyo., and w. Colo. (rare); migrates sparingly to Ariz. and N.M.

LINCOLN'S SPARROW. *Melospiza lincolni:* (1) Lincoln's Sparrow, *M. l. lincolni*; breeds in high mts. from Can. s. in Cascades, Sierras, and Rockies to s. Calif. and n. N.M.; migrates through lowlands of w. U.S.; winters from cent. Calif., Ariz., and cent. Tex. s. into Mex. (2) Forbush's Sparrow, *M. l. gracilis*; breeds in Alaska; winters in cent. Calif. s. to Monterey, casually to s. Calif.

SONG SPARROW. *Melospiza melodia.* Song Sparrows of seventeen races breed in the West from Can. s. to s. Calif., sw. Ariz., and n. N.M. They winter from Wash. and Mont. s. into Mex. Most of them are permanently resident or partially resident in the areas in which they breed. Races that migrate into areas where they do not breed are as follows: GREAT PLAINS, Dakota Song; SOUTHERN ROCKY MT. REGION, Mountain Song; GREAT BASIN REGION, Merrill's Song; WASHINGTON, Sooty Song (nw. coast), Yakutat Song (coast), and Merrill's Song (e.); OREGON, Yakutat Song (coast), and Merrill's Song (inland); CALIFORNIA, Mountain Song (se.), Yakutat Song (along n. coast), Rusty Song (coast to cent. Calif.), Modoc Song (w. and s. Calif.), Merrill's Song (chiefly e.). Breeding ranges are as follows: (1) Dakota Song Sparrow, *M. m. juddi*; extreme e. Mont. (2) Mountain Song Sparrow, *M. m. fallax*; Rocky Mt. district (ne. Ore., e. Nev., cent. and s. Idaho, w. Mont., Wyo., Colo., Ut., and n. N.M.). (3) Modoc Song Sparrow, *M. m. fisherella*; e. Ore. (except Blue Mt. section), sw. Idaho, nw. Nev., and ne. Calif. (e. of Sierras). (4) Merrill's Song Sparrow, *M. m. merrilli*; e. Wash. (e. of Cascades) and n. Idaho. (5) Rusty Song Sparrow, *M. m. morphna*; w. Wash. and w. Ore. (w. of Cascades). (6) Mendocino Song Sparrow, *M. m. cleonensis*; coast of nw. Calif. (Mendocino Co. to Ore. line; also coast of extreme sw. Ore.). (7) Samuels's Song Sparrow, *M. m. samuelis*; salt marshes of n. side of San Francisco Bay and s. side of San Pablo Bay, Calif. (8) Suisun Song Sparrow, *M. m. maxillaris*; lowlands surrounding Suisun Bay, w.-cent. Calif. (9) Modesto Song Sparrow, *M. m. mailliardi*; interior valleys of Calif. (Sacramento and n. San Joaquin Valleys s. to Stanislaus Co. except vicinity of Suisun Bay). (10) Alameda Song Sparrow, *M. m. pusillula*; salt marshes around s. arm of San Francisco Bay, Calif. (11) Heermann's Song Sparrow, *M. m. heermanni*; s. San Joaquin Valley, Calif. (Merced Co. to Kern Co.). (12) San Diego Song Sparrow, *M. m. cooperi*; coast district of s. Calif. n. to Santa Barbara. (13) Santa Cruz Song Sparrow, *M. m. santæcrucis*; coast district of cent. Calif. s. of San Francisco Bay to San Luis Obispo Co. (14) Santa Barbara Song Sparrow, *M. m. graminea*; Santa Barbara Id., Calif. (15) San Clemente Song Sparrow, *M. m. clementæ*; San Clemente, Santa Cruz, and Santa Rosa Ids., Calif. (16) San Miguel Song Sparrow, *M. m. micronyx*; San Miguel Id., Calif. (17) Desert Song Sparrow, *M. m. saltonis*; deserts of se. Calif., s. Nev., sw. Ut., and sw. Ariz. (18) Sooty Song Sparrow, *M. m. rufina*; se. Alaska.

HOME–REFERENCE SUGGESTIONS

THIS handbook is primarily a field guide. *The Book of Birds*, obtainable from the National Geographic Society, Washington, D.C., is recommended as a companion volume for home use. This contains an almost complete series of color portraits of both Eastern and Western birds. *Birds of the Pacific States*, by Ralph Hoffmann (Houghton Mifflin Company), is an excellent handbook for use in California, Oregon, and Washington. It gives seasonal dates and approximate abundance of different species in the three Pacific States, and also goes into more detail on voice than was possible in this volume. *Birds of New Mexico*, by Florence Merriam Bailey, which is available through the New Mexico Department of Game and Fish, Santa Fe, New Mexico, is a splendid volume for use anywhere in the Southwest. Be sure to consult your nearest museum or bird club about any available local publications or lists.

Following is a list of the most important or recent publications covering different States and major regions: WASHINGTON: *Distributional Check-List of the Birds of the State of Washington*, by E. A. Kitchin (Pacific Northwest Bird and Mammal Society, Seattle, Wash., 1934). OREGON: *Birds of Oregon*, by Gabrielson and Jewett (Oregon State College, Corvallis, Oregon, 1940). CALIFORNIA: (1) *Birds of the Pacific States*, by Ralph Hoffmann (Houghton Mifflin Company, 1927). (2) *Birds of California* (four large volumes), by William Leon Dawson, 1923; out of print. (3) *Animal Life in the Yosemite*, by Grinnell and Storer (University of California Press, 1924; out of print). ARIZONA: *A Distributional List of the Birds of Arizona*, by Harry S. Swarth (Pacific Coast Avifauna No. 10, Cooper Ornithological Club, University of California, 1914). NEVADA: *The Birds of Nevada*, by Jean M. Linsdale (Pacific Coast Avifauna No. 23, Cooper Ornithological Club, University of California, 1936). UTAH: No State publication at present, but one is contemplated. IDAHO: No State publication at present. MONTANA: *A Distributional List of the Birds of Montana*, by Aretas A. Saunders (Pacific Coast Avifauna No. 14, Cooper Ornithological Club, University of California, 1921). WYOMING: *Wyoming Bird Life*, by Otto McCreary (University of Wyoming, Laramie, 1937). COLORADO: (1) *A Guide to the Birds of Colorado*, by W. H. Bergtold (Smith-Brooks Printing Company, Denver, 1928). (2) *The Birds of Denver and Mountain Parks*, by Niedrach and Rockwell (Popular Series No. 5, Colorado Museum of Natural History, 1939). NEW MEXICO: *Birds of New Mexico*, by Florence Merriam Bailey (New Mexico Department of Game and Fish, Santa Fe, 1925).

TEXAS: Dr. H. C. Oberholser is completing a work on the Birds of Texas which should be of extreme value throughout the State. Until this comes out the following local publications, though treating limited areas, will be most useful. (1) *The Birds of Brewster County, Texas*, by Van Tyne and Sutton (Miscellaneous Publications No. 37, Museum of Zoölogy, University of Michigan, 1937). (2) *Birds of the Brownsville Region, Southern Texas*, by Griscom and Crosby (*The Auk* — July, 1925, October, 1925, and January, 1926).

For more complete data on ranges of Western birds, the *A.O.U. Check-List of North American Birds* (American Ornithologists' Union, Rudyerd Boulton, Treasurer, Field Museum of Natural History, Chicago, Ill.) is the standard. For reference in western Canada, use *Birds of Canada*, by P. A. Taverner (The Musson Book Company, Toronto).

INDEX

(Page numbers in italics refer to illustrations.)

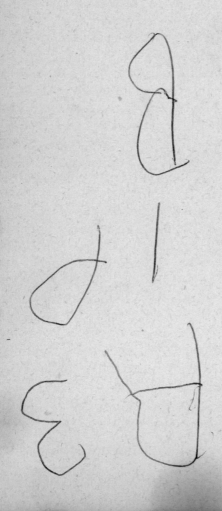